Urban Economics

Urban Economics

SIXTH EDITION

Arthur O'Sullivan

Department of Economics
Lewis & Clark College

McGraw-Hill Irwin

Boston   Burr Ridge, IL   Dubuque, IA   Madison, WI   New York   San Francisco   St. Louis
Bangkok   Bogotá   Caracas   Kuala Lumpur   Lisbon   London   Madrid   Mexico City
Milan   Montreal   New Delhi   Santiago   Seoul   Singapore   Sydney   Taipei   Toronto

McGraw-Hill Irwin

URBAN ECONOMICS, SIXTH EDITION
Published by McGraw-Hill/Irwin, a business unit of The McGraw-Hill Companies, Inc.,
1221 Avenue of the Americas, New York, NY, 10020. Copyright © 2007 by The
McGraw-Hill Companies, Inc. All rights reserved. No part of this publication may be
reproduced or distributed in any form or by any means, or stored in a database or retrieval
system, without the prior written consent of The McGraw-Hill Companies, Inc.,
including, but not limited to, in any network or other electronic storage or transmission,
or broadcast for distance learning.

Some ancillaries, including electronic and print components, may not be available to
customers outside the United States.

This book is printed on acid-free paper.

2 3 4 5 6 7 8 9 0 DOC/DOC 0 9 8 7 6

ISBN-13: 978-0-07-298476-7
ISBN-10: 0-07-298476-7

Editorial director: *Brent Gordon*
Publisher: *Gary Burke*
Executive sponsoring editor: *Paul Shensa*
Editorial assistant: *Robin Pille*
Executive marketing manager: *Rhonda Seelinger*
Project manager: *Kristin Bradley*
Lead production supervisor: *Michael R. McCormick*
Senior designer: *Adam Rooke*
Lead media project manager: *Becky Szura*
Cover design: *Jillian Lindner*
Typeface: *10/12 Times Roman*
Compositor: *Interactive Composition Corporation*
Printer: *R. R. Donnelley*

Library of Congress Cataloging-in-Publication Data
O'Sullivan, Arthur.
    Urban economics / Arthur O'Sullivan.—6th ed.
        p. cm.
    Includes index.
    ISBN-13: 978-0-07-298476-7 (alk. paper)
    ISBN-10: 0-07-298476-7 (alk. paper)
    1. Urban economics. I. Title
HT321.O88 2007
330.9173'2—dc22   2005054447

www.mhhe.com

To Professor Ed Whitelaw, the most talented teacher I've ever known. It has been almost 30 years since I've been in Ed's class, but whenever I start thinking about how to teach some new material, my first thought is, "How would Ed present this material?"

About the Author

ARTHUR O'SULLIVAN is a professor of economics at Lewis and Clark College in Portland, Oregon. After receiving his B.S. degree in economics at the University of Oregon, he spent two years in the Peace Corps, working with city planners in the Philippines. He received his Ph.D. degree in economics from Princeton University in 1981 and taught at the University of California, Davis and Oregon State University, winning teaching awards at both schools. He is the Robert B. Pamplin Junior Professor of Economics at Lewis and Clark College in Portland, Oregon, where he teaches microeconomics and urban economics. He is the coauthor of the introductory textbook, *Economics: Principles and Tools,* currently in its fourth edition.

Professor O'Sullivan's research explores economic issues concerning urban land use, environmental protection, and public policy. His articles appear in many economics journals, including *Journal of Urban Economics, Regional Science and Urban Economics, Journal of Environmental Economics and Management, National Tax Journal, Journal of Public Economics,* and *Journal of Law and Economics.*

Preface

This book is on urban economics, the discipline that lies at the intersection of geography and economics. Urban economics explores the location decisions of utility-maximizing households and profit-maximizing firms, and it shows how these decisions cause the formation of cities of different size and shape. Part I of the book explains why cities exist and what causes them to grow or shrink. Part II examines the market forces that shape cities and the role of government in determining land-use patterns. Part III looks at the urban transportation system, exploring the pricing and design of public transit systems and the externalities associated with automobile use (congestion, environmental damage, collisions). Part IV uses a model of the rational criminal to explore the causes of urban crime and the spatial consequences. Part V explains the unique features of the housing market and examines the effects of government housing policies. The final part of the book explains the rationale for our fragmented system of local government and explores the responses of local governments to intergovernmental grants and the responses of taxpayers to local taxes.

The text is designed for use in undergraduate courses in urban economics and urban affairs. It could also be used for graduate courses in urban planning, public policy, and public administration. All of the economic concepts used in the book are covered in the typical intermediate microeconomics course, so students who have completed such a course will be able to move through the book at a rapid pace. For students whose exposure to microeconomics is limited to an introductory course—or who could benefit from a review of the concepts covered in an intermediate microeconomics course—I have provided an appendix ("Tools of Microeconomics") that covers the key concepts.

CHANGES FOR THE SIXTH EDITION

This sixth edition of *Urban Economics* incorporates the remarkable progress in the field of urban economics in the last 10 to 15 years. The recent advances in theory, empirical analysis, and policy evaluation are fundamental and widespread. Early in the revision process I realized that the usual cut-paste-insert approach would not suffice, so I started from scratch. The result is an extreme makeover of a teenaged book. The makeover provided many opportunities to improve the book as a teaching instrument:

- **Leaner writing style.** The book has fewer pages but more content.

- **Axioms of urban economics.** The book starts with five axioms of urban economics, self-evident truths that provide the foundation for the economic analysis throughout the book.
- **Active learning.** In the words of William Shakespeare, "Action is eloquence." Each chapter ends with four or five exercises that allow students to apply the key concepts. These exercises can be incorporated into class sessions or exams.
- **User-friendly appendix, "Tools of Microeconomics."** I have rewritten the appendix to allow readers to review key concepts in a just-in-time fashion. In each chapter, callouts refer the reader to a specific section of the appendix for a review of the relevant concepts.

The makeover also provided an opportunity to reorganize the book to provide a better flow of topics. Here are the key organizational changes.

- The analysis of urban poverty is integrated throughout the book, with appearances in nine chapters.
- The key insights from the old chapter on land rent appear at the beginning of the chapter on urban land rent.
- The key insights from the old chapters on location theory and central place theory are integrated into various chapters in the first part of the book.
- A new appendix to the urban-growth chapter presents the neoclassical model of regional development.
- The section on land use starts with modern cities, and then looks back 80 to 150 years to the heyday of the monocentric city. This approach identifies the market forces behind the rise and demise of the monocentric city. The appendix to Chapter 7 presents the model of the monocentric city and two applications of the model.
- A new appendix to the chapter on urban rent uses economic choice models to explain (1) how consumer substitution generates a convex housing-price curve and (2) how input substitution generates a convex bid-rent curve.
- A new chapter explores the economics of neighborhood choice and segregation, focusing on the role of local public goods and neighborhood externalities related to education and crime.
- The first chapter on urban transportation focuses on three externalities from automobiles—congestion, environmental damage, and collisions—and explores various policy responses to the externalities.

INSTRUCTOR'S CD

The *Instructor Resource* CD for the book (ISBN 0-07-299662-5) has the following documents:

- A complete set of figures and tables in PowerPoint format
- Model answers to the exercises
- Lecture notes for each chapter
- Selected chapters from the 5th edition: Location Theory, Central Place Theory, Introduction to Land Rent
- Additional exercises and model answers for each chapter
- A chapter that presents the core-periphery model of regional development

These and other resources for instructors and students are available on the author's Web site: http://www.lclark.edu/~arthuro/

Acknowledgments

I am indebted to many people who read the book and suggested ways to improve the coverage and the exposition. In particular I would like to thank those instructors who participated in surveys and reviews that were indispensable in the development of the Sixth Edition of *Urban Economics*. The appearance of their names does not necessarily constitute their endorsement of the text or its methodology.

Richard Arnott
Boston College

Brian J. Cushing
West Virginia University

Maria N. DaCosta
University of Wisconsin–Eau Claire

Joseph Daniel
University of Delaware

Gilles Duranton
University of Toronto

Steven Durlauf
University of Wisconsin

Roxanne Ezzet-Lofstrom
University of Texas at Dallas

Julia L. Hansen
Western Washington University

Daryl Hellman
Northeastern University

Stanley Keil
Ball State University

Sukoo Kim
Washington University

Ken Lipner
Florida International University

Bruce Pietrykowski
University of Michigan–Dearborn

Florenz Plassmann
Binghamton University, State University of New York

Michael J. Potepan
San Francisco State University

Donald Renner
Minnesota State University

Jonathan Rork
Vassar College

Jeffrey Rous
University of North Texas

William A. Schaffer
Georgia Institute of Technology

Mary Stevenson
University of Massachusetts, Boston

Will Strange
University of Toronto

Timothy Sullivan
Towson University

Jacques-Francois Thisse
Universite Catholique de Louvain-la-Neuve

Wendine Thompson-Dawson
University of Utah

Mark R. Wolfe
University of California, Berkeley

In addition, dozens of instructors provided feedback and suggestions for earlier editions of the book.

Randall Bartlett
Smith College

Charles Berry
University of Cincinnati

Bradley Braun
University of Central Florida

Jerry Carlino
University of Pennsylvania

Ed Coulson
Pennsylvania State University

David Figlio
University of Oregon

Edward J. Ford
University of South Florida

Andrew Gold
Trinity College

Julia L. Hansen,
Western Washington University

Stanley Keil
Ball State University

Kenneth Lipner
Florida International University

Vijay Mathur
Cleveland State University

Florenz Plassmann
Binghamton University, State University of New York

Michael J. Potepan
San Francisco State University

Steven Raphael
University of California, San Diego

Stuart S. Rosenthal
Syracuse University

William Schaffer
Georgia Institute of Technology

Steve Soderlind
Saint Olaf College

Mary Stevenson
University of Massachusetts, Boston

Timothy Sullivan
Towson University

Mark R. Wolfe
University of California, Berkeley

Anthony Yezer
George Washington University

John Yinger
Syracuse University

Arthur O'Sullivan

Brief Contents

Contents

Part VI
LOCAL GOVERNMENT

321

CHAPTER 1

Introduction and Axioms of Urban Economics

Cities have always been the fireplaces of civilization, whence light and heat radiated out into the dark.
—THEODORE PARKER

I'd rather wake up in the middle of nowhere than in any city on earth.
—STEVE MCQUEEN

*T*his book explores the economics of cities and urban problems. The quotes from Parker and McQueen reflect our mixed feelings about cities. On the positive side, cities facilitate innovation, production, and trade, so they increase our standard of living. On the negative side, cities are noisy, dirty, and crowded. As we'll see in the first part of the book, firms and people locate in cities because the obvious costs of being in a city are more than offset by subtle benefits of producing in close proximity to other firms and people. As we'll see later in the book, policies that combat urban problems such as congestion, pollution, and crime are likely to increase the vitality of cities, causing them to grow.

WHAT IS URBAN ECONOMICS?

The discipline of urban economics is defined by the intersection of geography and economics. Economics explores the choices people make when resources are limited. Households make choices to maximize their utility, while firms maximize their profit. Geographers study how things are arranged across space, answering the question, Where does human activity occur? Urban economics puts economics and geography together, exploring the geographical or location choices of utility-maximizing households and profit-maximizing firms. Urban economics also identifies inefficiencies in location choices and examines alternative public policies to promote efficient choices.

Urban economics can be divided into six related areas that correspond to the six parts of this book.

1. **Market forces in the development of cities.** The interurban location decisions of firms and households generate cities of different size and economic structure. We explore the issues of why cities exist and why there are big cities and small ones.
2. **Land use within cities.** The intraurban location decisions of firms and households generate urban land-use patterns. In modern cities, employment is spread throughout the metropolitan area, in sharp contrast to the highly centralized cities of just 100 years ago. We explore the economic forces behind the change from centralized to decentralized cities. We also use a model of neighborhood choice to explore the issue of segregation with respect to race, income, and educational level.
3. **Urban transportation.** We explore some possible solutions to the urban congestion problem and look at the role of mass transit in the urban transportation system. One issue is whether a bus system is more efficient than a light-rail system or a heavy-rail system like BART (San Francisco) or Metro (Washington).
4. **Crime and public policy.** We look at the problem of urban crime and show the links between crime and two other urban problems, poverty and low educational achievement.
5. **Housing and public policy.** Housing choices are linked to location choices because housing is immobile. We'll discuss why housing is different from other products and how housing policies work.
6. **Local government expenditures and taxes.** Under our fragmented system of local government, most large metropolitan areas have dozens of local governments, including municipalities, school districts, and special districts. In making location choices, households consider the mix of taxes and local public goods.

WHAT IS A CITY?

An urban economist defines an urban area as a geographical area that contains a large number of people in a relatively small area. In other words, an urban area has a population density that is high relative to the density of the surrounding area. This definition accommodates urban areas of vastly different sizes, from a small town to a large metropolitan area. The definition is based on population density because an essential feature of an urban economy is frequent contact between different economic activities, which is feasible only if firms and households are concentrated in a relatively small area.

The U.S. Census Bureau has developed a variety of geographical definitions relevant to urban economics. Since much of the empirical work in urban economics is based on census data, a clear understanding of these definitions is important. The appendix to this chapter provides the details of the census definitions.

The key census definitions, some of which are new for the 2000 Census, are as follows.

1. **Urban area:** A densely settled geographical area with a minimum population of 2,500 people and a minimum density of 5,000 people per square mile. In 2000, there were 3,756 urban areas in the United States.
2. **Urban population:** People living in urban areas. In 2000, the urban population was 79 percent of the total population.
3. **Metropolitan area:** A core area with a substantial population nucleus, together with adjacent communities that are integrated, in an economic sense, with the core area. To qualify as a metropolitan area, the minimum population is 50,000 people. In 2000, there were 361 metropolitan statistical areas in the United States.
4. **Micropolitan area:** A smaller version of a metropolitan area with a concentration of 10,000 to 50,000 people. In 2000, there were 559 micropolitan statistical areas in the United States.
5. **Principal city:** The largest municipality in each metropolitan or micropolitan statistical area. A municipality is defined as an area over which a municipal corporation exercises political authority and provides local government services such as sewage service, crime protection, and fire protection.

This book uses three terms to refer to spatial concentrations of economic activity: *urban area, metropolitan area,* and *city.* These three terms, which will be used interchangeably, refer to the economic city (an area with a relatively high population density that contains a set of closely related activities), not the political city. When referring to a political city, we will use the term *central city* or *municipality.*

WHY DO CITIES EXIST?

This is the fundamental question of urban economics. People need land to produce food and other resources, and living in dense cities separates us from the land where food is produced. As Bartlett (1998) points out, no other creatures in the animal world form anything like cities. Herbivores such as wildebeests and bison form larger herds but constantly migrate to fresh land to ensure a steady supply of food. Coral is concentrated in stationary reefs, but ocean currents provide a steady supply of food to the stationary coral. Perhaps the closest thing to a city in the natural world is a bee hive or an anthill. Eusocial insects such as bees and ants form colonies with thousands of inhabitants, with highly specialized castes—soldier ants, drones, breeders, nurses, and cleanup crews. In contrast with human cities, these insect agglomerations are closed to non-natives and not based on voluntary exchange.

Cities exist because human technology has created systems of production and exchange that seem to defy the natural order. Three conditions must be satisfied for a city to develop.

1. **Agricultural surplus.** People outside cities must produce enough food to feed themselves and city dwellers.

2. **Urban production.** City dwellers must produce something—goods or services—to exchange for food grown by rural workers.
3. **Transportation for exchange.** There must be an efficient transportation system to facilitate the exchange of food and urban products.

Figure 1–1 shows the share of people living in cities in the United States from 1800 to 2000. Over this period, the urban share increased from 6 percent to 79 percent, a remarkable transformation that also occurred in other parts of the world. As we'll see in the next three chapters of the book, the transformation of a rural society into an urban one occurred because technological advances increased the agricultural surplus (condition 1), increased the productivity of urban workers (condition 2), and increased the efficiency of transportation and exchange (condition 3).

Figure 1–2 shows urbanization rates for different regions around the world, with projections for the year 2030. In 1950, urbanization rates were relatively low in Africa and Asia, and highest in Oceania and North America. Between now and the year 2030, urbanization rates are expected to increase everywhere, with the largest increases in Africa and Asia. For the world as a whole, the urbanization rate was 30 percent in 1950 and is expected to double by the year 2030.

Table 1–1 (page 6) shows the population figures for the nation's 30 largest metropolitan areas. The New York area tops the list, followed by Los Angeles, Chicago, Philadelphia, and Dallas. The third column shows the percentage growth of each metropolitan area over the period 1990 to 2000. The most rapidly growing metropolitan areas were in the South, the Mountain States, and the West. Over the longer

FIGURE 1–1 Percent of U.S. Population in Urban Areas, 1800–2000

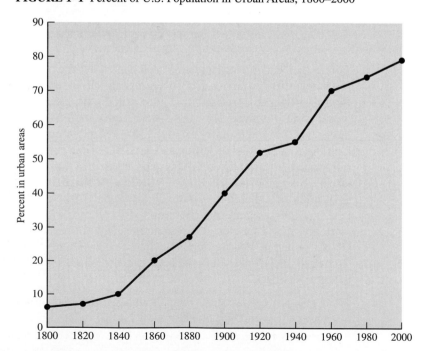

FIGURE 1–2 Urbanization Rates, by World Region, 1950–2030

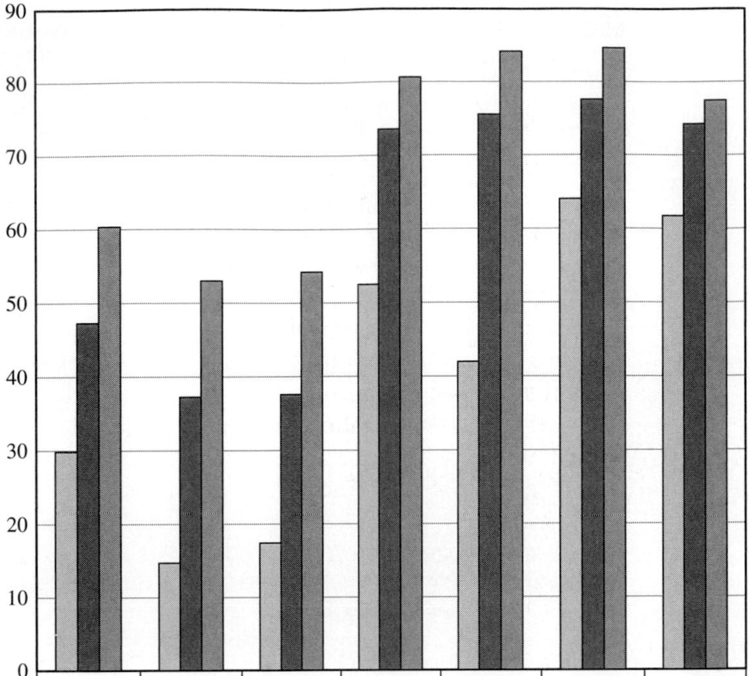

	World	Africa	Asia	Europe	Latin America and the Caribbean	Northern America	Oceania
▫ 1950	29.8	14.7	17.4	52.4	41.9	63.9	61.6
▪ 2000	47.2	37.2	37.5	73.4	75.4	77.4	74.1
▪ 2030	60.2	52.9	54.1	80.5	84	84.5	77.3

Percent in urban areas

Source: United Nations: World Urban Prospects, 2001 Revision.

period 1980–2000, two other metropolitan areas, Cleveland and Baltimore, lost population. These metropolitan areas experienced large losses in manufacturing employment, including losses in primary metals, motor vehicles, rubber, and non-electrical machinery industries.

Table 1–2 (page 7) shows the population figures for the world's largest metropolitan areas outside the United States. The table shows actual populations in 1995 and projected populations for the year 2015. Six metropolitan areas, all of which are in the developing world, are expected to grow by at least 50 percent over the 20-year period. In contrast, three cities in the developed world (Tokyo, Osaka, and Paris) are expected to grow at moderate to slow rates. In the United States, New York is expected to grow 8 percent over the period, and Los Angeles is expected to grow 15 percent.

TABLE 1–1 Largest Metropolitan Areas in the United States, 2000

Metropolitan Area	Population 2000	Percent Change 1990–2000
New York-Northern New Jersey-Long Island, NY-NJ-PA	18,323,002	8.8
Los Angeles-Long Beach-Santa Ana, CA	12,365,627	9.7
Chicago-Naperville-Joliet, IL-IN-WI	9,098,316	11.2
Philadelphia-Camden-Wilmington, PA-NJ-DE	5,687,147	4.6
Dallas-Fort Worth-Arlington, TX	5,161,544	29.4
Miami-Fort Lauderdale-Miami Beach, FL	5,007,564	23.5
Washington-Arlington-Alexandria, DC-VA-MD	4,796,183	16.3
Houston-Baytown-Sugar Land, TX	4,715,407	25.2
Detroit-Warren-Livonia, MI	4,452,557	4.8
Boston-Cambridge-Quincy, MA-NH	4,391,344	6.2
Atlanta-Sandy Springs-Marietta, GA	4,247,981	38.4
San Francisco-Oakland-Fremont, CA	4,123,740	11.9
Riverside-San Bernardino-Ontario, CA	3,254,821	25.7
Phoenix-Mesa-Scottsdale, AZ	3,251,876	45.3
Seattle-Tacoma-Bellevue, WA	3,043,878	18.9
Minneapolis-St. Paul-Bloomington, MN-WI	2,968,806	16.9
San Diego-Carlsbad-San Marcos, CA	2,813,833	12.6
St. Louis, MO-IL	2,698,687	4.6
Baltimore-Towson, MD	2,552,994	7.2
Pittsburgh, PA	2,431,087	−1.5
Tampa-St. Petersburg-Clearwater, FL	2,395,997	15.9
Denver-Aurora, CO	2,179,240	30.7
Cleveland-Elyria-Mentor, OH	2,148,143	2.2
Cincinnati-Middletown, OH-KY-IN	2,009,632	8.9
Portland-Vancouver-Beaverton, OR-WA	1,927,881	26.5
Kansas City, MO-KS	1,836,038	12.2
Sacramento-Arden–Arcade-Roseville, CA	1,796,857	21.3
San Jose-Sunnyvale-Santa Clara, CA	1,735,819	13.1
San Antonio, TX	1,711,703	21.6
Orlando, FL	1,644,561	34.3

Source: U.S. Census Bureau, Census 2000 and 1990 Census.

Figure 1–3 (page 8) shows the time trend of large urban agglomerations in the world, defined as metropolitan areas with at least 1 million people. The figure distinguishes between cities in the developed and less developed regions. In 1970, the two types of regions had roughly the same number of large cities. By 1996, however, the number of large cities in the less developed regions nearly doubled, and by 2015 there will be roughly four times as many large cities in less developed regions.

THE FIVE AXIOMS OF URBAN ECONOMICS

Urban economics explores the location choices of households and firms, and so it is natural to assume that people and firms are mobile. Of course, people don't instantly change their workplaces and residences when circumstances change; therefore, a model of perfect mobility tells us more about long-term changes than short-term

TABLE 1–2 Population and Expected Growth in Large World Cities

City	Population 1995 (million)	Population 2015 (million)	Percentage Increase, 1995–2015
Tokyo, Japan	26.96	28.89	7%
Mexico City, Mexico	16.56	19.18	16
Sao Paulo, Brazil	16.53	20.32	23
Bombay, India	15.14	26.22	73
Shanghai, China	13.58	17.97	32
Calcutta, India	11.92	17.31	45
Buenos Aires, Argentina	11.80	13.86	17
Seoul, Korea	11.61	12.98	12
Beijing, China	11.30	15.57	38
Osaka, Japan	10.61	10.61	—
Lagos, Nigeria	10.29	24.61	139
Rio de Janeiro, Brazil	10.18	11.86	17
Delhi, India	9.95	16.86	69
Karachi, Pakistan	9.73	19.38	99
Cairo, Egypt	9.69	14.42	49
Paris, France	9.52	9.69	2
Tianjin, China	9.42	13.53	44
Manila, Philippines	9.29	14.66	58
Moscow, Russian Fed.	9.27	9.30	0
Jakarta, Indonesia	8.62	13.92	61
Dhaka, Bangladesh	8.55	19.49	128

Source: United Nations Population Division, *Urban Agglomerations, 1950–2015,* rev. ed. (New York: United Nations, 1996).

ones. The average household changes its residence every seven years, meaning that about 14 percent of the population moves every year. Although most models of urban economics assume perfect mobility, there are exceptions, and we will highlight the analysis that assumes less than perfect mobility.

In this part of the chapter, we introduce five axioms of urban economics. An axiom is a self-evident truth, something that most people readily understand and accept. For our purposes, "most people" are people who have taken at least one course in economics. The five axioms lie at the heart of urban economics and together provide a foundation for the economic models of location choices. As you go through the book, these five axioms will appear repeatedly.

1. Prices Adjust to Achieve Locational Equilibrium

A locational equilibrium occurs when no one has an incentive to move. Suppose that you and Bud are competing for two rental houses, one along a beautiful beach and one along a noisy highway. If the two houses have the same price (the same monthly rent), you would prefer the beach house, and so would Bud. Flipping a coin and giving the beach house to the winner wouldn't generate a locational equilibrium because the unlucky person in the highway house would have an incentive to move to the more desirable house.

FIGURE 1–3 The Number of Large Agglomerations in the World, 1950–2015

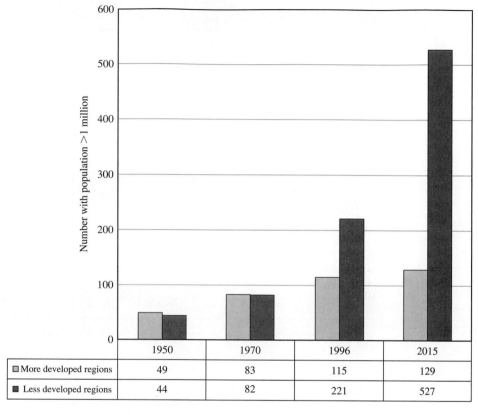

	1950	1970	1996	2015
☐ More developed regions	49	83	115	129
■ Less developed regions	44	82	221	527

Source: United Nations World Population Prospects (New York: United Nations, 2001).

Locational equilibrium requires a higher price for the beach house. To eliminate the incentive to move, the price of the beach house must be high enough to fully compensate for the better environment. The question is, How much money are you willing to sacrifice to live on the beach? If your answer is $300 and Bud agrees, then the equilibrium price of beach house will be $300 higher than the price of the highway house. In general, prices adjust to generate the same utility level in different environments, getting people to live in both desirable and undesirable locations.

The same sort of economic forces operate in the labor market. Workers compete for jobs in desirable locations, causing lower wages in more desirable locations. Suppose you are competing with Ricki for two jobs, one in Dullsville and one in Coolsville, a city with a more stimulating social environment. If a $500 gap in the monthly wage fully compensates for the difference in the social environment, the equilibrium wage will be $500 lower in Coolsville. The two workers will be indifferent between the two cities because a move to Coolsville means a $500 wage cut. In the labor market, wages adjust to get people to work in both desirable and undesirable environments.

The price of land also adjusts to ensure locational equilibrium among firms. Office firms compete for the most accessible land in a city, and land at the center is the most accessible and thus the most expensive. In equilibrium, office firms on less accessible land far from the center pay lower prices for land, and can be just as profitable as firms on the most accessible land.

2. Self-Reinforcing Effects Generate Extreme Outcomes

A self-reinforcing effect is a change in something that leads to additional changes in the same direction. Consider a city where the sellers of new automobiles are initially spread evenly throughout the city. If one seller relocates next to another seller on Auto Road, what happens next? Auto consumers compare brands before buying, and the pair of sellers on Auto Road will facilitate comparison shopping and thus attract buyers. The increased consumer traffic on Auto Road will make it an attractive site for other auto sellers, so they will move too. The ultimate result is an "auto row," a cluster of firms that compete against one another, yet locate nearby.

Self-reinforcing changes also happen in the location decisions of people. Suppose artists and creative types are initially spread out evenly across a dozen cities in a region. If by chance one city experiences an influx of artists, its creative environment will improve as artists (1) are exposed to more ideas and fabrication techniques and (2) can share studios, print shops, tool suppliers, and other facilities. The cluster of artists will attract other artists from the region, causing a concentration of artistic production in one city. In recent decades, cities that have attracted artists and creative folks have experienced relatively rapid growth (Florida, 2002).

3. Externalities Cause Inefficiency

In most transactions, the costs and benefits of the exchange are confined to the individual buyer and seller. The consumer pays a price equal to the full cost of producing the good, so no one else bears a cost from the transaction. Similarly, the consumer is the only person to benefit from the product. In contrast, an externality occurs when some of the costs or benefits of a transaction are experienced by someone other than the buyer or seller, that is, someone *external* to the transaction.

An external cost occurs when a consumer pays a price that is less than the full cost of producing a product. The price of a product always includes the costs of the labor, capital, and raw materials used to produce the product, but it usually does not include the environmental costs of producing the product. For example, if burning gasoline in automobiles generates air pollution, part of the cost of driving is borne by people who breathe dirty air. Similarly, when you enter a crowded highway, you slow down everyone else, meaning that other drivers bear a cost.

An external benefit occurs when a product purchased by one person generates a benefit for someone else. For example, painting my peeling house improves the appearance of my neighborhood, increasing the value of my neighbor's house as well as mine. Education generates external benefits because it improves communication and thinking skills, making a person a better team worker. In other words, some of the benefits of education are experienced by a person's fellow workers, who become more productive and thus earn higher wages.

When there are external costs or benefits, we do not expect the market equilibrium to be socially efficient. In the case of external cost, people pay less than the full social cost of an action like driving, so they drive too much. In the case of external benefit, people get less than the full social benefit from an action like education, so they stop short of the socially efficient level of education. As we'll see later in the book, cities have all sorts of external costs and benefits. In many cases there is a simple solution: Internalize the externality with a tax or a subsidy, and let individuals, who then bear the full social cost and benefits of their actions, decide what to do.

4. Production Is Subject to Economies of Scale

Economies of scale occur when the average cost of production decreases as output increases. For most products, if we start with a relatively small production operation and double all inputs, the average cost of production decreases. In the jargon of economics, when the long-run average cost curve is negatively sloped, we say that there are scale economies in production. Scale economies occur for two reasons:

- **Indivisible inputs.** Some capital inputs are "lumpy" and cannot be scaled down for small operations. As a result, a small operation has the same indivisible inputs as a large operation. For example, to manufacture frisbees you need a mold, whether you produce one frisbee per day or a thousand. Similarly, to produce microprocessors you need a clean room and other expensive equipment, whether you produce one processor per day or a thousand. As output increases, the average cost decreases because the cost of the indivisible input is spread over more output.
- **Factor specialization.** In a small one-person production operation, a worker performs a wide variety of production tasks. In a larger operation with more workers, each worker specializes in a few tasks, leading to higher productivity because of continuity (less time is spent switching from one task to another) and proficiency (from experience and learning). The notion of factor specialization is captured in the old expression, "A jack of all trades is master of none." Adding to this expression, we can say that a specialized worker is a master of one task.

As we'll see later in the book, scale economies play a vital role in urban economies. In fact, as we'll see in Chapter 2, if there are no scale economies, there will be no cities. It is costly to transport products from a production site to consumers, so centralized production in cities will be sensible only if there is some advantage that more than offsets transport costs.

The extent of scale economies in production varies across products. Microprocessors are produced in $5 billion fabrication facilities with a highly specialized workforce performing hundreds of complex tasks, resulting in large scale economies in production. In contrast, pizza is produced with a $5,000 pizza oven with just a few production tasks, so scale economies are exhausted sooner. In general, the extent of scale economies is determined by the lumpiness of indivisible inputs and the opportunities for factor specialization.

5. Competition Generates Zero Economic Profit

When there are no restrictions on the entry of firms into a market, we expect firms to enter the market until economic profit is zero. Recall that economic profit equals the excess of total revenue over total economic cost, where economic cost includes the opportunity costs of all inputs. Two key components of economic costs are the opportunity cost of the entrepreneur's time and the opportunity cost of funds invested in the firm. For example, suppose an entrepreneur could earn $60,000 in another job and invests $100,000 in the firm, taking the money out of a mutual fund that earns 8 percent. The economic cost of the firm includes $60,000 in time cost and $8,000 in investment cost. Once we account for all the opportunity costs, the fact that economic profit is zero means that a firm is making enough money to stay in business, but not enough for other firms to enter the market. Earning zero economic profit means earning "normal" accounting profit.

In urban economics, competition has a spatial dimension. Each firm enters the market at some location, and the profit of each firm is affected by the locations of other firms. Spatial competition looks a lot like monopolistic competition, a market structure in which firms sell slightly differentiated products in an environment of unrestricted entry. Although this sounds like an oxymoron such as "tight slacks" and "jumbo shrimp," the words are revealing. Each firm has a monopoly for its differentiated product, but unrestricted entry leads to keen competition for consumers who can easily switch from one differentiated product to another. With spatial competition, each firm has a local monopoly in the area immediately surrounding its establishment, but unrestricted entry leads to keen competition. Firms will continue to enter the market until economic profit drops to zero.

WHAT'S NEXT?

This introductory chapter sets the stage for the economic analysis of cities in the rest of the book. Here are some of the big questions we'll address in coming chapters:

- Why do cities exist?
- Are cities too big or too small?
- What causes urban economic growth?
- Why is employment in modern cities so widely dispersed?
- Why is there so much segregation with respect to race and income?
- Why do economists advocate a tax of about 7 cents per mile for all driving and about 27 cents per mile for driving on congested roads?
- Why do so few people take mass transit?
- Why is crime higher in cities?
- Why does the typical metropolitan area have dozens of municipalities?

In answering these and other questions, we will use the five axioms of urban economics. In addition, we will use a number of economic models to explore the spatial aspects of decision making. It's worth noting that much of the analysis in the book reflects advances in urban economics in the last 10 to 15 years, in both theoretical modeling and empirical analysis. In fact, so much is new that writing the sixth edition of the book involved an extreme makeover, with only a few paragraphs and figures surviving from the fifth edition.

REFERENCES AND ADDITIONAL READING

1. Audretsch, David, and Maryann Feldman. "Knowledge Spillovers and the Geography of Innovation," Chapter 61 in *Handbook of Regional and Urban Economics 4: Cities and Geography,* eds. Vernon Henderson and Jacques-Francois Thisse. Amsterdam: Elsevier, 2004.
2. Bartlett, Randall. *The Crisis of American Cities.* Armonk, NY: Sharp, 1998.
3. U.S. Government. "Standards for Defining Metropolitan and Micropolitan Statistical Areas." *Federal Register* 65, no. 249 (December 17, 2000).
4. Florida, Richard. *The Rise of the Creative Class.* New York: Basic Books, 2002.

Appendix: Census Definitions

The U.S. Census Bureau has developed a variety of geographical definitions relevant to urban economics. Since much of the empirical work in urban economics is based on census data, a clear understanding of these definitions is important. This appendix provides the details of the census definitions.

URBAN POPULATION

The first three definitions deal with the urban population and are based on the census block, the smallest geographical unit in census data. A *census block* is defined as an area bounded on all sides by visible features (streets, streams, or tracks) or invisible features (property lines or political boundaries). The typical census block has between a few dozen and a few hundred residents. A *block group* is a group of contiguous census blocks. There are two types of urban areas:

1. **Urbanized area.** An *urbanized area* is a densely settled core of census block groups and surrounding census blocks that meet minimum population density requirements. In most cases, the density requirement is 1,000 people per square mile for the core block groups and 500 people per square mile for the surrounding blocks. Together, the densely settled blocks must encompass a population of at least 50,000 people. In 2000, there were 464 urbanized areas in the United States.

2. **Urban clusters.** An *urban cluster* is a scaled-down version of an urbanized area. The total population of the census blocks that make up an urban cluster is between 2,500 and 50,000 people. In 2000, there were 3,112 urban clusters in the United States.
3. **Urban population.** The Census Bureau defines the nation's *urban population* as all people living in urbanized areas and urban clusters. Based on this definition, 79 percent of the population lived in urban areas in 2000.

METROPOLITAN AND MICROPOLITAN STATISTICAL AREAS

The census bureau has a long history of changing its definitions of metropolitan areas. The general idea is that a metropolitan area includes a core area with a substantial population nucleus, together with adjacent communities that are integrated, in an economic sense, with the core area. Over the years, the labels for metropolitan areas have changed from standard metropolitan area (SMA) in 1949, to standard metropolitan statistical area (SMSA) in 1959, to metropolitan statistical area (MSA) in 1983, to metropolitan area (MA) in 1990, which referred collectively to metropolitan statistical areas (MSAs), consolidated metropolitan statistical areas (CMSAs— the largest metropolitan areas), and primary metropolitan statistical areas (PMSAs— parts of CMSAs).

The new label for areas considered metropolitan, implemented in 2000, is *core based statistical area* (CBSA). Each CBSA contains at least one urban area (either an urbanized area or an urban cluster) with at least 10,000 people and is designated as either a metropolitan area or a micropolitan area.

1. **Metropolitan area.** A *metropolitan statistical area* includes at least one urbanized area with at least 50,000 people.
2. **Micropolitan area.** A *micropolitan statistical area* includes at least one urban cluster of between 10,000 and 50,000 people.

In 2000, there were 361 metropolitan statistical areas and 559 micropolitan statistical areas in the United States.

The building blocks for metropolitan and micropolitan areas are counties. For a particular CBSA, central counties are ones in which at least 5,000 people or 50 percent of the population resides within urban areas with at least 10,000 people. Additional outlying counties are included in the CBSA if they meet minimum thresholds of commuting rates to or from the central counties. Specifically, at least 25 percent of workers in an outlying county must work in one of the central counties, or at least 25 percent of the jobs in an outlying county must be filled by residents of one of the central counties.

Together CSBAs contain 93 percent of the nation's population, with 83 percent in metropolitan areas and 10 percent in the smaller micropolitan areas. The percentage of the population in CSBAs (93 percent) exceeds the percentage in urban areas (79 percent) because CSBAs encompass entire counties, including areas outside urban areas (defined by the smallest geographical unit, the census block).

PRINCIPAL CITY

The largest municipality in each metropolitan or micropolitan statistical area is designated a *principal city*. Additional cities qualify as "principal" if they meet minimum requirements for population size (at least 250,000 people) and employment (at least 100,000 workers). The title of each metropolitan or micropolitan statistical area consists of the names of up to three of its principal cities and the name of each state into which the metropolitan or micropolitan statistical area extends. For example, the name for Minneapolis metropolitan area is Minneapolis-St. Paul-Bloomington, MN-WI, indicating that it includes parts of two states with two other municipalities large enough to merit listing. For most metropolitan areas, the label includes only one principal city. About a dozen large metropolitan areas are divided into smaller groupings of counties called metropolitan divisions.

PART ONE

Market Forces in the Development of Cities

*I*n a market economy, individuals exchange their labor for wage income, which they use to buy consumer goods and services. How do these market transactions affect cities? As we'll see in Chapter 2, cities exist because of the benefits of centralized production and exchange. We'll look at the rationale for the development of cities based on trade, production, and processing raw materials. Chapter 3 explores agglomeration economies, the economic forces that cause firms to cluster in cities to share the suppliers of intermediate inputs, share a labor pool, get better skills matches between workers and firms, and share knowledge. Chapter 4 explores the economic forces behind the development of cities of different size and scope. We'll look at how worker utility varies with city size and see why the equilibrium city size often exceeds the optimum size. Chapter 5 explores the sources of urban economic growth (increases in per-capita income) and urban employment growth. It also addresses the question of who benefits from employment growth and describes some of the techniques used by economists to predict future employment growth.

CHAPTER 2

Why Do Cities Exist?

*Nobody ever saw a dog make a fair and deliberate exchange
of one bone for another with another dog.*

—ADAM SMITH

*C*ities exist because individuals are not self-sufficient. If each of us could produce everything we consumed and didn't want much company, there would be no reason to live in dirty, noisy, crowded cities. We aren't self-sufficient, but instead specialize in a labor task—writing software, playing the accordion, performing brain surgery—and use our earnings to buy the things we don't produce ourselves. We do this because labor specialization and large-scale production allow us to produce and consume more stuff. As we'll see in this chapter, production happens in cities, so that's where most of us live and work. By living and working in cities, we achieve a higher standard of living but put up with more congestion, noise, and pollution.

To explain why cities exist, we'll start with a model that implies that they don't. In the model of backyard production, every consumer is a producer, and all production occurs in backyards (or apartment roofs). In other words there is no need for concentrated production or population. As we drop the assumptions of the backyard-production model, the new models imply that cities will develop. In other words, the short list of assumptions in the model identifies the key factors behind the development of cities.

A REGION WITHOUT CITIES—BACKYARD PRODUCTION

Consider a region that produces and consumes two products, bread and shirts. People use the raw materials from land (wool and wheat) to produce the two consumer products. The following assumptions eliminate the possibility of cities.

- **Equal productivity.** All land is equally productive in producing wheat and wool, and all workers are equally productive in producing shirts and bread.

- **Constant returns to scale in exchange.** The unit cost of exchange (the cost of executing one transaction, including transportation cost) is constant, regardless of how much is exchanged.
- **Constant returns to scale in production.** The quantity of shirts produced per hour is constant, regardless of how many shirts a worker produces. The same is true for bread production.

Together these assumptions eliminate the possibility of exchange and guarantee that each household will be self-sufficient. If a person were to specialize in bread and then trade some bread for shirts, she would incur a transaction cost equal to the time required to execute the trade. Under the assumption of equal productivity, there is no benefit from specialization because everyone is equally productive. Under the assumption of constant returns to scale, there is no benefit from producing shirts in factories because an individual is just as efficient as a shirt factory. In sum, exchange has costs without any benefits, so every household will be self-sufficient, producing everything it consumes.

The absence of exchange guarantees a uniform distribution of population. If population were concentrated at some location, competition for land would bid up its price. People in the city would pay a higher price for land without any compensating benefit, so they would have an incentive to leave the city. In the locational equilibrium, the price of land would be the same at all locations, and population density would be uniform. Recall the first axiom of urban economics:

Prices adjust to ensure locational equilibrium

In this case, all sites are equally attractive, so locational equilibrium requires the same price of land at all locations.

A TRADING CITY

Now that we have a short list of assumptions under which cities don't develop, let's drop the assumptions, one by one, and see what happens. We'll start by dropping the assumption of equal productivity for all workers. Suppose households in the North are more productive in producing both bread and shirts. This could result from differences in soil conditions, climate, or worker skills. Table 2–1 shows the output per hour for the two regions. While each worker in the South can produce one shirt or one loaf per hour, workers in the North are twice as productive in producing bread and six times as productive in producing shirts.

TABLE 2–1 Comparative Advantage

	North		South	
	Bread	Shirts	Bread	Shirts
Output per hour	2	6	1	1
Opportunity cost	3 shirts	1/3 loaf	1 shirt	1 loaf

Comparative Advantage and Trade

A region has a comparative advantage in producing a particular product if it has a lower opportunity cost. For every shirt produced, the North sacrifices 1/3 loaf of bread, so that's the opportunity cost of a shirt. In the South, the opportunity cost of a shirt is one loaf. The North has a lower opportunity cost for shirts, so it has a comparative advantage in producing shirts. It is sensible for the North to specialize in shirts (and not produce any bread) because, although the North is twice as productive as the South in producing bread, the North is *six* times as productive in producing shirts.

Comparative advantage may lead to specialization and trade. Suppose the two regions are initially self-sufficient, with each household producing all the bread and shirts it consumes. Table 2–2 shows what happens if a North household switches one hour from bread to shirt production, and a South household goes the other direction, switching two hours from shirt to bread production. The first row shows the changes in production: -2 loaves and $+6$ shirts for North; $+2$ loaves and -2 shirts for South. As shown in the second and third rows, if the households exchange two loaves and four shirts, each has a gain from trade of two shirts. After specialization and exchange, each household has just as much bread as before and two additional shirts.

What about transaction costs? The transaction cost is the opportunity cost of the time required to exchange products and is equal to the amount of output that could be produced during that time. For example, a North household can produce six shirts per hour, so the opportunity cost for a 10-minute (1/6 hour) transaction is one shirt. As long as the transaction time is less than 1/3 hour (two shirts), trade is beneficial. The South household, with a lower opportunity cost, has a lower transaction cost.

Scale Economies in Exchange

The presence of specialization and trade will not necessarily cause a city to develop. The second assumption of the backyard-production model is that there are constant returns to scale in exchange. Under this assumption, an individual household is just as efficient in executing trades as a trading firm, so there is no reason to pay a firm to execute an exchange. Therefore, each North household will link up with a South household to exchange shirts and bread directly, without intermediaries.

TABLE 2–2 Specialization and Gains from Trade

	North		South	
	Bread	Shirts	Bread	Shirts
Change in production from specialization	-2	$+6$	$+2$	-2
Exchange 4 shirts for 2 loaves	$+2$	-4	-2	$+4$
Gain from trade	0	$+2$	0	$+2$

Trading firms will emerge if there are economies of scale associated with exchange and trade. Recall the fourth axiom of urban economics:

Production is subject to economies of scale

A trading firm could use indivisible inputs such as a large truck to transport output between North and South. Similarly, workers who specialize in transportation tasks will be more efficient than workers who spend most of their time producing bread or shirts. In general, because trading firms have lower transaction costs, individual households will pay trading firms to handle exchanges.

The emergence of trading firms will cause the development of a trading city. To fully exploit scale economies, trading firms will locate at places that can efficiently collect and distribute large volumes of output. The concentration of trade workers will bid up the price of land near crossroads, river junctions, and ports. The increase in the price of land will cause people to economize on land by occupying smaller residential lots. The result is a place with a relatively high population density—a city.

TRADING CITIES IN URBAN HISTORY

Our simple model of the trading city suggests that trading cities develop when comparative advantage is combined with scale economies in transport and exchange. This observation provides some important insights into the history of cities before the Industrial Revolution of the 1800s. Most of the workers in these trading cities didn't produce goods, but instead collected and distributed goods produced elsewhere, such as agricultural products from the hinterlands and handcrafted goods from various locations. Trade was a risky business, and firms in the trading city provided insurance, credit, investment opportunities, banking, and legal services.

Trading Cities in World History

Trading cities have a long history. In the third millennium B.C., Phoenicians used fast sailing ships to serve as traders for the entire Mediterranean basin, trading dye, raw materials, foodstuffs, textiles, and jewelry. They established trading cities along the Mediterranean coast in present-day Lebanon. Around 500 B.C., Athens was a thriving site for regional trade, exchanging household crafts and olive products for food and raw materials from the countryside. During the 11th and 12th centuries, Italian city-states forged agreements with the Byzantine and Islamic rulers for trade with North Africa and the East. The Europeans traded wood, iron, grain, wine, and wool cloth for medicines, dyes, linen, cotton, leather, and precious metals. This trade was the major force behind the growth of Venice, Genoa, and Pisa.

Some cities were built on coercive transfer payments rather than voluntary trade. The Athenian empire developed in the aftermath of the successful war against Persia in the fifth century B.C. After the Greek city-states repelled the Persian invasion, they formed the Delian League for joint defense and later to carry the war into

Asia Minor. By the end of the successful campaign, Athens controlled the league and transformed the voluntary contributions of member city-states into payments of tribute to Athens. The system of homage and tribute led to the Peloponnesian War between the Athenian Empire and Sparta (431 to 404 B.C.). The war ended when Athens renounced control over its empire and demolished its defensive walls.

By the third century A.D., Rome had a population exceeding 1 million. The Romans established colonial cities throughout Europe and focused on collecting the agricultural surplus while they neglected urban production activity (Hohenberg and Lees,1985). Instead of exchanging urban goods for agricultural products, Rome used conquest and tribute to feed its population. In the fourth and fifth centuries, attacks from Germanic tribes disrupted the Roman collection system. It appears that there was little interest outside of Rome in restoring the "trade" routes, so the losses from successive attacks were cumulative. If Rome had relied to a greater extent on voluntary exchange, the colonies would have had a greater stake in maintaining the exchange network and the Western empire might have recovered from the Germanic raids.

What are the lessons from the rise and fall of Athens and Rome? Early in its history, Athens thrived under a system of voluntary trade with other areas, exchanging urban goods for food from the countryside. The Athenians eventually switched to a system of conquest and tribute, resulting in war and the decline of the city. Mumford (1961) suggests that the city of Rome should have been called "Parasitopolis" to indicate its dependence on the labors of outsiders. The decline of Rome was caused in part by the disruption of its collection system by the Germanic raids. Perhaps the lesson is that cities based on coercive transfer payments are not sustainable.

Trading Cities in American History

The history of urban America illustrates the role of transport costs and comparative advantage in trading cities (Bartlett, 1998). In the 1700s, most cities served largely as trading posts for ocean trade. On the eastern seaboard, cities collected agricultural products from their hinterlands to the west and shipped them overseas. The volume of trade was limited by the dirt roads serving the interior: Travel was always slow and, in times of rain and melting snow, slippery. The Pennsylvania Turnpike, built with stone and gravel in 1792, increased travel speeds to a steady two miles per hour, increasing the market area and trading volume of the city of Philadelphia.

Farther to the north, New York State took more drastic steps, completing the 360-mile Erie Canal in 1825. The canal linked New York City, with its natural harbor, to vast agricultural areas to the north and west, and it cut freight costs from about 20 cents per ton mile to 1.5 cents. An additional canal connecting Lake Champlain to the Hudson River extended the market area of New York City to northern New England. The vast transportation network increased the volume of trade through New York City, increasing its size. By 1850, the city had a population of half a million, about 20 times its size at the end of the American Revolution. Other cities, including competitors to the south (Baltimore and Philadelphia), responded by building canals to connect hinterlands and ports, and by 1845 there were over 3,300 miles of artificial waterways in the United States.

Comparative advantage also plays a role in urban history. Eli Whitney's cotton gin (1794) provided a means of removing the sticky seeds of green-seed cotton, which could be grown throughout the south. The total output of cotton increased by a factor of 50 over a 15-year period, with most of the output coming from inland areas far from the east coast ports. American cotton was transported along rivers to New Orleans for shipment to textile firms in New England and Europe. The increase in cotton trade caused the rapid growth of New Orleans at the mouth of the Mississippi, and the development of upriver commercial cities such as Mobile, Alabama and Natchez, Mississippi.

Later innovations in transportation reduced transport costs and contributed to the development of trading cities. Before the introduction of the steamboat in 1807, traffic was strictly downstream: After cargo was unloaded at the terminal point, wooden boats were broken up for lumber. The steamboat allowed two-way traffic and cut river freight costs, increasing the volume of trade and the size of river cities. Later, the steam engine was used to power locomotives, and railroad freight replaced river shipping as the principal means of transporting goods. Between 1850 and 1890, the ratio of railroad freight to river freight went from 0.10 to 2.0, and the volume of railroad freight increased by a factor of 240. The shift from river to railroad caused the decline of commercial cities along rivers and the rise of cities along the vast railroad network.

A FACTORY TOWN

The third assumption of the backyard-production model is constant returns to scale in production. We'll maintain this assumption for bread production, but apply the fourth axiom of urban economics to shirt production:

Production is subject to economies of scale

A shirt factory will use indivisible inputs (machines) and allow workers to specialize in narrowly defined tasks, leading to a higher output per worker and lower average cost. Suppose a household can produce either a loaf of bread or one shirt per hour. A worker in a shirt factory is six times as productive as a home worker, so the factory worker produces six shirts per hour.

Determining Wages and Prices

We assume that workers are perfectly mobile, so the utility level of a city worker must be the same as the utility level for a rural worker. Recall the first axiom of urban economics:

Prices adjust to ensure locational equilibrium

A factory must pay its workers enough to make them indifferent between working in the factory town and in the rural area. A rural worker earns one loaf of bread

TABLE 2–3 Cost of Factory Shirt

Labor cost per hour	3/2 loaves
Cost of indivisible inputs per hour	1/2 loaf
Total cost per hour	2 loaves
Cost per shirt with 6 shirts produced per hour	1/3 loaf

per hour, so city workers must earn one loaf per hour plus an amount high enough to offset the higher cost of living in the factory town, such as higher land prices. For example, if the cost of urban living is 50 percent higher, locational indifference requires an hourly wage of 3/2 loaves of bread. A city worker will pay 1/2 loaf for land, leaving one loaf per hour of factory work, the same that she could earn producing bread in a rural area.

What's the price of factory shirts? The price must be high enough to cover the costs of labor and the indivisible inputs used to produce shirts. In Table 2–3 the labor cost per hour is the wage (3/2 loaves) and the hourly cost of indivisible inputs is 1/2 loaf. Adding these together, the hourly cost of producing shirts is two loaves of bread. To translate this into a cost per shirt, recall that a factory worker produces six shirts per hour, so the cost per shirt is one-sixth of the cost per hour, or $2/6 = 1/3$ loaf. Therefore, for zero economic profit, the price per shirt must be 1/3 loaf of bread.

Suppose there is a single shirt factory in the region. The factory competes with homemade shirts, and will sell shirts to any household for which the net price of factory shirts is less than the cost of a homemade shirt. The cost of a homemade shirt is the one loaf of bread that is sacrificed to produce a shirt. The net price of a factory shirt equals the price charged by the factory (1/3 loaf) plus the opportunity cost of travel to and from the factory to buy the shirt.

The Market Area of a Factory Town

Figure 2–1 (page 24) shows the net price of factory shirts and the market area of the shirt factory. As shown by point f, the net price for a consumer located just across the road from the factory (distance = 0) is the factory price, equal to $1/3 = 4/12$ loaf of bread. Other consumers bear a travel cost when they buy factory shirts, so the net price is higher. Suppose the travel time is 1/12 hour per round-trip mile: It takes 1/12 hour to complete a round trip of one mile in each direction. In an hour, a rural household can produce one loaf of bread, so in 1/12 of an hour of travel, it sacrifices 1/12 loaf. For example, at point g (two miles from the factory), the net price of a factory shirt is 6/12 loaves, equal to 4/12 paid at the factory plus 2/12 in travel cost (forgone bread production at home).

The market area of the factory is the area over which it underprices the home production of shirts. In Figure 2–1, the horizontal line shows the opportunity cost of homemade shirts, which is one loaf of bread. The net price of factory shirts is 4/12 at the factory and increases by 1/12 per mile, reaching one loaf at a distance of eight

FIGURE 2–1 Market Area of Factory

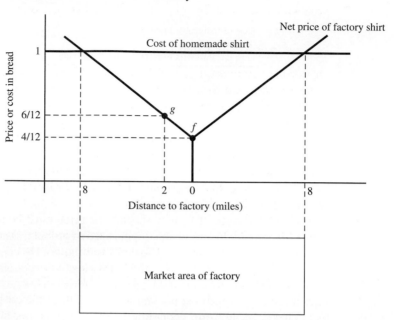

The net price of a factory shirt is the factory price (1/3 = 4/12 loaf of bread) plus transport cost (1/12 loaf per round-trip mile). The market area of the factory is the area over which the net price of a factory shirt is less than the cost of a homemade shirt (one loaf).

miles (4/12 + 8/12). In other words, the factory underprices home production up to eight miles away, so households within eight miles of the factory buy shirts rather than producing them at home. Beyond this point, households are self-sufficient, producing their own bread and shirts.

A factory town will develop around the shirt factory. Workers will economize on travel costs by living close to the factory, and competition for land will bid up its price. The higher price of land will cause workers to economize on land, leading to a higher population density. The result is a place of relatively high population density, a factory city. Note that we have already incorporated the higher land price into the factory wage and the factory price: Workers receive an hourly wage of 3/2 loaves to cover the opportunity cost of their time (1 loaf) and land rent (1/2 loaf).

THE INDUSTRIAL REVOLUTION AND FACTORY CITIES

Our simple model of the factory city suggests that a factory town develops because scale economies make factory shirts cheaper than homemade shirts. The Industrial Revolution of the 19th century produced innovations in manufacturing and transportation that shifted production from the home and the small shop to large factories in industrial cities. In contrast to the earlier trading cities, workers in factory cities produced products rather than simply distributing products produced elsewhere.

Innovations in Manufacturing

One of the key innovations of the Industrial Revolution was Eli Whitney's system of interchangeable parts for manufacturing, developed around 1800. Under the traditional craftsman approach, the component parts of a particular product were made individually—and imprecisely. Skilled craftsmen were necessary to produce the parts and then fit them all together. Under Whitney's system, the producer made a large batch of each part, using precise machine tools to generate identical parts. The identical parts were interchangeable, so unskilled workers could be quickly trained to assemble the parts. The replacement of handcraft production with standardized production generated large scale economies, causing the development of factories and factory cities.

Whitney applied this system to the production of muskets for the army. To prove to President-elect Jefferson and other government officials that his system would work with unskilled labor, he unloaded a random collection of parts onto the floor and had the officials assemble the muskets. He got the contract to manufacture 10,000 muskets and built a factory in New Haven, Connecticut, close to a stream that he used to power the factory. His system, which became know as the American System of Manufacturing, became the standard system for mass production.

The new system of manufacturing caused the development of factory cities. New machines, made of iron instead of wood, were developed to fabricate products in large factories. Manual production by skilled artisans was replaced by mechanized production using interchangeable parts, specialized labor, and steam-powered machines. Mass production decreased the relative cost of factory goods, causing the centralization of production and employment in large industrial cities.

As an illustration of the role of scale economies in the development of cities, consider the sewing machine, which was developed in the middle of the 19th century. At the beginning of the century, about four-fifths of the clothing worn in the United States was hand-sewn in the home for members of the household, and the rest was hand-sewn by tailors. The sewing machine (patented in 1846) allowed factories to underprice home producers, and by 1890 nine-tenths of U.S. clothing was being made in factories. New cities developed around the clothing factories.

A similar story line applies to shoes. Before 1700, most shoes were produced in the home or the local village. The cost of transportation was so high that local production was efficient. Over time, transportation costs decreased, and the putting-out system was implemented in the 1700s: Shoe producers distributed raw materials to cottage workers, collected their rough output, and finished the shoes in a central shop. As new shoemaking machines were developed, the number of operations performed in the central shops increased. The McKay sewing machine (for which a patent was granted to Lyman Blake in 1858) mechanized the process of sewing the soles to the uppers. The scale economies in shoe production increased to the point that shops became genuine factories, and cities developed around the shoe factories.

Innovations in Transportation

Innovations in intercity transportation contributed to industrialization and urbanization. As we saw earlier in the chapter, the dirt roads of the 1700s were replaced by turnpikes, and the construction of canals allowed a more dense network of inland water transport. The development of the steamship allowed two-way travel on major rivers, and the railroad system increased the speed and reach of the transportation system. All of these innovations decreased the relative price of factory goods, contributing to the growth of factory cities.

Innovations in Agriculture

One of the three conditions for the development of cities is an agricultural surplus to feed city dwellers. The Industrial Revolution generated a number of innovations that increased agricultural productivity. Farmers substituted machinery for muscle power and simple tools, increasing the output per farmer. The increased agricultural productivity freed people to work in urban factories and commercial firms. Between 1800 and 1900, the share of the population living in cities increased from 6 percent to 35 percent, reflecting the decrease in the number of agricultural workers required to feed city dwellers.

Consider first the sowing side of agriculture. At the start of the 19th century, plows were fragile, awkward, and often made of wood. These inefficient plows were replaced in the 1830s by the cast-iron plow, which was produced in factories in Pittsburgh and Worcester. In the 1840s, John Deere introduced the steel plow, which was lighter, stronger, and easier to handle. Later innovations allowed the farmer to adjust the depth and angle of the plow blade, increasing productivity further.

Consider next the reaping side of agriculture. In 1831, McCormick combined several earlier innovations into a horse-drawn harvesting machine that increased the productivity of the most labor-intensive part of agriculture. Using a horse-drawn reaper, two people could harvest the same amount of grain as eight people using traditional harvesting methods.

Other innovations contributed to higher agricultural productivity. The development of agricultural science led to innovations in planting, growing, harvesting, and processing. Innovations in transportation cut transport costs and allowed each farmer to serve a wider market area. Because of rising productivity, the share of employment in agriculture decreased over the 19th and 20th centuries, from over 90 percent to less than 3 percent.

Energy Technology and Location Decisions

During the Industrial Revolution, the location pattern of factory towns reflected changes in energy technology. The first factories used waterwheels turned by waterfalls and fast-moving streams to translate moving water into mechanical motion. The power was transmitted by systems of belts and gears. Textile manufacturers built factories along backcountry streams in New England and used waterwheels to run their machines. Some examples of waterwheel cities are Lowell, Lawrence, Holyoke, and Lewiston.

The refinement of the steam engine in the second half of the 19th century made energy a transportable input. A key innovation was John McNaught's development of a compounding engine (using steam twice, at descending pressures, to drive pistons) in 1845. The steam engine could be operated anywhere, with the only constraint being the availability of coal to fuel the engine. Some energy-intensive manufacturers located near the coal mines in Pennsylvania. Others located along navigable waterways and shipped coal from the mines to their factories. In New England, textile firms shifted from backcountry waterfall sites to locations along navigable waterways. Production shifted to the Fall River–New Bedford area along the south coast of New England. The later development of the railroad gave coal users another transport option, causing the development of factories along the vast network of rail lines. In general, the steam engine widened the location options for factories.

The development of electricity changed the location patterns of factories. Electricity generators were refined in the 1860s, and the electric motor was developed in 1888. Factories replaced belt-and-gear systems driven by a central steam engine with small electric motors for individual machines. The first factory to use electric power was adjacent to a hydroelectric generating facility at Niagara Falls. Rapid improvements in the electricity transmission soon allowed factories to be hundreds of miles from hydroelectric and coal-powered generating plants. Between 1900 and 1920, the share of factory horsepower from electric motors increased from 2 percent to 33 percent.

The development of electricity made factories more footloose. A firm could tap water power without locating close to the stream and use coal without shipping the bulky fuel to the factory. In general, the development of electricity decreased the importance of energy considerations in location decisions, causing firms to base their location choices on the accessibility to other inputs and to consumers.

A SYSTEM OF FACTORY TOWNS

We can widen our horizon by looking at the entire region and consider the possibility of additional factory towns. Firms can enter the shirt industry by building shirt factories at different locations, and each firm will have a local monopoly in the area surrounding its factory. Recall the fifth axiom of urban economics:

Competition generates zero economic profit

If there are no restrictions on entry, firms will continue to enter the market until economic profit is zero.

Figure 2–2 (page 28) shows the equilibrium in the region. The horizontal axis measures distance from a coastline. The rectangular region is 48 miles wide, and in equilibrium has three shirt factories, each with a market area 16 miles wide. The

FIGURE 2–2 System of Factory Towns

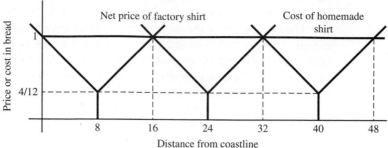

Each factory's market area is 16 miles wide, so a system of factory towns develops
with a distance of 16 miles between towns. In this equilibrium, workers specialize,
with shirt workers in towns and bread producers in rural areas between the towns.

market areas of the factories span the region: Every location in the region lies within
the market area of some factory. There is complete labor specialization: Workers in
factory towns produce shirts (and receive bread as wages), and workers in rural
areas produce bread (and pay bread to get factory shirts).

This is an equilibrium because each firm makes zero economic profit and workers are indifferent between rural and city life:

- **Zero economic profit.** The factory price of 4/12 loaf equals the average cost
  of producing shirts, including the cost of urban workers and the cost of indivisible inputs.
- **Locational indifference for workers.** The wage for factory workers is high
  enough to cover (1) the opportunity cost of working in factories rather than producing bread in the rural area and (2) the higher cost of urban living (land rent).

What about rural residents? For a rural resident just outside the factory towns,
the net price of a factory shirt is 4/12 loaf of bread, compared to a homemade cost
of one loaf. At the other extreme, a rural household eight miles from the factory
pays a net price of one loaf per shirt (4/12 + 8/12 in travel cost). Recall the first
axiom of urban economics:

Prices adjust to ensure locational equilibrium

In this case, the price of land in rural areas will adjust to make people indifferent between locations that differ in their accessibility to the shirt factory. The shorter the
distance to the factory, the lower the net price of factory shirts, and the more a
household is willing to pay for land. In other words, the price of land adjusts to fully
compensate for differences in accessibility.

Landowners benefit from the scale economies in production that generate the
regional system of factory towns. In the rural areas, the price of land is higher at locations close to the factory city. In the factory city itself, competition among workers for locations near the factory bids up the price of land.

MATERIALS-ORIENTED FIRMS AND PROCESSING TOWNS

Up to this point, we have ignored the cost of transporting the raw materials required to produce urban goods (shirts). We have implicitly assumed that factory workers harvest wool from wild sheep who wander by the factory at just the right time to be sheared for shirts. In the language of urban economics, we have assumed that the raw materials required for production are ubiquitous—available at all locations at the same price. This is an extreme case of a market-oriented industry, defined as an industry in which the cost of transporting output is large relative to the cost of transporting inputs.

Consider the opposite extreme. Suppose it is costly to transport material inputs, but output can be transported at zero cost. This is the extreme case of a materials-oriented industry, defined as an industry for which the cost of transporting material inputs is large relative to the cost of transporting output. For example, the sugar content of sugar beets is roughly 15 percent, so it takes seven tons of beets to produce one ton of sugar. Beet-sugar firms locate their plants close to the beet fields to economize on transport costs (Holmes and Stevens, 2004). Beet-sugar producers will cluster in the regions of the country where weather and soil conditions are favorable for the production of sugar beets.

Scale Economies and Market Areas

The process of transforming sugar beets into sugar is subject to scale economies. Processors use indivisible inputs and engage in factor substitution, so the average processing costs decrease as the quantity increases. The typical sugar-beet processing plant employs 186 workers, about four times the average number of employees per plant in manufacturing.

The market area of a processing plant is determined by the net price farmers receive. The net price equals the price paid by the processor minus the cost of transporting the beets from the farm to the processing plant. In Figure 2–3, the horizontal

FIGURE 2–3 System of Processing Towns

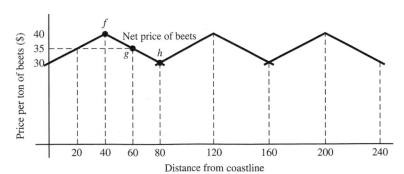

The net price of beets (received by farmers) decreases as the distance to the processing plant increases. The market area of the typical sugar-beet processing plant is 80 miles wide, so a system of processing towns develops with a distance of 80 miles between them.

axis measures the distance from a coastline. Consider a processing plant located 40 miles from the coastline. If the price paid by the processor is $40, the net price is $40 for a farmer across the road from the processor (point *f*), and drops to $35 for a farmer 20 miles away (point *g*). Farmers naturally sell to the processing plant that generates the highest net price, so this processing plant has a market from the coastline to 80 miles inland.

Figure 2–3 shows a regional equilibrium with three processing plants, each with a market area of 80 miles. Each firm is the single buyer of sugar beets within its 80-mile market area, so it has a local monopsony (as opposed to monopoly for a single seller). Recall the fifth axiom of urban economics:

Competition generates zero economic profit

If there are no restrictions on entry, firms will continue to enter the market until economic profit is zero.

System of Processing Towns

The location of sugar-beet processing plants leads to the development of a system of processing towns. The people who work in the processing plants live nearby to economize on commuting, resulting in a place with a relatively high population density: a small city or town. As Holmes and Stevens (2004) show, beet-sugar processing plants locate in the regions where beet production occurs, and they carve out input market areas within each beet-growing region.

Note the similarities of the beet-sugar industry and the shirt industry. In the shirt industry, with relatively high cost of transporting output, each firm gets a local monopoly, with all consumers patronizing the nearest factory. In the beet-sugar industry, with relatively high cost of transporting input, each firm gets a local monopsony, with all farmers selling their output to the nearest beet-sugar plant.

Other Examples of Materials-Oriented Industries

The same logic applies to other materials-oriented industries (Kim, 1999). The production of leather requires hides and tannin (from tree bark) for the tanning process. The tannin content of bark is only 10 percent, so it takes a lot of bark to produce a ton of leather. In 1900, U.S. leather producers located close to forests to economize on the transport costs of tannin. In the 20th century, improvements in the extraction process and the development of synthetic tannin reduced the orientation toward forest sites, and firms moved closer to other input sources.

The location decisions of steel producers reflected changes in the input requirements of coal and iron ore. Early in the history of the industry, a ton of steel required five tons of coal and two tons of ore, and steel production was concentrated near coal deposits. Technological innovations reduced the coal content, and steel producers were pulled toward locations that provided access to ore deposits, including sites on the Great Lakes that offered water access to ore from the Masabi Range in Minnesota. Each ton of steel required 175 tons of water, and the Great Lakes sites also provided a plentiful supply of water.

The location decisions of these and other materials-oriented industries caused the development of processing towns. Leather towns developed around tanneries and steel towns developed around steel mills. Lumber producers locate near forests, causing the development of lumber towns centered on sawmills. Ore processors locate near mineral deposits, causing the development of mining towns.

SUMMARY

Cities exist because of the benefits of centralized exchange (trading cities) and centralized production (factory and processing cities). We have focused on the market forces that generate cities. For a discussion of other possible reasons for cities, such as religion and defense and their role in the development of the first cities, see Mumford (1961) and O'Sullivan (2005). Here are the main points of this chapter:

1. A trading city develops when comparative advantage is combined with scale economies in exchange.
2. A factory city develops when there are scale economies in production.
3. The Industrial Revolution caused massive urbanization because of its innovations in agriculture, transportation, and production.
4. Changes in energy technology altered the location decisions of firms, with water power generating factories along streams, steam power generating factories along rivers and railroads, and electricity making firms more footloose.
5. Spatial competition among firms generates a market area for each firm and a system of cities.

APPLYING THE CONCEPTS

1. **Matter Transmitter in Trading City**
   Consider a region with two standardized products (bread and shirts) and a single trading city. Transport is initially by horse-drawn wagons. Predict the effects of a new matter transmitter, which can instantly transport goods (but not people), with a zero marginal cost of transport. The transmitter is an indivisible input, and it is expensive.
   a. Predict the effects of the transmitter on [i] the volume of trade and [ii] the population of the trading city. Will the matter transmitter cause the trading city to grow, shrink, or disappear?
   b. How would your answers to (a) change if the matter transmitter were relatively cheap?
2. **Self Singing, Choral Groups, and the Internet**
   Consider a region where households produce and consume two products, bread and live musical performances. All workers are equally productive at producing bread and music. The production of bread is subject to constant returns to scale, with one hour required to produce each loaf. In an hour, a single person can produce one unit of music for herself. A choral group of 20 people working for an hour (57 minutes of practice and 3 minutes of performance) can produce

one unit of music for an audience of 80 people. Assume that the opportunity cost of actually listening to the music is zero.

  a. What is the appropriate price for choral music, that is, the price (in bread) paid by each person who listens?
  b. If the travel cost is 1/8 hour per round-trip mile, what is the market area of the choral group? Defend your answer with a completely labeled graph.
  c. Suppose choral music becomes available on the Internet, and the provider charges 1/2 loaf per song. What is the new market area of the choral group? Illustrate with a completely labeled graph.

3. **Spring-Loaded Sneakers**

   Using Figure 2–1 as a starting point, suppose all consumers switch to spring-loaded sneakers, decreasing walking time per round-trip mile from 1/12 to 1/18 hours.

  a. Depict graphically the effects of the new sneakers on the market area of the shirt factory.
  b. Modify Figure 2–2 to generate a region of factory cities with market areas that span the entire region (48 miles wide). Do the new sneakers increase or decrease the number of cities?

4. **Beer and Wine**

   Most breweries locate close to their customers (far from their primary input sources), while most wineries locate close to their input sources (far from their consumers).

  a. Why?
  b. Consider a region that is 120 miles wide. Beer consumers are uniformly distributed throughout the region, while grapes are uniformly distributed through the western half of the region. There are two evenly spaced wineries and two evenly spaced breweries. Where do they locate? Illustrate with a graph.

5. **Helicopters and Cities in Retireland**

   Consider Retireland, where no one works and everyone consumes a single good (food), which is imported from another region and can be purchased (one meal at a time) from the nearest vending machine. Alternatively, food can be delivered by helicopter, by dropping a meal through a food slot on the roof. The price of a delivered helicopter meal is $6 and the price of a vending-machine meal is $2. The travel cost is $0.04 per round-trip meter ($0.02 per meter traveled).

  a. What is the market area of a vending machine? Illustrate with a graph.
  b. How does the price of land vary within the region?
  c. What are the implications for population density and cities?

REFERENCES AND ADDITIONAL READING

1. Bartlett, Randall. *The Crisis of American Cities.* Armonk, NY: M.E. Sharp, 1998.
2. Combes, P., and H. Overman. "The Spatial Distribution of Economic Activities in the European Union." Chapter 64 in *Handbook of Regional and Urban*

Economics 4: Cities and Geography, eds. V. Henderson and J.F. Thisse. Amsterdam: Elsevier, 2004.

3. Davis, Kingsley. "Urbanization." In *The Urban Economy,* ed. Harold Hochman. New York: W. W. Norton, 1976.

4. Fujita, Mashisa, and Jacques-Francois Thisse. *Economics of Agglomeration.* Cambridge: Cambridge University Press, 2002.

5. Hohenberg, Paul M., and Lynn H. Lees. *The Making of Urban Europe 1000–1950.* Cambridge, MA: Harvard University Press, 1985.

6. Holmes, T., and J. Stevens. "Spatial Distribution of Economic Activities in North America." Chapter 63 in *Handbook of Regional and Urban Economics 4: Cities and Geography,* ed. V. Henderson and J.F. Thisse. Amsterdam: Elsevier, 2004.

7. Kim, Sukkoo. "Regions Resources, and Economic Geography: Sources of U.S. Regional Comparative Advantage, 1880–1987." *Regional Science and Urban Economics* 29 (1999), pp. 1–32.

8. Mumford, Lewis. *The City in History.* New York: Harcourt Brace Jovanovich, 1961.

9. O'Sullivan, Arthur. "The First Cities." In *Λ Companion to Urban Economics,* ed. Richard Arnott and Daniel McMillen. Boston: Blackwell, 2005.

CHAPTER 3

Why Do Firms Cluster?

People don't go there anymore. It's too crowded.
—YOGI BERRA

*I*f two firms compete for customers in a region, will they locate close together or far apart? It is natural to imagine that the two firms will split the region into two halves, giving each firm a local monopoly. That's what happened in the theoretical models of Chapter 2, and it happens for many firms in the real world. Yet all sorts of competing firms locate close to one another, including carpet producers in Georgia and television producers in Los Angeles. Why?

This chapter explores agglomeration economies, the economic forces that cause firms to locate close to one another in clusters. The forces acting on firms in a single industry together are called localization economies, indicating that they are "local" to a particular industry. For example, firms in the software industry cluster in Silicon Valley. When agglomeration economies cross industry boundaries, they are called urbanization economies. The idea is that the presence of firms in one industry attracts firms in other industries. For example, the corporate headquarters of different industries cluster in cities. Urbanization economies lead to the development of large, diverse cities. As we'll see, localization and urbanization economies have common roots.

Before we explore the reasons for localization economies, it will be useful to look at some facts on industry clusters in the United States. As shown in Table 3–1, the information-technology industry has a number of clusters, with the largest cluster in the San Jose area and smaller concentrations around the country. Among the small metropolitan areas with large clusters of software jobs are Boise, Idaho and Burlington, Vermont. Moving down the table, firms producing aerospace engines cluster in Hartford, Cincinnati, Indianapolis, and Phoenix, and firms in financial services cluster in New York City and Boston.

Of course, not all industry clusters occur because of agglomeration economies. We saw in the previous chapter that beet-sugar production facilities are concentrated in beet-growing areas. Similarly, employment in the tobacco-products industry is

TABLE 3–1 Select Industrial Clusters in U.S. Metropolitan Areas, 2001

Product	Metropolitan Area	2001 Employment	National Share (%)
Information technology	San Jose, CA	92,453	10.15
	Boston, MA	54,811	6.02
	Dallas, TX	38,570	4.24
	Seattle, WA	37,469	4.12
Aerospace engines	Hartford, CT	14,207	15.81
	Cincinnati, OH	7,805	8.68
	Indianapolis, IN	7,745	8.62
	Phoenix, AZ	7,560	8.41
Financial services	New York, NY	316,922	9.36
	Boston, MA	158,727	4.69
Furniture	Hickory, NC	31,714	8.92
	Greensboro, NC	20,121	5.66
Biopharmaceuticals	Newark, NJ	21,619	8.23
	Middlesex, NJ	16,757	6.38
Jewelry and precious metals	New York, NY	29,807	24.55
	Providence, RI	11,850	9.76
Chemical products	Augusta, GA	20,053	4.77
	Chicago, IL	16,206	3.85
	Houston, TX	15,189	3.61
Analytical instruments	Boston, MA	77,637	10.38
	San Jose, CA	48,569	6.49
Hospitality and tourism	Las Vegas, NV	182,681	7.16
	Orlando, FL	93,850	3.68
	Atlantic City, NJ	43,002	1.68

Source: Author's calculations based on data from Cluster Mapping Project, Harvard Business School.

concentrated in tobacco-growing areas: North Carolina has about 31 percent of national employment in the industry. For the hospitality and tourism industry, two clusters occur in cities with legalized gambling (Las Vegas and Atlantic City).

SHARING INTERMEDIATE INPUTS

Some competing firms locate close to one another to share a firm that supplies an intermediate input. The conventional list of production inputs includes labor, raw materials, and capital (machines, equipment, structures), but usually ignores intermediate inputs. An intermediate input is something one firm produces that a second firm uses as an input in its production process. For example, buttons produced by one firm are used as inputs by a dressmaking firm. The classic example of a cluster motivated by sharing an intermediate input is a cluster of dressmakers around a buttonmaker (Vernon, 1972).

Dresses and Buttons

Consider the production of high-fashion dresses. The demand for dresses is subject to the whims of fashion, so the dressmaking firms must be small and nimble, ready to respond quickly to changes in fashion. The varying demand for dresses causes varying demands for intermediate inputs such as buttons. A dressmaker's demand for buttons changes from month to month, not in the quantity demanded, but in the type of buttons demanded. One month the dressmaker might use square blue buttons with a smooth finish and the next month round pink buttons with a rough finish.

Consider next the production of buttons, the intermediate input. The production technology for buttons is summarized in three assumptions. The first is one of the axioms of urban economics:

Production is subject to economies of scale

Because button producers use indivisible inputs and specialized labor, the cost per button decreases as the quantity increases. The scale economies are large relative to the button demand of an individual dressmaker, so dressmakers won't produce their own buttons but will buy them as intermediate inputs from button producers. There are two other assumptions in the dress-button model:

- **Face time.** A button for a high-fashion dress is not a standardized input that can be ordered from a catalog or a Web site, but requires interaction between dressmaker and buttonmaker to design and produce the perfect button for the dress of the month. The face time means that a dressmaker must be located close to its button supplier.
- **Modification cost.** Once a dressmaker buys a button from a buttonmaker, the dressmaker may incur a cost to modify the button to make a perfect match. For example, the dressmaker might have to shave the edges of a square button to make it a hexagon.

Figure 3–1 shows the average cost of buttons from the perspective of the dressmaker. Point *i* shows the cost for an isolated dressmaker, which has a relatively high button cost for two reasons. First, the buttonmaker produces for a single dressmaker, so output will be relatively low and the average cost (and price) of buttons will be relatively high. Second, the buttonmaker produces just one type of button (e.g., square buttons), so the dressmaker's modification costs will be relatively high. When the dress of the month calls for square buttons, modifications won't be necessary, but in all the other months, the dressmaker incurs a modification cost.

A dressmaker in a cluster has lower button costs for two reasons. First, a cluster of several dressmakers will generate sufficient button demand to allow buttonmakers to exploit scale economies, leading to lower button prices. Second, the larger total demand for buttons will allow buttonmakers to specialize in different varieties of buttons, reducing the modification costs of dressmakers. In a cluster, a dressmaker might be able to choose from buttons that are squares, hexagons, or triangles. In Figure 3–1, the average cost (and price) of buttons drops from $0.50 for

FIGURE 3–1 Clustering and the Unit Cost of Intermediate Inputs

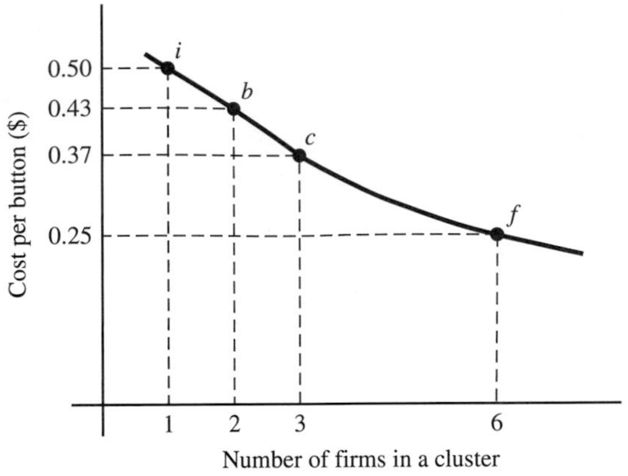

An isolated firm has a relatively high unit cost of buttons (point *i*). As the number of dressmakers in a cluster increases, the unit cost of buttons decreases because together the firms generate sufficient demand to realize scale economies in button production and support a wider variety of buttons.

an isolated firm to $0.43 for a two-firm cluster (point *b*), to $0.25 for a six-firm cluster. The lower cost provides an incentive for dressmakers to cluster to share a buttonmaker.

High-Technology Firms

The lessons from the button–dressmaker story apply to other industries. Firms producing high-technology products face rapidly changing demand for their cutting-edge products. The small, innovative firms share the suppliers of intermediate inputs, such as electronic components, and cluster to get the face time required to match components and new products. Innovative high-technology firms also share firms that provide product-testing services and locate close enough to quickly when needed tap the facilities.

SHARING A LABOR POOL

What do the producers of television programs and the producers of computer software have in common? Every year, dozens of new television programs are aired, and only a few are hits. In the rapidly changing software industry, hundreds of new products are introduced every year, and only a few succeed. For an individual firm in either industry, this year's new product—television program or computer program—may be wildly successful, and next year's may be a dud. In this environment of rapidly changing demand, unsuccessful firms will be firing workers at the same time that successful firms are hiring them. A cluster of firms facilitates the transfer of workers from unsuccessful firms to successful ones.

The key notion of sharing a labor pool is that the boom-bust process occurs at the level of the firm, not the industry. Suppose the total demand for output in an industry is constant over time, but the demand facing an individual firm varies from year to year. For example, the number of slots for television programs is fixed, so the success of one television firm (a hit) comes at the expense of another (a canceled dud). Similarly, the success of one firm's encryption software comes at the expense of other firms that introduce similar products.

In this part of the chapter, we develop a formal model of labor pooling. The total demand at the industry level is constant, but the demand for each firm varies from year to year. For each firm, there are two possibilities—high demand or low demand—and each outcome is equally likely. As we'll see, there is an incentive for firms in such an industry to cluster to share a pool of workers.

The Isolated Firm

Consider first the situation for an isolated firm outside any industry cluster. The isolated firm doesn't face any competition for labor within its town, and to simplify matters, we assume that labor supply in the isolated site is perfectly inelastic, fixed at 12 workers. This means that wages will rise and fall with the demand for the firm's product.

When the demand for the firm's product is high, so is the firm's demand for labor. In Panel A of Figure 3–2, the high-demand equilibrium is shown by the intersection of

FIGURE 3–2 Clustering to Share a Labor Pool

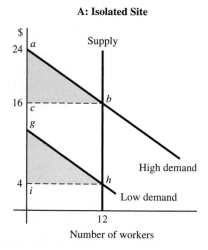

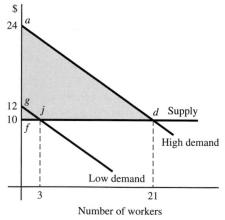

In an isolated site, the firm faces a perfectly inelastic supply of labor (12 workers). The firm hires the same number of workers during high demand and low demand but pays a higher wage during high demand.

In a cluster, the firm faces a perfectly elastic supply of labor, and the wage is fixed at $10. The firm hires 21 workers during high demand but only 3 workers during low demand.

the upper demand curve and the vertical supply curve at point b, generating a wage of $16. When demand for the firm's product is low, so is its demand for labor and the equilibrium wage ($4 at point h). To summarize, the isolated firm hires the same number of workers during high and low demand but pays a lower wage when demand is low.

Locating in a Cluster

The key difference between an isolated site and a cluster concerns the competition for labor and the variability of wages. Workers in the cluster can choose from a large number of firms. For every successful firm hiring workers, there is an unsuccessful firm firing them. Therefore, the total demand for labor in the cluster is constant, and so is the equilibrium wage.

Workers are mobile between the isolated site and the cluster, and in equilibrium they will be indifferent between the two locations. Recall the second axiom of urban economics:

Prices adjust to generate locational equilibrium

At the isolated site, the wage is uncertain, being either $16 during high demand or $4 during low demand. The two outcomes are equally likely, so the expected wage (the sum of the probabilities times the wages) is $10:

$$\text{Expected wage} = \frac{1}{2} \cdot \$16 + \frac{1}{2} \cdot \$4 = \$10$$

To make workers indifferent between the two sites, the certain (constant) wage in the cluster must be $10.

Panel B in Figure 3–2 shows the outcomes in the cluster. An individual firm can hire as many workers as it wants at the market wage. The typical firm hires 21 workers when demand is high (point d), but only 3 workers when demand is low (point j). When the demand for a firm's product goes from high to low, the firm fires 18 workers at the same time that another firm in the cluster is hiring 18 workers as its demand goes from low to high.

Expected Profits Are Higher in the Cluster

Expected profits will be higher in the cluster. To see why, consider what happens when a firm moves from the isolated site to a cluster and then experiences one year of high demand, followed by one year of low demand.

- **Good news when demand is high.** The move to the cluster cuts the wage (from $16 to $10) and allows the firm to hire more workers (21 instead of 12), generating higher profit in the cluster.
- **Bad news when demand is low.** The move to the cluster increases the wage (from $4 to $10), generating lower profit in the cluster.

Which is larger, the good news with high demand, or the bad news with low demand?

The good news will dominate the bad news because a firm in the cluster responds to changes in the demand for its product. When demand is high, the firm takes advantage of the lower wages (a $6 gap) in the cluster by hiring more workers (21). When demand is low, a firm in the cluster cushions the blow of low demand by hiring fewer workers (only 3). Because the firm changes its workforce when the demand for its product changes, the good news will be large relative to the bad news, and profit will be higher in the cluster.

Another way to show that profit is higher in the cluster is to compute the expected profits at the two sites. As shown in Section 3 of "Tools of Microeconomics" (the Appendix to the book), the labor-demand curve shows the marginal benefit of labor, the value of output produced by the marginal worker. A firm's profit from hiring a worker equals the difference between the worker's marginal benefit and the wage, and a firm's profit from its entire workforce is shown by the gap between the labor demand curve and the horizontal wage line. In Panel A of Figure 3–2, triangle *abc* shows the profit for an isolated firm when demand is high ($48), and triangle *ghi* shows the profit when demand is low ($48). In Panel B, the profit with high demand is shown by triangle *adf* ($147), and the profit with low demand is shown by triangle *gjf* ($3). So if the two outcomes are equally likely, the expected profit in the cluster is $75 (the average of $147 and $3), compared to $48 in the isolated site.

LABOR MATCHING

In a typical economic model of a labor market, we assume that workers and firms are matched perfectly. Each firm can hire workers who have precisely the skills the firm requires. In the real world, things are not so tidy. Workers and firms are not always perfectly matched, and mismatches require costly worker training. As we'll see, a large city can improve the matching of workers and firms in the untidy real world, decreasing training costs and increasing productivity.

As an illustration of the labor matching problem, consider a set of software firms that hire computer programmers. Programmers have different skill sets, depending on their facility with different programming languages (e.g., C, C++, Java) and their experience with different programming tasks (e.g., graphics, number crunching, artificial intelligence, operating systems, e-commerce). Although some programmers are more productive than others, what matters for the matching model is that they have different skill sets. A firm enters the market with a particular skill requirement and hires workers who provide the best skill matches.

A Model of Labor Matching

Helsley and Strange (1990) developed a formal model of labor matching. The model uses several key assumptions about workers and firms.

- **Variation in worker skills.** Each worker has a unique skill described by a position or "address" on a circle with a one-unit circumference. In Panel A of

FIGURE 3–3 Skills Matching

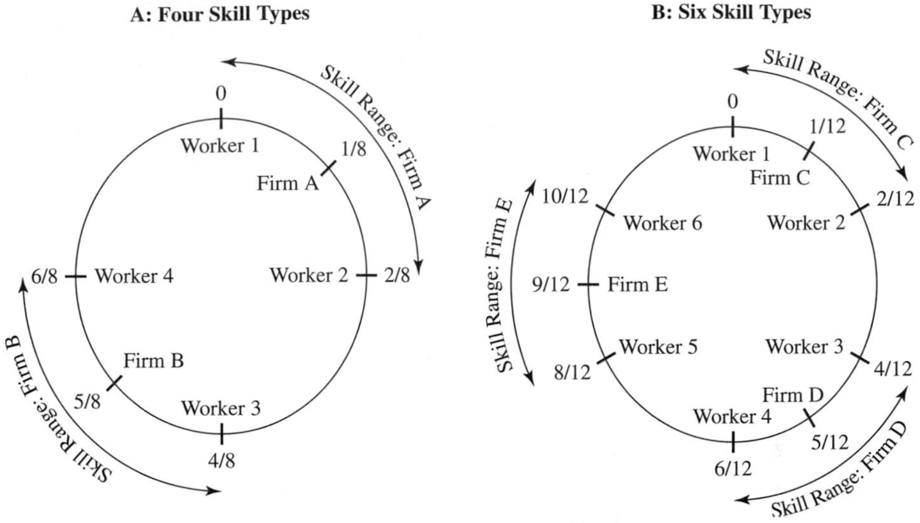

A: Four Skill Types

B: Six Skill Types

With four skill types, worker addresses are {0, 2/8, 4/8, 6/8}. There are two workers per firm, so two firms will enter with skill requirements {1/8, 5/8}, and the mismatch per worker is 1/8.

With six skill types, worker addresses are {0, 2/12, 4/12, 6/12, 8/12, 10/12}. There are two workers per firm, so three firms will enter the market with skill requirements {1/12, 5/12, 9/12}, and the mismatch per worker is 1/12.

Figure 3–3, there are four workers, and their skills are evenly spaced on the circle. The address of a worker is the distance between her skill position and the north pole of the circle. The addresses of the four workers are {0, 2/8, 4/8, 6/8}.

- **Firm entry.** Each firm enters the market by picking a product to produce and an associated skill requirement. In Panel A of Figure 3–3, one firm enters with skill requirement S = 1/8, and a second enters with S = 5/8.
- **Training costs.** Workers incur the cost associated with closing the gap between the worker's skill and the skills required by a firm.
- **Competition for workers.** Each firm offers a wage payable to any worker who meets its skill requirement, and each worker accepts the offer with the highest net income, which is equal to the wage minus the training cost required to close the skills gap.

The next two assumptions of the matching model are related to the axioms of urban economics:

Production is subject to economies of scale

Because of scale economies in production, each firm will hire at least one worker. This is important because in the absence of scale economies, each firm would hire just one worker, and each worker would be perfectly matched with a firm. To simplify matters, we will assume that scale economies require each firm to hire two workers. The final assumption is that entry is unrestricted, so firms will continue to enter the market until economic profit is zero.

Competition generates zero economic profit

In the labor-matching model, entry involves picking a skill requirement and hiring workers with closely matched skills. In other words, each firm gets a local monopsony (single buyer) in the skill interval surrounding its skill requirement.

Panel A of Figure 3–3 shows the equilibrium with four skill types and two firms. The equilibrium mismatch per worker is $1/8$. For example, the workers at $S = 0$ and $S = 2/8$ work in a firm with $S = 1/8$, so each worker has a skills gap of $1/8$. Each firm pays a gross wage equal to the value of output produced by a perfectly matched worker. The net wage earned by a worker equals the gross wage minus the training cost:

Net wage = Gross wage $-$ Skills gap $\cdot$ Unit training cost

Suppose the gross wage is \$12 and the unit training cost is \$24. In the equilibrium shown in Panel A of Figure 3–3, the skill gap is $1/8$, so the net wage is

$$\text{Net wage} = \$12 - \frac{1}{8} \cdot \$24 = \$9$$

Agglomeration Economies: More Workers Implies Better Matches

What happens to skills matching as an urban economy grows? We can represent an increase in the size of the workforce by increasing the number of workers on the unit circle. This increases the density of workers with respect to skills but doesn't change the range of skills. As we'll see, more workers means better skill matches and higher net wages.

Panel B of Figure 3–3 shows the effects of increasing the number of workers from four to six. Each firm still hires two workers, so three firms will enter the market. In Panel B of Figure 3–3, the six workers are equally spaced, with skill addresses $\{0, 2/12, 4/12, 6/12, 8/12, 10/12\}$. The three firms enter the market with skill requirements $\{1/12, 5/12, 9/12\}$, so the mismatch per worker drops to $1/12$. For example, workers at skill addresses 0 and $2/12$ are hired by the firm at address $1/12$, so each worker has a mismatch of $1/12$. Workers incur lower training cost, so the net wage increases to \$10:

$$\text{Net wage} = \$12 - \frac{1}{12} \cdot \$24 = \$10$$

In general, an increase in the number of workers decreases mismatches and training costs, increasing the net wage. This is shown in Table 3–2 for up to 12 workers.

What are the implications of skill matching for the clustering of firms and urban development? The presence of a large workforce attracts firms that compete for workers, generating better skill matches and higher net wages for workers. The higher net wage provides an incentive for workers to live in large numbers in cities,

TABLE 3–2 Number of Workers, Skills Gap, and Net Wage

Number of Workers	Skills Gap	Training Cost	Net Wage
4	1/8	$24/8 = $3	$12 − $3 = $9
6	1/12	$24/12 = $2	$12 − $2 = $10
12	1/24	$24/24 = $1	$12 − $1 = $11

so the attraction between firms and workers is mutual. Both firms and workers benefit from better skill matching.

KNOWLEDGE SPILLOVERS

A fourth agglomeration economy comes from sharing knowledge among firms in an industry. As Marshall (1920) explained,

> When an industry has chosen a locality for itself, it is likely to stay there for long; so great are the advantages which people following the same skilled trade get from near neighborhood to one another. The mysteries of the trade become no mysteries; but are as it were in the air, and children learn many of them unconsciously. Good work is appreciated; inventions and improvements in machinery, in processes and the general organization of the business have their merits promptly discussed; if one man starts a new idea, it is taken up by others and combined with suggestions of their own; and thus it becomes the source of new ideas.

There is ample evidence that knowledge spillovers cause firm clustering. Dumais, Ellison, and Glaeser (2001) show that knowledge spillovers increase the number of new plant births, with the largest effect on industries that employ college graduates. Their results suggest that knowledge spillovers are important in determining the locations of firms in idea-oriented industries. Rosenthal and Strange (2001) show that the most innovative industries are more likely to form clusters. They also show that knowledge spillovers are highly localized, petering out over a distance of a few miles.

There is also evidence that knowledge spillovers are more important for industries with small, competitive firms. A recent study compared two clusters of the electronics industry, California's Silicon Valley and Route 128 near Boston (Saxenian, 1994). Knowledge spillovers are more important in Silicon Valley because its network of specialized companies generates an atmosphere of collaboration, experimentation, and shared knowledge. In contrast, the firms in the Route-128 cluster are less interdependent so there are fewer knowledge spillovers.

SELF-REINFORCING EFFECTS CAUSE INDUSTRY CLUSTERS

So far we have seen that clustering is beneficial because it allows firms to take advantage of agglomeration economies from input sharing, labor pooling, skills matching, and knowledge spillovers. What about the costs? After we consider the cost side of clustering, we can compare the benefits to the costs. When agglomeration economies are strong enough to offset the costs, firms will form industry clusters, causing the development of specialized cities.

The Cost of Clustering

Consider a rectangular region and the location decisions of three firms producing shirts. In Panel A of Figure 3–4, each of the three firms (W for west; C for central; E for east) has an exclusive market area. For example, the territory of firm E is from mile 32 to mile 48. Suppose firm E moves to the center, joining firm C to form an industry cluster. What are the consequences of such a move?

Consider first the implications of the move for the demand facing firm E. After a move to the center, firm E will no longer have an exclusive market area (from mile 32 to mile 48) but instead will share this area with firm C. On the other hand, the firm will now share firm C's old market area from mile 16 to 32. Putting these two changes together, E trades an exclusive market over one-third of the region for half the market over two-thirds of the region. It may appear that the move doesn't change the total demand facing firm E. After all, 1/3 is half of 2/3.

If we ignore the effects of agglomeration economies for the moment, firm E's move to the center will actually decrease its total sales because consumers obey the law of demand. The move to the center increases the net price of shirts for all consumers between mile 32 and mile 48. They previously patronized firm E (at mile 40), but now must travel to the E&C cluster at mile 24. The increase in the net price of shirts decreases the quantity of shirts demanded, so a move to the center of the region decreases the quantity of shirts sold by firm E. Similarly, firm C will sell fewer shirts because it splits its original market area with E and picks up distant consumers whose demand is relatively low because of high travel costs.

FIGURE 3–4 Market Areas Before and After Clustering

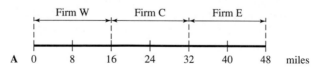

A

Three firms (W, C, E) divide the region into three exclusive market areas.

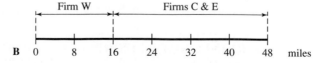

B

If firm E joins C at the center (mile 24), firm E trades its exclusive market area from mile 32 to mile 48, for half of the market between mile 16 and mile 48.

Benefits of Clustering

On the benefit side, a move to the central location allows firms to benefit from agglomeration economies. Firms in the cluster may share the suppliers of intermediate inputs, tap a labor pool, get better skill matches, or benefit from knowledge spillovers. These agglomeration economies lead to lower production costs. Lower production costs lead to lower output prices, and consumers will respond by purchasing more output. If agglomeration economies are strong enough, a move to the central cluster will lead to higher profits. If so, firms will have an incentive to cluster, giving up their exclusive market areas to benefit from agglomeration economies.

Self-Reinforcing Effects

Figure 3–5 shows the effects of firm E's move to the center of the region. The horizontal axis measures the number of firms at the center of the region. The vertical axis measures the profit gap, defined as the difference between the profit of the typical firm at the center of the region and the profit of an isolated firm. Point i shows the initial dispersed outcome: There is a single firm at the center of the region, and this isolated firm makes just as much profit as the other isolated firms. The profit gap is zero.

Suppose that firm E joins firm C at the central location. Referring back to Figure 3–1, suppose the average cost of buttons decreases from $0.50 to $0.43. If each firm uses 100 buttons, the savings in production cost from agglomeration economies is $7 for each firm. To simplify matters, assume that this is the only effect of clustering. Then the profit gap between the typical firm in a two-firm cluster and an isolated firm is $7—shown at point i in Figure 3–5.

FIGURE 3–5 Self-Reinforcing Effect and Clustering

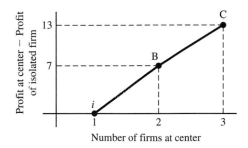

In the initial dispersed outcome, the single firm at the center location earns the same profit as other isolated firms, so the profit gap (profit at the center minus profit of an isolated firm) is zero. If there are two firms at the center, each firm makes $7 more profit than an isolated firm because of agglomeration economies. The extreme outcome is that all three firms are in the central cluster.

The move of one firm to the center may be self-reinforcing. Recall the second axiom of urban economics:

Self-reinforcing changes generate extreme outcomes

Once firm E moves to the center, the remaining isolated firm has an even greater incentive to join the cluster. Adding a third firm to the cluster would decrease the average cost of buttons and increase the profit of firms in the cluster. For example, suppose the average cost in a three-firm cluster would be $0.37, so the profit of a firm in the cluster would be $13 higher than an isolated firm (equal to 100 buttons times the cost gap of $0.13). As shown by point k in Figure 3–5, if firm W joins the cluster, its profit will increase by $13. The extreme outcome is that all three firms locate in the cluster, sacrificing exclusive market areas to benefit from agglomeration economies.

EVIDENCE OF LOCALIZATION ECONOMIES

A large volume of economics literature examines the magnitude of localization economies. In searching for evidence of localization economies, researchers focus on the effects of industry concentration on (1) worker productivity, (2) the number of new production plants (plant births), and (3) growth in industry employment. If there are localization economies, we expect industry clusters to generate higher productivity, more births, and more rapid employment growth.

Consider first the effect of concentration on worker productivity. Henderson (1986) estimates the elasticity of output per worker with respect to industry output, defined as the percentage change in output per worker divided by the percentage change in industry output. For the electrical machinery industry, the elasticity is 0.05, meaning that a 10 percent increase in the output of the industry increases output per worker by 0.50 percent. The elasticity estimates for other U.S. industries range from 0.02 for the pulp and paper industry to 0.11 for the petroleum industry.

Mun and Hutchison (1995) use data from Toronto to estimate agglomeration economies in the office sector. They estimate a productivity elasticity of 0.27, suggesting that localization economies are more powerful in the office sector than in the manufacturing sector. The productivity effects are larger for growth in central locations and are localized.

Consider next the implications of industry concentrations for the location of new production facilities. Carlton (1983) examines the location choices of firms in three industries: plastics products, electronic transmitting equipment, and electronic components. His estimated elasticity of firm births with respect to industry output is 0.43: A 10 percent increase in industry output increases the number of births by 4.3 percent. More recently, Head, Reis, and Swenson (1995) show that Japanese corporations locate their new plants close to other Japanese plants in the same industry. Rosenthal and Strange (2003) show that firm births are more numerous in locations close to concentrations of employment in the same industry.

Consider next the effects of industry concentration on employment growth. Henderson, Kuncoro, and Turner (1995) show that growth in mature industries is more rapid in areas that start with large concentrations of the industry. Rosenthal and Strange (2003) compute this localization effect for six industries, including computer software. A zip code area that starts out with 1,000 more software jobs than another zip code area experiences a larger increase in software employment—about 12 more jobs. On average, the localization effect peters out at a rate of about 50 percent per mile. The rapid attenuation of the localization economies explains the local in "localization economies."

URBANIZATION ECONOMIES

So far in this chapter, we have considered agglomeration economies experienced within a particular industry, also known as localization economies. These localization economies generate clusters of firms producing the same product. In contrast, urbanization economies—defined as agglomeration economies that cross industry boundaries—cause firms of different industries to locate close to one another. The result is the development of large, diverse cities. The four agglomeration economies that generate localization economies also generate urbanization economies.

Sharing, Pooling, and Matching

Consider first the notion of input sharing. Although some intermediate inputs such as buttons are specific to an industry, others are shared by firms in different industries. For example, most industries use business services such as banking, accounting, building maintenance, and insurance. Similarly, firms in different industries share hotels and firms providing transportation services. In addition, firms share public infrastructure such as highways, transit systems, ports, and universities. By sharing these intermediate inputs, firms in larger cities pay lower prices and tap a wider variety of inputs.

Another source of agglomeration economies is labor pooling. Recall that labor pooling is beneficial when the product and labor demand per firm varies while total industry demand remains constant. A cluster of firms in the same industry facilitates the movement of workers from firing firms to hiring firms. Labor pooling generates urbanization economies when demand varies across industries, with some industries expanding while others decline.

Consider next the benefits of labor matching. Recall that an increase in a city's workforce increases the density of worker skills, reducing the mismatches between workers' skills and firms' skill requirements. Because some skill requirements are common to multiple industries, the benefits of labor matching cross industry boundaries. For example, firms in many industries require computer programmers, and firms in these industries benefit from producing in a city with a high density of programmers.

Corporate Headquarters and Functional Specialization

Corporations locate their headquarters in cities to exploit urbanization economies. Corporate executives and managers perform a variety of tasks—developing

TABLE 3–3 Increase in Functional Specialization of Metropolitan Areas

	Percentage Gap between Metropolitan Ratio of Management to Production Workers and the National Ratio		
Population	1950	1970	1990
5–20 million	+10.2	+22.1	+39.0
1.5 to 5 million	+0.30	+11.0	+25.7
75,000 to 250,000	−2.1	−7.9	−20.7
67,000 to 75,000	−4.0	−31.7	−49.5

Source: Gilles Duranton and Diego Puga. "From Sectoral to Functional Specialization," *Journal of Urban Economics* 57 (2005), pp. 343–70.

marketing campaigns, picking locations for new plants, and fending off lawsuits—and draw on other firms to accomplish these tasks. Corporate expenditures on outsourced legal, accounting, and advertising services are equivalent to about two-thirds of their wage bill (Aarland, Davis, Henderson, Ono, 2003).

Corporations cluster to share firms that provide business services. For example, given the large economies of scale in producing advertising campaigns, corporations cluster to share advertising firms, and they get specialized marketing campaigns at a lower cost. Similarly, corporations are attracted by the large concentrations of firms providing financial and business services in midtown Manhattan, the Loop in Chicago, and the financial district of San Francisco.

In the last several decades, there has been a fundamental shift in the specialization of cities. Large cities have become increasingly specialized in managerial functions, while smaller cities have become more specialized in production. Duranton and Puga (2005) compute the ratio of managerial workers to production workers for the nation as a whole and for different metropolitan areas. Table 3–3 shows the percentage differences between the national ratio and the metropolitan ratio for metropolitan areas of different sizes. For example, in the largest metropolitan areas in 1950, the metropolitan ratio was 10.2 percent higher than the national ratio, indicating a slight specialization in managerial functions. At the other extreme, for the smallest areas, the metropolitan ratio was 4.0 percent lower than the national ratio, indicating slight specialization in production.

Over the 40-year period shown in Table 3–3, there was a dramatic change in specialization. By 1990, the ratio for largest cities was 39 percent higher than the national ratio, indicating substantial specialization in managerial functions. At the other extreme, the ratio for the smallest cities was nearly 50 percent lower than the national ratio, indicating a high degree of specialization in production. These changes in specialization were caused by decreases in the cost of managing production facilities from afar. Firms are better equipped to operate multiplant firms from headquarters in large cities where agglomeration economies generate lower production costs. The most important cost reductions have come from innovations in telecommunications, in particular the development of duplicators (photocopiers, fax machines, and e-mail) that have facilitated the rapid transmission of information and reduced the cost of coordination.

Knowledge Spillovers

The essential feature of knowledge spillovers is that physical proximity facilitates the exchange of knowledge between people, leading to new ideas. The ideas lead to new products as well as new ways to produce old products. Some knowledge spillovers occur within an industry, but knowledge spillovers often cross industry boundaries. A city that produces a wide variety of products is fertile ground for applying ideas refined in the design and production of one product to new products.

The evidence for the knowledge spillovers in large cities comes from data on new product innovations (Audretsch and Feldman, 2004). The bulk of patents for new products and production technology are issued to people in large cities. For example, in 1860 the incidence of patents (the number of patents per capita) in the largest 35 U.S. cities was over four times the national average. More recently, the most innovative metropolitan areas in the United States are San Francisco (8.9 innovations per 100,000 population), Boston (8.7), New York (4.2), and Philadelphia (3.6).

The evidence from the paper trail of patents provides additional evidence of knowledge spillovers in large cities. On each patent is a list of related patents—earlier patents that provide a foundation of knowledge for the new patent. A disproportionate number of these citations involve patents from the same metropolitan area. Specifically, the number of local citations (of patents from the same metropolitan area) is five times the number that would occur in the absence of knowledge spillovers.

Following the paper trail of innovation reveals two other features of knowledge spillovers. First, citations to a particular patent are highly localized in the first year following the patent, but the local nature of knowledge spillovers declines over time as knowledge is diffused geographically. Second, the fertility of patents (the number of subsequent citations) varies across the originating institutions: University patents are the most fertile, followed by corporate patents and government patents.

Evidence of Urbanization Economies

There have been many studies of urbanization economies. The general conclusion is that the elasticity of productivity with respect to population is in the range 0.03 to 0.08 (Rosenthal and Strange, 2004). In other words, a doubling of population increases output per worker by between 3 percent and 8 percent. Two studies (Glaeser, Kallal, Scheinkman, and Schleifer, 1992, and Henderson, Kuncoro, and Turner, 1995) suggest that diversity promotes employment growth, especially in new and innovative industries. Hanson (2001) concludes that long-run industry growth is higher in cities with a wider variety of industries, suggesting that diversity promotes growth.

OTHER BENEFITS OF URBAN SIZE

The urbanization economies discussed so far—input sharing, labor pooling, skills matching, and knowledge spillovers—generate higher productivity and lower production costs. In this part of the chapter, we'll consider three other advantages associated with a larger urban economy: better employment opportunities for families, a better learning environment for workers, and better social opportunities.

These advantages of size increase the relative attractiveness of large cities and increase the supply of labor to big cities. How does that contribute to the clustering of firms in cities? Recall the first axiom of urban economics:

Prices adjust to generate locational equilibrium

An increase in the relative attractiveness of a big city decreases the wage that workers are willing to accept to live and work in the city, generating lower production costs for firms. This is similar to the Dullsville versus Coolsville example in Chapter 1: A city that has superior opportunities for family employment, learning, and social interactions has lower wages, everything else being equal.

Joint Labor Supply

Most families have two workers, but are tied to a single residential location. In other words, families must confront the problem of joint labor supply. If the skills of the two workers are suited to different industries, the family will be attracted to locations with a mix of industries. Therefore, the joint supply of labor encourages firms in different industries to cluster. The role of cities in resolving the issue of joint labor supply has a long history. In the 1800s, mining and metal-processing firms (employing men) located close to textile firms (employing women), and each industry benefited from the presence of the other. More recently, "power couples" (defined as a pair of college graduates) are concentrated in large cities, where they are more likely to find good employment matches for both workers.

Learning Opportunities

Another benefit of urban size comes from the greater learning opportunities in cities. Human capital is defined as the knowledge and skills acquired by workers in formal education, work experience, and social interaction. Human capital can be increased through learning by imitation, that is, observing other workers and imitating the most productive workers. A larger city provides a wider variety of role models for workers so it attracts workers looking for learning opportunities.

The evidence for urban learning comes from data on the wages earned by workers who migrate to cities (Glaeser, 1999). Wages are higher in cities, reflecting the higher productivity of urban workers. But when a worker migrates from a rural area, she doesn't earn the higher urban wage immediately. Instead she experiences rising wages over time as learning increases her productivity. When a worker leaves the city, her wage does not drop back to the wage she earned prior to coming to the city. Instead, the higher productivity resulting from urban learning leads to a higher wage outside the city. In other words, the benefits of urban learning translate into higher wages everywhere.

Social Opportunities

A third benefit of city size comes from social interactions. An implicit assumption of the backyard-production model in Chapter 2 is that people do not value social interaction. Of course, people enjoy interacting with one another, and a larger city provides more opportunities for social interactions.

To think about the social dimension of cities, recall the labor-matching model. Suppose we replace labor skills with social interests: People have different hobbies, conversational topics, and social activities. In addition, suppose we replace firms seeking good skills matches with people seeking a network of friends with similar interests. In a model of social-interest matching, a larger city will generate better interest matches, with each network (like each firm) achieving a tighter range of social interests. Some people live in cities to take advantage of better opportunities for social-interest matching.

To illustrate the notion of social benefits of large cities, suppose you want to form a book club to discuss your favorite book, *Giles Goat Boy* (by John Barth). In a small town, you may be the only person who has read the book. In contrast, thousands of people in the typical large city have read the book and perhaps a dozen will be eager to discuss the masterpiece. A quick Internet search reveals that larger cities have more book clubs on a wider variety of topics, consistent with the notion that bigger cities provide better social matches.

SUMMARY

Firms cluster to exploit agglomeration economies, including localization economies at the industry level and urbanization economies at the city level. Here are the main points of the chapter:

1. Firms may cluster to share a supplier of an intermediate input if the input is subject to relatively large scale economies and requires face time for its design and production.
2. Firms may cluster to share a labor pool if the variation in product demand is greater at the firm level than at the industry level.
3. Larger cities provide better skill matches, leading to higher productivity and wages.
4. People and firms are attracted to cities because they facilitate knowledge spillovers, learning, and social opportunities.
5. Agglomeration economies cause self-reinforcing changes in location: The movement of one firm to a city increases the incentive for other firms to move to the city.

APPLYING THE CONCEPTS

1. **Corporate Clustering and Advertising**
   Consider corporations that use advertising firms to develop marketing campaigns. Each corporation buys one campaign per year, and the cost per campaign

is $36/n$, where $n =$ the number of campaigns produced per year. A corporation's profit equals $40 minus the cost of its marketing campaign. There are two location options: an isolated site ($n = 1$, so the cost of the campaign $= \$36$) or in a cluster with up to four corporations.

   a. Use a graph like Figure 3–5 to show the profit gap (profit in cluster − isolated profit) for clusters with one through four corporations.

   b. If initially all corporations are isolated and one joins another to form a two-corporation cluster, is the change self-reinforcing?

2. **Mr. Mullet's Carnival**

   Mr. Mullet runs a traveling carnival that hires local workers in each city it visits. The demand for carnival activities is uncertain, with low or high demand equally likely in any given city. At the end of the year, Mr. Mullet reviews his financial records and discovers some puzzling differences between his experiences in small and large cities.

   i. He always paid the same wage in large cities ($9) but paid different wages in small cities ($6 or $12).

   ii. He always hired the same quantity of labor in small cities (20 workers) but different quantities in big cities (10 or 30 workers).

   Which type of city has a higher expected profit? Illustrate with a completely labeled graph, assuming that the demand curves for labor are linear and parallel, with vertical intercepts of $18 (high demand) and $12 (low demand).

3. **Models on the Color Wheel**

   Consider the model-management industry, with firms that supply human models for advertisements. Workers (models) vary in skin tone along the color wheel, which can be divided into 24 colors. In other words, the color wheel is like a 24-hour clock. Firms enter the market with a specific skin tone requirement for their models. If a model's skin tone does not match the firm's tone requirement, the model must spend money on makeup to close the gap. The cost of makeup is $2 for each unit of color shift. For example, to go from color #3 to color #2, the cost is $2; to go from color #5 to color #2, the cost is $6. Each firm manages two models, and there are two cities in the region: Smallville has 4 models and Bigburg has 24. The gross wage is $50. Compute the net wage of models for the two cities.

4. **Agglomeration Economies and Auto Row**

   In Chapter 1, we used Auto Row as an example of self-reinforcing changes that lead to extreme outcomes. Consider a city with three isolated automobile dealers, each of which has six shoppers per day and sells three cars per day. The profit per car sold is $1,000, and half of the people who actively shop for cars actually buy one. A two-dealer cluster would get six times as many shoppers (36), and a three-dealer cluster would get nine times as many shoppers (72).

   a. Use a graph like Figure 3–5 to show the profit gap (the profit for a firm in a cluster minus the profit for an isolated firm) for one, two, and three dealers.

   b. Would a change from isolation (all dealers at different locations) to a two-dealer cluster be self-reinforcing?

c. Show the profit gap under the alternative assumption that the number of shoppers is proportional to the number of firms, that is, six times the number of firms. What does this tell us about the reasons for auto rows and other retail agglomerations?

REFERENCES AND ADDITIONAL READING

1. Aarland, K., J.C. Davis, J. Henderson, and Y. Ono, Spatial Organization of Firms: The Decision to Split Production and Administration. Providence, RI: Brown University Press, 2003.
2. Audretsch, David, and Maryann Feldman. "Knowledge Spillovers and the Geography of Innovation." Chapter 61 in Handbook of Regional and Urban Economics 4: Cities and Geography, eds. Vernon Henderson and Jacques-Francois Thisse. Amsterdam: Elsevier, 2004.
3. Carlton, D.W. "The Location and Employment Choices of New Firms." *Review of Economics and Statistics* 65 (1983), pp. 440–49.
4. Dumais, Guy, Glen Ellison, and Edward Glaeser. "Geographic Concentration as a Dynamic Process." *Review of Economics and Statistics* 84 (2002), pp. 193–204.
5. Duranton, Gilles, and Diego Puga. "Micro-foundations of Urban Agglomeration Economies." Chapter 48 in *Handbook of Regional and Urban Economics 4: Cities and Geography,* eds. Vernon Henderson and Jacques-Francois Thisse. Amsterdam: Elsevier, 2004.
6. Duranton, Gilles, and Diego Puga. "From Sectoral to Functional Specialization." *Journal of Urban Economics* 57 (2005), pp. 343–70.
7. Fujita, Mashisa, and Jacques-Francois Thisse. *Economics of Agglomeration.* Cambridge: Cambridge University Press, 2002.
8. Glaeser, Edward. "Learning in Cities." Journal of Urban Economics 46 (1999), pp. 254–277.
9. Glaeser, Edward L., Hedi D. Kallal, Jose A. Scheinkman, and Andrei Shleifer. "Growth in Cities." *Journal of Political Economy* 100 (1992), pp. 1126–52.
10. Hanson, Gordon. "Scale Economies and the Geographic Concentration of Industry." *Journal of Economic Geography* 1 (2001), pp. 255–76.
11. Harvard Business School, Cluster Mapping Project. http://data.isc.hbs.edu/isc/.
12. Head, K., J. Ries, and D. Swenson. "Agglomeration Benefits and Location Choice." *Journal of International Economics* 38 (1995), pp. 223–48.
13. Helsley, R., and W. Strange. Matching and Agglomeration Economies in a System of Cities." *Regional Science and Urban Economics* 20 (1990), pp. 189–212.
14. Henderson, J.V. "Efficiency of Resource Usage and City Size." *Journal of Urban Economics* 19 (1986), pp. 47–90.
15. Henderson, J.V., Kuncoro, A., and M. Turner. "Industrial Development and Cities." *Journal of Political Economy* 103 (1995), pp. 1067–81.
16. Jacobs, Jane. *The Economy of Cities.* New York: Random House, 1969.
17. Marshall, Alfred. *Principles of Economics.* London: Macmillan, 1920, p. 352.

18. Mun, Seil, and Bruce G. Hutchinson. "Empirical Analysis of Office Rent and Agglomeration Economies: A Case Study of Toronto." *Journal of Regional Science* 35 (1995), pp. 437–55.

19. Rosenthal Stuart and William Strange. "The Micro-Empirics of Agglomeration." Chapter 1 in *A Companion to Urban Economics,* eds. R. Arnott and D. McMillen. London: Blackwell, 2005.

20. Rosenthal, S. S., and W. C. Strange (2001). "The Determinants of Agglomeration," *Journal of Urban Economics* 50 (2001), pp. 191–229.

21. Rosenthal, S. S., and W. C. Strange. "Geography, Industrial Organization, and Agglomeration," *Review of Economics and Statistics* 85 (May 2003, pp. 377–93.

22. Rosenthal, Stuart, and William Strange. "Evidence on the Nature and Sources of Agglomeration Economies." Chapter 49 in *Handbook of Regional and Urban Economics 4: Cities and Geography,* eds. Vernon Henderson and Jacques-Francois Thisse. Amsterdam: Elsevier, 2004.

23. Saxenian, Annalee. *Regional Advantage: Culture and Competition in Silicon Valley and Route 128.* Cambridge, MA: Harvard University Press, 1994.

24. Vernon, Raymond. "External Economies." In *Readings in Urban Economics,* eds. M. Edel and J. Rothenberg. New York: Macmillan, 1972.

CHAPTER 4

City Size

There is no need to worry about mere size. Sir Isaac Newton was very much smaller than a hippopotamus, but we do not on that account value him less.
— BERTRAND RUSSELL

New York, the largest urban area in the United States, has a population of more than 18 million, while the smallest urban area (Andrews, Texas) has a population of about 13,000. As shown in Table 4–1 (page 56), there are a few very large cities, a moderate number of medium-size cities, and many small cities. In this chapter, we'll explore the economic forces responsible for the development of cities of different size. We'll also explore why cities differ in their economic scope—from highly specialized cities to diverse cities.

UTILITY AND CITY SIZE

The previous chapter explained how agglomeration economies cause firms to cluster. As we'll see in this chapter, these agglomeration economies increase productivity and wages, so workers in larger cities earn higher wages. As a city grows, the benefits of higher wages are at least partly offset by several undesirable features of larger cities, including longer commuting times, greater density, and more congestion and pollution. Given these tradeoffs, the key question is:

> *How does an increase in city size (population) affect the utility of the typical worker?*

Benefits and Costs of Bigger Cities

We are interested in the relationship between city size and the utility level of the typical worker. Consider a city where production occurs at a single point, and workers commute from a residential area to the production center. We'll start with the benefits of a larger city, then turn to the costs.

TABLE 4–1 Size Distribution of Urban Areas, 2000

Population Range	Number of Urban Areas
Greater than 10 million	2
5 million to 10 million	4
1 million to 5 million	43
100,000 to 1 million	324
Less than 100,000	549

TABLE 4–2 Utility and City Size

Workforce (millions)	Wage	Labor Income	Commuting Cost	Utility
1	$ 8	$64	$ 5	$59
2	$10	$80	$10	$70
4	$11	$88	$22	$66

As we saw in the previous chapter, agglomeration economies—from input sharing, labor pooling, skills matching, and knowledge spillovers—increase labor productivity. In a competitive labor market, competition among firms ensures that wages reflect labor productivity so wages are higher in larger cities. Table 4–2 provides a simple example of the relationship between wages and city size. As shown in the second column, the wage increases at a decreasing rate, reflecting the assumption that agglomeration economies diminish as the city grows: Labor productivity increases with the size of the workforce, but at a diminishing rate.

To simplify matters, let's assume that the only cost of population growth is longer commuting time. Suppose commuting time comes at the expense of leisure time, and we can place a dollar figure on the value of leisure time lost to commuting. As shown in the fourth column of Table 4–2, the cost of commuting increases with city size. A doubling of the workforce from 1 million to 2 million doubles the commuting cost per worker from $5 per day to $10. Doubling the workforce again more than doubles commuting cost.

The last column of Table 4–2 shows the utility level of the typical worker. For now, we'll define utility as income minus the value of leisure time lost from commuting. We assume that each person works an eight-hour day, so income is eight times the wage. Moving from a city of 1 million to a city of 2 million, the increase in productivity and labor income is large relative to the increase in commuting cost, so utility increases from $59 to $70. In Figure 4–1, this is shown as a move from point S to point M on the utility curve. In other words, agglomeration economies are stronger than the diseconomies of scale associated with commuting, so utility increases. In contrast, an increase in the workforce from 2 to 4 million decreases utility because agglomeration economies are weaker than the diseconomies from commuting. In Figure 4–1 the city's utility curve reaches $70 at a workforce of 2 million.

FIGURE 4–1 Utility and City Size

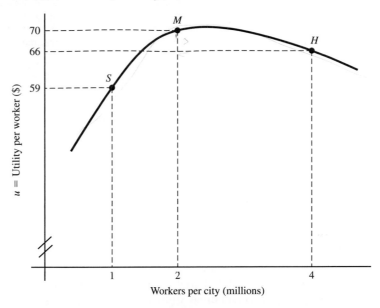

An increase in city size increases wages because of agglomeration economies and increases commuting costs. As long as agglomeration economies are stronger, utility increases with city size. When agglomeration economies are weaker than the diseconomies from commuting, utility decreases as city size increases.

Locational Equilibrium, Land Rent, and Utility within a City

So far we have ignored the location decisions of workers within a particular city. Consider a city with a workforce of 2 million (shown by point M in Figure 4–1), where workers commute from different residential locations to the city's production center. Workers differ in their commuting costs. Recall the first axiom of urban economics:

Prices adjust to achieve locational equilibrium

In this case, the price of residential land will adjust to make workers indifferent among all residential locations.

Table 4–3 (page 58) shows how differences in commuting generate differences in land rent. Let's compare two workers, one who lives near the production center and thus incurs no commuting cost, and a second who has a commuting cost of $10. If the worker at the center has a rent of $25, the rent for the other worker must be $10 lower, or $15. The same logic suggests that a worker 10 miles from the center will pay only $5 for land. Workers are indifferent between the three residential locations because the differences in commuting cost are exactly offset by differences in land rent.

TABLE 4–3 Commuting, Land Rent, and Utility within a City

A Commute Distance	B Commute Cost	C Land Rent Paid	D Labor Income	E Rental Income	F Utility
0	0	$25	$80	$15	$70
5 miles	$10	$15	$80	$15	$70
10 miles	$20	$ 5	$80	$15	$70

Who gets the rent from land? Suppose that workers own land, and to keep things simple, assume that land rent is shared equally among the city's workers. The average rent is $15 (the rent paid by the worker living 5 miles from the center), and as shown in column E of Table 4–3, each worker earns $15 of rental income to supplement labor income. For the average worker (5 miles from the center), land rent paid equals the rental income received. In contrast, for the worker living at the center, the rent paid exceeds rental income, while the opposite is true for the worker living 10 miles from the center.

The last column of Table 4–3 shows the utility for workers at different locations in the city. We can define utility as

Utility = Labor income + rental income − commute cost − rent paid

Each worker earns the same $95 of total income (labor plus rental income). For locational equilibrium, the differences in commuting costs are exactly offset by differences in land rent paid, so workers living at different locations reach the same utility level, $70.

A SYSTEM OF CITIES

We can use the utility curve to explore how a region's workforce can be distributed among its cities. The issue is whether the region will have a large number of small cities, a small number of large cities, or something between the two extremes. Consider a region with a total urban workforce of 6 million and three possible configurations:

- Six cities {A, B, C, D, E, F}, each with a workforce of 1 million.
- Three cities {D, E, F}, each with a workforce of 2 million.
- Two cities {E, F}, each with a workforce of 3 million.

Cities Are Not Too Small

We can use Figure 4–2 to explore the feasibility of the alternative configurations. Consider first the six-city outcome, with each city housing a workforce of 1 million. As shown by point S, utility in each of the six cities is $59. Is this a stable equilibrium, or will workers have an incentive to move from one city to another?

FIGURE 4–2 Cities May Be Too Large But Not Too Small

The utility curve reaches its maximum with 2 million workers in a city (point *M*), so a region with 6 million workers will maximize utility with 3 cities, each with 2 million workers. The outcome with six small cities (point *S*) is unstable because the utility curve is positively sloped. The outcome with two big cities (point *L*) is stable because the utility curve is negatively sloped.

To demonstrate the instability of the six-city outcome, imagine that a group of workers moved from city A to city D. The workforce of city D will grow, causing the city to move upward along the positively sloped portion of its utility curve, leading to a higher utility level, for example, $60. At the same time, the workforce of city A will shrink, moving the city downward along its utility curve to a lower utility level, for example, $58. In other words, the movement of workers from city A to city D opens a utility gap of $2, which will encourage more workers to move from A to D.

Because the utility curve is positively sloped near point *S*, migration is self-reinforcing. The more workers who migrate, the larger the utility gap between the two cities and the greater the incentive to relocate. For example, if the workforce of city D grows to 1.2 million and the workforce of city A shrinks to 0.8 million, utility in city D will be about $61, compared to about $57 in city A. Recall the second axiom of urban economics:

Self-reinforcing effects generate extreme outcomes

The extreme outcome is that everyone will relocate from city A to city D, so city A will disappear.

The same logic of self-reinforcing migration applies to other cities in the region. Suppose that cities A, B, and C shrink and eventually disappear, while D, E, and F grow, each eventually doubling in size. In this case, we reach point *M* in

Figure 4–2, with each of the region's three cities housing a workforce of 2 million and reaching a utility level of $70. The three-city outcome happens to be the optimum, where utility is maximized.

Cities May Be Too Large

What happens if we start out with a small number of large cities? Suppose we start with two large cities, each with a workforce of 3 million. In Figure 4–2, the starting point in each city is shown by point L. Each city (E, F) has a workforce of 3 million and reaches a utility level of $68. For all workers in the region, utility is lower than the maximum level. Is the two-city outcome a stable equilibrium?

To show why this is a stable equilibrium, consider the effects of migration from city E to city F. The workforce of city F will grow, so the city will move downward along the negatively sloped portion of the utility curve (from point L toward point z) and reach a lower utility level (e.g., $67). At the same time, the workforce of city E will shrink, moving the city upward along the utility curve to a higher utility level (e.g., $69). In other words, the migration of workers opens a utility gap of $2, but utility is higher in the smaller city, not the larger one.

In this case, migration is self-correcting, not self-reinforcing, and will be reversed. The migrant workers who migrated reach a lower utility level in their new city, so they'll regret the move and perhaps return to their original city. Alternatively, other workers in the larger city now have lower utility than is available in the smaller city, giving them an incentive to move, effectively swapping places with the original migrants. In either case, migration will be reversed, restoring the original workforces and utility levels in the two cities.

Why is the situation with small cities unstable, while the situation with large cities is stable? The reason is shown by the utility curve. With small cities, the utility curve is positively sloped because agglomeration economies are stronger than the diseconomies of scale resulting from commuting. The utility of the migrants increases because their new city is larger and more efficient, and the utility of people left behind decreases because they now live in a smaller city. In contrast, when we start with large cities, the utility curve is negatively sloped because agglomeration economies are weaker than commuting diseconomies. The utility of migrants decreases because their new city is larger but less efficient, and the utility of workers left behind increases because they now live in a smaller, more efficient city.

The general lesson from this discussion is that cities tend to be too large rather than too small. The too-small outcome occurs when a region has a city on the positively sloped portion of the utility curve. This triggers self-reinforcing migration that eliminates some of the small cities and causes the others to grow. These self-reinforcing changes do not occur when cities are too large, so cities that are inefficiently large persist.

SPECIALIZED AND DIVERSE CITIES

Do cities specialize in a narrow set of economic activities, or do they generalize, producing a diverse mix of products? It turns out that the "or" in this question is misplaced: The typical region contains a wide variety of cities, from highly specialized cites to highly diverse ones (Henderson, 1988). The specialized cities develop because of localization economies, while the diverse cities develop because of urbanization economies.

In fact, specialized and diverse cities are actually complementary, serving different roles in a market economy. Many firms start their lives in a diverse city and eventually relocate to a specialized city. Diverse cities foster new ideas and experimentation so they serve as laboratories for innovative firms. Once a firm settles on a product design and production process, production is likely to be more efficient in a specialized city that fully exploits localization economies. In other words, diverse cities foster innovation, while specialized cities facilitate efficient production.

A Model of Laboratory Cities

We can use a model developed by Duranton and Puga (2001) to explore the role of cities in innovation and production. Consider a firm that is looking for the ideal production process for a new product. By experimenting with different processes, the firm will eventually find the ideal one. At that point, the firm will switch to mass production and start earning a profit. Where should the firm experiment—in a diverse city or a specialized city?

Consider first the possibility that a firm experiments in a diverse city then relocates to a specialized city after discovering the ideal process. An experiment entails producing a prototype of the firm's new product with a particular production process. Suppose there are six potential processes, and the entrepreneur can observe other firms using these processes in the diverse city. Once the prototype from the ideal process is finished, the firm will immediately recognize that it has discovered the ideal process. This may take one year or six years, but on average it will take three years. Once the entrepreneur discovers the ideal process, the firm will move to a specialized city and start making a profit.

Figure 4–3 (page 62) shows the time path of profits under this scenario. If the cost of each prototype is $4, the firm will lose $4 in each of the three experimental years. In year four, the firm moves to a specialized city for mass production, incurring a moving cost of $7. Suppose the firm is expected to operate for a total of six years. In the last three years, the firm earns a gross profit of $12 each year. The firm's lifetime profit is

Net profit = Gross Profit − Prototype cost − Moving cost
Net profit = $36 − $12 − $7 = $17

The alternative scenario is to experiment—search for the ideal process—in the region's specialized cities. As usual, there are some trade-offs:

- **Good news: lower prototype cost.** The cost of producing a given prototype will be lower in a specialized city because each city has the specialized inputs for that production process. Suppose the cost per prototype is $3 lower in specialized cities, so the good news is a $9 savings in prototype costs ($3 per prototype times three prototypes on average).

FIGURE 4–3 Time Path of Profits in a Diversified City

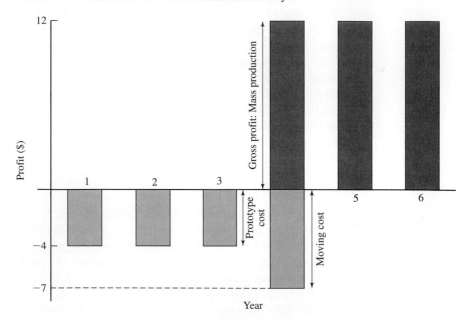

If there are six possible production processes, a firm in a diversified city can expect, on average, three years of prototype costs of $4, followed by a moving cost of $7 and three years of gross profits of $12 per year. Total expected profit is $17.

- **Bad news: Higher moving cost.** The search for the ideal process would require moves from one specialized city to another. On average, a firm adopting this strategy will have three moves, compared to a single move for the firm that experiments in the diverse city. Each move costs $7, so the bad news is $14 in additional moving cost.

In this example, moving costs are large relative to the savings in prototype costs, so profit is lower when the firm experiments in specialized cities.

This model of laboratory cities shows the roles of diverse and specialized cities in the product cycle. A diverse city has a rich variety of products and production processes, providing fertile ground for new ideas about how to produce new products. Once a firm finds its ideal production process, the benefits of being in a diverse environment diminish, so the firm relocates to a specialized city, where localization economies generate lower production cost.

Example: The Radio Industry in New York

Vernon (1972) identifies the radio industry in New York as the classic example of an industry that developed in a diversified city:

> In the 1920s that industry had all the earmarks of an activity whose establishments were heavily dependent on external [agglomeration] economies, speed, and personal contact. Its technology was unsettled and changing rapidly; its production methods were

untried; its market was uncertain. Accordingly, at that stage, producers were typically small in size, numerous, agile, nervous, heavily reliant upon subcontractors and suppliers. Mortality in the industry was high. In those circumstances, the attraction of an urban area like the New York Metropolitan Region was especially strong.

New York was attractive because it provided a wide variety of intermediate inputs and a large and diverse workforce. The area also provided production knowledge—embodied in a wide variety of production processes—that proved useful in developing a production process for the radio.

Vernon explains why the radio industry eventually left the New York metropolitan area:

> A decade or two later, however, the technology of the industry had settled down. Production methods were standardized and sets were being turned out in long runs. Now, the critical competitive questions had become transport and labor costs, rather than product design. The small firm faded from the picture and large assembly plants appeared at lower-range locations more centrally placed for national markets.

When a product reaches its mature stage, with a settled design and established production process, producers have less to gain from diversified cities, and they can relocate to places with lower production costs because of localization economies, lower wages, or lower land rent.

Evidence of Laboratory Cities

Duranton and Puga (2001) provide evidence for the notion that diversified cities serve as laboratories for firms in innovative industries. Using data from firms in France, they show that among firms that change locations, over 7 in 10 relocated from a diverse city to a specialized city. As firms mature, they relocate from diverse cities with urbanization economies to specialized cities with localization economies.

The most innovative industries have the highest frequency of relocations from diverse to specialized cities. For example, the frequency is 93 percent for research and development, 88 percent for pharmaceuticals and cosmetics, and 82 percent for information technology. The frequency is high for other industries, including business services, printing and publishing, aerospace equipment, and electronic equipment. In contrast, the frequency of movement to specialized cities is relatively low for less innovative sectors such as furniture, food, beverages, clothing, and leather.

Much of the recent work on urbanization economies focuses on the connection how city diversity affects plant births and employment growth. Rosenthal and Strange (2004) summarize the most recent studies and conclude that diversity encourages both births and growth in employment, especially in high-technology industries.

DIFFERENCES IN CITY SIZE

Table 4–1 shows the wide range of city sizes in the United States. Other countries have a similar pattern of differences in city sizes. In this part of the chapter, we'll explore the roles of localization and urbanization economies determining city size. We'll also explore the role of consumer goods.

Differences in Localization and Urbanization Economies

Figure 4–4 shows utility curves for three types of cities in a regional economy. The curve on the left applies to an industry for which localization economies are exhausted with a relatively small workforce. In this case, the diseconomies of commuting quickly overwhelm agglomeration economies, so the optimum city size is relatively small. The middle utility curve is for a specialized city with larger localization economies and thus a larger optimum size. Finally, the utility curve on the right is for a city that experiences large urbanization economies, generating a large optimum size.

Locational equilibrium requires that workers in the region are indifferent between the three cities, meaning that workers in the three cities must achieve the same utility level. Suppose the region has a total of 10 million workers. In Figure 4–4, points s, m, and b show one possible equilibrium. The utility level, u^* is the same in all three cities, and the city workforces (1 million in the small city, 3 million in the medium-size city, and 6 million in the big city) add up to the regional workforce (10 million). As we saw earlier in the chapter, this is a stable equilibrium because each city is on the negatively sloped portion of its utility curve.

Local Goods and City Size

So far our discussion of city size has focused on employment in industries subject to localization and urbanization economies. In other words, we have ignored the consumer side of the urban economy. We can distinguish between employment in

FIGURE 4–4 Differences in City Sizes from Differences in Agglomeration Economies

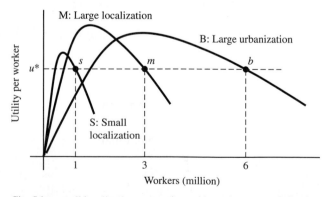

City S has small localization economies and its optimum population is smaller than that of city M with its large localization economies. City B has large urbanization economies and a large population. The set of points {s, m, b} shows a possible equilibrium, with all residents achieving the utility level u^* and populations of 1 million (city S), 3 million (city M), and 6 million (city B) adding up to the regional population of 10 million.

industries that export their output to people outside the city and those that sell their products locally to residents of the city. For example, most of the cars produced in Detroit are sold to people in other cities, while most of the donuts produced in Detroit are sold to city residents, as are most haircuts and groceries. Total employment in a city is the sum of export employment and local employment.

Some local products are available in all cities, large and small. If the per-capita demand for a product is large relative to the scale economies associated with producing it, even a small city will generate sufficient demand to support at least one firm. For example, it takes just a few thousand people to support a barber, so even a small city will have at least one barber. Similarly, a pizzeria can be supported by a few thousand people, so even a small city will have pizzerias and pizza workers. Of course, a larger city has more hair to cut and more people to feed, so it will have more barbers and pizza tossers. In fact, we expect the number of barbers and pizza tossers to increase proportionately with city size.

Some local products are available only in large cities. If the per-capita demand for a product is low relative to the scale economies in production, it will take a large city to generate enough demand to support a firm. For example, the per-capita demand for opera is relatively small, so it may take a million people to support an opera company. As a result, we will find opera companies in large cities but not small ones. Similarly, the per-capita demand for brain surgery is low relative to the scale economies in production, so brain surgeons operate in large cities.

Larger cities have a wider variety of consumer products. In a large city, consumers can get everything available in small cities (pizzas and haircuts) as well as products not available in small cities (opera and brain surgery). In fact, people in small cities travel to large cities to buy products that are not available locally. In contrast, consumers in large cities can buy almost anything they want locally so there is little reason to travel to smaller cities.

Local Employment Amplifies Size Differences

Figure 4–5 (page 66) shows the implications of local employment for the size of cities with different levels of export employment. Suppose that in a city with export employment of 1 million, each export job supports half a job in local industry. If so, total employment in the city is 1.5 times its export employment, or 1.5 million. We know that a larger city can support a wider range of consumer goods. Suppose that in a city with export employment of 3 million, each export job supports one local job. As shown in Figure 4–5, total employment in such a city is 6 million (3 million export jobs plus 3 million local jobs). Finally, suppose that in a city with 6 million export jobs, each export job supports two local jobs. In this case, total employment is 18 million (6 million export jobs plus 12 million local jobs).

As shown in Figure 4–5, local employment amplifies differences in population. Total employment increases by half in the small city (1 to 1.5 million), while it doubles in the medium-sized city (from 3 to 6 million) and triples in the large city (from 6 to 18 million). After incorporating local employment, the largest city has 12 times the total employment of the small city, up from 6 times before considering local

FIGURE 4–5 The Introduction of Local Goods Amplifies Differences in City Size

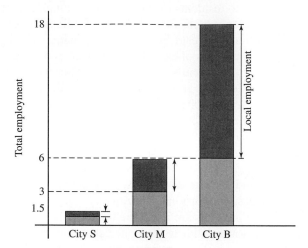

Introducing local consumer amplifies the differences in population arising from differences in export employment. The population of the small city increases by half, while the population of the medium city doubles and the population of the large city triples.

employment. This occurs because the large city has a larger consumer base and can support a wider variety of products.

THE SIZE DISTRIBUTION OF CITIES

Figure 4–6 shows the size distribution of cities split into two graphs, one for the top 50 urban areas and a second for the rest of the urban areas. The figure is drawn with the new census definitions of urban areas, with metropolitan areas (urban areas with populations exceeding 50,000) and micropolitan areas (smaller urban areas).

The Rank-Size Rule

Geographers and economists have estimated the relationship between city rank and size. One possibility is that the relationship follows the rank-size rule:

Rank times population is constant across cities

In other words, if the largest city (rank 1) has a population of 24 million, the second largest city will have a population of 12 million ($12 \cdot 2 = 24$), while the third largest will have a population of 8 million ($8 \cdot 3 = 24$), and so on.

Nitsche (2005) analyzes the results of 29 studies of the rank-size relationship, with data from countries around the world. The hypothesized relationship is

$$Rank = \frac{C}{N^b}$$

FIGURE 4–6 Size Distribution of U.S. Urban Areas, 2000

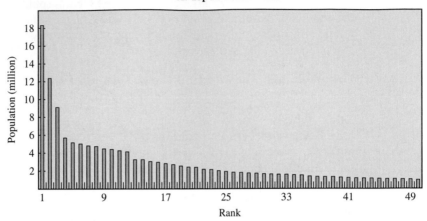

A: Top 50 Urban Areas

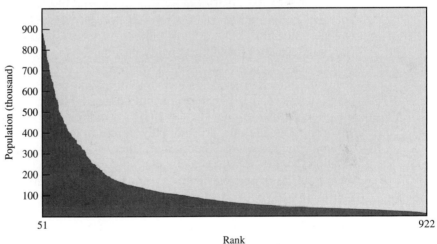

B: 51st through 922nd Urban Areas

where C is a constant, N is population, and the exponent b is to be estimated from the data on rank and population. If $b = 1.0$, the rank-size rule holds. In the studies considered by Nitsche, two-thirds of the estimates of b are between 0.80 to 1.20, and the median estimate is 1.09. This is consistent with earlier cross-country studies that generate estimates of b in the range 1.11 to 1.13. In other words, the urban population is more evenly distributed across cities than would be predicted by the rank-size rule.

An important qualification of this conclusion is that many of the studies use political definitions of cities rather than the economic definition. A political city is defined by boundaries that separate political jurisdictions. In contrast, the economic definition of a city ignores political boundaries and includes in a city's population all the people who are economically involved in a particular urban economy. In practical terms, the economic city is typically defined as a metropolitan area (e.g., the San Francisco Bay Area) that includes the central (political) city along with all the surrounding communities. For the studies of the rank-size rule that use economic cities rather than political cities, the median estimate for b is 1.02, which is much closer to the rank-size result.

Urban Giants: The Puzzle of Large Primary Cities

In many developing countries, the largest city has a relatively large share of population. Table 4–4 shows the populations and the national population shares for the largest cities in several countries. As a point of reference, the New York metropolitan area has only 6.5 percent of the population of the United States. In contrast, the other metropolitan areas listed in the table have national shares between 11 percent and 39 percent.

Economists have developed several models to explain the large concentrations of population in primary cities. One theory is based on the idea that large economies of scale in trade encourage the development of a single large trading city rather than several smaller ones. For example, the substantial investment in a port facility encourages nations to designate a primary port city. English trade grew rapidly between 1520 and 1670, a result of military victories against the Spanish, improved shipping technology, and the expansion of markets in Asia and the Americas. The population of London increased during this period from 55,000 to 475,000, and its share of England's population increased from 2 percent to 10 percent. In Argentina, between 1887 and 1914 exports quadrupled, and the population of Buenos Aires—the principal trading city—increased by 1.1 million (265 percent).

Transportation infrastructure plays a role in urban concentration. In many developing countries, a disproportionate share of investment in roads and telecommunication facilities occurs in and around the capital city. The relatively low investment in infrastructure outside the capital area generates high transport costs within the country and encourages the development of large primary cities.

What is the role of politics in the development of large primary cities? Andes and Glaeser (1995) suggest that nations run by dictators have larger primary cities than democracies. One way for a dictator to stay in power is to take resources from the hinterland (areas outside the capital city) and transfer these resources to the

TABLE 4–4 Population of Largest Cities as Share of National Population

Metropolitan Area	Population	Share of National Population
Tokyo	19,037,361	15.76%
Mexico City	16,465,487	20.97
São Paulo	15,538,682	11.46
Buenos Aires	10,759,291	35.47
Santiago, Chile	4,227,049	34.87
Montevideo, Uruguay	1,157,450	39.36

people who are most likely to overthrow him—people in the capital city. If a dictator pays off local agitators, the capital city will grow as some people migrate to the city to get the payoffs and others migrate for jobs in local industry that are supported by the bribes. Based on a study of cities in 85 countries, Andes and Glaeser conclude that capital cities in countries with dictatorships are 45 percent larger than capital cities in other countries.

The experience of Rome illustrates the role of redistribution policies on urban concentration. In the period 130–50 B.C., the population of Rome increased from 375,000 to 1 million, making Rome more than twice as large as any city up to that point in history. Military successes during this period extended the empire into Gaul and the eastern provinces of Asia, providing a large hinterland from which to extract resources. The rulers responded to political unrest in Rome by distributing free grain to the residents and staging the infamous—and very expensive—Roman circuses.

SUMMARY

This chapter explains why cities come in different sizes. Here are the main points of the chapter:

1. The utility curve shows the trade-offs from an increase in population: Agglomeration economies increase productivity and wages, but diseconomies of scale from increased commuting costs reduce utility.
2. Cities are unlikely to be too small because such an outcome is not a stable equilibrium: Migration is self-reinforcing because the growing city becomes more productive while the shrinking city becomes less productive.
3. Cities may be too large because such an outcome is a stable equilibrium: Migration is self-correcting because the shrinking city becomes more productive while the growing city becomes less productive.
4. Local employment amplifies differences in workforces and population across cities.
5. A diverse city fosters experimentation and leads to innovations in product design and production.
6. The rank-size rule provides a rough approximation to the size distribution of cities.

APPLYING THE CONCEPTS

1. **Jet Packs for Workers**
   Consider a region that initially has 12 identical cities, each with a workforce of 1 million (the optimum or utility-maximizing workforce). Suppose that commuting by automobile is replaced by commuting by jet pack (strap it on and fly to work), and the time and monetary costs of commuting decrease. The optimum workforce triples to 3 million.
   a. Depict graphically the effects of jet packs on the urban utility curve.
   b. Is the initial workforce of 1 million an equilibrium? Is it a stable equilibrium?
   c. Predict the new equilibrium workforce and number of cities.

2. City Formation and Efficiency

Consider a region with a workforce of 12 million. The urban utility curve reaches its maximum with 3 million workers and includes the following combinations:

Workers (millions)	1	2	3	4	6	8	9	10	11	12
Utility ($)	32	56	70	65	55	45	40	35	30	25

Initially, there is a single city with 12 million workers. Suppose the government establishes a new city with 1 million workers, leaving 11 million workers in the old city.

a. Assume that the number of cities remains at two. What happens next? What's the new equilibrium city size?

b. Suppose that the government establishes three new cities, each with 1 million workers (leaving 9 million in the old city). What happens next? Will the region reach the optimum configuration of four cities, each with 3 million workers?

c. Suppose your objective is to reach the optimum configuration and you establish three new cities. What is the minimum number of workers to be placed initially in each of the new cities?

3. One City Size

Consider a region with two export goods (gloves and socks), and two local products (tattoos and manicures). The production of each export good is subject to localization economies, so each city specializes in one export good. According to Mr. Wizard, "If my assumptions are correct, all the cities in the region will be the same size." Assume that Mr. Wizard's logic is correct. List his assumptions and explain why together they imply the cities will be the same size.

4. Experiments in Specialized Cities

In the example of the laboratory cities, firms did their prototype experiments in a diverse city rather than in specialized cities. Consider the changes in the numerical assumptions required to change the conclusion. Using only integers, fill in the blanks:

Firms will do their prototype experiments in the specialized cities if (a) the cost per prototype were _____ lower in the specialized city or (b) if the moving cost per move decreased to _____.
Explain the logic behind your numbers.

5. K-Mart Dresses

Most of the dresses sold in the United States are produced in large factories that are dispersed throughout the world, not concentrated in a single U.S. city. Reconcile this fact with the text discussion of localization economies that cause dressmakers to cluster.

REFERENCES AND ADDITIONAL READING

1. Andes, Alberto F., and Edward L. Glaeser. "Trade and Circuses: Explaining Urban Giants." *Quarterly Journal of Economics* (1995), pp. 195–227.
2. Abdel-Rahman, H., and A. Anas. "Theories of Systems of Cities." Chapter 52 in *Handbook of Regional and Urban Economics 4: Cities and Geography,* eds. V. Henderson and J.F. Thisse. Amsterdam: Elsevier, 2004.
3. Audretsch, D., and M. Feldman. "Knowledge Spillovers and the Geography of Innovation," Chapter 61 in *Handbook of Regional and Urban Economics 4: Cities and Geography,* eds. V. Henderson and J.F. Thisse. Amsterdam: Elsevier, 2004.
4. Duranton, G., and D. Puga. "Nursery Cities: Urban Diversity, Process Innovation, and the Life Cycle of Products." *American Economic Review* 91 (5), 1454–77 (2001).
5. Gabaix, X., and Y. Ioannides. "Evolution of City Size Distributions," Chapter 53 in *Handbook of Regional and Urban Economics 4: Cities and Geography,* eds. V. Henderson and J.F. Thisse. Amsterdam: Elsevier, 2004.
6. Glaeser, E. "Learning in Cities." *Journal of Urban Economics* 46 (1999), pp. 254–77.
7. Henderson, V. *Urban Development: Theory, Fact, and Illusion.* Oxford: Oxford University Press, 1988.
8. Nitsche, V. "Zipf Zipped." *Journal of Urban Economics* 57 (2005), pp. 86–100.
9. Rosenthal, S., and W. Strange, "Evidence on the Nature and Sources of Agglomeration Economies," Chapter 49 in *Handbook of Regional and Urban Economics 4: Cities and Geography,* eds. V. Henderson and J.F. Thisse. Amsterdam: Elsevier, 2004.
10. U.S. Department of Transportation. *Summary of Travel Trends: 2001 National Household Travel Survey.* Washington D.C., December 2004.
11. Vernon, Raymond. "External Economies." In *Readings in Urban Economics,* ed. M. Edel and J. Rothenberg. New York: Macmillan, 1972.

CHAPTER 5

Urban Growth

An economic forecaster is like a cross-eyed javelin thrower: He doesn't win many accuracy contests, but he keeps the crowd's attention.

—ANONYMOUS

*I*n an urban economy, there are two sorts of growth. First, economic growth is defined as an increase in a city's average wage or per-capita income. Second, employment growth is defined as an increase in a city's total workforce. In this chapter, we explore the various sources of income and employment growth and look at the consequences of increases in a city's total employment. One of the key questions is, Who benefits when total employment increases?

ECONOMIC GROWTH: INCREASE IN PER-CAPITA INCOME

Economic growth is defined as an increase in per-capita income. The traditional—nongeographical—sources of economic growth are as follows:

- **Capital deepening.** Physical capital includes all the objects made by humans to produce goods and services, such as machines, equipment, and buildings. Capital deepening is defined as an increase in the amount of capital per worker—it increases productivity and income because each worker works with more capital.
- **Increases in human capital.** A person's human capital includes the knowledge and skills acquired through education and experience. An increase in human capital increases productivity and income.
- **Technological progress.** Any idea that increases productivity—from a worker's commonsense idea about how to better organize production, to a scientist's invention of a faster microprocessor—is a form of technological progress. The resulting increase in productivity increases income per worker.

Non Geographic

As we saw earlier in the book, the geographical perspective adds a fourth source of economic growth.

Geographic

- **Agglomeration economies.** Physical proximity increases productivity through input sharing, labor pooling, labor matching, and knowledge spillovers.

Cities increase productity and income because they bring the inputs to the production process together and facilitate face-to-face communication. According to Lucas (2001), cities are the engines of economic growth.

It is important to distinguish between a change in a city's income level and a change in its growth rate of income. Suppose a city's annual per-capita income increases from $20,000 to $21,000 and then remains at the higher level. This city has experienced an increase in its income level but no change in its long-term economic growth rate, which is zero. In contrast, suppose a city whose income was growing at a rate of 1 percent per year starts to grow at a rate of 3 percent per year. If the higher growth rate persists, the city has experienced an increase in its long-term economic growth rate. A city's economic growth rate is determined by the rate of capital deepening (how rapidly capital per worker increases each year), the rate of technological progress (how many new ideas are developed each year), and the rate of increase in human capital.

To illustrate the distinction between level and growth effects, consider the effects of an increase in human capital. Suppose the fraction of a city's population that completes college increases from 30 to 35 percent and remains at the higher level. If the resulting increase in productivity increases per-capita income from $20,000 to $21,000, we measure economic growth as a $1,000 increase in the city's income level. By itself, the increase in human capital does not affect the city's long-term growth rate. However, if better-educated people generate more and better ideas every year, the rate of technological progress will increase, leading to a higher long-term economic growth rate.

CITY-SPECIFIC INNOVATION AND INCOME

We can use the urban utility curve derived in Chapter 4 to show the connection between technological progress and per-capita income. Consider a region of 12 million workers and two cities that are initially identical. In Figure 5–1 (page 74), the initial utility curve has the familiar hump shape, reflecting the tension between agglomeration economies and diseconomies of scale (from rising commuting times; more congestion, noise, and pollution; and higher density). The two cities have the same initial utility curve, and the initial equilibrium is shown by point *i*. The region's workforce is split equally between two cities of 6 million workers, and the common utility level is $70 per worker.

Suppose one of the two cities experiences technological progress that increases worker productivity. In Figure 5–1, the city's utility curve shifts upward, with a higher productivity (and average income) for each level of the workforce. For

FIGURE 5–1 Urban Economic Growth from Technological Progress

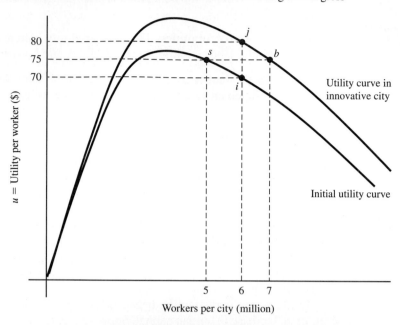

In the initial equilibrium shown by point *i*, a region's workforce is divided equally
between two cities of 6 million workers. Innovation in one city shifts its utility
curve upward, and in the absence of migration, the innovative city moves to point *j*.
Migration to the innovative city generates points *b* (innovative city) and *s* (other
city). The innovation increases utility in both cities and shifts population to the
innovative city.

example, with a workforce of 6 million in the innovative city, the income level
would increase from $70 (point *i*) to $80 (point *j*). So in the absence of migration,
utility in the innovative city would exceed utility in the other city by $10. In re-
sponse to the utility gap, workers will migrate to the innovative city, and migration
will continue until utility is equalized.

The new equilibrium is shown by points *s* and *b*. This is a locational equilibrium because both cities have the same utility level ($75), and the workforces in the
two cities add up to the fixed regional population: The innovative city (shown by
point *b*) gains 1 million workers, while the other city (shown by point *s*) loses the
same number. Utility increases from $70 to $75 in both cities, meaning that workers in both cities benefit from innovation in one city. Workers in the other city benefit because the decrease in population causes the city to move upward along its
negatively sloped utility curve to a higher utility level.

One of the lessons from Figure 5–1 is that the benefits of innovation in a single
city spread to other cities in the region. Any initial gap in the utility levels of cities
will be eliminated by labor migration to the city with the higher utility level, and
migration will continue until the utility gap is eliminated. In our two-city region, the

initial utility gap (shown by points *i* and *j*) is $10, and in equilibrium, each of the two cities experiences an increase in utility equal to half this initial gap ($5): Utility increases from $70 to $75.

In a larger region, the increase in per-capita utility would be smaller. If the region had 10 cities instead of 2, there would be five times as many workers to share the benefits of the innovation. For example, the initial $10 utility gap, spread over 10 cities, translates into a $1 increase in per-capita utility.

Regionwide Innovation and Income

Consider next the effect of simultaneous innovation in both cities. Suppose the two cities experience the same innovation, and thus experience the same upward shift of the utility curve. In this case, both cities would move from point *i* to point *j*, and point *j* would be the new equilibrium. There would be no utility gap to overcome with migration because both cities would experience the same change in productivity. As a result, each city would maintain its workforce of 6 million workers.

We've seen that technological innovation—represented by an upward shift of the utility curve—increases the equilibrium utility and per-capita income throughout the region. The same logic applies to other sources of higher productivity—capital deepening, increases in human capital, and productivity boosts from localization and urbanization economies.

HUMAN CAPITAL AND ECONOMIC GROWTH

Urban economists have explored the effects of human capital on urban productivity and income. An increase in the education or job skills of a specific worker increases the worker's productivity, and competition among employers increases the wage to match the higher productivity. In addition, workers learn from one another by sharing knowledge—in both formal and informal settings—and a worker with more human capital has more knowledge to share and better communication skills. If better-educated workers generate more ideas, an increase in human capital also increases the rate of technological innovation. Glaeser, Scheinkman, and Shleifer (1995) show that cities with relatively high levels of human capital experienced relatively large increases in per-capita income over the period 1960–1990, suggesting a link between human capital and the rate of technological progress.

In recent decades, the share of metropolitan residents with college degrees has increased significantly. Between 1980 and 2000, the overall share for U.S. metropolitan areas increased from 0.17 to 0.23. There is substantial variation in the college share across cities, with a range of 0.11 to 0.44 in 2000. The cities with above-average shares experienced more rapid growth in the college share since 1990, so the variation across metropolitan areas has actually increased since then. For example, three cities that started the decade among the top seven cities in terms of college shares experienced the largest increases in the college share during the decade.

There is evidence that the largest beneficiaries of educational spillovers are less-skilled workers. One study estimated that a 1 percent increase in a city's share of college-educated workers increases the wage of high-school dropouts by 1.9 percent, while it increases the wage of high-school graduates by 1.6 percent and the wage of college graduates by 0.4 percent (Moretti, 2004). This reflects the general observation that urban economic growth tends to reduce income inequality (Wheeler, 2004).

A recent study of the biotechnology industry shows that physical proximity to top-notch "star" researchers is an important factor in the birth of biotechnology firms (Zucker, Darby, Brewer, 1998). The new biotechnology firms located close to scientists with specific human capital (those involved in the discovery of genetic sequences). Although many of the scientists were connected to universities and research centers, the key location factor was the human capital of the scientists, not the presence of a university or research center.

In less developed countries, secondary (high-school) education is an important factor in income growth. According to a recent study of Chinese cities (Mody and Wang, 1997), when enrollment in secondary education increases from 30 percent to 35 percent of the eligible population in a city, the growth rate of total output increases by 5 percentage points. This effect diminishes as the enrollment rate increases: An increase in the enrollment rate from 55 percent to 60 percent increases the growth rate by only 3 percentage points. The largest productivity boost from secondary education occurs in cities with relatively high levels of foreign investment, suggesting that foreign investment and human-capital investments are complementary inputs.

URBAN EMPLOYMENT GROWTH

A model of the urban labor market can help us explore the reasons for changes in total urban employment. We assume that the metropolitan area is part of a larger regional economy and that households and firms move freely between cities in the region. The demand for labor comes from firms in the city, while supply comes from households living in the city. The model shows the effects of changes in demand and supply on equilibrium employment and wages in the city.

Export versus Local Employment and the Multiplier

We can divide production in the urban economy into two types, export and local. Export goods are sold to people outside the city. For example, steel producers sell most of their output to customers outside the city where steel is produced. In contrast, local goods are sold to people within the city. Most of the output of bakeries, bookstores, and pet salons are sold within the city. Total employment is the sum of export employment and local employment.

The two types of employment are related to one another through the multiplier process. Suppose a steel producer expands its operation by hiring 100 additional workers to produce goods for exports. These workers earn an income, and they spend part of it on local goods such as groceries, haircuts, and books. The firms producing these local goods hire more workers to produce additional output, so the increase in export employment leads to increases in local employment. These new local workers in turn spend part of their income on local goods, supporting additional local jobs. The spending and respending of income in the local economy supports local jobs, so the increase in total employment exceeds the initial increase in export employment.

How many additional local jobs are generated by the increase in export employment? To answer this question, policy makers examine the interactions between firms in an urban economy and estimate the employment multiplier, defined as the change in total employment per unit change in export employment. If the multiplier is 2.10, for example, a one-unit increase in export employment increases total employment directly by one export job, and indirectly by 1.10 local jobs, for a total effect of 2.10 jobs.

Table 5–1 shows the estimated multipliers for select industries for the Portland Metropolitan Area. The multipliers vary across industries, from a low of 1.46 for

TABLE 5–1 Metropolitan Employment Multipliers

Industry	Portland Metropolitan Multiplier
Frozen food manufacturing	2.40
Wineries	2.74
Textile and fabric finishing mills	1.82
Carpet and rug mills	1.88
Footwear manufacturing	1.92
Envelope manufacturing	2.13
Photographic film and chemical manufacturing	2.53
Optical instrument and lens manufacturing	1.46
Fiber optic cable manufacturing	2.71
Heavy duty truck manufacturing	2.55
Motorcycle, bicycle, and parts manufacturing	1.92
Software publishers	2.17
Insurance carriers	2.49
Legal services	1.76
Architectural and engineering services	1.74
Custom computer programming services	1.58
Computer systems design services	2.21
Other computer-related services	1.60
Management consulting services	1.66
Environmental and other technical consulting	1.78
Scientific research and development services	1.51
Advertising and related services	1.67
Hospitals	2.13
Spectator sports	1.54
Independent artists, writers, and performers	2.77
Museums, historical sites, zoos, and parks	2.19

Source: ECONorthwest

optical instruments to a high of 2.77 for independent artists. For the service sectors (legal, architecture, programming, computer, consulting, scientific, advertising), the multipliers are between 1.51 and 2.21. The average multiplier for the 423 industries for which multipliers are estimated is 2.13, indicating that on average, a one-unit increase in export employment increases total employment in the metropolitan area by 2.13 jobs.

The Labor Demand Curve

Figure 5–2 shows the city's negatively sloped labor-demand curve. An increase in the wage decreases the quantity of labor demanded for two reasons:

- **The substitution effect.** An increase in the city's wage causes firms to substitute other inputs (capital, land, materials) for the relatively expensive labor.
- **The output effect.** An increase in the city's wage increases production costs, increasing the prices charged by the city's firms. Consumers respond by purchasing less output, so firms produce less and hire fewer workers.

The demand curve is negatively sloped because an increase in wages generates both a substitution effect and an output effect.

FIGURE 5–2 Direct and Multiplier Effects of an Increase In Export Employment

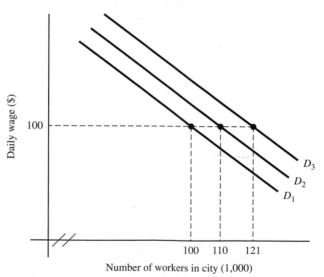

If export employment increases by 10,000, the labor demand curve shifts to the right (D_1 to D_2) because of the direct effect (10,000 workers) and shifts further to the right (D_2 to D_3) because of the multiplier effect (11,000 additional local workers).

What causes the demand curve to shift to the right or the left? The following factors determine the position of the curve:

Demand Curve Shift —

1. **Demand for exports.** An increase in the demand for the city's exports increases export production and shifts the demand curve to the right: At every wage, more workers will be demanded.
2. **Labor productivity.** An increase in labor productivity decreases production costs, allowing firms to cut prices, increase output, and hire more workers. As we saw earlier in the chapter, labor productivity increases with capital deepening, technological progress, increases in human capital, and agglomeration economies.
3. **Business taxes.** An increase in business taxes (without a corresponding change in public services) increases production costs, which in turn increases prices and decreases the quantity produced and sold, ultimately decreasing the demand for labor.
4. **Industrial public services.** An increase in the quality of industrial public services (without a corresponding increase in taxes) decreases production costs and thus increases output and labor demand.
5. **Land-use policies.** Industrial firms require production sites that (a) are accessible to the intracity and intercity transportation networks and (b) have a full set of public services (water, sewerage, electricity). By coordinating its land-use and infrastructure policies to ensure an adequate supply of industrial land, a city can accommodate existing firms that want to expand their operations and new firms that want to locate in the city.

Figure 5–2 shows the effects of an increase in export sales on a city's labor-demand curve. Suppose that an increase in exports increases the demand for export workers by 10,000. The city's demand curve will shift to the right from D_1 to D_2, and an additional 10,000 export workers would be demanded at a wage of $100 per day. If the employment multiplier is 2.10, every export job supports 1.10 local jobs, so the demand curve shifts to the right by an additional 11,000 workers (from D_2 to D_3). Total labor demand increases by 21,000 (2.1 times the increase in the demand for export labor).

The Labor Supply Curve

Consider next the supply side of the urban labor market. The supply curve is positively sloped, indicating that the higher the wage, the larger the number of workers in the city. We make two simplifying assumptions for the supply curve:

- **A fixed number of work hours per worker.** The empirical evidence on labor supply suggests that an increase in the wage has a negligible effect on the aggregate hours worked; some people work more and others work less, but on average, people work about the same number of hours.
- **A fixed labor-force participation rate.** We assume that a change in the wage does not change the fraction of the city's population in the workforce.

Given these two assumptions, an increase in the wage increases the supplied labor because more workers move to the city.

Why is the supply curve positively sloped? An increase in total employment in the city increases the total demand for housing and land, pulling up their prices. Recall the first axiom of urban economics:

Prices adjust to generate locational equilibrium

To ensure locational equilibrium in the labor market, a growing city must offer a higher wage to compensate workers for the higher cost of living. The elasticity of the cost of urban living with respect to the size of the labor force is 0.20 (Bartik 1991):

[handwritten: elasticity]

$$e(C, N) = \frac{\% \text{ change in Cost of living}}{\% \text{ change in Labor force}} = 0.20$$

[handwritten: rate change of cost / rate change in employment]

For example, a 10 percent increase in the labor force increases the cost of living by about 2 percent. This means that to keep real wages constant, the elasticity of the wage with respect to the labor force must be 0.20:

[handwritten: wage w resp. to emp.]

$$e(W, N) = \frac{\% \text{ change in Wage}}{\% \text{ change in Labor force}} = 0.20$$

We can use these numbers to compute the elasticity of supply of labor, defined as the percentage change in the quantity of labor supplied divided by the percentage change in the wage. This is of course just the inverse of the elasticity of the wage with respect to the labor force.

[handwritten: elasticity of wages]

$$e(N, W) = \frac{\% \text{ change in Labor force}}{\% \text{ change in Wage}} = 5.0$$

With an elasticity of labor supply of 5.0, a 2 percent increase in the wage increases the labor force by five times 2 percent, or 10 percent. This elasticity applies to an individual city and is much larger than the national labor-supply elasticity (close to zero) because there is less migration between nations than between cities.

What causes the supply curve to shift to the right or left? The position of the supply curve is determined by the following factors:

[handwritten: increases/decrease shift in supply curve]

1. **Amenities.** Anything that increases the relative attractiveness of the city (other than the wage) shifts the supply curve to the right. For example, an improvement in air or water quality causes migration that increases the supply of labor. Similarly, an increase in the variety of consumer goods (restaurants, entertainment) will increase the supply of labor.
2. **Disamenities.** Anything that decreases the relative attractiveness of a city decreases labor supply and shifts the supply curve to the left. For example, an increase in the crime rate causes people to flee the city, decreasing labor supply.
3. **Residential taxes.** An increase in residential taxes (without a corresponding change in public services) decreases the relative attractiveness of the city, causing out-migration that shifts the supply curve to the left.

[handwritten: ↑ taxes = ↓ attractiveness]

Public service = ↑ attractiveness

4. **Residential public services.** An increase in the quality of residential public services (without a corresponding increase in taxes) increases the relative attractiveness of the city, causing in-migration that shifts the supply curve to the right.

Equilibrium Effects of Changes in Supply and Demand

Figure 5–3 shows the effects of an increase in export sales on the urban labor market. The labor-demand curve shifts to the right by 21,000 workers, reflecting the effect of an increase in 10,000 export jobs. As the population of the city increases, the prices of housing and land increase, requiring an increase in the wage to compensate workers for the higher cost of living. In other words, the city moves upward along its supply curve. The equilibrium wage rises from $100 per day to $103, and the equilibrium number of laborers increases from 100,000 to 115,000.

Figure 5–3 suggests that predicting the effects of an increase in export employment is tricky. The simple approach is to use the employment multiplier to predict the change in total employment from a projected change in export employment. In the numerical example, the predicted change in total employment from this method would be 21,000 (2.1 times 10,000). This approach tells us the horizontal shift of the demand curve, not the change in equilibrium employment. To accurately predict the change in total employment, one must also know the slopes of the supply and demand curves.

Multiplier 2.1
new export jobs results in 2.1 total job increase. ie. 1.1 local jobs increase.

FIGURE 5–3 Equilibrium Effects of an Increase in Export Employment

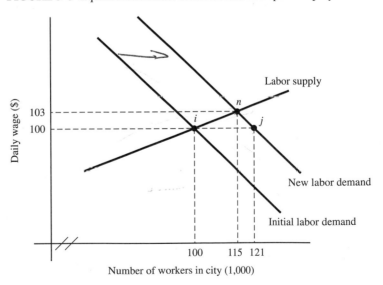

An increase in export employment shifts the demand curve to the right, reflecting both the direct and multiplier effects. The equilibrium moves from point *i* to point *n*, with an increase in the wage and total employment.

We can use two simple formulas to predict the effect of an increase in demand on a city's equilibrium wage and employment. The formula for the change in the equilibrium wage is

$$\text{Percentage change in equilibrium wage} = \frac{\text{Percentage change in Demand}}{E_d + E_s}$$

where the percentage change in demand is the percentage horizontal shift of the demand curve, E_s is the elasticity of supply, and E_d is the absolute value of the elasticity of demand. In the example depicted in Figure 5–3, the demand curve shifts horizontally by 21 percent (equal to 21,000/100,000). Suppose the absolute value of the demand elasticity is 2.0, and the supply elasticity is 5.0. Then the predicted wage change is

$$\text{Percentage change in equilibrium wage} = \frac{21\%}{2 + 5} = 3\%$$

The market moves upward along the supply curve, so we can use the supply elasticity to predict the change in quantity:

$$\% \text{ change in quantity of labor} = E_s \cdot \% \text{ change in Wage}$$

$$\% \text{ change in quantity of labor} = 5 \cdot 3\% = 15\%$$

In this case, a 21 percent increase in demand leads to a 3 percent increase in the wage and a 15 percent increase in total employment.

Figure 5–4 shows the effects of an increase in the supply of labor. Suppose the city improves its residential public services. For example, the city could improve its

FIGURE 5–4 Equilibrium Effects of an Improvement in Public Services

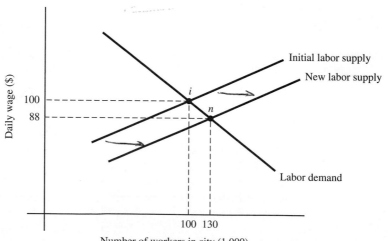

An improvement in residential public services increases labor supply and shifts the supply curve to the right. The equilibrium moves from point i to point n, with a decrease in the wage and an increase in total employment.

public-safety programs or alter its transportation system to decrease commuting costs. In Figure 5–4, the labor-supply curve shifts to the right: At each wage, more people are willing to work and live in the city. The shift of the supply curve increases equilibrium employment and decreases the equilibrium wage. Figure 5–4 is consistent with the empirical evidence provided by Eberts and Stone (1992) concerning the effects of improvements in local infrastructure on wages and total employment. Workers accept lower wages in cities that provide a superior mix of local public goods.

PUBLIC POLICY AND EQUILIBRIUM EMPLOYMENT

Policies change demand/supply which effects size of city

Public policy affects equilibrium employment in a city by shifting the labor supply curve or the labor demand curve. As explained earlier in the chapter, local government can shift the curves through its decisions concerning local education, public services, business infrastructure, and taxes. In this part of the chapter, we take a closer look at the effects of various public policies on the location decisions of firms—the demand side of the labor market. The question is whether a particular policy attracts firms or repels them.

Taxes and Firm Location Choices

In the last few decades, there have been dozens of studies examining the effect of local taxes on firm location choices and urban employment growth. Bartik (1991) draws some general conclusions from these studies. There is evidence that local taxes have a strong negative effect on employment growth: A high-tax city will grow at a slower rate than a low-tax city, *everything else being equal*. Of course, one of the items included in *everything else* is public services. The evidence suggests that if two cities have the same level of public services but different tax liabilities, the high-tax city will grow at a slower rate.

We can distinguish between two types of business location decisions, intercity decisions (choosing a city or metropolitan area) and intracity decisions (choosing a site within a city or metropolitan area). The elasticity of business activity with respect to tax liabilities is defined as the percentage change in business activity divided by the percentage change in tax liabilities.

- **Intercity location decisions.** The elasticity is between −0.10 and −0.60: A 10 percent increase in taxes in a particular metropolitan area decreases business activity in the metropolitan area by 1 percent to 6 percent.
- **Intracity location decisions.** The elasticity is between −1.0 and −3.0: If an individual municipality increases its taxes by 10 percent, business activity in the municipality decreases by 10 percent to 30 percent.

The elasticity for the intracity decision is larger because firms are more mobile within metropolitan areas than between them. The locations within a metropolitan area are better substitutes than locations in different metropolitan areas.

Two other results from recent empirical studies are worth noting. First, manufacturers are more sensitive than other firms to tax differences. This is sensible because manufacturers are oriented toward the national market and thus have a wider
range of location options. Second, metropolitan areas with relatively high taxes on
capital (in the form of taxes on business property) tend to repel capital-intensive
industries and attract labor-intensive industries.

Public Services and Location Decisions

There is evidence that local public services have a strong positive effect on regional
business growth. If two cities differ only in the quality of their local public services,
the city with better public services will grow at a faster rate. Similarly, if a city improves its public services, it will grow faster, everything else (including taxes) being
equal. The public services that have the largest positive effect on business growth
are education and infrastructure.

How would simultaneous increases in taxes and spending on public services affect location choices and business activity? Studies by Helms (1985) and Munnell
(1990) suggest that the effect of a tax increase depends on how the extra tax revenue
is spent. If the extra revenue is spent on local public services (infrastructure, education, or public safety), the tax/expenditure program increases the relative attractiveness of the city and promotes employment growth. In contrast, if the extra tax revenue is spent on redistributional programs for the poor, the tax decreases the relative
attractiveness of the jurisdiction and decreases the growth rate.

Subsidies and Incentive Programs

Many cities try to attract new firms by offering special subsidies. One approach is
to lure firms with special tax abatements, for example an exemption from paying
property taxes for 10 years. Some cities loan money directly to developers, and others guarantee loans from private lenders. Some cities subsidize the provision of land
and public services for new development. The city purchases a site, clears the land,
builds roads and sewers, and then sells the site to a developer at a fraction of the cost
of acquiring and developing the site.

Studies of economic-development programs suggest that they have relatively
small effects. A study of economic-development policies of municipalities in the
Detroit area shows that the programs have a positive effect on business activity in
only 5 of 16 cases (Wassmer, 1994). For the other 11 cases, the programs have either no effect on business activity or a negative effect. Studies of enterprise zones
(areas of a city where firms pay low tax rates, receive subsidies for worker training,
and are exempted from local regulations) suggest that such zones are not very
effective in luring firms (Boarnet and Bogart, 1996).

A study of property-tax abatement (Anderson and Wassmer, 1995) discusses
how cities sometimes get into bidding to lure firms. The classic example is a firm
that secretly decides to locate in a particular city but then asks an inferior city for a
tax-abatement package. With the "bid" of the inferior city in hand, the firm then

asks the preferred city to match the tax package. The preferred city matches the tax package, and the firm locates in that city, which it had intended to do even in the absence of any tax incentives.

Professional Sports, Stadiums, and Jobs

In 1997, billboards around the San Francisco metropolitan area read, "Build the Stadium. Create the Jobs." That was the slogan for a campaign to get citizens to approve $100 million of public money for a new football stadium for the San Francisco 49ers. Although the campaign failed in San Francisco, many cities have subsidized the construction of facilities for professional sports (Noll and Zimbalist, 1997). Between 1989 and 1997, 31 new stadiums were built, at an average cost of about $150 million. Are sports stadiums effective tools of economic development? Do they create jobs?

The logic behind the job-creation effects of sports stadiums is straightforward. A new stadium can be used to attract a professional sports team or to retain an existing team. Like other organizations, a professional team sells a product and hires workers, including athletes, groundskeepers, ticket takers, accountants, and media personnel. In addition, some of the money the team's employees earn is spent in the local economy, generating multiplier effects that increase employment in restaurants, dental offices, and hardware stores. How many additional jobs does a professional team generate?

Despite the hyperbole of stadium proponents, the job-creation effects of stadiums are modest. The stadium for the Arizona Diamondbacks cost $240 million but increased total employment in the area by only 340 jobs. This figure includes both the direct effect (people hired by the team) and the multiplier effect (local jobs). In other words, the cost per job was $705,882. Employment gains were modest for other host cities, with between 128 and 356 additional jobs in Denver, Kansas City, and San Diego. A comprehensive study of cities that host professional teams showed small positive effects in only one-quarter of cases (Baade and Sanderson, 1997). In about a fifth of the cases, the presence of a sports team actually decreased total employment.

Why are the employment effects of sports teams so small? Most of the money consumers spend on professional sports events comes at the expense of local goods such as movies and restaurant meals. When a sports team comes to town, a large fraction of the money spent on the team is diverted from local consumer products. For example, there may be more popcorn sellers in the stadium, but fewer popcorn sellers in movie theaters. Similarly, a sports event provides a different place to drink beer. To the extent that consumers switch from movies and other local goods to sport events, the employment effects of sports teams will be small.

The real power of sports teams to increase employment comes from their ability to attract money from outside the metropolitan area. When someone travels from Providence to Boston to see the Red Sox, the $50 spent on tickets, souvenirs, and food adds money to the Boston economy—and subtracts it from the Providence economy. As a result, total spending and employment in the Boston economy increases. However, because most of the money spent on sporting events comes from local consumers, sports teams don't create many jobs.

Environmental Quality and Employment

Is there a trade-off between environmental quality and total employment? Consider a city with two industries, a polluting steel industry and a clean industry. Suppose the city imposes a pollution tax: Steel producers pay $100 for every ton of pollution they generate. The pollution tax affects both sides of the urban labor market as follows:

1. **Shift of demand curve.** The tax increases the production costs of steel producers, which increases the price of steel. Consumers respond by purchasing less steel, and the decrease in steel output decreases the demand for labor. In Figure 5–5, the labor demand curve shifts to the left.
2. **Decrease in pollution.** The tax decreases air pollution for two reasons. First, steel producers will reduce pollution to decrease their pollution taxes (installing abatement equipment or changing their inputs or production process), so the volume of pollution generated per ton of steel drops. Second, the increase in the price of steel decreases total steel production.
3. **Shift of supply curve.** The improvement of the city's air quality increases the relative attractiveness of the city. People sensitive to air quality will move to the city, shifting the supply curve to the right.

FIGURE 5–5 The Equilibrium Effects of a Pollution Tax

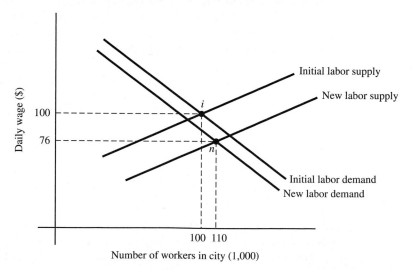

A pollution tax increases production costs, decreasing the demand for labor. It also improves environmental quality, increasing the supply of labor. The equilibrium moves from point *i* to point *n*. In this example, the supply shift is large relative to the demand shift, so the equilibrium employment increases. The tax decreases the equilibrium wage.

Figure 5–5 shows one possible outcome of the pollution tax. Because supply increases and demand decreases, the program decreases the equilibrium wage from $100 (point i) to $76 (point n). The cleaner city has a lower wage, consistent with the first axiom of urban economics:

Prices adjust to generate locational equilibrium

To make workers indifferent among the cities in the regional economy, the wage must be lower in a city with a better environmental quality. In this example, the rightward shift of the supply curve is large relative to the leftward shift of the demand curve, so equilibrium employment increases from 100,000 to 110,000. The supply shift will be relatively large if households are very responsive to changes in environmental quality, meaning that a large number of households will migrate to the city as environmental quality improves.

How does the pollution tax affect the distribution of employment between the polluting industry and the clean industry? As the wage falls, the production costs of both industries decrease. For the steel industry, the decrease in the wage only partly offsets the pollution taxes, so its production cost increases and its workforce decreases. In contrast, the clean industry simply pays lower wages, so its production costs decrease and its workforce increases. In Figure 5–5, the increase in employment in the clean industry more than offsets the decrease in employment in the steel industry, so total employment increases.

Of course, the pollution tax could actually decrease total employment in the city. If households are not very responsive to improvements in environmental quality, the supply curve will shift by a relatively small amount, generating a relatively small wage reduction. In this case, the increase in employment in the clean industry will not be large enough to offset the decrease in employment in the steel industry, so total employment will decrease. In general, the policy will decrease total employment if the shift of the supply curve is small relative to the shift of the demand curve.

PROJECTING CHANGES IN TOTAL EMPLOYMENT

It is sometimes necessary to project future employment in a city. Cities use employment projections to plan public services such as roads and schools, and firms use employment projections to predict the future demand for their products. The projected change in total employment is computed as follows:

$$\text{Change in total employment} = \text{Change in export employment} \cdot \text{Employment Multiplier}$$

As we saw in Table 5–1, multipliers are available for all sorts of industries. Armed with a set of multipliers and a projected change in export employment, policy makers and firms can project a city's future employment. Given the uncertainties associated with predicting future events, the projection of employment is more of an art than a science.

The employment-multiplier approach suffers from a number of problems that limits its applicability. As we saw earlier in the chapter, the approach projects the horizontal shift of the city's labor-demand curve, not the equilibrium change in employment. A second problem is that the appoach focuses attention on jobs rather than per-capita income. A third problem is that the approach seems to suggest that a city's economic fate is in the hands of outsiders—the people who buy the exports. If exports determine a city's fate, why has the earth's economy grown without any exports?

WHO BENEFITS FROM INCREASED EMPLOYMENT?

This part of the chapter explores the benefits from an increase in employment, addressing two questions:

- How many of the new jobs are filled by newcomers and how many are filled by original residents of the city who would otherwise not be employed?
- How does an increase in total employment affect real income per capita?

Who Gets the New Jobs?

Bartik (1991) studied the effects of increases in employment on unemployment rates, labor-force participation rates, and migration rates in 89 metropolitan areas. His results suggest that if a city starts with 100,000 jobs, a 1 percent increase in employment (1,000 additional jobs) has the following effects:

- The unemployment rate (the number of unsuccessful job searchers divided by the workforce) decreases from 5.40 percent to 5.33 percent.
- The labor-force participation rate (the workforce divided by the number of adults) increases from 87.50 percent to 87.64 percent.
- The employment rate (jobs divided by the number of adults) increases from 82.78 percent to 82.97 percent.

Figure 5–6 shows how the new jobs are divided between old and new residents. Newcomers fill 770 of the 1,000 jobs, leaving 230 jobs for the original residents. The 230 jobs filled by original residents are split between people who were unemployed (70 jobs) and people who were not in the labor force (160 jobs). The simple lesson from Figure 5–6 is that increases in employment causes in-migration and population growth, so a small fraction of the new jobs are filled by original residents.

Effects on Real Income per Capita

How does an increase in total employment affect a city's real income per capita? Income could increase in several ways:

1. **Increase in the real wage.** As explained earlier in the chapter, an increase in total employment causes offsetting changes in nominal wages and living costs, so the real wage for a given occupation will be unaffected.
2. **Promotions.** Bartik (1991) shows that an increase in total employment hastens movement upward in the job hierarchy. An increase in the demand for labor causes firms to promote workers to higher-paying jobs more rapidly. The

FIGURE 5–6 Distribution of 1,000 New Jobs between Original Residents and Newcomers

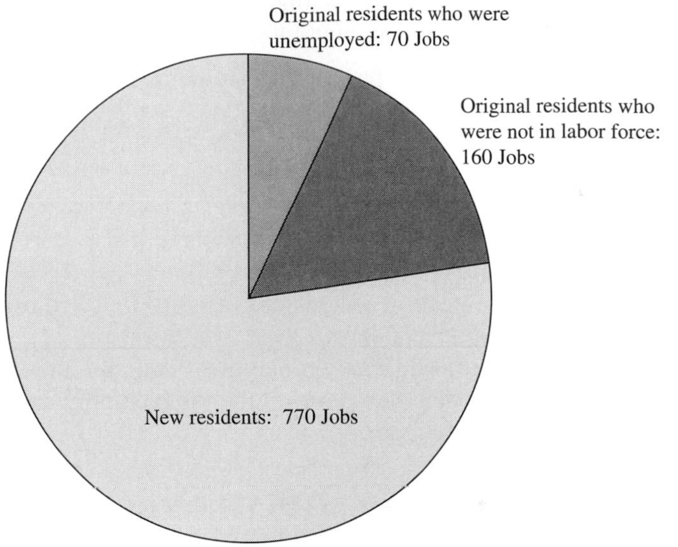

Original residents who were
unemployed: 70 Jobs

Original residents who
were not in labor force:
160 Jobs

New residents: 770 Jobs

Source: Timothy Bartik. *Who Benefits from State and Local Economic Development Policies?*
Kalamazoo, MI: Upjohn Institute, 1991.

largest moves up the hierarchy are experienced by workers who are less educated, young, or black.

3. **Increase in the employment rate.** As explained earlier, an increase in total employment decreases the unemployment rate and increases the participation rate, so it increases the fraction of the working-age population that is employed.

Table 5–2 shows the combined effects of changes in real wages, occupational rank, unemployment rates, and participation rates. For the average household, a 1 percent increase in employment increases real income per capita by 0.40 percent. The most important factors behind higher income are the promotion effect (promotion to higher-paying jobs) and participation effect (higher labor-force participation). The elasticities are larger for households that experience relatively large promotion effects (less educated, young, or black).

TABLE 5–2 Effects of 1 Percent Increase in Total Employment
on Real Income Per Capita

	Average	Less Educated	Younger	Black
Percent increase in real income	0.40	0.47	0.41	0.49

Source: Bartik, Timothy J. *Who Benefits from State and Local Economic Development Policies?* Kalamazoo, MI:
Upjohn Institute, 1991.

SUMMARY

This chapter explores the determinants of increases in urban income and employment. Here are the main points of the chapter:

1. An increase in per-capita income results from capital deepening, increases in human capital, technological progress, and agglomeration economies.
2. An increase in export employment increases local employment through the multiplier process.
3. The urban labor supply curve is positively sloped because a larger city has higher housing prices, requiring firms to pay higher wages to compensate workers for higher living costs.
4. A large fraction of new jobs in a city are filled by newcomers, leaving few jobs for original residents.
5. An increase in total employment in a city increases real income per capita by (*a*) hastening the move up the job hierarchy and (*b*) increasing the labor-force participation rate.

APPLYING THE CONCEPTS

1. **TV Abuse and Economic Decline**
   Consider a two-city region where the initial equilibrium generates a common utility level of $70, with the workforce of 8 million divided equally between the two cities. In each city, the equilibrium workforce exceeds the utility-maximizing level. Over a 10-year period, workers in one city (Tubeton) watch a lot of television, and each worker's human capital decreases. In the other city, each worker's human capital doesn't change.
   a. Use utility curves to show the effects of the decade of TV abuse on city sizes and utility for the two cities.
   b. Who bears the cost of TV abuse?
2. **Predicting Wages and Employment**
   In the city of Growville, equilibrium employment is 100,000 workers, and the equilibrium wage is $100 per day. The elasticity of demand for labor is 1.0 (in absolute value) and the elasticity of supply of labor is 5.0. The employment multiplier is 2.0. Suppose the demand for export labor increases by 6,000 jobs. Predict the new equilibrium values for the wage and total employment. Illustrate your answer with a graph.
3. **Growth Control and Equilibrium Wages**
   Consider a city with an equilibrium wage of $80 per day and equilibrium employment of 100,000 jobs. The city will experience a 20 percent increase in labor demand next year.
   a. Show the effects of the increase in demand on the equilibrium wages in three policy environments.
   i. The government does not intervene.
   ii. The government sets the maximum total employment at the current level of 100,000 jobs.

      iii. The government restricts the supply of housing, setting the maximum total square footage in the city at its current level of 100 million square feet of living space. New housing can be built, but every square foot of new housing requires that one square foot of old housing be retired from the market.

  b. Suppose that the demand for labor decreases next year instead of increasing. Should policies (ii) and (iii) have any effect on the urban labor market? If your graphs predict any effects, you should reconsider your logic and redo your graphs.

4. Inefficient Environmental Policy

Consider a city where each polluting firm initially generates two tons of pollution. Half the polluters (type L) could cut back pollution at a cost of $4 per ton, and the other half (type H) could cut back at a cost of $20 per ton. The city is considering two different environmental policies:

  i. Pollution tax: Each firm would pay a tax of $5 for each unit of pollution.

  ii. Uniform-reduction: Each firm would be required to cut its pollution in half, to one ton.

Each polluting firm increases its output price to cover the cost of the pollution policy.

  a. Depict graphically the effect of each policy on the city's labor demand curve and explain any differences.

  b. Under which policy is the city more likely to shrink?

5. Economic Impact of a Football Team

Consider the results of a consultant's report on the possible economic impacts of moving the Raiders (a professional football team) to Sacramento. The consultant estimated that the team would increase total spending in the Sacramento economy by $61.6 million per year, based on the following assumptions: (1) The average fan will spend $40 on admission, parking, food, and merchandise; (2) total attendance will be 700,000; (3) the spending multiplier is 2.2, the average multiplier across the city's export activities. The spending impact was computed by multiplying the spending per fan ($40), total attendance (700,000), and the multiplier (2.20)

  a. Suppose the numbers for spending per fan and attendance are correct. Is the conclusion of a $61.6 million spending impact sound? If not, list the implicit assumptions of the analysis that are troublesome.

  b. Ms. Wizard recently said, "If my assumptions are correct, the spending impact on the Sacramento economy will actually be negative." Assume that her logic is correct and list her assumptions.

REFERENCES AND ADDITIONAL READING

1. Anderson, John E., and Robert W. Wassmer. "The Decision to 'Bid for Business': Municipal Behavior in Granting Property Tax Abatements." *Regional Science and Urban Economics* 25 (1995), pp. 739–57.
2. Baade, Robert A., and Allen R. Sanderson. "The Employment Effects of Teams and Sports Facilities." *Sports, Jobs and Taxes,* eds. Roger Noll and Andrew Zimbalist. Washington, D.C.: Brookings, 1997.

3. Bartik, Timothy J. *Who Benefits from State and Local Economic Development Policies?* Kalamazoo, MI: Upjohn Institute, 1991.

4. Black, Duncan, and Vernon Henderson. "A Theory of Urban Growth." *Journal of Political Economy* 107 (1999), pp. 252–84.

5. Boarnet, Marlon, and William T. Bogart. "Enterprise Zones and Employment: Evidence from New Jersey." *Journal of Urban Economics* 40 (1996), pp. 198–215.

6. Dowall, David. "An Evaluation of California's Enterprise Zone Programs." *Economic Development Quarterly* 10 (1996), pp. 352–68.

7. Eberts, Randall W., and Joe A. Stone. *Wage and Adjustment in Local Labor Markets*. Kalamazoo, MI: Upjohn Institute, 1992.

8. Glaeser, Edward, Jose Scheinkman, and Andrei Shleifer. "Economics Growth in a Cross-Section of Cities." *Journal of Monetary Economics* 36 (1995), pp. 117–43.

9. Helms, L. Jay. "The Effect of State and Local Taxes on Economic Growth: A Times Series-Cross Section Approach." *Review of Economics and Statistics* 68 (1985), pp. 574–82.

10. Lucas. Robert. "On the Mechanics of Economic Development." *Journal of Monetary Economics* 22 (1988), pp. 3–22.

11. Lucas. Robert. "Externalities and Cities." *Review of Economic Dynamics* 4 (2001), pp. 245–74.

12. Mody, Ashoka, and Fang-Yi Wang. "Explaining Industrial Growth in Coastal China: Economic Reforms . . . and What Else?" *World Bank Economic Review* 11 (1997), pp. 293–325.

13. Moretti, Enrico. "Human Capital Externalities and Cities." Chapter 51 in *Handbook of Regional and Urban Economics 4: Cities and Geography,* eds. V. Henderson and J.F. Thisse. Amsterdam: Elsevier, 2004.

14. Munnell, Alicia H. "How Does Public Infrastructure Affect Regional Economic Performance?" *New England Economic Review,* (1990), pp. 11–33.

15. Noll, Roger G., and Andrew Zimbalist. "Build the Stadium—Create the Jobs!" *Sports, Jobs and Taxes,* eds. Roger Noll and Andrew Zimbalist. Washington D.C.: Brookings, 1997.

16. Papke, Leslie. "Tax Policy and Urban Development: Evidence from the Indiana Enterprise Zone Program." *Journal of Public Economics* 54 (1994), pp. 37–49.

17. Papke, Leslie. "What Do We Know about Enterprise Zones?" In *Tax Policy and the Economy,* ed. James Poterba. Cambridge, MA: MIT Press, 1993.

18. Rauch, J.E. "Productivity Gains from Geographic Concentration of Human Capital: Evidence from the Cities." *Journal of Urban Economics* 34 (1993), pp. 380–400.

19. Robak, Jennifer. "Wages, Rents, and the Quality of Life." *Journal of Political Economy* 90 (1982), pp. 1257–78.

20. Wassmer, Robert W. "Can Local Incentives Alter a Metropolitan City's Economic Development?" *Urban Studies* 31 (1994), pp. 1251–78.

21. Wheeler, Christopher H. "On the Distributional Aspects of Urban Growth." *Journal of Urban Economics* 55 (2004), pp. 1371–97.

22. Zucker, L.G., M.R. Darby, and M.B. Brewer. "Intellectual Human Capital and the Birth of U.S. Biotechnology Enterprises." *American Economic Review* 88 (1998), pp. 290–306.

Appendix: The Regional Context of Urban Growth

In this Appendix, we broaden our geographical perspective, looking at regions as parts of a national economy. The growth of cities is affected by economic forces at the regional level, and in turn affects those forces. We start with a discussion of the neoclassical model of regional development, then use the model to explain the general trend of region concentration followed by dispersion.

THE NEOCLASSICAL MODEL

The neoclassical model of regional development focuses on the location decisions of workers, who are assumed to be perfectly mobile between two regions. In the simplest version of the model, the two regions have equal endowments of natural resources. In Figure 5A–1, the horizontal axis measures the number of workers in

FIGURE 5A–1 Neoclassical Model of Regional Development

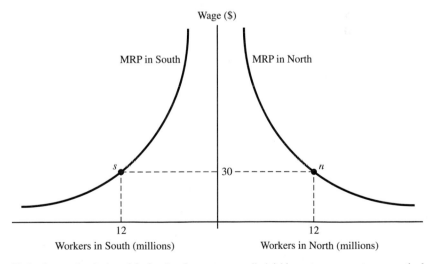

Under the neoclassical model of regional convergence, diminishing returns generates a negatively sloped marginal revenue product (MRP) curve. With perfect mobility, wages are equal in the two regions ($30). In the absence of a natural advantage, the nations's workforce is split equally between the two regions (12 million in each).

the regions. The two curves show the marginal revenue product of labor (MRP), which is equal to the marginal product of labor times the price of the export good. The MRP curves are negatively sloped, reflecting the assumption of diminishing marginal returns: As the workforce of a region expands, the marginal product of labor decreases, pulling down the MRP.

In this simple neoclassical model, the two regions are identical. Workers are perfectly mobile, and locational equilibrium requires that the two regions have the same wage. The two regions have the same MRP curve, so the only way to accommodate all the workers with a common wage is an equal division of workers between the two regions. In Figure 5A–1, the initial equilibrium is shown by points *s* (for South) and *n* (for North). At a wage of $30, the nation's population is split equally between the two regions, with 12 million workers in each.

Differences in Natural Advantage Cause Concentration

Consider the implications of differences in natural advantage between the two regions. For example, suppose the North has deposits of iron ore and coal, so the cost of transporting raw materials is zero for firms in the North. In contrast, the South must import iron ore and coal to produce steel, incurring transport costs in the process.

The natural advantage of the North will result in migration that increases the size of the North economy. As shown in Figure 5A–2, the North's superior access to raw materials make its workers more productive, generating a higher MRP curve. If we start with 12 million workers in each region, the MRP in the North (shown by

FIGURE 5A–2 Natural Advantage and Size of the Regional Economy

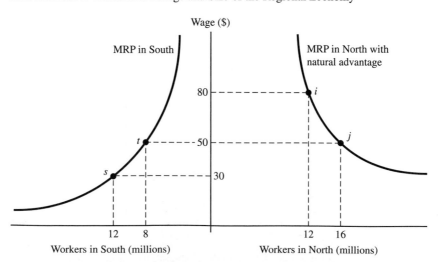

The North has a natural advantage (e.g., access to raw materials), and
has a higher MRP curve. Equilibrium occurs at points *t* (South) and *j*
(North), with the same wage but a larger workforce in North.

point i) is $80, compared to only $30 in the South (point s). Workers are paid a wage equal to their MRP, and the higher wage in the North will cause workers to migrate there. As they migrate, we move downward along the North MRP curve and upward along the South MRP curve.

Locational equilibrium will be restored when the two regions have the same wage. In other words, migration will continue until we reach points t and j, with equal wages ($50) and a larger workforce in the North (16 million), the region with the natural advantage. To summarize, the region with a natural advantage has a larger economy.

A Decrease in Transport Costs Causes Regional Dispersion

How would a decrease in transportation cost affect the distribution of economic activity across regions? In our example, the North has a natural advantage because it bears no transport costs for iron ore and coal, but the South does. A decrease in transport costs will reduce the North's natural advantage and narrow the economic difference between the two regions.

Figure 5A–3 shows the effects of a decrease in transport costs. The productivity of South workers increases, shifting the South MRP curve upward and increasing the wage in the South. Workers will migrate to the South, and migration will continue until the wages are equalized. Equilibrium is restored at points u and k. The equilibrium wage rises to $60, and the workforce in the South increases by 2 million workers at the expense of the North.

FIGURE 5A–3 Decrease in Transport Cost Causes Regional Dispersion

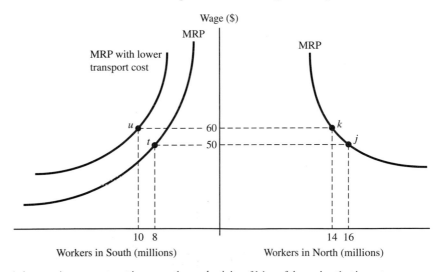

A decrease in transport cost increases the productivity of labor of the region that imports raw materials (South). The upward shift of the South's MRP curve generates a new equilibrium with a higher common wage ($60, up from $50), and the South workforce grows (from 8 million to 10 million), while the workforce of the North shrinks (from 16 million to 14 million). Lower transport costs narrows the gap in the economic activity between the two regions.

A decrease in transport costs reduces the differences in the regional economy because it reduces the natural advantage that caused the differences in the first place. As we've seen in earlier chapters, there is a long history of decreasing transport costs, and the neoclassical model predicts that differences across regions will diminish over time.

REGIONAL CONCENTRATION AND DISPERSION IN THE U.S.

The economic history of the United States shows periods of regional concentration followed by dispersion (Kim, 1998). During the colonial period, the national economy was dominated by agriculture, extraction, and fishing. Regional specialization was based on natural comparative advantages generated by differences in soil, climate, and geography. Most nonagricultural products were produced in the home or by artisans in towns and cities.

In the first half of the 19th century, production shifted from artisan shops to mechanized and nonmechanized factories. Among the products produced in factories were shoes, wagons, furniture, hats, paper, leather, and textiles. Factories were concentrated in the Northeast region, where in 1840, about 36 percent of the labor force produced nonagricultural goods (compared to 21 percent for the nation and 9 percent for the South).

During the second half of the 19th century, a manufacturing belt developed in the Northeast and Great Lakes regions. Innovations in production allowed firms to exploit scale economies, and many of the production processes required large volumes of relatively immobile resources (e.g., coal and iron ore). The manufacturing belt had a natural advantage in its access to these resources, so manufacturing was concentrated there. As late as 1947, the manufacturing belt contained 70 percent of the nation's manufacturing employment. In 1954, the manufacturing industry employed about 28 percent of workers nationwide. In three of nine regions, the manufacturing share was well above the national average; in the remaining six, the share was well below the average.

In the second half of the 20th century, economic activity became more widely dispersed. In 1987, seven of the nation's nine regions had manufacturing employment shares within 2.4 percentage points of the national share of 17.6 percent. By the year 2000, the traditional manufacturing belt contained only about 40 percent of the nation's manufacturing employment, just above its share of total employment. An important factor in the dispersion of manufacturing was a general reduction in transport costs that reduced the natural advantage of the old manufacturing belt. In addition, producers switched to alternative raw materials as well as recycled inputs.

Figure 5A–4 shows the time trend in the concentration of manufacturing from 1860 to 1987. The index of concentration measures the differences in the mix of economic activities between two regions. If two regions have the same mix (the same shares of employment in manufacturing, services, agriculture, and trade), the value of the index is zero. The maximum value is 2, indicating completely different economic mixes. Figure 5A–4 shows the average index for the nine regions of the

FIGURE 5A–4 Regional Concentration of Manufacturing

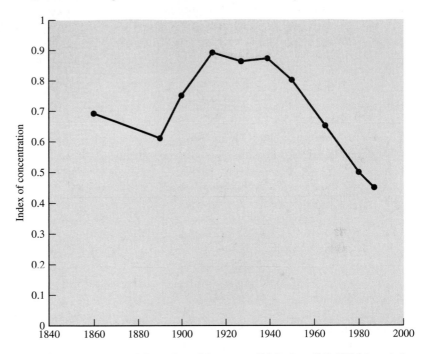

Source: Kim, Sukkoo. "Economic Integration and Convergence: U.S. Regions, 1840–1987." *Journal of Economic History.* (1998), pp. 659–83.

U.S. The index increases between 1860 and the turn of the century, levels off for about 30 years, and then declines steadily.

The experience of the U.S. is consistent with the neoclassical model of regional development. The manufacturing belt developed because of natural advantage (access to material inputs such as coal and iron ore), and declined because the relative cost of transporting inputs decreased. The decrease in transport costs diminished the natural advantage that played a key role in the development of the manufacturing belt, causing manufacturing to disperse to other regions.

REFERENCES AND ADDITIONAL READING

1. Kim, Sukkoo. "Economic Integration and Convergence: U.S. Regions, 1840–1987." *Journal of Economic History* (1998), pp. 659–83.
2. Kim, Sukkoo. "Regions Resources, and Economic Geography: Sources of U.S. Regional Comparative Advantage, 1880–1987." *Regional Science and Urban Economics* 29 (1999), pp. 1–32.
3. Fujita, Masahisa, and Jacques-Francois Thisse. *Economics of Agglomeration.* Cambridge: Cambridge University Press, 2002.

4. Vernon Henderson, and Jacques-Francois Thisse, eds., *Handbook of Regional and Urban Economics 4: Cities and Geography.* Amsterdam: Elsevier, 2004.
   - Chapter 63: Holmes, Thomas and John Stevens. "The Spatial Distribution of Economic Activities in North America."
   - Chapter 64: Combes, Pierre-Philippe and Henry Overman. "The Spatial Distribution of Economic Activities in the European Union."
   - Chapter 65: Fujita, Masahisa, Tomoya Mori, Vernon Henderson, and Yoshitsuga Kanemoto. "The Spatial Distribution of Economic Activities in Japan and China."
   - Chapter 66: Kim, Sukkoo and Robert Margo. "Historical Perspectives on U.S. Economic Geography."

PART TWO

Land Rent and Land-Use Patterns

This part of the book examines the spatial structure of cities, exploring the market forces and government policies that determine land-use patterns within metropolitan areas. In Chapter 6, we divide the urban economy into three sectors—manufacturing, offices, and households—and see how much each sector is willing to pay for land in different parts of the city. Land usually goes to the highest bidder, so once we know how much each sector is willing to pay for land, we can predict what goes where. An appendix to Chapter 6 uses the economic choice model to explain why land-rent curves are convex rather than linear. In Chapter 7, we examine the actual land-use patterns in modern cities and see how things have changed in the last 100 years. In the heyday of the monocentric city, most jobs were close to the center. In modern cities, jobs are divided between central business districts, subcenters, and "everywhere else." We'll explore the economic forces behind the spatial transformation of cities and discuss the causes and consequences of urban sprawl. An Appendix to Chapter 7 describes and applies a model of a monocentric city. Chapter 8 explores the economics of neighborhood choice, focusing on how decisions of where to live are affected by local public goods, schools, and crime. The chapter shows why we observe so much sorting of households with respect to income, educational level, and race. Chapter 9 discusses the role of local governments in the urban land market, exploring the market effects of zoning and growth controls.

CHAPTER 6

Urban Land Rent

The trouble with land is that they're not making it anymore.
—WILL ROGERS

T ake a walk from the outskirts of a metropolitan area to the center, and you'll observe some curious changes along the way. Early in your trip, the price of land will increase slowly and sometimes decrease, but eventually the price will start to increase exponentially. As you approach the center, building heights will increase exponentially too, so buildings near the center will tower over buildings just a few blocks away. In this chapter, we explain why the price of land varies within cities and show the connection between expensive land and tall buildings.

This is the first of three chapters on the spatial structure of cities. In this chapter, we divide the urban economy into three sectors—manufacturing, offices, and households—and see how much each sector is willing to pay for land in different parts of the city. Land usually goes to the highest bidder, so once we know how much each sector is willing to pay for land, we can predict what goes where. In the next chapter, we'll look at the actual land-use patterns in modern cities and see how things have changed in the last 100 years. In the third chapter on spatial structure, we'll explore the effects of government policy on land-use patterns.

INTRODUCTION TO LAND RENT

It will be useful to define two terms, *land rent* and *market value*. Land rent is the periodic payment by a land user to a landowner. For example, a firm may pay $9,000 per month to use an empty lot as a parking lot. In contrast, the market value of land is the amount paid to become the land owner. In this book, the "price" of land is land rent, a periodic payment to a landowner. This is sensible because many other economic variables are expressed as periodic payments, including household income, firm profits, and interest payments.

The rent on a particular plot of land is determined by how much money can be earned by using the land. David Ricardo (1821) is credited with the idea that the

TABLE 6–1 Fertility and Land Rent

	Price of Corn	Quantity Produced	Total Revenue	Nonland Cost	WTP for Land	Bid Rent for Land
Low fertility	$10	2	$20	$15	$ 5	$ 5
High fertility	$10	4	$40	$15	$25	$25

price of agricultural land is determined by its fertility. Consider an agricultural county where farmers grow corn on two types of land, highly fertile and less fertile. The price of corn, determined in national markets, is $10. Farmers rent land from landowners, and there are no restrictions on entry into the corn market.

Table 6–1 shows how to compute the maximum amount a tenant farmers is willing to pay for land. The less fertile land produces two units of corn per hectare, so total revenue per hectare is $20. The cost of nonland inputs (capital, labor, fertilizer) is $15, so the farmer's profit before paying for land is $5. This is the maximum amount a farmer is willing to pay (WTP) for a hectare of low-fertility land. In contrast, highly fertile land produces twice as much output per hectare for the same cost. The more fertile land generates $20 of extra revenue, so the farmer is willing to pay $20 more to use the more fertile land.

How much will farmers offer to pay (bid) for land? Recall the fifth axiom of urban economics:

Competition drives economic profit to zero

There are no restrictions on entry into corn farming, and we assume that all farmers have access to the same production technology and the same inputs. Therefore, competition among prospective farmers will bid up the price of land until economic profit is zero. Farmers are willing to pay up to $25 per hectare for the high-fertility land, and that's how much they bid for it. If a farmer bid less than $25, the landowner could find another farmer willing to pay $25 to use the land. This is the *leftover principle:* Because of competition among farmers for land, the landowner gets the leftovers, equal to total revenue minus total nonland costs. Less fertile land has a lower rent ($5) because there is less money left over after paying the nonland production cost.

BID-RENT CURVES FOR THE MANUFACTURING SECTOR

In an urban environment, the willingness to pay for land depends on its accessibility rather than its fertility. Suppose manufacturing firms in a city assemble bicycles, using land, labor, and imported parts (such as wheels and frames), and then export their output to consumers outside the city. Imported parts and finished bikes are transported by truck on a highway that runs through the city. Let's assume that the price of bikes is determined in the world market and is unaffected by changes in the city.

TABLE 6–2 Computing the Manufacturing Bid Rent

Distance	Total Revenue	Nonland Production Cost	Freight Cost	WTP for Land	Production Site (hectares)	Bid Rent (per hectare)
0	$250	$130	—	$120	2	$60
1	$250	$130	$20	$100	2	$50
2	$250	$130	$40	$ 80	2	$40
3	$250	$130	$60	$ 60	2	$30

We can use the leftover principle to determine how much bike producers will bid for land at different locations in the city. We are interested in the bid rent per hectare of land, which equals the firm's willingness to pay for a lot large enough for its factory (revenue minus cost) divided by the size of the factory lot (in hectares).

$$\text{Rent per hectare} = \frac{\text{Total revenue} - \text{nonland production cost} - \text{freight cost}}{\text{Lot size (quantity of land)}}$$

Suppose each firm produces five units of output and its output price is $50, so its total revenue is $250. The nonland production cost is $130. As shown in the first row of numbers in Table 6–2, a firm at the highway has no freight cost, so its willingness to pay for a factory lot (the numerator of the rent expression) is $120. If a firm occupies two hectares of land, its bid rent per hectare is $60.

The firm's bid rent for land decreases as the distance to the highway increases. Suppose the unit freight cost, defined as the cost of transporting one unit of output one mile, is $4. The firm produces five units of output per day, so its daily freight cost is $20 at a site one mile from the highway, $40 two miles from the highway, and so on. As shown in the last column of Table 6–2, the firm bids $50 per hectare for a site one mile from the highway, $40 for a site two miles away, and so on.

In Figure 6–1 (page 104), the manufacturing bid-rent curve is negatively sloped, reflecting rising freight cost as the firm moves away from the highway. The slope is the change in the bid rent from a one-unit increase in distance:

$$\frac{\Delta R}{\Delta x} = -\frac{\text{Unit freight cost} \cdot \text{output}}{\text{Lot size}} = -\frac{\$4 \cdot 5}{2} = -\$10$$

For a one-mile move away from the highway, freight cost increases by the unit freight cost ($4) times the output transported (5), or $20 in total. Dividing this by the size of the production site (two hectares), we get a slope of −$10. A one-mile move away from the highway increases freight cost by $10 per hectare and decreases the bid rent for land by the same amount. Recall the first axiom of urban economics:

Prices adjust to generate locational equilibrium

In this case, variations in the bid rent for land make firms indifferent among all locations: Differences in freight cost are exactly offset by differences in land rent.

FIGURE 6–1 Freight Cost and Manufacturing Bid-Rent Curve

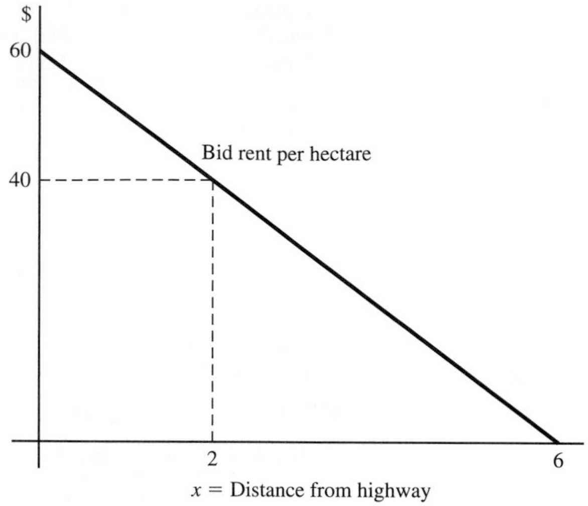

Freight cost increases with distance to the highway, so the bid rent
for land decreases to generate zero economic profit at every location.

BID-RENT CURVES FOR THE INFORMATION SECTOR

Consider next the city's office sector. Although firms that produce their output in offices provide a wide variety of services, they have a common input and output: information. The firms gather, process, and distribute tacit information, defined as information that cannot be codified in an encyclopedia or operating manual. The transmission of tacit information requires face-to-face contact between people exchanging information—typically high-skilled workers who face a high opportunity cost of travel. Some examples of workers who transmit input and output in this way are accountants, financial consultants, marketing strategists, designers, and bankers. Office firms have an incentive to cluster in an area that provides ready access to information provided by other office firms.

Travel for Information Exchange

Suppose there are seven firms in a central business district (CBD), spaced one block apart in a straight line. Each firm travels to each of the other firms to exchange information. In Figure 6–2, firms A through G are located one block apart in the CBD, with D at the center. As shown in Table 6–3, firm D travels west to firms C (one block), B (two blocks), and A (three blocks), so its westward travel distance is six blocks. Similarly, the firm travels to the east to firms E, F, and G, so its eastward travel distance is six blocks. The firm's total travel distance, the sum of westward and eastward travel, is 12 blocks. (All these figures are for one-way travel.)

FIGURE 6–2 Travel Distances for Information Exchange

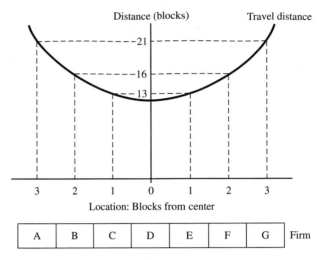

Each office firm interacts with all other office firms in the CBD to exchange information. The total travel distance for information exchange is minimized at the center of the CBD and grows at an increasing rate as the distance to the center increases.

TABLE 6–3 Travel Distance for Firms in a CBD

Firm	Location	Travel Distance: West	Travel Distance: East	Total Travel Distance
D	0	6 = 1 + 2 + 3	6 = 1 + 2 + 3	12
E	1	10 = 1 + 2 + 3 + 4	3 = 1 + 2	13
F	2	15 = 1 + 2 + 3 + 4 + 5	1	16
G	3	21 = 1 + 2 + 3 + 4 + 5 + 6	0	21

The total travel distance for a firm increases as we move away from the center. For firm E, located one block east of the center, the westward distance is longer (10 blocks for travel to A, B, C, and D), and the eastward distance is shorter (3 blocks for travel to F and G), for a total distance of 13 blocks. Travel distance is 16 blocks for firm F and 21 blocks for firm G. As shown in Figure 6–2, travel distance is minimized at the central location.

Why does the central location minimize total travel distance? The center is the median location, the location that splits travel destinations into two equal halves. One of the fundamental concepts in location theory is the principle of median location:

The median location minimizes total travel distance

When a firm moves away from the median location (the CBD center), its total travel distance increases because the firm moves *farther from at least half* of its destinations and moves *closer to fewer than half* of its destinations. To illustrate, suppose firms D and E swap places, meaning that firm D moves one block away from the median location. Firm D is now one block farther from three firms (A, B, C) and one block closer to only two firms (F, G), so its total travel distance increases by one block (from 12 to 13).

As shown in Table 6–3 and Figure 6–2, as we move away from the center location, travel distance increases at an increasing rate. As we move to the east in one-block increments, travel distance increases from 12 to 13 to 16 to 21. This occurs because as a firm moves to the east, it is moving farther from progressively *more* firms to its west and closer to progressively *fewer* firms to its east. For example, if firm E swaps locations with firm F, E gets closer to one firm (G), but farther from four firms (A, B, C, D). At the extreme, when F swaps places with G, firm F gets farther away from five firms and closer to none.

Office Bid-Rent Curve with a Fixed Lot Size

We can apply the leftover principle to the office sector. Suppose each office firm has a four-story building on 1/4 hectare of land. Each firm produces $500 worth of output per day and has two types of production costs: the capital cost of the building ($100) and other costs (for labor, materials, and other inputs) of $150. For zero economic profit, land rent is computed as follows:

$$\frac{\text{Rent}}{\text{per hectare}} = \frac{\text{Total revenue} - \text{capital cost} - \text{other production cost} - \text{travel cost}}{\text{Lot size (quantity of land)}}$$

As before, the numerator is the firm's willingness to pay for a lot large enough for the production facility, and the denominator is the lot size. For a firm with zero travel cost, the bid rent per hectare is $1,000:

$$\text{Rent per hectare} = \frac{\$500 - \$100 - \$150}{0.25} = \$1,000$$

Table 6–4 shows the computed bid rents for different distances from the center. As we move away from the center and travel cost increases, the bid rent for

TABLE 6–4 Office Bid Rent without Factor Substitution

Distance (blocks)	Building Height (floors)	Total Revenue	Capital Cost of Building	Other Nonland Cost	Travel Cost	WTP for Land	Production Site (hectares)	Bid Rent per Hectare
0	4	$500	$100	$150	$ 0	$250	0.25	$1,000
1	4	$500	$100	$150	$ 36	$214	0.25	$ 856
5	4	$500	$100	$150	$200	$ 50	0.25	$ 200

FIGURE 6–3 The Office Bid-Rent Curve without Factor Substitution

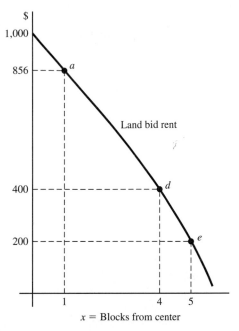

The bid-rent curve of office firms is negatively sloped because as we move away from the center, the cost of travel for information exchange increases. The curve is concave because travel cost increases at an increasing rate.

land decreases. If the travel cost at a distance of one block is $36, the bid rent is $856:

$$\text{Rent per hectare} = \frac{\$500 - \$100 - \$150 - \$36}{0.25} = \$856$$

Similarly, if the travel cost at a distance of five blocks is $200, the bid rent is $200.

In Figure 6–3, the bid-rent curve is negatively sloped and concave. The slope is negative because travel cost increases with the distance to the center. The curve is concave because as we move away from the center, travel cost increases at an increasing rate, so rent decreases at an increasing rate. For example, a move from the center to one block away increases travel cost by $36 and decreases the bid rent per hectare by $144 (point *a*). A move from four blocks to five blocks increases travel cost by $50 and decreases the bid rent per hectare by $200 (point *d* to point *e*). The farther from the center, the larger the increase in travel cost and the larger the reduction in the bid rent for land. Recall the first axiom of urban economics:

Prices adjust to generate locational equilibrium

Differences in the cost of travel for information exchange are fully offset by differences in land rent, so economic profit is zero at all locations.

OFFICE BID-RENT CURVES WITH FACTOR SUBSTITUTION

A key assumption for the bid-rent curve in Figure 6–3 is that each office firm uses a standard office building on the same amount of land. In other words, office buildings at all locations are assumed to be the same height. In fact, office firms near the center occupy tall buildings on small lots.

Building Options: The Office Isoquant

An office firm bases its choice of a building height on the trade-offs between the costs of land and capital. Suppose each office produces the same quantity of output per day and occupies 10,000 square meters of office space (a 100-meter square, which is one hectare). The office space could be in a tall building on a small lot or in a short building on a big lot. The first two rows of Table 6–5 show three options, a 25-story building on 1/25 hectare, a 4-story building on 1/4 hectare, and a 1-story building on one hectare.

    If every office building contains one hectare of office space, do they all have the same amount of capital? A taller building requires more capital because it requires extra reinforcement to support its more concentrated weight, along with extra equipment for vertical transportation (elevators). To see why taller buildings are more expensive, imagine that you borrow a crane and build a 25-story office building by stacking 25 regular mobile homes on top of one another. In addition to the accordion problem (upper floors crushing lower ones), the lack of a vertical transportation system would require workers to rappel from one floor to another. We can avoid these problems by putting more capital in taller buildings. As shown in the third row of numbers in Table 6–5, the tallest building, which is 25 times taller than the shortest building, requires 5 times as much capital ($250 versus $50).

    Figure 6–4 shows the production isoquant for an office building with one hectare of office space. An *isoquant* shows different combinations of inputs (land

TABLE 6–5 Lot Size, Building Heights, and Capital Cost

	Tall	Medium	Short
Land (hectares)	0.04	0.25	1.0
Building height (floors)	25	4	1
Capital cost ($)	250	100	50

FIGURE 6–4 Isoquant for Office Building

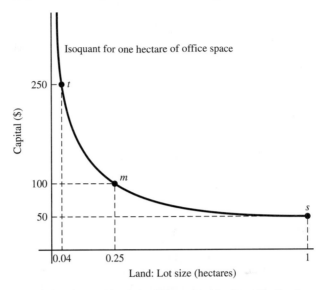

The building isoquant shows the different combinations of land and capital that provide a fixed amount of office space (one hectare = 10,000 square meters). A taller building requires more capital for reinforcement and vertical transportation, so the isoquant is negatively sloped.

and capital in this example) that produce a fixed amount of output (*iso* is Greek for equal). The isoquant in Figure 6–4 is simply a graphical representation of the numbers in the first and third rows of Table 6–5. Point *t* shows the input combination for the tall building, while point *m* represents the medium building and point *s* represents the short building.

Factor Substitution: Choosing a Building Height

The isoquant shows the building options for the office firm, and we can use it to explain why buildings are taller near the city center. The firm's objective is to minimize the cost of the building, equal to the sum of land and capital costs. The question is, Which point on the isoquant minimizes the building cost? The answer is that it depends on the prices of land and capital.

We've seen that office firms are willing to pay more for land near the city center. In contrast, the price of capital will be the same at all locations within the city. Table 6–6 (page 110) continues our example of the three types of buildings and shows how the total building cost varies with land rent.

- **Low Rent ($40).** Total cost is minimized (at $90) with a short building (point *s* on the isoquant). When land is cheap, it doesn't make sense to build up because the savings from using less land are dominated by the higher capital cost of a

TABLE 6–6 Lot Size, Building Heights, and Building Costs

	Tall	Medium	Short
Land (hectares)	0.04	0.25	1.0
Capital ($)	250	100	50
Building cost with rent = $40			
Land cost	1.6	10	40
Total cost	251.6	110	**90**
Building cost with rent = $200			
Land cost	8	50	200
Total cost	258	**150**	250
Building cost with rent = $1,600			
Land cost	64	400	1,600
Total cost	**314**	500	1,650

taller building. For example, a firm could save $30 in land cost with a medium building ($40 − $10), but would pay $50 more in capital cost ($100 − $50).

- **Medium Rent ($200).** Total cost is minimized (at $150) with a medium building (point m on the isoquant). The cost of land is high enough to justify a nine-story building but not a taller one. A taller building would save $42 in land cost but would require $150 more in capital cost.
- **High Rent ($1,600).** Total cost is minimized (at $314) with a tall building (point t on the isoquant). When land is expensive, the savings in land costs from using less land dominate the extra capital costs of a tall building.

As the price of land increases, a firm responds by substituting capital for land, a process known as input substitution or factor substitution.

How much does an office firm save by engaging in factor substitution? Let's use the medium building as a reference point. An office firm on expensive land ($1,600) builds a tall building at a cost of $314 rather than a medium building at a cost of $500, so the savings from building up (factor substitution) is $186. In the opposite direction, a firm on cheap land builds a short building at a cost of $90 rather than a medium building at a cost of $110, so the savings from factor substitution is $20.

Factor Substitution Generates a Convex Bid-Rent Curve

Figure 6–5 shows the implications of factor substitution for the office bid-rent curve. The concave curve is the bid-rent curve without factor substitution (from Figure 6–3). Suppose that at a site five blocks from the center, a four-story building is efficient. As we saw earlier in Table 6–4, the bid rent at this location is $200 (shown by point e in Figure 6–5). If an office firm moved to a site one block from the center and continued to use a four-story building, its bid rent would increase to $856 (point a; computed in the second row of Table 6–4). The increase in bid rent reflects the savings in travel cost at the more central location.

Factor substitution increases the slope of the bid-rent curve. Land is more expensive closer to the center, so it will be rational to occupy a taller building.

FIGURE 6–5 The Office Bid-Rent Curve with Factor Substitution

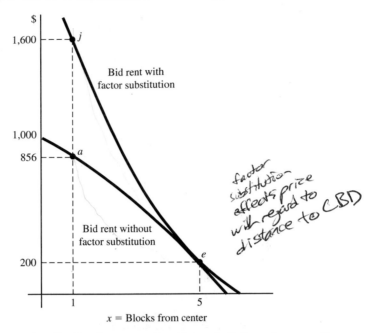

The bid-rent curve for office firms is concave without factor substitution and convex with factor substitution. A move from five blocks from the center to one block increases the bid rent because travel cost decreases (point *e* versus point *a*) and factor substitution saves on building costs (point *a* versus point *j*).

TABLE 6–7 Office Bid Rent with Factor Substitution

Distance (blocks)	Building Height (floors)	Total Revenue	Capital Cost of Building	Other Nonland Cost	Travel Cost	Total Rent Paid	Production Site (hectares)	Bid Rent per Hectare
1	25	$500	$250	$150	$ 36	$64	0.04	$1,600
5	4	$500	$100	$150	$200	$50	0.25	$ 200

Suppose at a site one block from the center, the efficient building height is 25 stories. As shown in the first row of Table 6–7, the bid-rent per acre is $1,600.

$$\text{Rent per hectare} = \frac{\$500 - \$250 - \$150 - \$36}{0.04} = \frac{\$64}{0.04} = \$1,600$$

In other words, factor substitution increases the bid rent for land from $856 to $1,600. So a move closer to the center increases the bid rent for land because (1) travel cost decreases and (2) factor substitution cuts the cost of an office building.

The same logic applies to moves away from the center, with a slight twist. Suppose an office firm starts at a site five blocks from the center and then moves farther from the center. In Figure 6–5, if the firm were to use a four-story building at the more distant location, the bid for land would decrease by an amount equal to the increase in travel cost. But given the lower price of land at a more distant location, a shorter building will be efficient, and the cost savings from factor substitution partly offset the effect of higher travel costs. Because of factor substitution, the bid rent decreases by an amount less than the increase in travel cost.

The general effect of factor substitution is to increase the office firm's bid rent for land. An office firm will engage in factor substitution only if it decreases production costs and thus increases its ability to pay land rent. In Figure 6–5, factor substitution transforms a concave bid-rent curve into a convex curve, meaning that as we approach the city center, the price of land rises at an increasing rate. The rapidly increasing price of land in turn encourages more factor substitution, resulting in tall office buildings close to city centers.

We have explained factor substitution with an isoquant and a numerical example. In the appendix to this chapter, we use the full input choice model (with isoquants and isocosts) to provide a more general analysis of factor substitution and its implications for land rent.

HOUSING PRICES

Consider next the residential sector of the urban economy. Our goal is to derive the residential bid-rent curve, which shows the bid rent of housing producers for land at different locations in the city. Their bids for land depend on how much consumers are willing to pay for housing, so we'll start by showing how the price of housing varies within the city.

Our model of the housing market focuses attention on commuting as the key location factor for households.

1. The cost of commuting is strictly monetary, a cost of $t per mile. We ignore the time cost of commuting.
2. One member of each household commutes to a job in an employment area, either the CBD or a manufacturing district.
3. Noncommuting travel is insignificant.
4. Public services and taxes are the same at all locations.
5. Amenities such as air quality, scenic views, and weather are the same at all locations.

These assumptions make the employment area the focal point for city residents. The other things that people care about (e.g., public services, taxes, amenities) are distributed uniformly throughout the city. Later in the chapter, we will relax these assumptions and explore the implications for the price of housing.

Linear Housing-Price Curve: No Consumer Substitution

Suppose for the moment that households do not obey the law of demand. Regardless of the price of housing, each household occupies a standard dwelling, with

FIGURE 6–6 The Housing-Price Curve Without Consumer Substitution

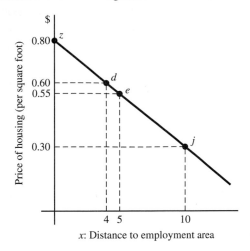

The price of housing decreases as the distance to the employment area increases, offsetting commuting costs and ensuring locational equilibrium for households. In the absence of consumer substitution, the housing-price curve is linear.

1,000 square feet of living space. Suppose the typical household has a fixed amount ($800) to spend on housing and commuting each month. The cost of commuting is $50 per month per mile: A household living one mile from the employment district incurs $50 per month in commuting costs, compared to $100 for a household two miles away, and so on. The price of housing is defined as the price per square foot of housing per month. If a household rents a 1,000 square-foot house (a "standard" house) for $600, the price of housing is $0.60 per square foot ($600/1,000).

Figure 6–6 shows the equilibrium housing-price curve. For a standard dwelling next to the employment area ($x = 0$), commuting cost is zero, so the household can spend its entire $800 budget on housing, paying $0.80 per square foot for a 1,000 square-foot dwelling (point z). In contrast, at a distance of 4 miles from the employment area, commuting cost is $200 (equal to $50 per mile times four miles), so the household has $600 of its $800 budget left over to spend on housing and is willing to pay $0.60 per square foot for a standard dwelling (point d). Similarly, at a distance of 10 miles, the household is willing to pay $0.30, as shown by point j.

To see the logic of the negatively sloped housing-price curve, consider what would happen if it were horizontal, with a constant price of $0.60 at all locations in the city. For a household living 10 miles from the employment area, a move to a location next to the employment area would eliminate $500 of commuting cost without any change in housing costs. Other households have the same incentive to move closer to the employment area. The demand for housing near the employment area will increase, pulling up housing prices. At the same time, the demand will decrease at more remote locations, pushing down housing prices. In other words, a horizontal housing-price curve will be transformed into a negatively sloped curve.

The equilibrium housing-price curve makes residents indifferent among all locations. Recall the first axiom of urban economics:

Prices adjust to generate locational equilibrium

A move toward or away from the employment area changes commuting cost by the change in distance (Δx) times the commuting cost per mile (t) and changes housing cost by the change in price of housing (ΔP) times housing consumption (h). For locational indifference, the two changes must sum to zero: *size of house (amount of land)*

$$\Delta P \cdot h + \Delta x \cdot t = 0$$

We can rewrite this expression to show that the change in housing cost equals the negative of the change in commuting cost:

$$\Delta P \cdot h = -\Delta x \cdot t$$

In Figure 6.6, if a household moves from $x = 10$ to $x = 5$ and the price increases by 0.25, a 250 increase in housing cost is exactly offset by a 250 decrease in commuting cost.

$$\$0.25 \cdot 1,000 = -(-5) \cdot \$50 = \$250$$

We can use the trade-off expression to get an equation for the slope of the housing-price curve. Dividing each side of the expression by Δx and h,

$$\frac{\Delta P}{\Delta x} = -\frac{t}{h}$$

In our example, $t = \$50$ and $h = 1,000$ square feet, so the slope of the housing-price curve is $-\$0.05$:

$$\frac{\Delta P}{\Delta x} = -\frac{t}{h} = -\frac{\$50}{1,000} = -\$0.05$$

In Figure 6–6, points e and d show the direct computation of the slope: a one-mile move toward the employment center increases the price per square foot of housing by $0.05.

Consumer Substitution Generates a Convex Housing-Price Curve

The linear housing-price curve in Figure 6–6 reflects the assumption of perfectly inelastic demand for housing. Everyone lives in a 1,000-square-foot house, regardless of the price of housing. In fact, real households obey the law of demand, responding to a higher price by consuming fewer square feet of housing. What are the implications for the housing-price curve?

We saw earlier that a move closer to the employment area generates offsetting changes in commuting costs and housing costs. For a five-mile move inward, commuting cost falls by $250 (equal to $50 times five miles) and the price of housing increases by $0.25. Therefore, a household could use the $250 savings in commuting costs to exactly cover the higher cost of a 1,000-square-foot dwelling. But if a 1,000-square-foot dwelling is affordable, is that the best use of the consumer's money?

In the appendix to this chapter, we use the consumer choice model to show that the consumer will in fact consume less housing at the higher price. The economic intuition for this result is as follows. When the price of housing increases, the opportunity cost of housing increases: The amount of other goods sacrificed for each square foot of housing increases. For example, if the price per square foot increases from $0.30 at 10 miles to $0.55 at 5 miles, the opportunity cost of 100 square feet of housing increases from $30 worth of meals to $55 worth. Given the higher opportunity cost, the consumer will rent a house with fewer square feet of space and get more restaurant meals.

As shown in Figure 6–7, consumer substitution increases the slope of the housing-price curve. We can modify the expression for the slope to incorporate consumer substitution by simply replacing h with $h(x)$:

$$\frac{\Delta P}{\Delta x} = -\frac{t}{h(x)}$$

FIGURE 6–7 Consumer Substitution and the Price of Housing

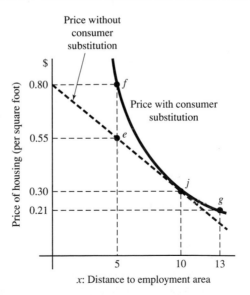

Consumer substitution generates a convex rather than a linear housing-price curve. As distance (x) decreases and the price rises, housing consumption (square feet of space) decreases, increasing the slope of the curve (in absolute value).

As we approach the employment area (as x decreases), the price of housing increases, so housing consumption decreases. Therefore, the denominator of the slope equation decreases, and the slope increases (in absolute value). The housing-price curve is steeper closer to the employment area, meaning that the curve is convex, not linear. For example, if housing consumption at $x = 5$ is 500 square feet, the slope is

$$\frac{\Delta P}{\Delta x} = -\frac{t}{h(x)} = -\frac{50}{500} = -\$0.10$$

THE RESIDENTIAL BID-RENT CURVE

We can use the housing-price curve to derive the residential bid-rent curve, which shows how much housing producers bid for land at different locations. As in the case of manufacturing and office firms, the leftover principle applies: The bid rent generates zero economic profit at each location.

Fixed Factor Proportions

Consider first the situation in which housing is produced with fixed factor proportions. Suppose each housing firm produces Q square feet of housing, using one hectare of land and $\$K$ worth of capital. Once the firm erects a building, it can be used as a single dwelling (with Q square feet of space), or divided into q units, each of which has (Q/q) square feet of living space. For example, a building with 10,000 square feet could be divided into 10 units, each with 1,000 square feet of living space.

In Figure 6–8, we derive the residential land bid rent at different distances from the employment area. The firm's total revenue is the fixed quantity per hectare (Q) times the price of housing $P(x)$, which decreases as the distance to the employment area increases. Because the housing-price curve is negatively sloped and convex, so is the firm's total-revenue curve. The gap between the total-revenue curve and the cost curve shows the firm's willingness to pay for a one-hectare lot for a housing complex. Since each firm occupies one hectare of land, the bid-rent per hectare equals the willingness to pay.

Factor Substitution

The bid-rent curve shown in Figure 6–8 is based on the assumption that housing is produced with fixed factor proportions. Housing firms produce the same amount of housing on each hectare at all locations, regardless of the price of land. How would things change if housing firms engaged in factor substitution?

As we saw earlier in the chapter, an increase in the price of land causes firms to substitute capital for land, economizing on land by building taller buildings. As we approach the employment area and the price of land increases, housing firms will build taller buildings on smaller lots. The cost savings from factor substitution are incorporated into the bid-rent curve, causing the bid rent for land to increase more

FIGURE 6–8 Residential Land Bid-Rent Curve

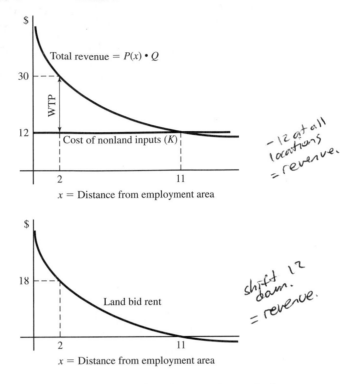

The land bid rent of housing producers equals total revenue minus nonland cost (*C*). The bid-rent curve is negatively sloped and convex, reflecting the negatively sloped and convex housing-price curve. At $x = 11$, total revenue = total nonland cost, so the bid rent is zero.

rapidly as we approach the city center. In other words, factor substitution makes the convex residential bid rent curve even more convex.

Residential Density

How does population density vary within the city? Density increases as we approach employment areas for two reasons:

- **Consumer substitution.** The price of housing increases, and households respond by consuming fewer square feet. In Table 6–8 (page 118), a suburban resident occupies a 2,000-square-foot house, while a central-city resident occupies a 1,000-square-foot apartment.
- **Factor substitution.** Housing firms respond to higher land prices by using less land per unit of housing. In Table 6–8, a suburban resident lives on a lot that is twice the living area of the house, while a central-city resident lives in a 10-story apartment building, with 0.10 square feet of land for each square foot of housing.

TABLE 6–8 Population Density in Suburbs versus Central City

	Housing (square feet)	Land per Square Foot of Housing	Land per Household (square feet)
Suburb	2,000	2	4,000
City center	1,000	0.10	100

Putting these two factors together, the city-center resident uses 100 square feet of land, while the suburbanite uses 4,000 square feet. Therefore, in this example, population density is 40 times higher in the central city.

RELAXING THE ASSUMPTIONS: TIME COSTS, PUBLIC SERVICES, TAXES, AMENITIES

As explained earlier in the chapter, the basic model of residential land use has a number of convenient but unrealistic assumptions.The first assumption is that commuting has no time cost. In fact, commuting time comes at the expense of work or leisure, so there is an opportunity cost. Studies of travel behavior suggest that the typical person values commuting time at between one-third and one-half the wage rate. The higher the opportunity cost of commuting, the steeper the housing-price curve and the residential bid-rent curve.

The model also assumes that there is one worker per household. For the more realistic case of two-earner households, we must keep track of two commuters and their costs. If the two earners have the same workplace, the savings in commuting costs from moving toward the employment area would double, increasing the slope of the housing-price curve. If the two earners work at different locations, things are not so tidy. The housing-price curve could be steeper, flatter, or even positively sloped.

The basic model also assumes that noncommuting travel—for shopping, entertainment, and other activities—is insignificant. If the destinations for noncommuting travel are distributed uniformly throughout the urban area, this assumption is harmless. A change in residence in one direction would decrease travel costs to some destinations but increase travel costs to others, and the net change in total travel costs would be relatively small. In contrast, if noncommuting trips are concentrated, households will be oriented to this destination, along with the employment area. Everything else being equal, a move away from the noncommuting destination would decrease the price of housing.

The fourth assumption is that public services and taxes are the same at all locations. Suppose instead that a city has two school districts with the same taxes, but one district has better schools. Competition among households will bid up the price of housing in the superior district. Instead of paying directly for better schools with higher taxes, people pay indirectly with higher housing prices. The same logic applies to variation in taxes. If two communities have the same level of public services but different taxes, competition among households will bid up the price of housing in the low-tax community.

The model also assumes that environmental quality is the same at all locations in the city. Suppose instead that a polluting factory moves into the center of a previously clean city, and the smoke and smell from the factory are heaviest in the central area. The factory will decrease the relative attractiveness of dwellings near the city center, decreasing the price of housing. For the opposite case of positive amenities, housing prices will be higher for sites that provide scenic views or access to parks.

LAND-USE PATTERNS

We can use the bid-rent curves of different land users to determine a city's equilibrium land-use patterns. In the market equilibrium, land is allocated to the highest bidder. In our simple model of the urban economy, three sectors compete for land: manufacturers, office firms, and residents.

The first step in determining land-use patterns is to specify the features of the urban transportation system. We will assume that manufacturers export their output from the urban area, using trucks that travel on intercity highways. An intercity highway goes through the center of the metropolitan area, and a circumferential highway (a beltway) is connected to the intercity highway. Firms in the office sector exchange information in a central business district. Residents work in offices and firms and travel by automobile from their homes to their workplaces.

Bid-Rent Curves for Business

Figure 6–9 (page 120) shows the bid-rent surfaces of the office and manufacturing sectors. Panel A shows bid rent for the office sector, which peaks at the center of the metropolitan area. Because of the face-to-face contact required in the exchange of information in the office sector, the bid rent curve is relatively steep. As an office firm moves away from the center, the cost of interacting with other office firms increases rapidly, so the bid rent decreases rapidly. As shown in Panel B of Figure 6–9, the bid rent of manufacturers reaches its highest level for sites along the highway (shown by the straight ridge) and the beltway (shown by the circular ridge four miles from the city center). As we move away from the highway or beltway, intracity freight costs increase, decreasing the bid rent for manufacturing land.

Panel C of Figure 6–9 puts the two sets of business bid-rent curves together and shows the maximum bid rents for business land users. At the city center, the office bid rent exceeds the manufacturing bid, indicating that the office sector has more to gain from being in the center. This is sensible because the transportation cost of office firms involves the travel of people rather than the shipping of goods. Because the office bid rent falls rapidly as distance to the center increases, manufacturing firms outbid the office firms for more distant locations. Along the highway, manufacturing takes over once we reach about half a mile from the center (where the highway ridge meets the office bid-rent cone). The beltway is far enough from the city center that office firms don't provide any competition for manufacturing firms.

FIGURE 6–9 Panel A: Bid Rent of the Office Sector

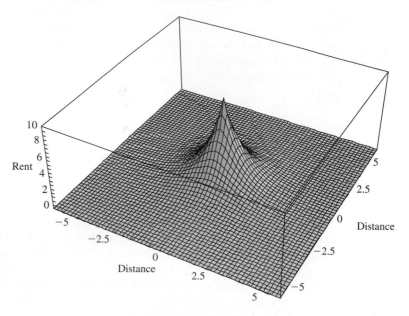

FIGURE 6–9 Panel B: Bid Rent of the Manufacturing Sector

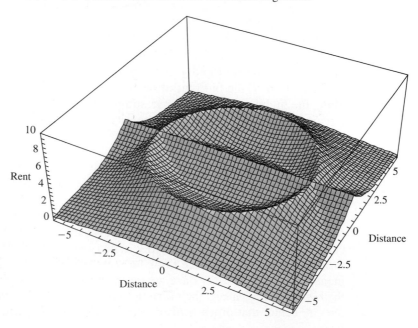

FIGURE 6–9 Panel C: Maximum Bid Rent of Employers

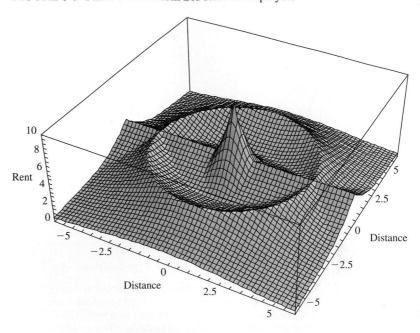

Territories of Different Sectors

In our simplified model of the urban economy, we assume that each household is oriented toward its workplace. There are three employment districts: the circular CBD, the area close to the highway, and a ring surrounding the beltway. If we superimposed all the residential bid-rent curves, one for each employment area, we could show the different residential and business areas.

To provide a clearer picture of the different territories, we use Figure 6–10 (page 122) to take a two-dimensional perspective, with distance from the center on the horizontal axis. This figure omits the highway manufacturing districts, but it includes the beltway districts. The office sector has a negatively sloped bid-rent curve that peaks at the city center. The first residential bid-rent curve is for office workers who travel inward to the CBD. The beltway is located x_4 miles from the center, and the bid rent of the manufacturing sector peaks at the beltway location. There are two bid-rent curves for manufacturing workers, one for those who travel outward and one for those who travel inward.

Figure 6–10 shows competition between workers and firms for urban land. Land is occupied by the highest bidder, and the intersection of the bid-rent curves of office firms and office workers shows the boundary between the business and residential area, x_1. Similarly, the boundary between office workers and manufacturing workers occurs where the bid-rent curves of the two worker types intersect, at x_2. Manufacturing firms outbid their workers for locations between x_3 and x_5, defining the manufacturing district. The outer residential district, defined as the area over which

FIGURE 6–10 Bid Rents and Land Use Patterns

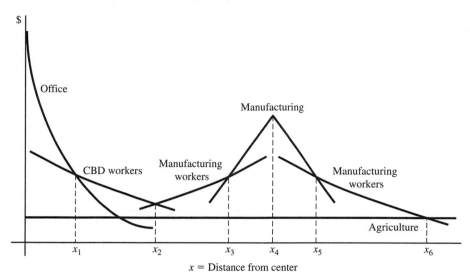

x = Distance from center

The equilibrium land-use pattern is determined by the bid-rent curves of firms and residents. The CBD is the area over which office firms outbid other users (from $x = 0$ to x_1). The area between x_1 and x_2 is occupied by residents who work in the CBD. Manufacturing workers live in the areas between x_2 and x_3 and x_5 and x_6. Manufacturers occupy the area between x_3 and x_5.

manufacturing workers outbid their employers and a nonurban land use (agriculture), is between x_5 and x_6.

SUMMARY

In this chapter, we've shown that the price of urban land is determined by its accessibility. Here are the main points of the chapter:

1. The leftover principle tells us that the bid rent for land equals the excess of total revenue over nonland cost.
2. Manufacturing firms are oriented toward highways that link the city to markets outside the city. Intracity freight cost increases with distance to the highway, so the bid-rent curve is negatively sloped.
3. Office firms exchange information, and the median location has the minimum travel cost and the maximum bid rent.
4. Tall buildings result from factor substitution in response to high land prices. The savings in production costs from factor substitution increase the bid rent for land.
5. Residents are oriented toward employment areas, and commuting costs generate negatively sloped and convex housing-price curves.
6. Land is allocated to the highest bidder, so we can use the bid-rent curves of different land users to predict land-use patterns.

APPLYING THE CONCEPTS

1. Gandhi and the Leftover Principle

In 1917, Mahatma Gandhi settled a dispute between Indian farmers and British landowners. Under a share-cropping arrangement, each indigo farmer gave 15 percent of the harvest to the landowner. When landowners heard about the development of synthetic indigo, they quickly sold the land to the farmers, who at the time didn't know about synthetic indigo and the upcoming collapse of indigo prices. When the price of indigo dropped, the farmers who had purchased land demanded their money back. Gandhi negotiated a partial refund of the payments. Imagine that you are Gandhi's research assistant and must compute the appropriate refund for the typical new landowner.

- The initial price of indigo is $10. The annual output is 100 units per hectare, and the annual nonland cost is $850.
- To purchase land, farmers borrow money at an interest rate of 10 percent per year.
- The alternative crop is rice, which has a price of $8, an annual output of 100 units, and a nonland cost of $700.
  - **a.** Before farmers find out about synthetic indigo, at what price will they be indifferent about buying land? In other words, what is their maximum willingness to pay when the price of indigo is $10?
  - **b.** Suppose that the development of synthetic indigo decreases the price of indigo to $5. What is the appropriate refund, to be paid by the old landowners to the new landowners?

2. Matter Transmitter for Manufacturers

Consider a manufacturing industry that exports its output by ship. Each firm has total revenue per month of $1,400 and a monthly nonland production cost of $400. Each firm initially transports its output from the factory to the port on trucks. A firm's freight cost is $100 per block from the port. Suppose a matter transmitter is introduced. For a monthly cost of $300, a firm can use a transmitter to transport its output, at zero cost, for up to seven blocks.

- **a.** Draw two bid-rent curves for manufacturers, one for firms that use the truck and one for firms that use the transmitter, for up to 10 blocks from the port.
- **b.** Over what interval do firms use the matter transmitter? Do any firms continue to use trucks?

3. Human Transporter for Information Workers

The Segway Human Transporter is a self-balancing personal transportation vehicle that is clean (battery powered) and small (its footprint is 19 by 25 inches) so it can be used on sidewalks and inside buildings. Suppose the vehicle is introduced into a CBD, doubling the speed of travel for information exchange. Depict graphically the effects on the bid-rent curve for the office sector in two circumstances:

- **a.** Fixed building heights: Office firms do not engage in factor substitution.
- **b.** Variable building heights.
- **c.** Who benefits from the innovation?

4. **Dink Commuting**

Consider the Dinks (double income, no kids). Mr. Dink commutes to a job in the city center ($u = 0$), while Ms. Dink commutes to a suburban subcenter four miles east of the city center. The Dinks consume the same quantity of housing at all locations. Travel speed is the same in both directions.

   a. Draw the household's housing-price curve up to a distance of seven miles.
   b. Draw the housing-price curve under the assumption that the speed of inward commuting (toward the city center in the morning and away from the center in the evening) is half the travel time of outward commuting.
   c. Draw the housing-price curve under the assumption that travel speed is the same in both directions, but Ms. Dink has a higher opportunity cost of travel time.

5. **Crime and Housing Prices**

Consider a city where everyone commutes to the city center, and commuting cost per mile per month is $40. Each household occupies a 1,000-square-foot dwelling and has $7,000 worth of possessions in its dwelling. The probability that any particular household will be burglarized (involving the uninsured loss of all possessions) is 0.10 at the city center and decreases by 0.01 per mile (to 0.09 at one mile, 0.08 at two miles, and so on). The housing price is $1.00 per square foot at the city center.

   a. Draw the housing-price curve for locations up to five miles from the city center.
   b. Compute the slope of the housing-price curve.

REFERENCES AND ADDITIONAL READING

1. Fujita, Mashisa, and Jacques-Francois Thisse. *Economics of Agglomeration.* Cambridge: Cambridge University Press, 2002.
2. O'Hara, D.J. "Location of Firms within a Square Central Business District." *Journal of Political Economy* 85 (1977), pp. 1189–1207.

Appendix: Consumer and Factor Substitution

In this appendix, we provide more rigorous analysis of two results in Chapter 6. First, consumers obey the law of demand, consuming less housing as the price of housing increases. This result explains the convex shape of the housing-price curve. Second, firms engage in factor substitution, substituting capital for land as the relative price of land increases. This result explains why the bid-rent curve of the office sector is convex rather than concave. For a review of the consumer choice model and the input choice model, see the appendix at the end of the book, "The Tools of Microeconomics."

CONSUMER CHOICE AND THE LAW OF DEMAND

The consumer choice model is a model of constrained maximization. It shows how consumers make choices to maximize their utility, subject to the constraints imposed by their income and the prices of consumer goods.

A consumer's budget set shows all the affordable combinations of two goods. In Panel A of Figure 6A–1, the shaded area is the budget set for a household located 10 miles from the employment area. The two goods are housing (measured in square feet) and all other goods (measured in dollars). Suppose the household has an income of $2,000 and its commuting cost is $500 per month ($50 per month per mile times 10 miles). The price of housing at 10 miles is $0.30 per square foot. The budget line *AB* shows the combinations of housing and other goods that exhaust the household's budget. Consider two points on the budget line.

- **Point *A*.** If housing consumption is zero, the household can spend $1,500 on other goods: $1,500 = $2,000 income − $500 spent on commuting.
- **Point *i*.** If housing consumption is 1,000 square feet, the household spends $300 on housing and $500 on commuting, leaving $1,200 for other goods.

FIGURE 6A–1 Economic Choice Model

A: Location *x* = 10 miles

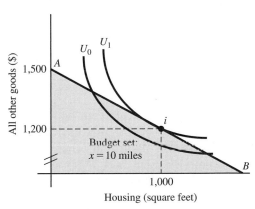

B: Location *x* = 5 miles

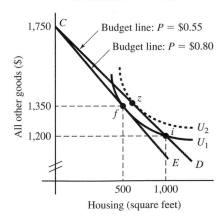

At location *x* = 10 miles, utility is maximized where the budget line is tangent to an indifference curve (point *i*), where MRS equals the price ratio of $0.30.

At location *x* = 5, commuting cost is $250 lower and the price of housing is higher. Although point *i* is affordable, it does not maximize utility. Location equilibrium is restored at point *f*, with a price of $0.80 and the same utility as at *x* = 10.

The slope of the budget line shows the market trade-off between housing and other goods. The slope is the quantity of other goods that must be sacrificed for each additional square foot of housing. If the price of housing is $0.30, each square foot of housing reduces the amount of other goods by $0.30. In other words, the slope is simply the price of housing.

Consumer preferences are represented by indifference curves. Each indifference curve shows the different combinations of two products that generate the same level of utility. The marginal rate of substitution (MRS) is the amount of other goods the consumer is willing to sacrifice to get one more square foot of housing, and it is shown by the slope of the indifference curve. For example, if the slope is $0.50, the household is willing to sacrifice $0.50 units of other goods for one square foot of housing: MRS = 0.50.

Maximizing Utility: MRS = Price Ratio

To maximize utility, a consumer finds the highest indifference curve within its budget. In Panel A of Figure 6A–1, the indifference curve U_1 is the highest indifference curve within the consumer budget set, so utility is maximized at point i, with 1,000 square feet of housing and $1,200 of other goods. At this point, the indifference curve is tangent to the budget line, meaning that the slope of the budget line (the price ratio = 0.30) equals the slope of the indifference curve (the marginal rate of substitution). In fact, this is the rule for utility maximization:

Marginal rate of substitution = Price ratio

If the price ratio (the market trade-off) equals the marginal rate of substitution (the consumer's own trade-off), the consumer can't do any better.

Consumer Substitution

Panel B of Figure 6A–1 shows budget lines for a location five miles from the employment area. When a household moves inward from 10 miles to 5 miles, its commuting cost decreases by $250. If the price of housing at 5 miles is $0.55 per square foot, CD is the budget line.

- **Point C.** If housing consumption is zero, the household can spend all the money it saves on commuting costs ($250) on other goods. The maximum for other goods increases from $1,500 (point A in Panel A) to $1,750.
- **Point i.** If housing consumption remains at 1,000 square feet and the price of housing is $0.55, the change in commuting cost ($250) is exactly offset by higher housing cost ($250), so the original combination shown by point i is still affordable.

Although point i is still affordable, the household will not choose it. Given the higher price of housing ($0.55, up from $0.30), the indifference curve U_1 is not tangent to the budget line at point i, so utility is no longer maximized at point i. Point i violates the utility-maximizing rule MRS = price ratio: The price ratio is 0.55 and the MRS (the consumer's own trade-of) is, of course, still 0.30. As a result, the household can do better.

Will housing consumption increase or decrease? At a price of $0.55, the household now sacrifices $0.55 of other goods for every square foot of housing, but it is willing to sacrifice only $0.30 of other goods (given the MRS). The household has too much housing and will reduce its consumption. For each square foot reduced, the household gets $0.55 of other goods—more than the amount the household needs to be indifferent about the change (MRS = 0.30 at point i). If the price of housing were to remain at $0.55, the household would move up the budget line CD to a higher indifference curve (U_2) and a higher utility level, consuming less housing and more of other goods (shown by point z).

Locational Equilibrium

Unfortunately for the household, the price of housing at location $x = 5$ will not be $0.55 but will be higher. Imagine for the moment that a household at $x = 5$ reaches utility level $U_2 > U_1$. Everyone will want to live at $x = 5$, and the resulting increase in demand for housing there will bid up its price until households are indifferent between the two locations ($x = 5$ and $x = 10$). For locational equilibrium, the utility level at $x = 5$ must be the same as the utility level at $x = 10$ (equal to U_1). To equalize utility, the price of housing at $x = 5$ rises above $0.55, causing the budget line to tilt inward, with a steeper slope. The price will continue to increase until we get a tangency between the new budget line and the indifference curve associated with the original utility level U_1. In Panel B of Figure 6A–1, this happens at point f: When the price of housing is $0.80, utility is maximized at level U_1.

This analysis shows how households living in different locations can achieve the same level of utility. Compared to the household living 10 miles from the employment area, the household living at 5 miles consumes less housing (500 square feet compared to 1,000) but consumes more of other goods ($1,350, compared to $1,200). Both households reach the same utility level because points i (chosen by the 10-mile household) and f (chosen by the 5-mile household) lie on the same indifference curve. Housing consumption is lower with the higher housing price, consistent with the law of demand.

INPUT CHOICE AND FACTOR SUBSTITUTION

Consider next the input choices of office firms. As we saw in the chapter, the isoquant shows the different combinations of land and capital that generate a fixed amount of office space (one hectare). The objective of the office firm is to find the input combination on its isoquant that has the lowest building cost, equal to the sum of capital and land costs.

Figure 6A–2 (page 128) shows how a firm picks the least costly input combination. The linear curve is an isocost line, the analog of the consumer's budget line. An isocost shows the combinations of two inputs that exhaust a fixed input budget.

FIGURE 6A–2 Factor Substitution and the Price of Land

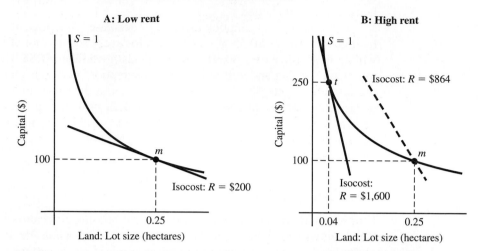

A: When land rent = $200, cost is minimized at point *m*, where the isocost line is tangent to the isoquant.

B: With offsetting changes in land rent and travel cost, the firm could still choose point *m*, but because the land rent is higher, factor substitution will decrease cost. The resulting increase in the bid rent for land increases the slope of the isocost, and cost is minimized at point *t*.

The slope of the isocost line is the market trade-off between the two inputs, the price of land (on the horizontal axis) divided by the price of capital (on the vertical axis). The price of capital is assumed to be $1, so the slope is simply the price of land. A higher (more northeasterly) isocost represents a bigger budget (more spent on both inputs). To minimize cost, the firm gets on the lowest (most southwesterly) isocost that touches the isoquant.

Panel A of Figure 6A–2, shows the firm's choice when the price of land is $200 per hectare. Cost is minimized at point *m*, with 0.25 hectares of land and 100 units of capital. Point *m* minimizes cost because it is on the lowest feasible isocost. The two curves are tangent at the cost-minimizing point, consistent with the cost-minimizing rule for input choices:

Marginal rate of technical substitution = Input price ratio

The marginal rate of technical substitution (MRTS) is the analog of the marginal rate of substitution. The MRTS of capital for land is the change in capital per unit change in land, keeping the quantity produced constant. When the MRTS equals the input price ratio, the production trade-off between two inputs equals the market trade-off, so the firm can't produce its target output at any lower cost. At point *m*, the MRTS = 200, equal to the input price ratio (land price = $200 and capital price = $1).

Suppose the firm moves toward the city center from a location five blocks from the center to a location one block from the center. If the firm does not engage in factor substitution, the decrease in travel cost will be exactly offset by higher rent, so point m will still be possible with the original budget: The firm takes its savings in travel cost and puts it into land. Using the leftover principle, the rent is $856:

$$\text{Rent per hectare} = \frac{\$500 - \$100 - \$150 - \$36}{0.25} = \frac{\$214}{0.25} = \$856$$

Although point m is affordable, the firm will not choose it. The higher price of land generates a steeper isocost: In Panel B of Figure 6A–2, the dashed isocost is steeper than the original isocost. As a result, point m is not the cost-minimizing point. The MRTS (still 200 at point m) is less than the price ratio (now 856), so the firm will substitute capital for the more expensive land, moving upward along the isoquant to a lower isocost line (lower cost).

Factor substitution cuts the firm's cost and increases its bid rent for land. The leftover principle tells us that the cost savings from factor substitution bid up the price of land, tilting the isocost line and increasing its slope. In Panel B of Figure 6A–2, cost is minimized at point t, with a 25-story building and 250 units of capital. The MRTS equals the price ratio of 1,600. As in the case of consumer substitution, factor substitution is caused by an increase in land rent, and in turn increases the bid rent for land.

CHAPTER 7

Land-Use Patterns

Otis's apparatus (the elevator) recovers the uncounted planes
that have been floating in the thin air of speculation.
—REM KOOLHAAS

*I*n modern metropolitan areas, jobs are divided between central business districts, suburban subcenters, and "everywhere else." It turns out that most jobs are elsewhere—widely dispersed throughout the metropolitan area—and most people work and live far from the center. In this chapter, we describe the spatial distributions of employment and population within cities, then look back about 100 years to a different urban reality. In the heyday of the monocentric city, between two-thirds and three-fourths of jobs were near the center. We'll explore the market forces behind the transformation of cities and discuss the causes and consequences of urban sprawl.

THE SPATIAL DISTRIBUTION OF JOBS AND PEOPLE

We will use two notions of urban geography to describe the distribution of jobs and people in metropolitan areas. The first is the distinction between a central city and the surrounding area. Recall that the *central city* is defined as the territory of the municipality at the center of the metropolitan area. The *suburban area*—the rest of the metropolitan area—is defined as the land area covered by the other municipalities. The second geographical distinction is between a central area within three miles of the center and the rest of the metropolitan area.

The Spatial Distribution of Employment

We'll start by looking at the spatial distribution of employment in U.S. metropolitan areas. Figure 7–1 shows the number of metropolitan jobs inside and outside central cities. In 1980, central cities had about 11 percent more jobs. The suburbs grew faster than the central cities, and by 1994, there were more jobs in the

FIGURE 7–1 Employment Inside and Outside Central Cities, 1980–2000

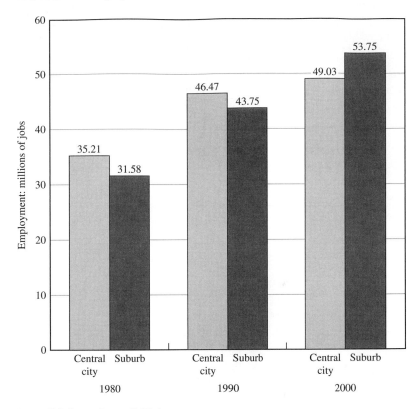

Source: U.S. Census, Journey To Work.

TABLE 7–1 Employment and Population within 3 Miles and 10 Miles

	Employment	Population
3-mile share	22%	20%
10-mile share	65%	65%
Median location (miles)	7	8

Source: Computations based on Edward Glaeser, Matthew Kahn, and Chenghuan Chu, "Job Sprawl: Employment Location in U.S. Metropolitan Areas." *Brookings Institution Survey Series,* May 2001, pp. 1–8.

suburbs. This is actually a continuation of a long trend of employment decentralization. Back in 1948, central cities had roughly twice as many jobs as suburban areas.

Table 7–1 shows the shares of metropolitan employment within 3 miles and 10 miles of the center. Just over one-fifth of jobs in the 100 largest metropolitan areas are within 3 miles, and about two-thirds are within 10 miles. The median location (where half of jobs are closer and half farther away) is 7 miles. For the four regions of the country (Northeast, Midwest, South, West), the 10-mile employment shares are remarkably close. All four are in the range of 64 percent to 67 percent. The 3-mile employment shares are similar for all but the Northeast region, whose share of 29 percent lies well outside the 19 percent to 21 percent range of the other regions.

Figure 7–2 provides another perspective on the spatial distribution of employment. The vertical axis measures the number of jobs in a central area within three miles of the

FIGURE 7–2 Central Employment in Metro Areas

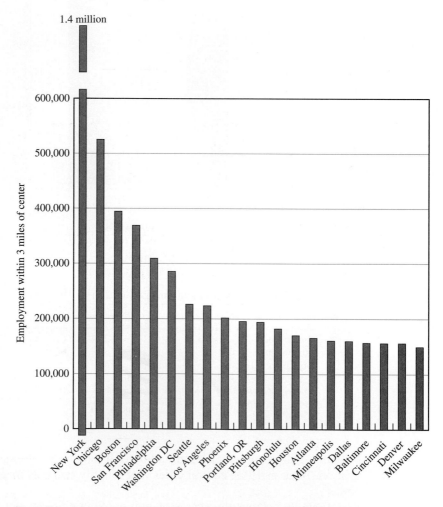

Source: Computations based on Glaeser, Edward, Matthew Kahn, Chenghuan Chu. "Job Sprawl: Employment Location in U.S. Metropolitan Areas." *Brookings Institution Survey Series,* May 2001.

center. The figure shows the three-mile job count for the 20 metropolitan areas with the most centralized employment. New York, with about 1.4 million jobs in the central area, is off the chart. For the remaining metropolitan areas, the number of central jobs ranges from over 500,000 for Chicago to about 160,000 for Milwaukee.

We can distinguish between three employment locations in a metropolitan area: the central business district (CBD), suburban subcenters, and everywhere else (dispersed). A subcenter is typically defined as an area with at least 10,000 workers and at least 10 workers per acre or 25 workers per hectare (a hectare is a 100-meter square). Figure 7–3 shows the job shares for four medium-size metropolitan areas. For three of the metropolitan areas, the CBD shares are between

FIGURE 7–3 Employment in Centers, Subcenters, and Elsewhere

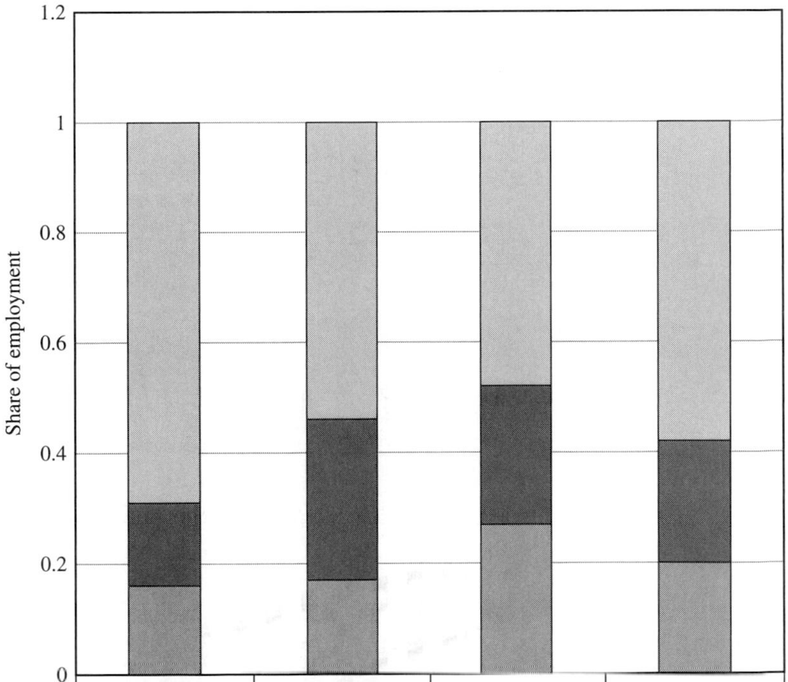

	Cleveland	Indianapolis	Portland, OR	St. Louis
□ Dispersed	0.69	0.54	0.48	0.58
■ Subcenters	0.15	0.29	0.25	0.22
▨ Central	0.16	0.17	0.27	0.2

Computations based on: Anderson, Nathan, and William Bogart. "The Structure of Sprawl: Indentifying and Characterizing Employment Centers in Polycentric Metropolitan Areas." *American Journal of Economics and Sociology* 60 (2001), pp. 147–69.

16 percent and 20 percent. Cleveland has the largest dispersed share (69 percent) and Portland has the smallest (48 percent).

The Distribution of Office Space

Consider next the distribution of office space. An office subcenter is defined as an area with at least 5 million square feet of office space in a relatively compact area. A recent study of 13 large U.S. metropolitan areas revealed a total of 81 office subcenters (Lang, 2003). For the 13 cities as a whole, 38 percent of office space is located in the CBD; 26 percent is in subcenters; and 36 percent is in dispersed locations. As shown in Figure 7–4, in New York and Chicago, over half the office space is in CBDs, but no other area has a CBD share of more than 38 percent. In the other 11 metropolitan areas, the dispersed share exceeds the CBD share.

FIGURE 7–4 Office Space in Centers, Subcenters, and Elsewhere

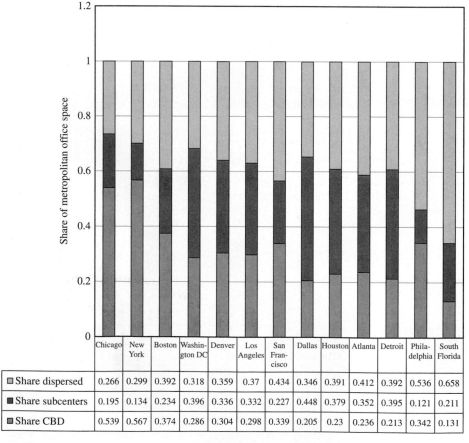

	Chicago	New York	Boston	Washington DC	Denver	Los Angeles	San Francisco	Dallas	Houston	Atlanta	Detroit	Philadelphia	South Florida
☐ Share dispersed	0.266	0.299	0.392	0.318	0.359	0.37	0.434	0.346	0.391	0.412	0.392	0.536	0.658
■ Share subcenters	0.195	0.134	0.234	0.396	0.336	0.332	0.227	0.448	0.379	0.352	0.395	0.121	0.211
■ Share CBD	0.539	0.567	0.374	0.286	0.304	0.298	0.339	0.205	0.23	0.236	0.213	0.342	0.131

Computations based on: Lang, Robert E. "Office Sprawl: The Evolving Geography of Business." *The Brookings Institution Survey Series*, October 2000.

FIGURE 7–5 Metropolitan Commuting Patterns, 2000

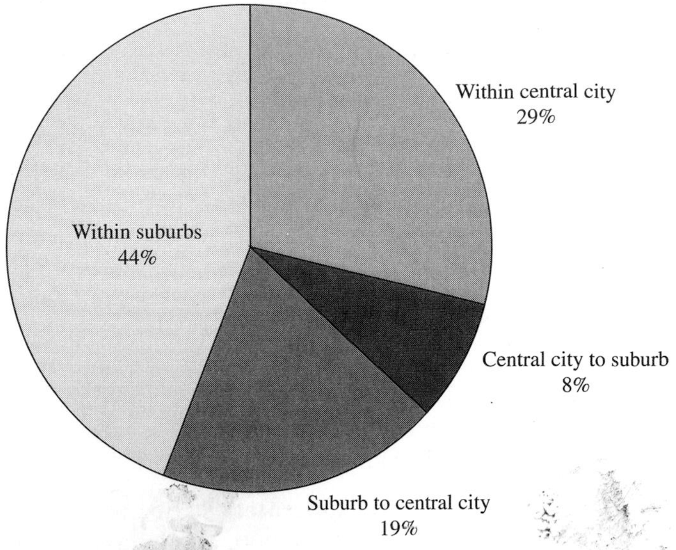

Within central city
29%

Within suburbs
44%

Central city to suburb
8%

Suburb to central city
19%

Source: U.S. Census, Journey To Work.

The Spatial Distribution of Population

Consider next the spatial distribution of population within metropolitan areas. For U.S. metropolitan areas as a whole, the central-city share is 36 percent and the suburban share is 64 percent. Looking back at the third column of Table 7–1, the share of the population living within three miles of the city center is 20 percent, while the 10-mile share is 65 percent. The median residential location is eight miles from the city center, meaning that the urban population is a bit more decentralized than urban employment.

Commuting Patterns

We've seen that the majority of jobs are outside central cities, and so is the majority of the population. It should be no surprise that the most frequent commuting trip is within suburban areas. As shown in Figure 7–5, about 44 percent of commuter trips are within suburban areas, while 29 percent are within central cities, and 19 percent are from a suburban residence to a central-city job. The least frequent trip is from a central city residence to a suburban job.

A CLOSER LOOK AT SUBCENTERS

As we saw in Chapter 3, agglomeration economies encourage firms to locate close to one another, and one manifestation of clustering is a subcenter. For example, manufacturing firms in a cluster can purchase maintenance and repair services from a common supplier, and office firms in a cluster can purchase glossy brochures from the same printing firm. Firms in office clusters also share restaurants and hotels. One rule of thumb is that a cluster of 2.5 million square feet of office space can support a 250-room hotel.

Subcenters in Los Angeles and Chicago

Giuliano and Small (1991) explore the spatial distribution of employment in the Los Angeles metropolitan area. The CBD had total employment of 496,000 (11 percent of total employment), with a density of 90 workers per hectare. They define a subcenter as an area where employment density is at least 25 workers per hectare and total employment is at least 10,000 workers. In 1990, there were 28 subcenters, with an average employment density of 45 workers per hectare. Together the subcenters contained 23 percent of the metropolitan employment, leaving about two-thirds of employment as dispersed—outside the center and the subcenters.

Giuliano and Small divide the 28 subcenters in Los Angeles into five types, according to the products produced:

- **Mixed-industrial subcenters** started out as low-density manufacturing areas near a transport node (airport, port, or marina) and grew as they attracted other activities.
- **Mixed-service subcenters,** like traditional downtowns, provide a wide range of services, and many functioned as independent centers before they were absorbed into the metropolitan economy.
- **Specialized-manufacturing subcenters** include old manufacturing areas as well as newer areas near airports that produce aerospace equipment.
- **Service-oriented subcenters** employ workers in service activities such as medical care, entertainment, and education.
- **Specialized entertainment subcenters** employ workers in television and film.

McMillen and McDonald (1998) explore the spatial distribution of employment in the Chicago metropolitan area. They define a subcenter as a set of adjacent land tracts with at least 25 workers per hectare and a total of at least 10,000 workers. They identified 20 subcenters, including 9 old industrial areas, 3 old satellite cities, 2 subcenters that mix new industry and retailing, and 3 that mix services and retailing.

Edge Cities

Garreau (1991) introduced the notion of edge cities, defined as relatively new concentrations of office and retail space. An edge city is a place with

- At least 5 million square feet of office space.
- At least 600,000 square feet of retail space.
- More jobs than bedrooms.

The bulk of the office and retail space in an edge city is less than 30 years old. Garreau identified dozens of edge cities in U.S. metropolitan areas. In many cases,

TABLE 7–2 The Number and Office-Space Shares of Edge Cities

	Number of Edge Cities	Percent of Metropolitan Office Space in Edge Cities
Atlanta	2	25
Boston	4	19
Chicago	6	20
Dallas	6	40
Denver	4	29
Detroit	2	40
Houston	6	38
Los Angeles	6	25
Miami	2	17
New York	6	6
Philadelphia	2	9
San Francisco	4	14
Washington D.C.	8	27

Source: Computations based on Robert E. Lang. *Edgeless Cities.* Washington DC: Brookings, 2003.

a single development company or individual controlled the initial development and building of the edge city.

More recent work focuses on total office space as the defining characteristic of an edge city, using the threshold of 5 million square feet (Lang, 2003). Edge cities are distinguished from other subcenters by their more recent development. Table 7–2 shows the number of edge cities and their shares of metropolitan office space.

Subcenters and City Centers

Based on recent studies, we can draw several conclusions about the nature and role of subcenters in the metropolitan economy (Anas, Arnott, and Small, 1998; Sivitanidou, 1996, McMillen, 1996; Schwartz, 1992).

1. Subcenters are numerous in both new and old large metropolitan areas.
2. In most metropolitan areas, most jobs are dispersed rather than concentrated in CBDs and subcenters.
3. Many subcenters are highly specialized, indicating the presence of large localization economies.
4. Subcenters have not eliminated the importance of the main center. In 7 of the 13 cities studied by Lang, the ratio of CBD office space to the space in the largest subcenter is at least 4. At the top of the list are New York (32) and Chicago (12). Detroit is the only metropolitan area with a ratio less than 1.
5. In the typical metropolitan area, employment density (jobs per hectare) decreases as distance from the center increases, despite the fact that the center contains a relatively small fraction of total employment.
6. Firms in subcenters interact with the center, and the value of access to firms in the center is reflected in higher land prices near the center.
7. Firms in different subcenters interact, indicating that subcenters have different functions and are complementary.

What is the economic relationship between a central business district and the surrounding subcenters and dispersed firms? The central business district provides better opportunities for the face time required for the production of services such as advertising, accounting, legal counsel, and investment banking. Although advances in telecommunications have reduced the need for some types of interaction, face time is still required to exchange complex and tacit information as well as to establish trust.

URBAN DENSITY

A city is defined as a place with relatively high population density. The conventional measure of urban density is the total population of a metropolitan area divided by the amount of land in urban use, including residential areas, industrial districts, commercial areas, roads, schools, and city parks. This is called built-up density, as opposed to residential density. As we'll see in this part of the chapter, urban density varies dramatically across cities and continents.

Densities of World Cities

Figure 7–6 shows the urban density in selected cities around the world. Asian cities are at the top of the list, and U.S. cities are at the bottom. New York is the densest U.S. metropolitan area, yet its density is about half the density of Paris, one-fourth the density of Barcelona, and one-tenth the density of Mumbai (formerly known as Bombay). Los Angeles, the second densest U.S. metropolitan area, is roughly half as dense as New York. All the European cities shown rank above Los Angeles in density, and most rank above New York.

Density Gradients

As we saw in the previous chapter, the price of land generally decreases as we move away from the city center, reflecting the superior accessibility of central locations. As a result, people economize on land close to the center, leading to higher population density. Figure 7–7 (page 140) shows densities at different distances from the city center for several cities. In Paris, the density decreases from 300 people per hectare close to the center to fewer than 50 people at a distance of 20 kilometers. New York has a lower density close to the center but is more dense than Paris between 10 and 20 kilometers. In the two other U.S. cities shown, densities start at a relatively low level at the center and decline at a moderate rate.

The density gradient is defined as the rate at which population density decreases with distance. For example, the density gradient is 0.13 in Boston, indicating that population density decreases by 13 percent for each additional mile from the city center. For most large metropolitan areas in the United States, the density gradient is currently in the range 0.05 to 0.15.

FIGURE 7–6 Population Density in World Cities

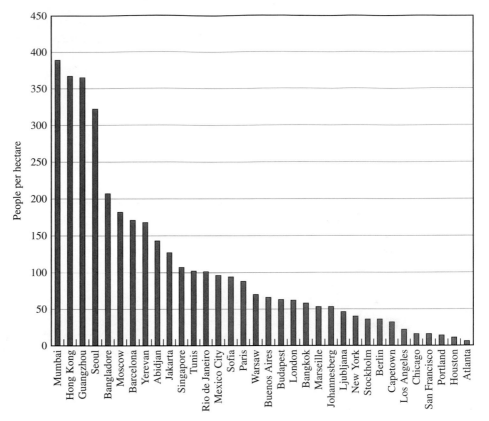

Based on: Alain, and Stephen Malpezzi. "The Spatial Distribution of Population in 48 World Cities: Implications for Economies in Transition." Working Paper, Center for Urban Land Economics Research, University of Wisconsin, 2003.

THE RISE OF THE MONOCENTRIC CITY

Cities looked very different just 100 years ago. At the start of the 20th century, jobs were concentrated near the city center. Manufacturing firms located close to railroad terminals and ports to economize on the cost of transporting inputs and outputs within the city. Office firms clustered in the CBD to facilitate the rapid exchange of information. Workers either lived near the central city and commuted by foot or rode streetcars from suburbs to the city center.

Before exploring the reasons for the demise of the monocentric city, we will explore why it arose in the first place. Recall the fourth axiom of urban economics:

Production is subject to economies of scale

As we saw in Chapter 2, the Industrial Revolution of the 19th century generated innovations in production and energy that increased the scale of production. Firms

FIGURE 7–7 Population Density for Selected Cities

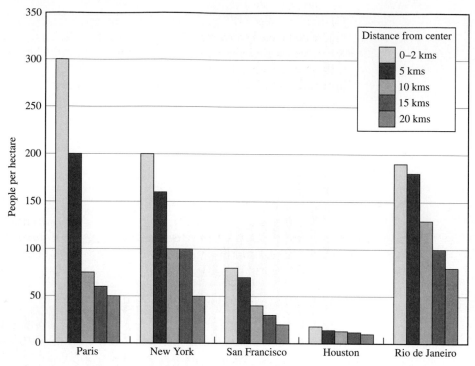

Computations based on: Bertaud, Alain, and Stephen Malpezzi. "The Spatial Distribution of Population in 48 World Cities: Implications for Economies in Transition," Working Paper, Center for Urban Land Economics Research, University of Wisconsin, 2003.

used indivisible inputs and specialized labor to produce on a large scale, and they located in cities to exploit agglomeration economies. The Industrial Revolution also generated innovations in intercity transportation that allowed the wider exploitation of comparative advantage, leading to increased trade and larger trading cities.

Innovations in Intracity Transportation

The Industrial Revolution also generated a series of innovations in intracity transportation that decreased commuting costs. Before the 1820s, most urban travel was by foot, although a few wealthy people traveled by private horse-drawn carriage. Beginning in the late 1820s, innovations in transportation included the following:

- **Omnibus (1827).** The omnibus, a horse-drawn wagon introduced in New York, was the first public transit mode. The name means "for all" (French via Latin), indicating the public nature of the mode, and is the predecessor of "bus." When the horse wagons were put on rails, the travel speed increased to six miles per hour.

- **Cable cars (1873).** Steam-powered cable cars were introduced in San Francisco and spread to other cities.
- **Electric trolley (1886).** The trolley was powered by an on-board electric motor connected to overhead power lines with dangling wires that apparently reminded harried city dwellers of fishing (trolling). Chicago built its elevated trolley line (with a dedicated throughway) in 1895.
- **Subways (1895).** The world's first subway started operation in London in 1890. Boston built the first U.S. subway, a 1.5-mile line that used streetcars. It was followed by systems in New York (1904) and Philadelphia (1907).

These innovations decreased commuting costs and increased the feasible radius of cities. One rule of thumb is that the radius of a city is the distance that can be traveled in an hour. In the "walking city" of the early 19th century, the maximum radius was about two miles. The series of innovations in intracity transport increased travel speeds and increased the feasible radius of cities.

The design of the public transit systems of the 19th century facilitated the large concentrations of employment near city centers. These were hub-and-spoke systems, with spokes radiating out from a central hub. They were designed to transport workers and shoppers from suburban areas along the spokes to the city center.

The Technology of Building Construction

Another limit to city size comes from the costs of building high-density housing to accommodate workers. In the early 1800s, wood buildings were made of posts and beams, with 16-inch timbers, and the practical height limit was three floors. The construction of a three-story building required highly skilled labor to fasten the posts and beams, so urban buildings were relatively expensive. Masonry buildings could be a bit taller but were inflexible because every wall was a load-bearing wall.

The balloon-frame building, introduced in 1832, used smaller pieces of lumber, fastened by nails using less skilled labor. The first balloon-frame building was a warehouse in Chicago. A critical element in the spread of the balloon-frame building was the introduction of inexpensive manufactured nails. Before they were introduced in the 1830s, handcrafted nails were expensive enough to be listed as valued possessions in wills (Bartlett, 1998). The combination of the balloon frame and manufactured nails decreased the cost of urban buildings significantly, contributing to the growth of monocentric cities.

Office buildings were transformed by the switch from masonry to steel frames. In 1848, a five-story building in New York used cast-iron columns instead of masonry walls. The switch to steel followed, providing framing material that was stronger and more elastic and workable than cast iron. The world's first skyscraper, an 11-story building housing the Home Insurance Company, was built in 1885 with a steel skeleton frame.

One limit on building heights is the cost of vertical transportation. The burden of walking up stairs imposed a practical height limit on buildings. In 1854, Elisha

Otis demonstrated the safe use of a steam-powered elevator. The key innovation was a safety latch that prevented the elevator car from plummeting down when the rope connecting the car to the pulley system broke. By 1857, the Otis elevator was being used in a five-story building. When the dedicated steam engine was replaced by electricity, the cost of running elevators decreased and their range increased. In the world's first skyscraper, a bank of elevators carried people up and down at a speed of 500 feet per minute.

The elevator changed the pricing of space on different floors of an office building. Recall the first axiom of urban economics:

Prices adjust to achieve locational equilibrium

In a tall office building, locational equilibrium requires firms to be indifferent between different floors. Before the elevator, upper floors were rented at a discount to offset the cost of climbing four or five flights of stairs. The elevator reduced the cost of vertical travel, and the upper floors became more desirable, inverting the bid-rent curve: Upper floors, with their better views, rented at a premium rather than a discount (Bartlett, 1998).

The Primitive Technology of Freight

Consider finally the technology of freight transportation in the 19th century. As we saw earlier in the book, most intercity freight traveled by railroad or water (on rivers or oceans). For transportation within the city, manufacturers used horse-drawn wagons to transport their freight from factories to the city's port or railroad terminal. This, of course, was the most primitive and costly part of the transportation system, and it tied manufacturers to the central export node—a railroad terminal or port.

THE DEMISE OF THE MONOCENTRIC CITY

What caused the demise of the monocentric city, with its large concentration of employment in the central area? We'll discuss the decentralization of manufacturing, office activity, and population.

Decentralization of Manufacturing: Trucks and Highways

The share of metropolitan manufacturing employment in central cities decreased from about two-thirds in 1948 to less than half in 2000. Mills (1972) provides evidence that the decentralization of manufacturing started long before 1948. What caused the suburbanization of manufacturing employment?

Moses and Williamson (1972) explain the role of the intracity truck in the suburbanization of manufacturing. The truck was developed about 1910, providing an alternative to the horse-drawn wagon used for the trip from factory to port or rail terminal. The truck was twice as fast as a horse-drawn wagon and half as costly, with a unit freight cost of only $0.15 per ton per mile. Between 1910 and 1920, the number of trucks in Chicago increased from 800 to 23,000.

Consider the trade-offs faced by a manufacturing firm that moves away from a central port to a suburban location:

- **Higher freight cost.** The cost of transporting output to the port increases.
- **Lower wages.** As the factory moves closer to its workforce, commuting time decreases, decreasing wages.

In the era of the horse-drawn wagon and the streetcar, the cost of moving freight was high relative to the cost of moving workers, so as a firm moved away from the city center, freight costs increased more rapidly than wages dropped. It was cheaper to ship the workers from the suburbs to the central factory than to ship output from a suburban factory to the export node.

The intracity truck decreased the unit cost of freight. For many firms, the cost of moving freight was now less than the cost of moving workers, so relocating to the suburbs reduced wages by more than it increased freight cost. The truck allowed manufacturers to benefit from lower wages in the suburbs without a large penalty in terms of freight cost, so many firms moved to the suburbs.

Two decades after the truck was first introduced, manufacturers started using it for intercity transport. Improvements in the truck made long-distance travel feasible, and the expansion of the intercity highway system facilitated intercity truck traffic. Eventually, the truck became competitive with the train and the ship for intercity freight. As manufacturers switched from trains and ships to trucks, they were freed from their dependence on the railheads and ports in city centers, and they moved to sites accessible to the intercity highways. In modern cities, manufacturers locate close to highways and beltways to get easy access to the interstate system.

Other Factors: Automobile, Single-Story Plants, and Airports

The automobile contributed to the suburbanization of manufacturers. In a streetcar city, a firm that drew workers from locations throughout the metropolitan area located near the hub of the streetcar system to be accessible to the metropolitan workforce. In a modern auto-based city, production sites along highways and beltways are accessible to the metropolitan workforce, so firms have more location options, including suburban locations.

Two other factors contributed to the suburbanization of manufacturing. First, the switch from the traditional multistory plants of the 19th century to modern single-story plants increased the relative attractiveness of suburbs, where land prices are lower. Second, an increase in the importance of air freight caused firms to locate near suburban airports. For some firms, the suburban airport has replaced the port as the point of orientation.

Decentralization of Office Employment

Before the early 1970s, most office firms located in the CBD because the central location facilitated face time with other office firms. There was some suburban office activity, but most of it involved back-office operations—paper processing rather than information exchange. For most office activities, the advantages of a CBD location (timely contact with other firms) outweighed the disadvantages (high wages and rents).

In the last 30 years, advances in communications technology have allowed more office activities to be performed outside CBDs. The electronic transmission of information allows workers to exchange a wider variety of information without face time. Firms can decouple their operations, with information processing in the suburbs and activities requiring face time in the CBD. For example, a firm's accountants can locate in the suburbs and transmit reports electronically to executives in the CBD, who then use the reports in their interactions with other firms.

Decentralization of Population

We can use the population density gradient, defined as the rate at which population density decreases with distance, to document the suburbanization of population. A smaller gradient indicates that density decreases less rapidly with distance and population is less centralized. As Mills (1972) shows, the U.S. density gradients have been decreasing for the last 120 years. The average gradient for four cities (Baltimore, Milwaukee, Philadelphia, Rochester) was 1.22 in 1880, indicating that 88 percent of the population lived within three miles of the center. By 1948, the gradient had dropped to 0.50 (a three-mile population share of 44 percent), and by 1963, the gradient had dropped to 0.31 (a three-mile share of 24 percent).

The decentralization of metropolitan population is a worldwide phenomenon (Anas, Arnott, and Small, 1998). Between 1801 and 1961, London's density gradient decreased from 1.26 to 0.34, meaning that the percentage of its population living within three miles of the city center dropped from 88 percent to 28 percent. In Paris, the gradient decreased from 2.35 in 1817 to 0.34 in 1946. In cities throughout the world, population has been shifting outward away from the city center.

What factors contributed to the decentralization of population over the last several decades? One factor is rising income. The demand for housing increases with income, and because housing prices are generally lower in suburban areas, rising income increases the relative attractiveness of suburban locations. Of course, an increase in income also increases the opportunity cost of commuting, increasing the relative attractiveness of locations close to workplaces. So it is not clear, in theory, whether higher income leads to more distant residential locations. There is evidence that income growth encourages suburbanization (Anas, Arnott, and Small, 1998).

Another factor in suburbanization of population is lower commuting costs. As we saw earlier in the chapter, technological innovations over the last 180 years, from the omnibus of 1827 to the fast and comfortable automobiles of today, have decreased the monetary and time costs of commuting. A decrease in commuting costs decreases the relative cost of living far from the city center, contributing to suburbanization. In addition, the suburbanization of jobs and people reinforce one another: Jobs follow workers to the suburbs, and workers follow jobs to the suburbs.

Several other factors contribute to the suburbanization of population:

1. **Old housing.** The deterioration of central-city housing encourages households to move to the suburbs, where most of the new housing is built.
2. **Central-city fiscal problems.** Many central cities have relatively high taxes, encouraging households to move to low-tax suburbs. The causality goes both ways: Fiscal problems cause suburbanization, and suburbanization contributes to central-city fiscal problems.
3. **Crime.** Most central cities have relatively high crime rates, encouraging households to move to the suburbs. Later in the book, we'll explore the reasons for higher crime rates in central cities.
4. **Education.** Suburban schools are often considered superior to central-city schools, encouraging households to relocate to the suburbs. Later in the book we'll explore the reasons for differences between central-city and suburban schools.

Empirical studies of the suburbanization process provide support for these other factors in suburbanization. Bradbury, Downs, and Small (1982) show relatively rapid suburbanization in metropolitan areas in which the central city had (1) a relatively old housing stock, (2) relatively high taxes, (3) a relatively large black population, and (4) a large number of suburban governments. Frey (1979) found that suburbanization was relatively rapid in metropolitan areas with high taxes, high crime rates, and low spending on schools. Cullen and Levitt (1999) estimate that for each additional central-city crime, one additional person relocates from the central city to a suburb.

URBAN SPRAWL

There is a spirited debate among economists and policy makers about "urban sprawl." As a city's population increases, the city can grow up by building taller buildings, or it can grow out by occupying more land. The people concerned about urban sprawl suggest that there is too little "up" and too much "out." Between 1950 and 1990, the amount of urbanized land in the United States increased by 245 percent while the urban population increased by only 92 percent. The "footprint" of the typical metropolitan area increased more rapidly than its population, so urban density decreased.

Sprawl Facts

One measure of urban sprawl is the density of economic activity. The lower the density, the larger the land area required to accommodate a given population, and the greater the spread or sprawl of the metropolitan area. We saw earlier in the chapter that U.S. cities are much less dense than cities in the rest of the world, including cities in Europe with similar education and income levels. Metropolitan areas in Germany are four times as dense as U.S. metropolitan areas, and Frankfurt is three times as dense as New York City.

Table 7–3 compares Barcelona to Atlanta. Barcelona is 28 times as dense as Atlanta, and the land used per person is 58 square meters, compared to 1,712 in Atlanta. A trip between the two most distant points in Atlanta is 86 miles, compared to only 23 miles in Barcelona. Reflecting its greater density, Barcelona has more trips by public transit and walking.

Population density varies considerably among U.S. metropolitan areas (Fulton, Pendall, Nguyen, Harrison, 2001). Among the 20 most densely populated areas, the range is 40 people per hectare in New York to 14 per hectare in Santa Barbara. The median value for the top 20 metropolitan areas is 18 people per hectare. In contrast with popular perceptions, 12 of the top 14 metropolitan areas (and 13 of the top 20) are in the West, including 8 cities in California. The high density in western cities reflects relatively high land prices. In fact, the two poster-cities for sprawl, Los Angeles (number 2, with 21 people per hectare) and Phoenix (number 11, with 18 per hectare), are more dense than Chicago (number 15, with 15 per hectare) and Boston (number19, with 14 per hectare).

Over the last few decades, the density of U.S. cities has decreased significantly. One way to convey the change is by computing the elasticity of urbanized land (the percentage change in land in urban use) with respect to the population (the percentage change in the urban population). Table 7–4 shows the elasticities for different regions over the period 1982–1997. In the United States, urbanized land grew 2.76 times faster than the urban population. The largest elasticities—and the largest decreases in density—occurred in the Northeast and the Midwest. In Chicago between 1970 and 1990, the urbanized land area increased by 46 percent while population grew by only

TABLE 7–3 Population Density in Atlanta and Barcelona

	Atlanta	Barcelona
Population in 1990 (million)	2.5	2.8
Average density (people per hectare)	6	171
Land per person (square meters)	1,712	58
Maximum distance between two locations (kilometers)	138	37
Percent of trips walking	Less than 1	20
Percent of trips on public transit	4.5	30

Source: Computations based on Alain Bertaud. "The Spatial Organization of Cities: Deliberate Outcome or Unforeseen Consequence?" Working Paper, Institute of Urban and Regional Development, University of California, Berkeley, 2004.

TABLE 7–4 Changes in Urban Land and Population, 1982–1997

Region	Percentage Increase in Urban Land	Percentage Increase in Urban Population	Elasticity of Urban Land with Respect to Urban Population
United States	47	17	2.76
West	49	32	1.53
South	60	22	2.73
Northeast	39	7	5.57
Midwest	32	7	4.57

Source: Computations based on William Fulton, Rolf Pendall, Mai Nguyen, and Alicia Harrison. "Who Sprawls Most? How Growth Patterns Differ across the U.S." *The Brookings Institution Survey Series,* July 2001, pp. 1–23.

4 percent. In Cleveland over the same period, urbanized land area increased by 33 percent while the population actually decreased by 8 percent.

The Causes of Sprawl

What causes urban sprawl—low density cities? Living at a low density means consuming a large quantity of land. Land is a normal good, so the higher the income, the larger the consumption of land and the lower the population density. A second factor is a low cost of travel, which allows workers and shoppers to live relatively long distances from jobs, shops, and destinations for social interaction. Distant land is cheaper, so lot sizes are larger and population density is lower. Putting these two factors together, high income makes people demand large lots, and a low travel cost allows them to move to the suburbs where land is relatively cheap. So we get low-density development at distant locations, also known as urban sprawl.

Is there a cultural dimension to urban density and sprawl? Bertaud and Malpezzi (2003) suggest that cultural differences explain some of the dramatic differences in urban density across world cities. Asia has much higher urban density than other continents, much higher than could be explained by other factors such as income. Similarly, the variation in density across other continents could reflect differences in preferences for living space. In U.S. metropolitan areas, the presence of immigrants tends to increase density, suggesting that culture is relevant (Fulton, Pendall, Nguyen, Harrison, 2001).

A number of government policies in the United States encourage low densities in large metropolitan areas.

- **Congestion externalities.** As we discuss later in the book, people who use streets and highways during the peak travel period slow other drivers down, imposing an external cost. This underpricing of urban transportation encourages people to commute relatively long distances from locations far from the city center where the low price of land encourages large lots.
- **Mortgage subsidy.** Interest on housing mortgages is a deductible expense for federal and state income taxes, providing a subsidy for housing that increases housing consumption. Land and housing are complementary goods, so the mortgage subsidy increases lot sizes, decreasing density.
- **Underpricing of fringe infrastructure.** In some metropolitan areas, the infrastructure cost of new development at the urban fringe is not fully borne by developers and their customers. Many states use development fees (impact fees) to impose the cost of fringe development on developers and their customers.
- **Zoning.** Many suburban municipalities use zoning to establish minimum lot sizes. One motivation is to exclude low-income households, whose tax contribution may fall short of the costs they impose on municipal government.

Glaeser and Kahn (2004) argue that sprawl is caused mainly by the automobile and the truck. These two travel modes eliminated the orientation of firms and workers toward the indivisible transportation infrastructure near the city center. The authors show that sprawl is ubiquitous across metropolitan areas with all levels of income, poverty, and government fragmentation, suggesting that something else—the internal combustion engine—is the driving force behind sprawl. The authors suggest that the subsidies for highways and housing are too small to have much of an effect.

European Policies

Why is urban population density higher in European cities? Nivola (1998) discusses various public policies that promote higher urban density in European cities. One factor is a higher cost of personal transportation. Because of high taxes, the price of gasoline in Italy is roughly four times the price in the United States. Another factor is the policy of heavier taxes on consumption rather than income. Sales taxes on cars sold in Europe are much higher than in the United States—nine times higher in the Netherlands and 37 times higher in Denmark.

A number of policies in Europe promote the small neighborhood shops that facilitate high-density urban living. Electricity is more costly in Europe, so it would be very expensive to operate the huge refrigerators and freezers that allow Americans to make infrequent trips to suburban megastores. As a result, most Europeans rely to a greater extent on more frequent trips to neighborhood stores. In addition, many European countries restrict the pricing and location of large retailers, protecting small shops from competition. The result is more neighborhood shops—and higher prices for consumers.

Several other policies in Europe promote higher density living. Large agricultural subsidies allow small farmers on urban fringes to outbid city dwellers for land. In 1995, the subsidy per hectare was $791 in the European Union, compared to $79 in the United States. In Europe, investment in transportation infrastructure favors mass transit rather than highways. Britain and France allocate between 40 percent and 60 percent of their transport investment to mass-transit networks, compared to 17 percent in the United States.

The Consequences of Sprawl

A recent study measures some of the consequences of low-density living in U.S. cities (Kahn, 2000). Compared to the typical central-city household, a suburban household requires 58 percent more land (1,167 square meters versus 739). A suburban household actually consumes about the same amount of energy: Although suburban dwellings are larger, they are newer and more energy-efficient. A suburban household drives about 30 percent more than a central-city household. In general, low density means more travel: The elasticity of vehicle miles traveled with respect to urban density is −0.36, meaning that a 10 percent decrease in density increases vehicle miles by 3.6 percent.

What about air pollution? In the last several decades, urban density decreased and urban travel increased, but urban air quality actually improved. Between 1980 and 1995, the annual number of days exceeding the ozone standard in Los Angeles dropped by 27. Although vehicle miles traveled increased, improvements in emissions technology cut emissions per mile. Since most of the "dirty" pre-1975 cars are now off the road, the opportunity to drive more and still get better air quality is evaporating.

What about greenhouse gases, the gases responsible for rising levels of carbon dioxide in the atmosphere? The volume of greenhouse gases generated from a car is determined by the amount of fuel burned. Every gallon of gasoline emits about 20 pounds of greenhouse gases. Over the period 1983–1990, vehicle miles traveled increased by about 4 percent per year, and the average fuel efficiency didn't change much, so the volume of greenhouse gases increased. Since then, vehicle miles traveled have continued to increase, while average fuel efficiency has decreased—a result of the popularity of SUVs, vans, and pickup trucks—so greenhouse emissions have continued to rise.

As we saw earlier in the chapter, the amount of urban land has increased in the last few decades. Between 1980 and 1990, the total urban land increased from 18.9 million hectares to 22.4 million hectares. Counties that experienced urban growth lost agricultural land, but the effect was relatively small. For the nation's counties as a whole, the elasticity of farmland acreage with respect to population is -0.02: a 10 percent increase in population causes a 0.2 percent decrease in farmland. The elasticity is much larger (-0.20) for a subset of states (Illinois, Indiana, Michigan, North Carolina, and Pennsylvania).

The loss of farmland at the city fringe indicates that the land is more valuable in urban use. As we saw earlier in the chapter, various public policies increase the residential value of fringe land, and the solution is to correct the distortionary policies. There is no evidence that urban sprawl has created a shortage of either agricultural land or agricultural products. If it had, the prices of agricultural products would increase, pulling up the price that farmers are willing to pay for land, allowing them to outbid developers for land on the urban fringe.

Bertaud (2004) discusses the challenges associated with providing mass transit in low-density areas. Mass transit is feasible only if density around bus stops or transit stations is high enough to attract a sufficient number riders. For most people, the maximum walking time to a transit stop is about 10 minutes, so a transit stop can serve households within an 800-meter radius. To support a bus system with an intermediate service level (2 buses per hour and $1/2$ mile between lines), the population density in the service area must be at least 31 people per hectare. There are two U.S. metropolitan areas with at least 31 people per hectare—New York (40) and Honolulu (31). Of course, density is higher closer to centers and subcenters, and these areas are likely to have high enough density to support mass transit. For example, the density of New York City is 80 people per hectare (compared to 40 for the metropolitan area). Later in the book, we'll explore various issues concerning the provision and pricing of mass transit.

A comparison of Barcelona to Atlanta reveals the transit challenge for U.S. cities (Bertaud, 2004). As shown in Table 7–3, Barcelona is 28 times as dense as Atlanta. In Barcelona, 60 percent of the population lives within 600 meters of a transit station, compared to only 4 percent living within 800 meters of a transit station in Atlanta. To duplicate the accessibility and ridership of the Barcelona system, Atlanta would have to build an additional 3,400 kilometers of metro tracks and 2,800 more stations. In contrast, the Barcelona system has just 99 kilometers of tracks and 136 stations.

Policy Responses to Sprawl?

There are many factors behind urban sprawl. It partly reflects consumer choice—a rational choice of a large lot at the expense of other consumer products. A number of public policies contribute to urban sprawl, and the appropriate response is to eliminate these distortions. Would land-use patterns change by a little or a lot? If the relatively low density in U.S. cities results in large part from high income, low transport costs, and strong preferences for space, eliminating the policy distortions won't change density very much. But if the distortions—from congestion externalities, mortgage subsidies, underpricing of fringe infrastructure, and large-lot zoning—are significant, we would expect larger changes in density.

An alternative approach is to adopt antisprawl policies such as urban growth boundaries and development taxes. We'll discuss the trade-offs associated with these policies later in the book. If an antisprawl policy succeeds in increasing density, what are the benefits and costs?

SUMMARY

In modern cities, most jobs are dispersed, and most people live and work far from the city center. Over the last 200 years, innovations in transportation have caused the rise of the monocentric city and then its demise. Here are the main points of the chapter.

1. The median job location is seven miles from the city center, and the median residential location is eight miles.
2. Cities in the United States are much less dense than cities in the rest of the world.
3. The key factors in the rise of the large monocentric city were innovations in intraurban transportation that decreased the cost of commuting and innovations in construction that decreased the cost of tall buildings.
4. The key factors in the decentralization of jobs and people were the development of the truck, the automobile, and the highway system; increases in income; and the switch to one-story production facilities.
5. Between 1950 and 1990, the amount of urban land increased more than twice as fast as the urban population.

APPLYING THE CONCEPTS

1. **By Land or by Air?**
   Consider a manufacturing firm in a rectangular city that produces 10 tons of output per day and transports four-fifths of its output on trucks via a highway four miles east of the city center and transports the remaining fifth on airplanes that leave from an airport seven miles east of the city center. Intraurban transportation is via trucks, with a unit cost of $20 per ton per mile. The firm does not engage in factor substitution as the price of land changes.
   a. Draw the firm's bid-rent curve for land from the city center to 10 miles east. A kinked curve is OK.
   b. Suppose the shipping proportions reverse; four-fifths of transport is via airplane and one-fifth by truck. Draw a new bid-rent curve.

2. Software Firm: CBD or Subcenter?

Consider a software firm with 10 workers, each of whom lives in a suburb due east of the city center and commutes by automobile. The firm exchanges products and information with other software firms in the center, and the savings in exchange costs from being the center as opposed to the suburb is $180 per day. The daily cost of automobile commuting from the suburb to the center (including the opportunity cost of time) is $10 per worker.

a. Where will the firm locate—in the city center or the suburb?

b. Suppose a large increase in the gas tax doubles the daily commuting cost. Where will the firm locate?

c. Suppose that commuting via mass transit is slower than automobile commuting and has a daily cost (including time cost) of $15. How would your answer to (b) change?

3. Urban Villages?

The traditional monocentric city was a segregated city in the sense that all employment was in the central core and most residents lived outside the core. The modern city is less segregated in the sense that employment is dispersed. According to Mr. Wizard, "If my assumptions are correct, land use in the typical American city will soon be completely integrated, with each manufacturer and each office firm surrounded by its workforce. Every worker will travel less than a mile to work." Assume that Mr. Wizard's reasoning is correct. What are his assumptions? Are the assumptions realistic?

4. Was the Monocentric City a Fluke?

According to Ms. Wizard, "The large, traditional, monocentric city of the 19th century was a fluke, a result of a particular sequence of technological transportation innovations over the 19th and 20th centuries. If the sequence of innovations had been slightly different, the large monocentric city never would have developed. Instead, we would have gone directly from the small cities of the 18th century to the large, multicentric, suburbanized cities that we see today."

a. List the sequence of innovations that caused the rise and then demise of the large monocentric city.

b. List an alternative sequence under which the large monocentric city would not have developed.

REFERENCES AND ADDITIONAL READING

1. Anas, Alex, Richard Arnott, and Kenneth A. Small. "Urban Spatial Structure." *Journal of Economic Literature* 34 (1998), pp. 1426–64.
2. Bartlett, Randall. *The Crisis of American Cities.* Armonk, NY: Sharp, 1998.
3. Bertaud, Alain. "The Spatial Organization of Cities: Deliberate Outcome or Unforeseen Consequence?" Working Paper, Institute of Urban and Regional Development, University of California, Berkeley, 2004.
4. Bertaud, Alain. "Clearing the Air in Atlanta: Transit and Smart Growth or Conventional Economics?" *Journal of Urban Economics* 54 (2003), pp. 379–400.

5. Bertaud, Alain, and Stephen Malpezzi. "The Spatial Distribution of Population in 48 World Cities: Implications for Cities in Transition." Working Paper, The Center for Urban Land Research, University of Wisconsin, 2003.

6. Bradbury, Katharine L., Anthony Downs, and Kenneth A. Small. *Urban Decline and the Future of American Cities.* Washington DC: Brookings Institution, 1982.

7. Brueckner, Jan K., Jacques-Francois Thisse, and Yves Zenou. "Why Is Central Paris Rich and Downtown Detroit Poor? An Amenity-Based Theory." *European Economic Review* 43 (1999), pp. 91–107.

8. Cullen, J.B., and S.D. Levitt. "Crime, Urban Flight, and the Consequences for Cities." *Review of Economics and Statistics* 81 (1999), pp. 159–69.

9. Frey, W.H. "Central City White Flight: Racial and Non-Racial Causes." *American Sociological Review* 44 (1979), pp. 425–88.

10. Fulton, William, Rolf Pendall, Mai Nguyen, and Alicia Harrison. "Who Sprawls Most? How Growth Patterns Differ across the U.S." *The Brookings Institution Survey Series.* July 2001, pp. 1–23.

11. Garreau, Joel. *Edge City: Life on the New Frontier.* New York: Doubleday, 1991.

12. Giuliano, Genevieve, and Kenneth Small. "Subcenters in the Los Angeles Region." *Regional Science and Urban Economics* 21 (1991).

13. Glaeser, Edward, and Matthew Kahn. "Decentralized Employment and the Transformation of the American City." NBER Working Paper, March 2001.

14. Glaeser, Edward, and Matthew Kahn. "Sprawl and Urban Growth." Chapter 56 in *Handbook of Regional and Urban Economics 4: Cities and Geography,* eds. Vernon Henderson and Jacques-Francois Thisse. Amsterdam: Elsevier, 2004.

15. Glaeser, Edward, Matthew Kahn, and Chenghuan Chu. "Job Sprawl: Employment Location in U.S. Metropolitan Areas." *Brookings Institution Survey Series,* May 2001, pp. 1–8.

16. Hohenberg, Paul M., and Lyann H. Lees. The Making of Urban Europe 1000–1950. Cambridge, MA: Harvard University Press, 1986.

17. Kahn, Matthew. "The Environmental Impact of Suburbanization." *Journal of Policy Analysis and Management* 19 (2000).

18. Lang, Robert E. "Office Sprawl: The Evolving Geography of Business." *The Brookings Institution Survey Series,* October 2000.

19. Lang, Robert E. *Edgeless Cities.* Washington DC: Brookings, 2003.

20. McMillen, Daniel P. "One Hundred Fifty Years of Land Values in Chicago: A Nonparametric Approach." *Journal of Urban Economics* 40 (1996), pp. 100–24.

21. McMillen, Daniel P., and John F. McDonald. "Suburban Subcenters and Employment Density in Metropolitan Chicago." *Journal of Urban Economics* 43 (1998), pp. 157–80.

22. Mills, Edwin S. *Studies in the Structure of the Urban Economy.* Baltimore: Johns Hopkins, 1972.

23. Moses, Leon, and Harold Williamson. "The Location of Economic Activity in Cities." In *Readings in Urban Economics,* eds. Matthew Edel and Jerome Rothenberg. New York: Macmillan, 1972.

24. Nivola, Pietro. "Fat City: Understanding American Urban Form from a Transatlantic Perspective." *Brookings Review,* Fall 1998, pp. 17–20.

25. Schwartz, Alex. "Corporate Service Linkages in Large Metropolitan Areas: A Study of New York, Los Angeles, and Chicago." *Urban Affairs Quarterly* 28 (1992), pp. 276 –96.
26. Sivitanidou, Rena. "Do Office-Commercial Firms Value Access to Service Employment Centers? A Hedonic Value Analysis within Polycentric Los Angeles." *Journal of Urban Economics* 40 (1996), pp. 125–49.
27. Wheaton, William. "Income and Urban Residence: An Analysis of Consumer Demand for Location." *American Economic Review* 67 (1977), pp. 620–31.

Appendix: The Monocentric Model and Applications

This appendix describes and applies the model of a monocentric city, the prevailing urban form until the early 20th century. After describing the model and its implications, we apply the model in two ways. First, we explore the reasons for the concentration of low-income households in central cities. Second, we develop a general-equilibrium model of the urban economy that captures the interactions between the urban labor market and the land market.

THE MONOCENTRIC MODEL

We can summarize the transportation technology of the monocentric city as follows:

- **Central export node.** Manufacturing firms export their output from the city through a central export node—a railroad terminal or a port.
- **Horse-drawn wagons.** Manufacturing firms transport their output on horse-drawn wagons from their factories to the central node.
- **Hub-and-spoke streetcar system.** Workers travel by streetcar from residential areas to their jobs in the central business district (CBD).
- **Central information exchange.** The employees of different office industries meet in the city center to exchange information.

Under these assumptions, the city center is the focal point of the metropolitan area: Manufacturers are oriented toward the export node, office firms are oriented toward each other, and households are oriented toward manufacturing and office jobs.

Figure 7A–1 (page 154) shows the allocation of land in the monocentric city. The office district is the area over which the bid rent of office firms exceed the bid rents of manufacturing firms, generating an office area with a radius of x_1 miles. Moving outward, manufacturing firms outbid other land users for land between x_1 and x_2, so the manufacturing district is a ring of width $x_2 - x_1$. Residents have the maximum bid rent for the area between x_2 and x_3, so the residential district is a ring of width $x_3 - x_2$.

In the monocentric city, both manufacturers and office firms are oriented toward the central business district. Why is the central area of the city occupied by the

FIGURE 7A–1 Bid Rents and Monocentric Land Use

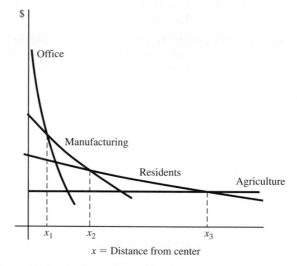

x = Distance from center

The equilibrium land-use pattern is determined by the bid-rent curves of firms and residents. The office area is the area over which office firms outbid other users (from $x = 0$ to x_1). The area between x_1 and x_2 is the manufacturing district. Residents live in the area between x_2 and x_3.

office industry? The geometric answer is that the activity with the steeper bid-rent curve occupies more central land. As we saw in Chapter 7, the slope of the bid-rent curve is determined by transport costs. The office industry has higher transport costs because it uses people—with a high opportunity cost of travel time—to transmit output. In contrast, manufacturing firms use horses and wagoneers.

Does the land market allocate land efficiently? In the terms used by land developers, is land allocated to its "highest and best use"? The office industry, with its higher transport costs, occupies the land closest to the city center. This allocation is efficient because the office industry has more to gain from proximity to the city center. If an office firm were to swap places with a manufacturing firm, the travel cost of the office firm would increase by a relatively large amount, while the freight cost of the manufacturing firm would decrease by a relatively small amount. As a result, total transport costs would increase. The market allocation, which gives central land to the office industry, economizes on transport costs.

The second feature of the monocentric model is that employment is concentrated in the central area, not distributed throughout the metropolitan area. Why do all the manufacturers and office firms locate in the central area? As we saw in this chapter, the cost of commuting on streetcars was low relative to the cost of moving output on horse-drawn wagons, so it was cheaper to transport workers from the suburbs to central factories rather than transporting output from a suburban production site to the central export node. The same logic applies to the office sector: A firm that moved to the suburbs would experience a large increase in the travel cost for information exchange and a relatively small reduction in wages.

INCOME AND LOCATION

In U.S. cities, the wealthy tend to locate in the suburbs, and the poor tend to locate near the city center. In other words, average household income increases as one moves away from the city center. Because the most expensive land is near the city center, this location pattern is puzzling: Why should the poor occupy the most expensive land?

Trade-off between Commuting and Housing Costs

The traditional theory of income segregation suggests that central locations provide the best trade-off between commuting and housing costs for the poor, while suburban locations provide the best trade-off for the wealthy. Consider a household that is thinking about a move outward from a central location. An outward move of one mile generates costs and benefits.

- **Lower housing costs.** The price of housing will decrease, and the marginal benefit of moving outward equals the change in price times housing consumption. For example, consider a household that consumes 2,000 square feet. If the price of housing drops by $0.10 per square foot, the marginal benefit of moving outward is $200 (equal to $0.10 times 2,000).
- **Higher commuting costs.** The marginal cost of a move outward is the marginal cost of commuting.

Figure 7A–2 (page 156) shows how two types of households, low-income and high-income, pick a residential location. The marginal-cost curves are horizontal, based on the assumption that the commuting cost per mile is constant with respect to distance. The marginal cost for the high-income household is more because it has a higher opportunity cost of commuting time. In Figure 7A–2, the marginal cost of the high-income household is $100, compared to $50 for the low-income household.

The marginal-benefit curves are negatively sloped. This reflects the convexity of the housing-price curve. Moving outward, the reduction in the price of housing for the first mile exceeds the reduction for the second mile, and so on. For example, suppose the price of housing drops by $0.10 for the first mile and then $0.095 for the second mile. For a household that consumes 2,000 square feet, the marginal benefit for the first mile is $200, and the marginal benefit for the second mile is $190. The marginal-benefit curve for the high-income household is higher because it consumes more housing. In this example, the high-income household consumes four times as much housing as the low-income household (2,000 versus 500 square feet). At point L, the marginal benefit for the first mile is $50 for the low-income household (a price reduction of $0.10 times 500 square feet).

In Panel A of Figure 7A–2, the low-income household lives in the central city and the high-income household lives in a suburb. For the low-income household, the marginal benefit equals the marginal cost at one mile from the center (point L). Moving farther outward generates an additional cost of $50 and an extra benefit less than $50, so the more central site is better. The relatively large housing

FIGURE 7A–2 Income and Location in Monocentric City

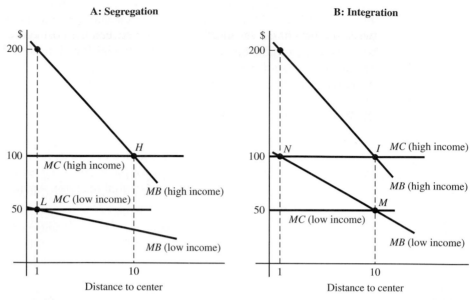

If the income elasticity of housing demand is larger than the income elasticity of commuting costs, the gap between the benefit curves will be large relative to the gap between the cost curves, and the low-income household will locate closer to the center.

If the income elasticity of housing demand equals the income elasticity of commuting costs, both types of households choose the same location.

consumption of the high-income household means that the marginal benefit of moving outward exceeds the cost for up to 10 miles (point *H*). Low-income households locate close to the center because their relatively low housing consumption means they have little to gain by moving outward.

The income segregation result shown in Panel A of Figure 7A–2 is based on specific assumptions about the relationships between income, commuting costs, and housing consumption. Specifically, it assumes that housing consumption increases more rapidly with income. The high-income household has four times the housing consumption but just twice the commuting cost. In other words, the income elasticity of demand for housing is larger than the income elasticity of commuting cost. Speaking geometrically, the gap between the benefit curves is larger than the gap between the cost curves, so the high-income household lives farther from the center.

Other Explanations

Wheaton (1977) provides empirical evidence that questions the validity of this conclusion. His results suggest that the income elasticity of demand for housing is roughly equal to the income elasticity of commuting cost. Therefore, the gap between the benefit curves will be roughly the same as the gap between the cost curves. In Panel B of Figure 7A–2, the high-income household has twice the housing consumption (2,000 versus 1,000) and twice the commuting cost, so the gap between the benefit curves matches the gap between the cost curves. As a result, the two households will choose the same residential location 10 miles from the city center.

This suggests that the observed pattern of income segregation cannot be explained by the trade-off between commuting cost and housing cost, so we must look for other explanations:

1. **New suburban housing.** If high-income households prefer new housing to old housing, they are pulled to the suburbs, where new housing is built.
2. **Fleeing central-city problems.** High-income households are relatively sensitive to crime and other problems, so they are willing to pay more for suburban housing.
3. **Suburban zoning.** As explained later in the book, suburban governments use zoning to exclude low-income households.

Other countries have different patterns of location by income. According to Hohenberg and Lees (1986), European cities, have large concentrations of high-income households near the center. A good example of the European pattern is the Paris metropolitan area, where the average income in the central city exceeds the average income in the surrounding suburbs.

Brueckner, Thisse, and Zenou (1999) contrast Paris and Detroit. Paris has a rich mixture of cultural amenities (museums, restaurants, parks, street life) that make central Paris attractive relative to the suburbs. The demand for these cultural amenities increases rapidly with income, so the forces pulling the rich toward the central city (access to jobs and cultural amenities) dominate the forces pulling them toward the suburbs (lower housing prices). In contrast, Detroit has few cultural opportunities in the city center, so there is little to counteract the pull of the low housing prices in the suburbs.

A GENERAL EQUILIBRIUM MODEL OF A MONOCENTRIC CITY

We can use the model of the monocentric city to explore the interactions between the urban labor market and land market. The model considers a city that is small (one of many in a nation) and open (people move freely between cities). The utility level of residents is determined at the national level and is unaffected by changes in the city. In other words, the utility level of city residents is fixed, but the population of the city varies.

Interactions between the Land and Labor Markets

To simplify matters, we adopt two assumptions. First, we assume for the moment that there is no consumer substitution or factor substitution. Therefore, population

FIGURE 7A–3 Interactions Between Land and Labor Markets and the Streetcar

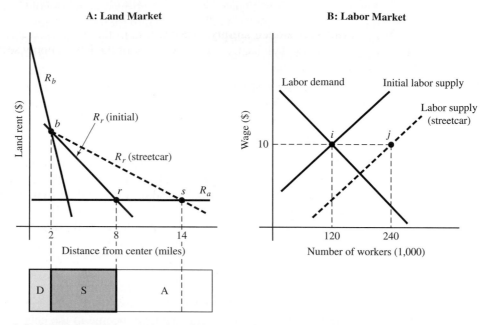

A: In the initial equilibrium, the business bid-rent curve intersects the residential bid-rent at point *b*, generating a two-mile business district. The residential bid-rent curve intersects the agriculture bid-rent curve at point *r*, generating a six-mile residential district.

The streetcar decreases commuting cost and tilts the residential bid-rent curve outward, and the new curve intersects the agriculture bid-rent curve at 14 miles, increasing the size of the residential area. B: In the initial equilibrium, shown by point *i*, the wage is $10 and there are 120,000 workers. The streetcar increases labor supply, shifting the supply curve to the right and causing excess supply of labor.

density is the same at all residential locations and employment density (workers per square mile) is the same at all business locations. Later we'll see how variation in density affects the analysis. The second assumption is that the city is not circular, but rectangular with a one-mile width.

Panel A of Figure 7A–3 shows the urban land market. The business bid-rent curve intersects the residential curve at point *b*, generating a two-mile CBD. The total demand for labor in the city equals the land area of the CBD (two square miles) times the employment density (workers per square mile, equal to 60,000), or 120,000 workers. The residential bid-rent curve intersects the agricultural curve at point *r*, generating a six-mile residential area (from mile 2 to mile 8). The total supply of labor in the city equals the land area of the residential area (six square miles) times residential density (workers per square mile, equal to 20,000), or 120,000 workers.

Panel B of Figure 7A–3 shows the urban labor market, with a negatively sloped demand curve and a positively sloped supply curve.

- **Negatively sloped demand.** An increase in the wage increases production costs and decreases the bid rent for businesses land, so the business territory shrinks, decreasing the quantity of labor demanded.
- **Positively sloped supply.** An increase in the wage increases the bid rent for residential land, increasing the territory of the labor-supply sector.

In the initial equilibrium shown by point i, the wage is $10 and the quantity of labor demanded (from the business district) equals the quantity supplied (from the residential district), with 120,000 workers.

The General-Equilibrium Effects of the Streetcar

Consider the effects of introducing a streetcar into the monocentric city. In Panel A of Figure 7A–3, the streetcar decreases the unit commuting cost so it tilts the residential bid-rent curve outward. The residential area expands into the previously agricultural area (at point s, the residential area has doubled), increasing labor supply. In Panel B, this is shown as a rightward shift of the labor supply curve, which causes an excess supply of labor at the original wage.

The excess supply of labor will cause the city's wage to fall. The wage drop causes two changes in the urban land market:

- The residential bid-rent curve shifts downward because residents' income decreases.
- The business bid-rent curve shifts upward because the decrease in wages decreases production costs.

These changes in the land market eliminate the excess supply of labor. The downward shift of the residential curve decreases the territory of the residential sector, decreasing the quantity of labor supplied. The upward shift of the business curve increases the territory of the business sector, increasing the quantity of labor demanded.

Figure 7A–4 (page 160) shows the new equilibrium. In Panel A, point c shows that the business district grows to three miles. Point t shows that the residential district is now nine miles (from mile 3 to mile 12). Compared to the initial equilibrium, land rent is higher in both the business and residential areas. In the residential area, the streetcar increases land rent because it decreases commuting costs and improves accessibility. In the business district, the streetcar increases land rent because it increases labor supply and reduces the wage and firm's production costs. In Panel B, the new equilibrium is shown by point f: The wage is $7 (down from $10) and there are 180,000 workers in the city (up from 120,000).

So far, we have assumed that both employment density and residential density are fixed. If we relax this assumption, the streetcar will increase density, reinforcing the changes shown earlier. The general effect of the streetcar is to increase land rent, and increases in land rent increase density: Households will economize on land by living on smaller lots; firms will economize on land by producing in taller buildings on smaller production sites.

FIGURE 7A–4 Equilibrium After the Streetcar

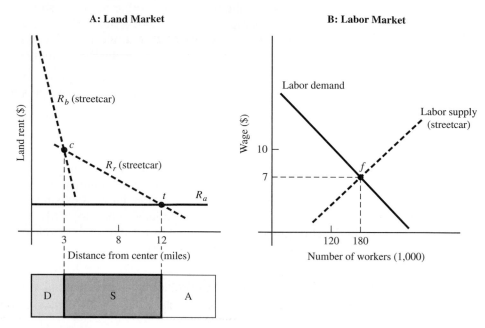

A: In the streetcar equilibrium, the business bid-rent curve intersects the residential bid-rent at point *c*, so the business district is three miles (up from two miles). The residential bid-rent curve intersects the agriculture bid-rent curve at point *t*, so the residential district is 9 miles (up from 6 miles).
B: In the streetcar equilibrium shown by point *f*, the wage is $7 (down from $10) and there are 180,000 workers (up from 120,000).

APPLYING THE CONCEPTS

1. **Paris versus Detroit**
   Suppose the benefit and cost curves of the high-income households shown in Figure 7A–2 are relevant for Detroit. In contrast, high-income households in Paris take 50 percent more trips to the city center (for work and cultural opportunities). While Detroiters commute in air-conditioned land yachts, tuna boats, and Suburban Parcels, Parisians pack into mass transit. The armpit factor (visualize Parisians in packed buses hanging onto overhead straps) makes the unit cost of travel one-third higher in Paris. Use a graph like Figure 7A–2 to predict where high-income Parisians live.
2. **Global Warming and Rising Sea Level**
   Consider Aquaville, a rectangular monocentric city depicted in Figure 7A–3. Suppose that global warming raises the sea level, flooding one-fifth of the CBD. Depict graphically the effects of the flooding on (1) the city's wage, (2) land rent within the CBD, (3) land rent in the residential area, (4) the size of the CBD, and (5) the size of the residential area. Assume that flooding eliminates one-fifth of CBD land at each distance from the central export node.

CHAPTER 8

Neighborhood Choice

Love thy neighbor as yourself, but choose your neighborhood.
—LOUISE BEAL

W hen a household chooses a house or apartment, it is choosing much more than a dwelling. It is also choosing a set of local public goods (schools, parks, and public safety) and a set of taxes to finance the public goods. The household is also choosing a set of neighbors who provide opportunities for social interactions and send their kids to the same schools. In this chapter, we explore the economics of neighborhood choice. In contrast with our earlier analysis of commuting-based residential choice, the analysis in this chapter considers a variety of neighborhood characteristics.

DIVERSITY VERSUS SEGREGATION

Our discussion of neighborhoods considers the issue of diversity. At one extreme is a city of diverse neighborhoods, each with an equal representation of households of different races and income levels. At the other extreme is a segregated city with a neighborhood for each type of household, rich and poor, black and white.

Cities in the United States experience a high degree of residential segregation with respect to income, education level, and ethnicity. Figure 8–1 (page 162) shows median incomes across the 176 census tracts in Suffolk County, the county containing Boston. If neighborhoods were perfectly integrated with respect to income, the median income would be the same in all census tracts. Instead, the range of median income across tracts is $12,100 to $98,900. Table 8–1 (page 162) shows the distribution of median income across census tracts in several U.S. cities. The data is for the county containing the central city. The first row of numbers shows the 10th percentile of median income, defined as the median income in the tract whose median income is higher than 10 percent of the city's tracts. At the opposite extreme, the fifth row shows the median income for the 90th percentile. In seven of the eight cities, the median income of the 90th percentile is between twice and three times the median income of the 10th percentile.

FIGURE 8–1 Median Income by Census Tract, Boston (Suffolk County)

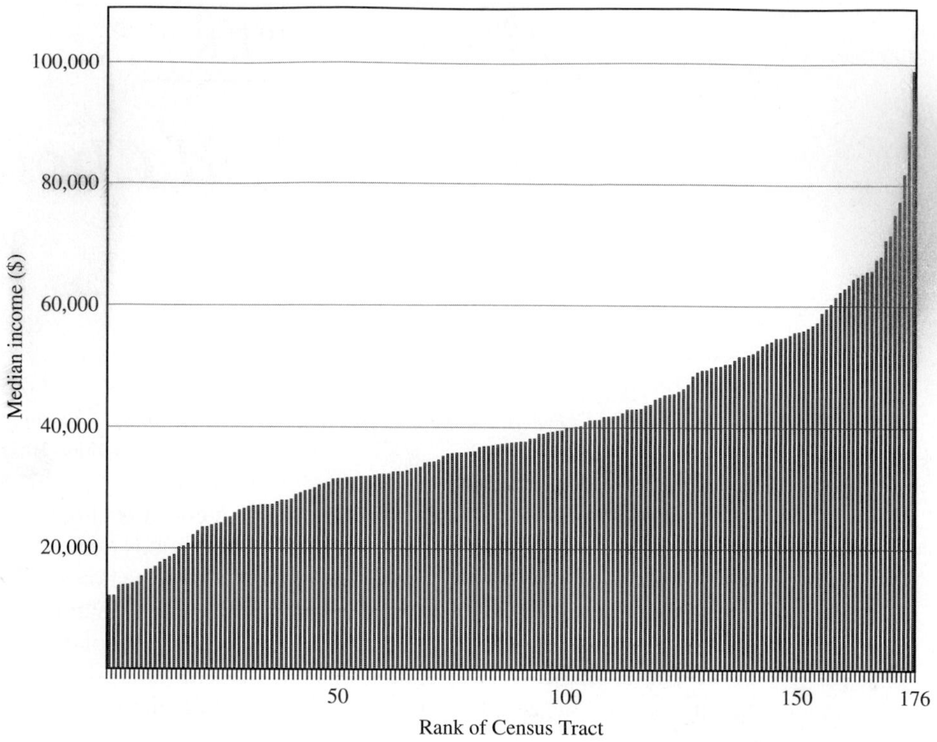

Source: U.S. Census, 2000.

TABLE 8–1 Distribution of Median Incomes across Census Tracts

Percentile	Salt Lake City, UT	Providence, RI	Minneapolis/ St. Paul, MN	Boston, MA	Honolulu, HI	Miami, FL	San Francisco, CA	Phoenix, AZ
10	30,285	20,153	28,038	20,576	29,391	18,705	29,060	26,996
20	36,132	24,382	33,300	27,165	35,224	23,712	44,541	31,113
50	50,678	36,683	47,790	37,432	51,966	34,356	58,817	45,322
80	67,559	50,036	66,427	52,160	73,667	51,414	73,571	65,833
90	77,957	58,410	78,633	60,878	82,113	62,218	85,264	76,077

Source: U.S. Census, 2000.

SORTING FOR LOCAL PUBLIC GOODS

In the typical metropolitan area, there are dozens of municipalities, each with a different mix of local public goods and taxes. In addition, there are many school districts, each with a different education program. The wide variety of munici-palities and school districts allows citizens to "vote with their feet," choosing the jurisdiction with the best combination of public services and taxes. In this part of the chapter, we'll explore the role of local public goods and local taxes in neighborhood choice. Later in the book, we'll take a more detailed look at local public goods and taxes.

Diversity in Demand for Local Public Goods

Consider a three-person city that provides a local public good, a park. The park is a public good because it is nonrival in consumption: The fact that one person in the city benefits from the park doesn't reduce the benefit for another person. If the benefits of the park are confined to people in the city, the park is a *local* public good. Citizens in the city vary in their demand for park acreage and will collectively decide how big the park will be.

Figure 8–2 shows three individual demand curves for parks, one for each citizen. As shown in Section 2.1 of "Tools of Microeconomics," the appendix at the end of the book, a demand curve shows how much a person is willing to pay for one more unit of a product, so it is a marginal-benefit curve. Lois has a relatively low demand for parks and a low marginal-benefit curve (MB_L). For example, point l indicates that she is willing to pay \$20 for the sixth acre. In contrast, Marian has a medium demand for park acres, and her marginal-benefit curve (MB_M), shows that she is willing to pay \$28 for the sixth acre (point k). Hiram, with a high demand (MB_H), is willing to pay \$48 for the sixth acre (point j).

FIGURE 8–2 Diversity of Demand for Local Public Good

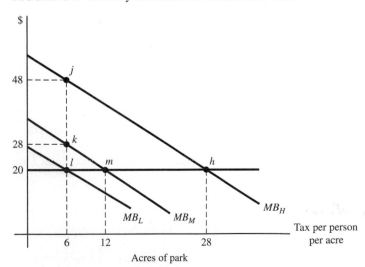

The demand curves of the individual citizens show their marginal benefits of park acres. With a tax of \$20 per person per acre, Lois prefers 6 acres, Marian prefers 12 acres, and Hiram prefers 28 acres.

The three citizens must collectively pick a park size. Suppose the cost per acre of parks is $60, and the city pays for the park with a tax of $20 per citizen per acre. In Figure 8–2, the horizontal line at $20 shows the marginal cost of park acreage for each citizen. For each additional acre, each citizen pays $20, one-third of the $60 cost. For each citizen, the preferred park acreage is the quantity at which his or her marginal benefit equals the $20 marginal cost. Lois prefers 6 acres (point *l*), while Miriam prefers 12 acres (point *m*), and Hiram prefers 28 acres (point *h*). In other words, diversity in demand for park acreage means that citizens disagree about how large the park should be.

Problems with Majority Rule and Formation of Municipalities

Under majority rule, the city will choose Marian's preferred park of 12 acres. Suppose the city holds a series of elections between pairs of parks of different sizes. As shown in Table 8–2, in an election between 6 acres (Lois' favorite) and 12 acres (Marian's favorite), Hiram joins Marian to approve Marian's choice because 12 acres is closer to his preferred level. In an election between Marian's favorite and a larger park (28 acres), Lois joins Marian to approve Marian's choice. Marian's preferred size wins both elections because she is the median voter, defined as the voter who splits the rest of the voting public into two equal halves. Marian wins because she can always get one voter to join her to defeat any alternative to her preferred option.

Majority rule leaves two of three citizens unhappy with local government. The park is too big for Lois, who would prefer 6 acres, and too small for Hiram, who would prefer 28 acres. The necessity of choosing one park size for citizens with different preferences means that two of three citizens will be dissatisfied and will look for alternative arrangements.

One alternative is to form a new municipality with citizens with similar park preferences. Consider a metropolitan area that starts with three heterogeneous municipalities: Each municipality initially has one citizen of each type (Lois, Marian, Hiram). Under majority rule, each municipality will have two dissatisfied citizens looking for alternatives. For example, the three Lois-type citizens could leave their old municipalities and form Loisville, a municipality that will provide a 6-acre park. Similarly, Marianville (with three Marians) would provide a 12-acre park, and Hiramville would provide a 28-acre park. By voting with their feet and sorting themselves into homogeneous communities, each citizen gets her or his preferred park size.

Median wins.

TABLE 8–2 The Median Voter Always Wins

Election	Votes for Median (12 acres)	Votes for Nonmedian
6 acres vs. 12 acres	Marian and Hiram	Lois
28 acres vs. 12 acres	Marian and Lois	Hiram

results in segregation of population

Variation in Consumption of the Taxed Good

Up to this point, we have assumed that the local public good is financed with a common head tax. In Loisville, the head tax would be $120 per head ($20 per acre times six acres), just high enough for each citizen to pay one-third of the cost of providing $360 worth of parks ($60 per acre times six acres). Suppose the government switches to a variable head tax: the heavier your head, the higher your tax. Assume that there are three head sizes in Loisville: Pin has a 2-pound head, while Avner has a 10-pounder, and Gordo has a 24-pounder. As shown in the first row of Table 8–3, a tax of $10 per pound would generate tax bills of $20 for Pin ($10 times 2 pounds), $100 for Avner, and $240 for Gordo, just enough to cover the $360 cost of the city park.

Although every citizen in Loisville has the same preferences for parks and benefits equally from the park, they have different tax bills. Gordo pays 12 times as much as Pin and has an incentive to form a new municipality with other big-head people. As shown in the last row of Table 8–3, if Gordo forms a big-head municipality with two other people, they could raise $120 per capita with a tax rate of only $5 per pound ($5 times 24 = $120). In other words, forming the big-head municipality cuts the head tax in half. Similarly, the average-head people have an incentive to form a municipality and exclude the pinheads. As shown in the second row of Table 8–3, a pinhead municipality needs a tax of $60 per pound to generate the $120 per person required to support the preferred park acreage.

The introduction of taxes that vary across individuals increases the equilibrium number of municipalities. In this example, there are nine municipalities, equal to the number of consumer types (three) times the number of head types (three). In equilibrium there will be three low-demand municipalities, each with a different head size. Similarly, there will be three medium-demand municipalities and three high-demand municipalities.

Real municipalities don't tax heads but instead use property taxes to finance local public goods. The basic logic of sorting with respect to head sizes applies to taxation based on housing consumption. Instead of big-head and pinhead municipalities, there will be big-house and small-house municipalities. People who own relatively expensive houses have an incentive to form municipalities with other big-house citizens in order to avoid paying more than their share of taxes. So if there are

[handwritten margin note: after segregation, more segregation will occur in the smaller groups.]

[handwritten margin note: Sorting of households with respect to Demand.]

TABLE 8–3 Municipality Formation for Tax Purposes

Outcome	Tax Rate per Pound	Pin (small head)	Avner (average head)	Gordo (big head)
		Tax Bill		
Mixed municipality	$10	$ 20	$100	$240
Exclusive small head	$60	$120	—	—
Exclusive average head	$12	—	$120	—
Exclusive big head	$ 5	—	—	$120

three types of preferences for local public goods (low, medium, and high) and three house sizes (small, medium, and big), there will be nine municipalities.

The sorting of households with respect to the demand for local public goods and the demand for taxed goods contributes to income segregation. If the demands for local public goods and the taxed goods depend on income, sorting will lead to municipalities with different income levels. Later in the book, we will develop a formal model of this sorting process and explore some of its consequences. Specifically, we will show how sorting with respect to public goods and tax bases generates a fragmented system of local government, with dozens of municipalities in each metropolitan area. We will also discuss the efficiency implications of fragmented government.

NEIGHBORHOOD EXTERNALITIES

Interactions among neighbors generate neighborhood externalities (Durlauf, 2004). Recall the third axiom of urban economics:

Externalities cause inefficiency

As we saw in Chapter 1, an externality is an unpriced interaction, and it can be positive or negative. A positive externality occurs when a person is not compensated for an action that benefits someone else. A negative externality occurs when a person does not pay for an action that imposes a cost on someone else. Social interactions at the neighborhood level generate several types of externalities for both children and adults.

Consider first the externalities relevant for children. Children imitate adults, and a neighborhood of educated and successful adults provides good role models for kids. Successful adults don't get a dollar every time they inadvertently encourage kids to stay in school, so there is a positive externality. In schools, the most important factor in student learning is the peer group: Kids learn more when they are surrounded by other kids who are motivated and focused. Motivated kids don't get a dollar every time they do their homework, so there is a positive externality. Troublesome kids don't pay a dollar every time they disrupt class, so there is a negative externality.

An important facet of children's externalities is imitative or self-reinforcing behavior. A person who joins a group benefits from social interaction but also tends to imitate the behavior—good or bad—of the members of the group. Imitation occurs for three reasons:

- There is a psychological payoff from behaving like others.
- A group provides a wider set of opportunities. For example, a chess club or a drama club will provide opportunities to interact with other high achievers.
- A group generates better information about future opportunities. For example, college recruiters target high-achieving students in chess and drama clubs.

Although the social aspects of a chess club or a drama club may be similar to those of a street gang, the self-reinforcing or imitative aspects generate very different long-term employment prospects.

[handwritten margin note: wealthier neighborhoods have better externalities but wealthier areas, pay more]

Consider next the externalities relevant for adults. In addition to regular social interactions, adults may get better information about job opportunities from their neighbors. Much of the information about employment opportunities comes from informal sources such as neighbors and friends. On the negative side, drug abuse among neighbors generates an unpleasant living environment. These are externalities because neighbors don't charge each other for information that leads to job prospects, and drug abusers don't compensate their neighbors for the unpleasant environment.

These neighborhood externalities affect a household's choice of a neighborhood. Most households have the same preferences with respect to adult role models and school peers, so they all would prefer the same sort of neighborhood. The positive externalities generated by a household generally increase with income and education level, so people generally prefer neighborhoods with large numbers of high-income, educated households. Of course, the number of such households is limited, so, who gets them as neighbors?

NEIGHBORHOOD CHOICE

Households compete for places in a desirable neighborhood by bidding for housing and land in the neighborhood. In this part of the chapter, we focus on competitive bidding for neighborhoods that differ in their income mixes. We assume that the positive externalities from neighbors increase with income. This means that the attractiveness of a neighborhood increases with the number of high-income households. Will neighborhoods be integrated, with a mixture of high-income and low-income households, or will they be segregated?

We will use a model developed by Becker and Murphy (2000). Consider a city with two neighborhoods (A and B) and two income groups (high income and low income), each with 100 households. The only difference between the two neighborhoods is in their income mixes and the resulting neighborhood externalities. Each household occupies one unit of land, and there is a fixed amount of land in each neighborhood—just enough to accommodate 100 households. In Figure 8–3 (page 168), the horizontal axis measures the number of high-income households in neighborhood A. Since each neighborhood has a total of 100 households, the number of low-income households in a neighborhood is 100 minus the number of high-income households.

The vertical axis in Figure 8–3 measures the difference in land rent between the two neighborhoods. Specifically, it measures the rent in the high-income neighborhood minus the rent in the low-income neighborhood. The horizontal axis starts at 50 high-income households, so under the assumption that high-income households generate positive externalities from role models and school peers, the rent premium is always positive, and the larger the number of high-income households, the larger the premium.

Segregation Equilibrium

The positively sloped curves in Figure 8–3 show the rent premiums for the two income groups. For example, suppose neighborhood A has 55 high-income households

FIGURE 8–3 Segregation Equilibrium

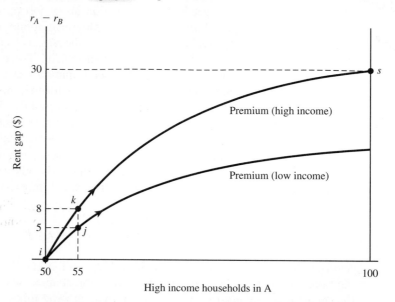

If high-income households have a steeper premium curve, the integrated outcome
(point *i*, with 50 of each type of household in A) is unstable. Segregation (shown by
point *s*) is the equilibrium, with all 100 high-income households in A. The equilibrium
rent gap is $30: Rent is $30 higher in neighborhood A.

and 45 low-income households, and the numbers are reversed in neighborhood B. As
shown by point *k*, a high-income household is willing to pay $8 more to live in neigh-
borhood A rather than B. Similarly, point *j* shows that the low-income household is
willing to pay a $5 premium for neighborhood A. At point *i*, the two neighborhoods
are identical (50 high-income and 50 low-income households in each), so the rent
premium is zero. The premium curves are positively sloped, reflecting the positive
externalities from the high-income population.

Equilibrium requires that all households in a particular neighborhood pay the
same rent. If they didn't, landowners with low prices would have an incentive to
raise them, and households on expensive land would have an incentive to change
locations. In our model of two household types, equilibrium requires that high-
income and low-income households in a particular neighborhood pay the same rent.

The integrated outcome shown by point *i* is a symmetric but unstable equilibrium. It is symmetric because the two neighborhoods are identical. It is an equilibrium
because the two premium curves intersect, meaning that both types pay the same rent
premium for neighborhood A (zero when the neighborhoods are identical). Point *i* is
unstable because a small movement of population will generate a different equilibrium. Suppose a group of five high-income households moves from neighborhood
B to A, displacing five low-income households who move the other direction.
Neighborhood A, with 55 high-income households, now has a more favorable

mix of households than B, and both types of households are willing to pay more to live in A.

- High-income households are willing to pay an $8 premium (point k).
- Low-income households are willing to pay a premium of only $5 (point j).

High-income households will outbid low-income households, so after the first five high-income households move into the neighborhood, others will join them, displacing low-income households and leading us away from point i, not back toward it.

A deviation from the integrated outcome triggers self-reinforcing changes. In Figure 8–3, the arrows on the premium curves indicate the direction of movement. Whenever the high-income premium curve is above the low-income curve, high-income households will outbid low-income households, and the high-income population will increase (we move to the right). The high-income curve lies everywhere above the low-income curve, so the high-income population will continue to increase at the expense of the low-income population until neighborhood A has only high-income households (shown by point s). Recall the second axiom of urban economics:

Self-reinforcing changes lead to extreme outcomes

In this case, the self-reinforcing change is an increase in the number of high-income households in neighborhood A. This change makes the neighborhood even more attractive to high-income households, and the extreme outcome is that all high-income households locate in one neighborhood.

Point s represents income segregation because all the high-income households are in neighborhood A and all the low-income households are in neighborhood B. Although low-income households value proximity to high-income households, the high-income households value proximity to high-income households even more, so they outbid low-income households for the limited number of places in the more desirable neighborhood. In graphical terms, segregation happens because high-income households have a steeper premium curve, reflecting a larger marginal benefit of living close to high-income households. A one-unit increase in the number of high-income households increases the premium of high-income households by a larger amount, so they outbid low-income households for the more desirable neighborhood.

Integration as a Stable Equilibrium

We've seen an example in which income integration is an unstable equilibrium. Under what circumstances would the integrated equilibrium be stable? The stability of integration is determined by the slopes of the premium curves.

Figure 8–4 (page 170) shows integration as a stable equilibrium. In this case, low-income households have a steeper premium curve. Suppose we start at point i, and five high-income households move to neighborhood A. What happens next?

- As shown by point h, a low-income household is willing to pay a premium of $12 for a neighborhood with 55 high-income households.
- As shown by point k, a high-income household is willing to pay a premium of only $8 for a neighborhood with more high-income households.

FIGURE 8–4 Integration is a Stable Equilibrium

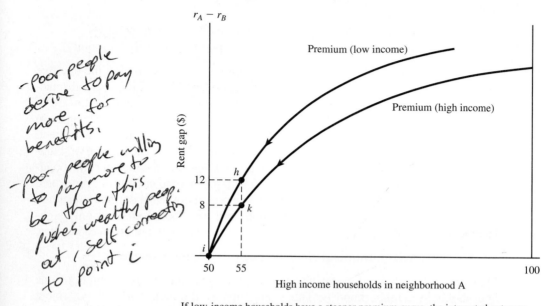

(handwritten margin notes:)
- poor people desire to pay more for benefits.
- poor people willing to pay more to be there, this pushes wealthy peop. at i self correcting to point i

If low-income households have a steeper premium curve, the integrated outcome (point *i*, with 50 of each type of household in neighborhood A) is stable. Any deviation from the integrated outcome is self-correcting. In equilibrium, rent is the same in the two neighborhoods.

Low-income households will outbid high-income households, so the number of low-income households will increase at the expense of high-income households.

The arrows along the premium curves indicate the direction of the change if we start at any point other than the integrated outcome (point *i*). If high-income households outnumber low-income households (if the number of high-income households exceeds 50), low-income households will outbid high-income households, and we will move back toward point *i*. In other words, any deviation from the integration outcome is self-correcting, not self-reinforcing. Integration is stable because low-income households are willing to pay more than high-income households to live in a neighborhood with more high-income households.

Mixed Neighborhoods

A third possibility is a mixed neighborhood, with an income mix between perfect segregation and perfect integration. For example, we could have one neighborhood with 70 percent high-income households and a second with 70 percent low-income households. This is shown in Figure 8–5, where the two premium curves for neighborhood A intersect at a quantity of 70 high-income households (and 30 low-income households). That leaves 30 high-income households and 70 low-income households for neighborhood B.

FIGURE 8–5 Mixed Neighborhood Equilibrium

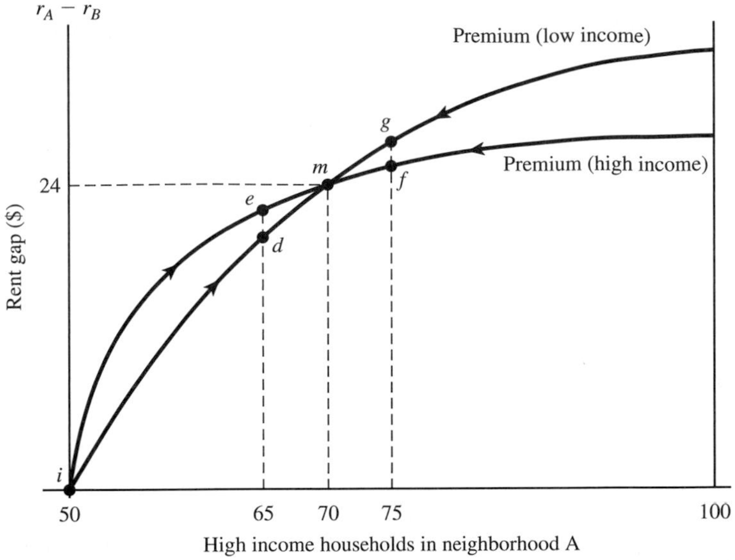

If the two premium curves cross, with a steeper curve for low-income households, the intersection point is a stable equilibrium. At point *m*, 70 of 100 households in neighborhood A are high-income, and the rent gap is $24.

Point *m* is a stable equilibrium. It is an equilibrium because the two premium curves intersect there, indicating that in neighborhood A, both types of households pay the same premium. Point *m* is stable because the premium curve for the low-income households is steeper at that point. To test for stability, consider two deviations from point *m*.

- **More high-income households.** Suppose the number of high-income households increases from 70 to 75. As shown by points *f* and *g*, low-income households are now willing to pay a bigger premium so they will outbid high-income households, and the high-income population will shrink back to 70.

- **Fewer high-income households.** Suppose the number of high-income households shrinks from 70 to 65. As shown by points *d* and *e*, high-income household are now willing to pay a bigger premium so they will outbid low-income households, and the high-income population will expand back to 70.

In the equilibrium with mixed neighborhoods, the equilibrium premium is $24. Recall the first axiom of urban economics:

Prices adjust to generate locational equilibrium

For equilibrium in the market for neighborhoods, each type of household, high-income and low-income, must be indifferent between the two neighborhoods. With a premium of $24, each household in neighborhood A pays $24 extra to live in the neighborhood with the more favorable income mix. This premium exactly offsets the benefits of the more favorable income mix, so we have a locational equilibrium.

Lot Size and Public Policy

Up to this point, we have assumed that each household occupies one unit of land. Of course, land is a normal good, and consumption increases with income. What are the implications of variable lot sizes for neighborhood choice and income segregation?

As we'll see, when high-income households consume more land, integration is more likely. As a starting point, consider the situation shown in Figure 8–3. A high-income household is willing to pay a premium of $8 to live in a neighborhood with 55 high-income households, while the premium for the low-income household is only $5. If both types of households occupy one unit of land, high-income households outbid low-income households, leading to segregation.

Things are different when the high-income household consumes more land. Suppose high-income households occupy two units of land, compared to only one unit for low-income households. The high-income premium of $8 translates into only a $4 premium *per unit of land*. As shown in Table 8–4, the high-income household has a lower premium per unit of land, so low-income households will outbid high-income households for land in the more desirable neighborhood. As a result, any deviation from the integrated equilibrium (e.g., 55 high-income households) will cause self-correcting (not self-reinforcing) changes as low-income households outbid high-income households. The result is integration, the symmetric equilibrium with 50 households of each type in each neighborhood.

Another way to think about the effects of lot size is to take the perspective of landowners, who of course maximize their rental income. If you have two units of land to rent, you can either rent to a single high-income household for $8 or to a pair of low-income households, each paying $5 for a total of $10. Obviously the pair of low-income households is a better choice. A high-income household loses the bidding battle because it competes against two low-income households.

This example illustrates the importance of land consumption in neighborhood choice and diversity. If the difference in land consumption between the two types of households is large relative to the difference in the premium, the low-income household will have a larger premium per unit of land, and integration will occur. On the other hand, if the difference in land consumption is relatively small, segregation will occur. For example, if the high-income household occupied only 1.33 units of

TABLE 8–4 Lot Size and Integration

	Premium for High-income Community	Lot Size	Premium per Unit of Land
Low income	$5	1	$5
High income	$8	2	$4

land, its premium per unit of land would be $6 per unit of land ($8/1.33), and segregation will persist.

Minimum Lot Size Zoning and Segregation

Some local governments use minimum lot size zoning to control land use. Under this policy, the government specifies a minimum lot size for residential development and outlaws higher density. As we'll see in a later chapter, one motivation for such a policy is to exclude people whose tax contributions fall short of the costs they impose on local government.

One of the consequences of this zoning policy is income segregation. In Table 8–4, integration is a stable equilibrium when high-income households occupy twice as much land as low-income households. Suppose the government specifies a minimum lot size of two units of land, the quantity chosen by high-income households. This policy imposes an extra cost on low-income households—they have to buy twice as much land as they want—and it decreases their premium per unit of land to $2.5, now less than the $4 premium of the high-income household. Once low-income households are forced to consume the same amount of land as high-income households, they lose the bidding war for land in the more desirable neighborhood. The result is that integration (the market-equilibrium outcome) is replaced by segregation.

SCHOOLS AND NEIGHBORHOOD CHOICE

In this part of the chapter, we take a closer look at the role of schools in neighborhood choice. One piece of evidence that schools matter in neighborhood choice is that real-estate agents provide prospective home buyers all sorts of data about the test scores and college-attendance rates of neighborhood schools.

Educational Achievement and Attainment across Neighborhoods

In the typical metropolitan area, educational achievement varies across schools. Table 8–5 shows the distribution of test scores in New York City and Portland. At the top 10 percent of New York schools, 94 percent of students scored above the

TABLE 8–5 Student Performance across Schools

	New York: Percentage of Students above Lowest Level	Portland: Percentage Meeting State Standard
Top 10% of schools	94	77
Top 20% of schools	90	72
Bottom 20% of schools	58	27
Bottom 10% of schools	45	24

Sources: "Quality Counts.," *Education Week,* 1998; Oregon Department of Education Report Cards.

TABLE 8–6 Percentage of Adults with College Degrees across Census Tracts

	Boston	Seattle
Minimum	5%	7%
10th percentile	12%	25%
20th percentile	16%	30%
Median	32%	48%
80th percentile	57%	64%
90th percentile	69%	70%
Maximum	89%	90%

Source: 2000 Census.

lowest performance level, compared to only 45 percent of students at the bottom 10 percent of schools. At the top 10 percent of high schools in Portland, 77 percent of students meet the state standard for mathematical problem solving, compared to only 24 percent at the bottom 10 percent of schools.

One measure of the educational attainment of a community is the share of the population that has a college degree. Table 8–6 shows the distribution of college degrees among adults (25 years or older) across census tracts in two cities. For Boston, the college rate ranges from a minimum of 5 percent to a maximum of 89 percent. The degree rate for the 10th percentile (10 percent of tracts have lower degree rates) is 12 percent, about one-sixth the rate for the 90th percentile. The data for Seattle shows roughly the same range but has a higher median and a more even distribution.

Another measure of educational attainment in a neighborhood is the high-school dropout rate. In Boston, the median dropout rate is 25 percent and the maximum is 89 percent. Seattle has a lower median (8 percent) and maximum (47 percent). In Cleveland, most of the neighborhoods with high dropout rates are in the central city, where only one neighborhood had a dropout rate less than 20 percent, but 11 had dropout rates above 50 percent.

The Education Production Function

The education production function shows the relationship between inputs to the education process and educational achievement. Achievement is typically measured by scores on standardized cognitive tests. The production function can be written as

$$\text{Achievement} = f(H, P, T, S)$$

where the inputs are the student's home environment (H), the quality of the peer group (P), the quality of the teacher (T) and the size of the class (S).

Dozens of studies have explored the relationship between inputs and achievement. The key question is, Which inputs are most productive in increasing test scores?

1. **Home environment.** This is the most important input. Parents can provide a favorable home environment by encouraging reading and studying. In general, the higher the income and education level of the parents, the better the home environment and the higher the child's educational achievement.

2. **Peer group.** A student learns more when he or she is surrounded by fellow students who are smart, motivated, and not disruptive. Good peers come from home environments that encourage achievement. There is some evidence that the largest peer group effects are experienced by low achievers: The students at the bottom of the class have the most to gain from adding smart and motivated students to the class. There is also evidence that these peer effects are most important in the middle and upper grades (grades 5 through 12).

3. **Teachers.** Teachers are not standardized inputs like blackboards but vary in effectiveness. A study of inner-city schools found that during a single academic year, a student taught by a high-quality teacher outperforms a child taught by a low-quality teacher by up to one full grade level. Rivkin, Hanushek, and Kain (1998) provide evidence of substantial variation in teacher productivity, with the largest difference among math teachers. The most productive teachers have superior communication skills. Studies have consistently shown that graduate coursework (e.g., a Master's degree) does not affect teacher productivity. The effectiveness of teachers increases with experience, but only for the first few years of teaching.

4. **Class size.** In the STAR experiment in Tennessee, students and their teachers were randomly assigned to different class sizes for the first four years of school. Krueger (1999) and Krueger and Whitmore (2001) show that students in small classes had higher test scores in grade school, and later were more likely to take college-entrance exams. The largest benefits from small classes were experienced by minority students.

A traditional study of the education production function uses test scores as a measure of output. An alternative approach uses the wages earned by adults as the "output" from earlier schooling. There is an ongoing debate among economists about the relationship between school spending and future earnings. Card and Krueger (1996) conclude that increases in school spending increase adult earnings. Heckman, Layne-Farrar, and Todd (1996) question the validity of the Card-Krueger results concluding that, "The evidence . . . is not decisive on the question of whether schooling inputs can increase earnings."

Education Production and Neighborhood Choice

The studies of the education production function shows that a family's choice of a neighborhood affects the education level of its children. One of the most important inputs to the production process is the peer group, and there is substantial variation in peer groups across neighborhoods, reflecting differences in income and educational level. In addition, spending per student varies across schools, generating differences in the quality of teachers and class sizes, and differences in educational achievement.

What are the implications for income segregation? We saw earlier that neighborhood externalities such as school peer effects encourage income segregation if high-income households are willing to pay more than low-income households to get access to superior school peers. Looking back at our discussion of local public goods, if high-income households have a higher preferred level of spending on schools, another reason for income segregation is sorting with respect to the demand for schooling.

CRIME AND NEIGHBORHOOD CHOICE

Another factor in neighborhood choice is crime. Table 8–7 shows the distribution of crime rates across census tracts in Cleveland and Portland. The Cleveland crime rate is the number of property crimes per 100,000 population per year. On the low end, the crime rate for the 10th percentile (10 percent of census tracts have lower crime rates) is 3,059. At the other end, the crime rate for the 90th percentile is over six times higher. Crime rate generally increases with the number of low-income households in the census tract.

The Portland data is the victim cost per capita per year. The victim costs of crime include the opportunity cost of lost work time, monetary losses, and the costs of injuries. Miller, Cohen, and Wiersema (1996) estimated the costs for different crimes as follows: $370 for larceny, $1,500 for burglary, $4,000 for auto theft, $13,000 for armed robbery, and $15,000 for assault. The median crime cost is $244 per person per year, and the crime rate for the 90th percentile is almost nine times the rate for the 10th percentile. As in Cleveland in other cities, crime is generally higher in low-income neighborhoods.

The substantial variation in crime rates mean that a household's choice of a neighborhood is influenced by crime. Households are willing to pay a premium to live in low-crime neighborhoods. A study of property crime (Thaler, 1977) estimates an elasticity of property values with respect to the crime rate of –0.067: A 10 percent increase in the crime rate decreases the market value of housing by about 0.67 percent, or $1,340 on a house worth $200,000.

What are the implications of crime for income segregation? Crime rates are generally lower in high-income neighborhoods, providing another attraction for all households, high-income and low-income. Which type of household is willing to pay more for low-crime neighborhoods? A recent study suggests that the willingness to pay for crime reduction increases with income (Cohen, Rust, Steen, and

TABLE 8–7 Distribution of Crime Rates across Census Tracts

	Cleveland: Property Crime per 100,000 Population	Portland: Crime Cost per Capita
10th Percentile	3,059	$ 69
20th Percentile	4,158	$122
Median	5,403	$244
80th Percentile	11,541	$451
90th Percentile	19,668	$616

Sources: Author's calculations from data from Portland Police Bureau and Center for Urban Poverty and Social Change, Case Western Reserve University.

Tidd, 2004). Cullen and Levitt (1999) conclude that high-income households are more sensitive to crime: They flee in larger numbers when crime rates increase. These studies suggest that high-income households are willing to pay more than low-income households to live in low-crime (high-income) neighborhoods, so crime encourages income segregation.

RACIAL SEGREGATION

The framework we've used to explore income segregation can also be used to explore the issue of racial segregation. In the United States, more than two-thirds of the blacks living in metropolitan areas reside in central cities, leaving one-third of metropolitan blacks for suburban areas. For whites, the fractions are reversed: One-third live in central cities, leaving two-thirds for the suburbs.

One way to quantify the degree of racial segregation in a metropolitan area is the index of dissimilarity. This index shows the proportion of one race (e.g., blacks or African Americans) that must relocate to achieve racial integration, with each census tract in the metropolitan area having the same racial mix. For the United States, the index of 0.64 indicates that to achieve complete integration, 64 percent of blacks (or whites) would need to relocate. The dissimilarity index is highest for metropolitan areas in the Northeast (0.75) and lowest in the West (0.48).

Between 1980 and 2000, racial segregation as measured by the dissimilarity index decreased in 203 of 220 metropolitan areas. The average reduction was 12 percent, and 13 of the 43 largest metropolitan areas experienced reductions of at least 15 percent, while 6 experienced reductions of at least 20 percent. In 2000, the six most segregated metropolitan areas were Detroit, Milwaukee, New York, Newark, Chicago, and Cleveland. Between 1980 and 2000, these metropolitan areas experienced relatively small reductions in segregation.

Racial Preferences and Neighborhood Choice

What causes racial segregation? One factor is household preferences for the racial mix of neighborhoods. While a majority of blacks would prefer to live in integrated neighborhoods, a majority of whites prefer segregated neighborhoods. Whites and blacks also differ in what they consider an integrated neighborhood. For the typical black household, an integrated neighborhood is one that is equally divided between whites and blacks. For the small number of whites who prefer integrated neighborhoods, an integrated neighborhood is one in which 80 percent of the residents are white and only 20 percent are black.

Figure 8–6 (page 178) applies the neighborhood choice model to the issue of racial preferences and segregation. The positively sloped premium curve reflects the general preferences of whites for whiter neighborhoods. In contrast, the inverted U shows the premium curve for blacks, who prefer integrated neighborhoods to segregated ones. The black curve reaches its maximum at a neighborhood population that is 64 percent white. We assume that beyond this point, black households are willing to pay less for whiter neighborhoods.

FIGURE 8–6 Racial Segregation

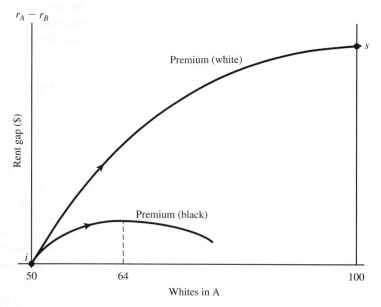

The premium curves reflect racial preferences: White households prefer to live in segregated neighborhoods, while black households prefer integration. Because the white curve lies everywhere above the black curve, the equilibrium in this case is segregation (point *s*).

Because the white curve lies everywhere above the black curve, the only stable equilibrium involves racial segregation. As we saw earlier, although the integration outcome (point *i*), is an equilibrium, it is not stable. If one or more white households moved to neighborhood A, the premium of whites would exceed the premium of blacks, so the white population will grow at the expense of the black household. The segregation equilibrium shown by point *s* is the only stable equilibrium.

What would be required to generate a stable integrated equilibrium? The slope of the black premium curve must be steeper than the white curve at the origin (50 white and 50 black households in neighborhood A). In this case, a deviation from the integrated outcome would be self-correcting because if the white population increased above 50, blacks would outbid whites for the limited number of places in the neighborhood.

Other Reasons for Racial Segregation

We've seen that racial preferences can lead to the extreme outcome of complete segregation. A second reason for racial segregation is income segregation. Black households have lower incomes on average. As explained by Mills and Lubuele (1997) housing is less expensive in the inner city, and this attracts low-income households, some of which are black. Several studies have shown that income segregation explains only a part of racial segregation.

- schools
- crime rates
- lot sizing
- result in racial segregation

A related factor is exclusionary zoning by suburban governments. As we saw earlier in the chapter, minimum lot-size zoning encourages income segregation, and so do other policies such as the prohibition of multifamily units, maximum densities, requirements for two-car garages, and development fees. Since black households have lower incomes, on average, than white families, exclusionary zoning has a larger effect on black households.

Another factor in racial segregation is racial discrimination by real-estate brokers. One technique is *racial steering*: The broker directs individual buyers away from predominantly white neighborhoods. According to Yinger (1998), blacks are treated differently from otherwise identical whites: Blacks are shown fewer dwellings, steered into certain neighborhoods, and given less advice and assistance on financing options. For example, 1 in 10 black renters is denied access to housing made available to white renters, and 1 in 4 learns about fewer vacant dwellings.

Until recently, federal housing policies have indirectly encouraged segregation. Historically, most public housing was concentrated in low-income areas, and until recently, housing vouchers (coupons used to help pay for private housing) could be used only in the city where the recipient lived when the voucher was issued. More recently, the federal government made most housing vouchers portable, so more recipients can use them to rent suburban housing.

CONSEQUENCES OF SEGREGATION

Why should we care about income and racial segregation? The concentration of low-income workers in the central city, far from suburban jobs, will reduce employment opportunities for low-income households. In addition, the imitative behavior that generates neighborhood externalities may transmit poverty from one generation to another. If there aren't many successful adults in a low-income neighborhood, youngsters won't have many good role models. If there aren't many high-achieving students in schools, children won't learn as much in schools.

The Spatial Mismatch

The concentration of low-income and minority households in central-city areas increases urban poverty because the bulk of metropolitan jobs are in suburban areas. The first evidence for the spatial mismatch is from Kain (1968), who estimated that racial segregation in Chicago decreased employment opportunities for blacks by more than 20,000 jobs.

Figure 8–7 (page 180) shows recent changes in employment in different areas in the San Francisco Bay Area (Rafael, 1998). Total employment increased by 23 percent in mostly white areas, but increased by only 1 to 2 percent in areas with larger black populations. Manufacturing employment increased slightly in mostly white areas, but decreased substantially in areas with larger black populations. Over half of low-skilled black workers are employed in manufacturing, transportation, communication, utilities, construction, or public administration. Employment in these sectors increased by 4 percent in the metropolitan area but decreased near areas with larger black populations.

FIGURE 8–7 Changes in Employment by Neighborhood Racial Composition

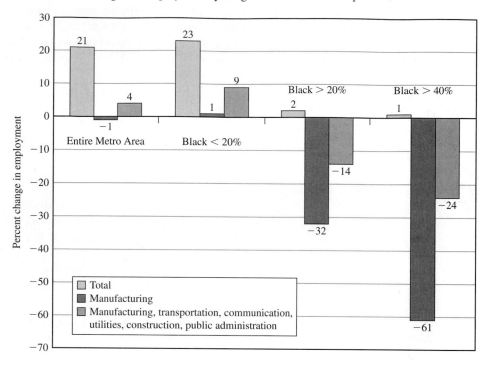

Source: Author's calculations based on Steven Rafael. "The Spatial Mismatch Hypothesis and Black Youth Joblessness: Evidence from the San Francisco Bay Area." *Journal of Urban Economics* 43 (1998), pp. 79–111

The spatial mismatch means that blacks have relatively high commuting costs. For low-income workers, the average one-way commute in 1990 was 26 minutes for white workers and 30 minutes for black workers (O'Regan and Quigley, 1998). After controlling for various factors such as earnings, housing prices, and neighborhood amenities, Gabriel and Rosenthal (1989) conclude that black workers commute roughly 22 percent longer than comparably skilled white workers. The longer commuting distances decrease the net wage of black workers and reduce the time available for work and other activities.

The longer commuting also decreases the employment rates of young black workers (Ihlanfeldt and Sjoquist,1990). Black youths in Philadelphia had an employment rate of 27 percent, compared to 49 percent for white youths. One reason for the relatively low employment rate is that the average commute time for blacks was 26 minutes, compared to only 19 minutes for whites. The difference in commuting distances explains between a third and a half of the differences in employment rates in Philadelphia.

What do we know about the relative importance of the spatial mismatch? Ihlanfeldt and Sjoquist (1990) tested the mismatch hypothesis in 50 metropolitan areas and came to the following conclusions.

- Overall, inferior access to jobs explains about 25 percent of the gap between the employment rates of black and white workers and about 31 percent of the gap between Hispanic and white employment rates.
- The spatial mismatch is more important in larger metropolitan areas. The mismatch explains only 3 percent of the black-white gap in small cities, compared to 14 percent in medium-sized cities and 25 percent in large cities.

Schools and the Poverty Trap

The allocation of school resources can contribute to a poverty trap. A low-income community is likely to spend less on schools, so its children are likely to get an inferior education. Many low-income neighborhoods have severe problems with drug abuse, crime, marital instability, and health. Schools in these neighborhoods must devote far more time and resources to family and health crises and spend more on security and school safety. In addition, many kids in low-income neighborhoods have limited skills in English and are not well prepared for school (Orfield, 1998). These problems make it more costly to deliver a particular education program. In low-income neighborhoods, the combination of lower school funding and higher production costs leads to inferior education.

The facts on central-city education are grim. Students in central-city school districts are twice as likely as suburban students to drop out of high school. Schiller (1995) suggests that the education received by a black central-city high-school graduate is roughly equivalent to the education received by a white suburban dropout. In high-poverty urban school districts (defined as districts where at least 40 percent of the residents are below the poverty line), scores on standardized tests are very low. At grade eight, only six percent of students in high-poverty urban districts are proficient in math, and only nine percent are proficient in reading (Institute on Race and Poverty, 1998).

Some natural experiments have demonstrated the differences between central-city and suburban schools. The Gautreaux program in Chicago gives residents of public housing in the central city the opportunity to move to affordable housing in the suburbs. Among the children who moved to the suburbs, the high-school dropout rate was one-quarter of the rate for their central-city counterparts, and the college-attendance rate was twice that of the central-city students (Orfield, 1998). In Norfolk, Virginia, black students in integrated schools had much higher test scores than black students in more segregated schools (Meldrum and Eaton, 1994).

Racial Segregation Increases Poverty

Are black households better or worse off in cities that are more racially segregated? A recent study (Cutler and Glaeser, 1997) provides evidence that young black adults (people in their 20s) are much worse off in more segregated cities: They earn less income, have lower high school graduation rates and are more likely to be idle. Specifically, a 10 percent increase in segregation increases the probability of dropping out of high school by 4.9 percent and increases the likelihood of being idle (neither in school nor working) by 8.8 percent.

The study suggests that segregation has powerful effects on the economic prospects of black households, leading to lower employment rates and higher rates of single parenthood. An important factor in these adverse outcomes is that young people living in a highly segregated, low-income environment have fewer contacts with positive role models—educated and successful people—and so they are less likely to be successful themselves. In other words, neighborhood externalities matter.

SUMMARY

This chapter discusses the conditions that lead households to sort themselves into neighborhoods according to their demand for local public goods, their demand for taxed goods, income, and race. Here are the main points of the chapter:

1. If there is diversity in demand for local public goods, households will sort into municipalities and school districts that provide different levels of the public good.
2. If there is variation in the demand for a locally taxed good, people with relatively high demand for the good will have an incentive to form new municipalities with other high-demand households.
3. Neighborhood externalities occur because neighbors provide role models, share classrooms, and provide information about job prospects.
4. Income segregation occurs when high-income households are willing to pay a bigger premium than low-income households for high-income neighbors.
5. Large-lot zoning promotes income segregation by requiring low-income households to consume more land.
6. Racial segregation increases the frequency of unfavorable outcomes, such as dropping out of school and idleness, and increases poverty.

APPLYING THE CONCEPTS

1. **Property Tax versus Square Footage Tax**
   In Metro, there are three types of houses: E (expensive), M (medium), and C (cheap). All households prefer the same spending on public education. Schools are financed with the property tax (based on market value), and initially there are three school districts. Suppose the property tax is replaced by a square-foot tax (e.g., $2 per square foot of living space per year).
   a. Under what circumstances will the equilibrium number of school districts decrease to one?
   b. Under what circumstances will the equilibrium number of school districts increase to a number greater than three?
2. **Allocating Space on the Space Plane**
   Consider an organization that provides rides on a space plane, an aircraft that takes off like an airplane, flies up and away from the earth until it is just about to

go into orbit, and then returns to the earth. There will be a single trip, and the total weight limit for passengers is 20,000 pounds. The objective of the organization is to maximize its total revenue. There are two income groups: low and high.

  a. Under what conditions will all the space plane riders come from the low-income group? Defend your answer with a numerical example.
  b. How is this exercise related to the material in the chapter?

3. Age Sorting

Consider a metropolitan area where people prefer to live close to aged people. The larger the number of aged neighbors, the greater the willingness to pay to live in the neighborhood. There are two income groups, young and old.

  a. Depict graphically three different outcomes: integration, segregation, and mixed.
  b. Some communities have a minimum age for their residents, for example 50 years old. What do you suppose is the rationale for such a limit?

4. Multiple Equilibria with Race

Using Figure 8–6 as a starting point, suppose the premium curve for black households is an inverted U and lies above the white curve for a white population in the range 50–60 whites, but below the white curve for a larger white population. In other words, the two premium curves intersect at 60 white households.

  a. Identify the three equilibria.
  b. Which of the equilibria is stable, and which are unstable?
  c. What are the implications for the feasibility of mixed neighborhoods?

REFERENCES AND ADDITIONAL READING

1. Becker, G., and K. Murphy. *Social Economics.* Cambridge: Harvard University Press, 2000.
2. Card, David, and Alan Krueger. "Labor Market Effects of School Quality: Theory and Evidence." In *Does Money Matter?* ed. Gary Burtless. Washington DC: Brookings, 1996.
3. Cohen, M., R. Rust, S. Steen, S. Tidd. "Willingness-to-pay for Crime Control Programs." *Criminology* 42 (2004), pp. 89–109.
4. Cullen, J. B., and S. D. Levitt. "Crime, Urban Flight, and the Consequences for Cities." *Review of Economics and Statistics* 81 (1999), pp. 159–69.
5. Cutler, David M., and Edward L. Glaeser. "Are Ghettos Good or Bad?" *Quarterly Journal of Economics* (1997), pp. 827–72.
6. Durlauf, Steven. "Neighborhood Effects." Chapter 50 in *Handbook of Regional and Urban Economics 4: Cities and Geography,* eds. Vernon Henderson and Jacques-Francois Thisse. Amsterdam: Elsevier, 2004.
7. Gabriel, Stuart A., and Stuart S. Rosenthal. "Household Location and Race: Estimates of a Multinomial Logit Model." *Review of Economics and Statistics,* 1989, pp. 240–49.
8. Heckman, James, Anne Layne-Farrar, and Petra Todd. In *Does Money Matter?* ed. Gary Burtless. Washington DC: Brookings, 1996.

9. Ihlanfeldt, Keith R., and David L. Sjoquist. "Job Accessibility and Racial Differences in Youth Employment Rates." *American Economic Review* 8 (1990), pp. 267–76.
10. Institute on Race and Poverty. *Examining the Relationship between Housing, Education, and Persistent Segregation: Final Report.* Minneapolis: Institute on Race and Poverty, 1998.
11. Kain, John F. "Housing Segregation, Negro Employment, and Metropolitan Decentralization." *Quarterly Journal of Economics* 82 (1968), pp. 175–97.
12. Krueger, Alan. "Experimental Estimates of Education Production Functions." *The Quarterly Journal of Economics* 114 (1999), pp. 497–532.
13. Krueger, Alan and Diane Whitmore. "The Effect of Attending a Small Class in the Early Grades on College-Test Taking and Middle School Test Results: Evidence from Project STAR." *The Economic Journal* 111 (2001), pp. 1–28.
14. Meldrum, Christina, and Susan Eaton. "Resegregation in Norfolk, Virginia: Does Restoring Neighborhood Schools Work?" Report of the Harvard Project on School Desegregation (1994).
15. Mills, Edwin S.; and Luan Sende Lubuele, "Inner Cities." *Journal of Economic Literature* 35 (1977), pp. 727–56.
16. O'Regan, Katherine M., and John M. Quigley. "Cars for the Low-income." *Access* 12 (Spring 1998), pp. 20–25.
17. Orfield, Gary. "Desegregation, Resegregation, and Education." Part I of *In Pursuit of a Dream Deferred: Linking Housing and Education.* Minneapolis: Institute on Race and Poverty, 1995.
18. Rafael, Steven. "The Spatial Mismatch Hypothesis and Black Youth Joblessness: Evidence from the San Francisco Bay Area." *Journal of Urban Economics* 43 (1998), pp. 79–111.
19. Rivkin, Steven G., Eric A. Hanushek, and John F. Kain. "Teachers, Schools, and Academic Achievement." NBER Working Paper Number 6691 (1998).
20. Schiller, Bradley. *The Economics of Poverty and Discrimination,* 6th ed. Englewood Cliffs, NJ: Prentice-Hall, 1995.
21. Miller, T., M.A. Cohen, B. Wiersema. *Victim Costs and Consequence—A New Look.* Washington DC: National Institute of Justice, 1996.
22. Thaler, Richard. "Econometric Analysis of Property Crime—Interaction between Police and Criminals." *Journal of Public Economics* 8 (1977), pp. 37–51.
23. Yinger, John. "Evidence on Discrimination in Consumer Markets." *Journal of Economic Perspectives* 12, no. 2 (Spring 1998), pp. 23–40.

CHAPTER 9

Zoning and Growth Controls

Nimby (not in my back yard) is for wimps. The new acronym is Banana: build absolutely nothing anywhere near anybody.
—THE ECONOMIST 17 APRIL 1993

A tranquil city of good laws, fine architecture, and clean streets is like a classroom of obedient dullards, whereas a city of anarchy is a city of promise.

—MARK HELPRIN

*T*his chapter explores the government's role in the urban land market. So far we have assumed that land is allocated to the highest bidder. In fact, cities regulate land use, using land-use zoning plans to segregate different types of land use—commercial, industrial, and residential—into separate zones. Residential zones are typically divided into separate zones for low-density and high-density housing. We'll explore the causes and consequences of zoning, focusing on who wins and who loses.

Municipalities use a variety of policies to limit their population growth. Some cities tax new development to discourage growth, and others limit the number of building permits. Some cities limit the amount of land that can be developed, either by limiting the extent of urban services such as roads, sewers, and water or by establishing an urban growth boundary. In the Portland area, a metropolitan authority overseas an urban growth boundary over the entire metropolitan area. We'll explore the trade-offs associated with growth controls, showing who wins and who loses.

LAND-USE ZONING

Urban land-use zoning dates back to 1870 in Germany and was first implemented in the United States in New York City in 1916. The basic idea of zoning is to separate land uses that are "incompatible" in some sense. As we'll see, local governments have adopted a flexible definition of "incompatible."

The Early History of Zoning

Fischel (2004) summarizes the history of land-use zoning in the United States. Before comprehensive zoning, many cities used ordinances to control land use in specific areas. For example, to address concerns that skyscrapers would block views and light, cities regulated tall buildings. New York City implemented the first comprehensive zoning plan in 1916, and eight other cities adopted zoning plans in the same year. By 1936, zoning had spread to over 1,300 cities.

Why didn't zoning develop earlier? Fischel argues that the urban transportation technology of the late 19th and early 20th centuries made zoning unnecessary, at least from the perspective of suburban homeowners. As we saw earlier in the book, manufacturers transported their output on horse-drawn wagons, a slow and expensive mode that required firms to locate close to the city's central port or railroad terminal. The main form of public transit was the hub-and-spoke streetcar system. Low-income households lived in apartments close to the city center or along the spokes of the streetcar system. Commercial activities and apartments located along the streetcar lines, generating neighborhoods with mixed land use. Most homeowners lived a few blocks from the streetcar lines—inside the spokes—in neighborhoods separated from industry, commerce, and apartments. Homeowners placed a high value on their quiet, low-density neighborhoods and organized to prevent the extension of streetcar lines that would disturb their peace.

Innovations in transportation increased the location options for business, setting the stage for industrial zoning. Before the intracity truck, the externalities generated by industry and commerce (pollution, noise, congestion) were confined to the central areas of the city, far from the homes of suburban homeowners. The intracity truck (which dates to 1910), allowed firms to move away from the city's central export node and closer to their suburban workers. Once firms became more footloose, cities implemented zoning to separate industry from homes. A headline from the *New York Times* in 1916 read "Zoning Act Removes Fear of Business Invasion."

Innovations in mass transit increased the location options for workers, setting the stage for residential zoning. The motorized passenger bus, developed in 1920, allowed low-income workers to live between the spokes of the streetcar systems, where homeowners had been insulated from high-density housing. Cities developed residential zoning to keep apartments out of homeowner neighborhoods. In the leading case on the constitutionality of zoning (*Euclid* v. *Ambler* [1924]), U.S. Supreme Court Justice Sutherland wrote that apartments are "a mere parasite, constructed in order to take advantage of the open spaces and attractive surroundings created by the residential character of the district."

Zoning as Environmental Policy?

Zoning can be used to separate pollution sources from residential areas. Recall the third axiom of urban economics:

Externalities cause inefficiency

Industrial firms generate all sorts of externalities, including noise, glare, dust, odor, vibration, and smoke. Zoning is appealing as an environmental policy because it is simple: The easiest way to reduce the exposure to pollution is to put a buffer between a polluter and its potential victims. The problem with zoning as an environmental policy is that it doesn't reduce pollution to its socially efficient level but simply moves it around.

The economic approach to pollution is to impose a tax on pollution equal to the external cost it imposes on society. A pollution tax forces a firm to pay for pollution in the same way that it pays for raw materials, capital, and labor. As a result, a firm has an incentive to economize on pollution in the same way that it economizes on raw materials and labor. In other words, a pollution tax reduces pollution to its socially efficient level.

What would happen if we simply replaced zoning with a pollution tax that didn't vary across space? We would expect some polluting firms to move closer to residential areas, so the exposure to pollution in some areas would increase. One approach would be to combine pollution taxes with zoning: By placing polluters in industrial zones and also imposing a tax, pollution could be reduced to the socially efficient level and exposure could be controlled. In fact, if zoning reduces the exposure to pollution, it also decreases the external cost of pollution and thus the pollution tax.

Retailers generate a number of externalities that affect nearby residents. Traffic generates congestion, pollution, noise, and parking conflicts. A traditional zoning plan deals with these externalities by confining retailers to special zones. A more flexible approach is to give retailers more location options while enforcing performance standards for parking, traffic, and noise. For example, a city can require retailers to provide adequate off-street parking, pay for improvements in the transportation infrastructure to handle extra traffic, and design the retail site to control noise and other externalities.

High-density housing may generate externalities. Like retailing activity, apartment and condominium complexes increase traffic, causing noise, congestion, and parking problems. In addition, tall buildings may block views and sunlight. An alternative to traditional zoning, which simply bans high-density housing in certain areas, is to use performance standards to prevent these externalities. Traffic problems can be prevented by street improvements, and parking problems can be avoided by requiring off-street parking. In addition, buildings can be designed to deal with the issues of lost views and sunlight.

Fiscal Zoning

Another motivation for zoning is to ensure that households or firms generate a fiscal surplus, not a deficit. A fiscal surplus occurs when a land user's tax bill exceeds the cost of public services provided. For example, a large retailer may pay a lot in property and sales taxes but not require much in local public services. If a commercial or industrial land user generates a fiscal surplus, the surplus will at least partly offset any negative externalities such as noise, traffic, or pollution. Some communities eagerly host firms and use the fiscal surplus to cut tax rates and spend more on local public services. In general, low-income communities more frequently make this trade-off between environmental quality and fiscal benefits (Evenson and Wheaton, 2003).

A fiscal deficit occurs when a firm or household pays less in taxes than it gets in public services. Local governments get about three-fourths of their tax revenue from the property tax, so a household's local tax liability is determined largely by the value of its house or apartment. A household's use of local public services such as education, recreation, and public safety depends in part on the number of people in the household. A large household in a small dwelling is more likely to generate a fiscal deficit for the local government.

One way to decrease the likelihood of fiscal deficits is to zone for minimum lot sizes. Housing and land are complementary goods, and in general the larger the lot, the higher the market value of the property (dwelling and land combined). A minimum lot size excludes some households that would generate fiscal deficits. For example, suppose a city breaks even on a family living in a house worth $200,000: The family's tax liability equals the cost of providing public services. One rule of thumb is that the market value of a property (for land and dwelling) is about five times the value of land. Therefore, requiring a household to live on a lot worth at least $40,000 is roughly equivalent to requiring the household to live in a $200,000 house.

We can use a simple formula to determine the minimum lot size. Given the rule of thumb that the property value is five times the land value,

$$v^* = 5 \cdot r \cdot s$$

where v^* = the target (breakeven) market value of the property, r is the price of land per acre, and s is the lot size (in acres). Rearranging the expression, we can solve for the target lot size:

$$s = \frac{v^*}{5 \cdot r}$$

For example, if the target value is $200,000 and the price of land is $80,000 per acre, the target lot size is 1/2 acre:

$$s = \frac{\$200,000}{5 \cdot \$80,000} = 0.50$$

Minimum Lot Zoning and the Space Externality

Another motivation for minimum lot-size zoning is to internalize an externality associated with residential space (Evenson and Wheaton, 2003). People value space between houses, and a larger lot size means more space between houses and higher utility for everyone in the neighborhood. Your neighbors benefit from your lot-size decision but don't pay for it, so there is an externality. Recall the third axiom of urban economics:

Externalities cause inefficiency

In this case, the positive space externality means that lots will be smaller than the socially efficient size. In picking a lot size, people ignore the benefits experienced by their neighbors, so lots are too small.

One response to the space externality is minimum-lot zoning. It establishes a minimum space between houses, with equal contributions of space by each household. For example, if zoning has the effect of establishing a 100-foot gap between houses, each household buys 50 feet of space between its house and the property line. In addition to increasing lot size, minimum-lot zoning enforces reciprocity in space decisions.

Provision of Open Space

Local governments provide open space in two ways. First, they provide public land in parks and greenbelts. Second, they use zoning to restrict the use of private land. For example, zoning may prevent agricultural land from being subdivided into small parcels for residential or commercial development.

Is zoning for open space efficient? The alternative is to purchase the land for public use. When a city pays for open space in the same way that it pays for fire trucks and schools, it bears the full cost of providing it. As a result, the city weighs the costs and benefits of open space and picks the socially efficient quantity. In contrast, when a city simply zones land as open space, the cost of the public good is shifted to the property owner. The government and voters face less than the full cost of open space and have an incentive to provide too much of it.

We can use Figure 9–1 to illustrate the inefficiency of open-space zoning. The marginal-benefit curve is negatively sloped, reflecting the assumption that citizens'

FIGURE 9–1 Open-Space Zoning

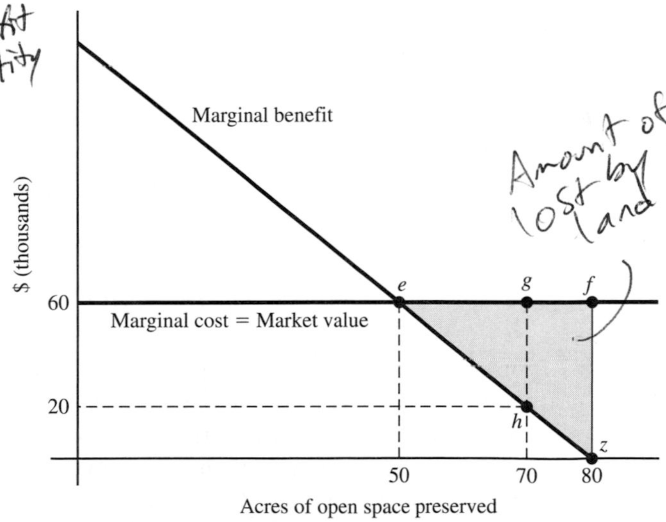

The marginal cost of open space is the market value of land in an alternative use. Point *e* shows the socially efficient quantity of open space, where the marginal benefit equals the marginal cost. If land is simply zoned for open space without compensation, the city will choose point *z*. The shaded triangle shows the deadweight loss.

compensation? According to Fischel (1985), the courts have provided mixed and confusing signals to local zoning authorities. The courts routinely uphold zoning laws that cause large losses in property values, suggesting that as long as the landowner is left with some profitable use of his land, compensation is not required. The courts have developed several rules to determine whether compensation is required.

1. **Physical invasion.** Compensation is required if the government physically occupies the land. The invasion rule is applicable only when the government actually occupies the land. It does not apply to most zoning actions in which the government merely restricts private land use.

2. **Diminution of value and reasonable beneficial use.** The origin of this rule is *Pennsylvania Coal* v. *Mahon* (1922), in which Justice Holmes states, ". . . while property may be regulated to a certain extent, if regulation goes too far it will be recognized as a taking." In other words, compensation is required if zoning decreases the property value by a sufficiently large amount. Unfortunately, the courts have not indicated how far zoning must go before compensation is required. A related rule is reasonable beneficial use: If zoning leaves the landowner with options that provide a reasonable rate of return, no compensation is required.

3. **Harm prevention.** According to this rule, compensation is not required if the zoning ordinance prevents a harmful use of the land. In other words, zoning is not a taking if it prevents the landowner from using land in ways that are detrimental to the general public. The harm-prevention rule suggests that a landowner, like a car owner, has limited property rights. The car owner has the right to drive her car, but she must stop at red lights. Should the driver be compensated for the opportunity cost of time spent waiting for the light to turn green? Since the traffic lights prevent a harmful use of the car, compensation is not required. Similarly, landowners have limited property rights: If zoning prevents the landlord from building a polluting factory in a residential district, compensation is unnecessary because zoning prevents a harmful use of the land. Most zoning ordinances are judged by a broad interpretation of the harm-prevention rule: If an ordinance promotes public health, safety, or welfare, compensation is usually not required.

A CITY WITHOUT ZONING?

What would an unzoned city look like? Would glue factories and pizza parlors invade quiet residential neighborhoods? Would land use be disorderly and ugly? Some tentative answers to these questions come from Siegan's (1972) analysis of Houston, the only metropolitan area in the United States without zoning. Land use in the city is controlled by restrictive covenants, voluntary agreements among landowners that limit land uses and structures. The covenants governing residential subdivisions (over 7,000 in number) are typically more strict than conventional zoning. They have detailed restrictions on architectural design, external appearance, and lot maintenance. The covenants for industrial parks limit the activities that can locate in the park.

Not tested?

Current zoning laws are the result of over 60 years of legal decisions. In the last six decades, individuals affected by specific zoning laws have sued local governments, forcing state and federal courts to rule on the constitutionality of zoning ordinances. If a particular type of zoning is declared unconstitutional, all cities get the message from the courts and rewrite their zoning ordinances to drop the illegal practices. On the other hand, if a zoning practice is upheld as constitutional, the practice spreads to other local governments. Court decisions have established three criteria for the constitutionality of zoning: substantive due process, equal protection, and just compensation.

Substantive Due Process

The case of *Euclid* v. *Ambler* (1924) established the standards for **substantive due process.** According to the due-process criterion, zoning must be executed for a legitimate public purpose using reasonable means. In the early 1920s, the city of Euclid, Ohio, enacted a zoning ordinance that restricted the location, size, and height of various types of buildings. Ambler Realty had purchased some property between the railroad tracks and a major thoroughfare and expected to sell the land to an industrial developer. When the city zoned its land for residential use, Ambler sued. The Supreme Court ruled against Ambler, concluding that the zoning ordinance satisfied the standards for substantive due process because it had some "reasonable relation" to the promotion of "health, safety, morals, and general welfare." In other words, zoning to separate different land uses is a legitimate use of the city's police power because it promotes public health and safety.

One interpretation of the *Euclid* v. *Ambler* decision is that a zoning ordinance is constitutional as long as it generates some benefit for the local community. The court did not say that the benefit of zoning must exceed its cost, only that the benefit must be positive. Fischel (1985) calls this benefit analysis, as opposed to benefit-cost analysis. The court defined the possible social benefits from zoning in broad terms, to include monetary, physical, spiritual, and aesthetic benefits.

As an example of the use of the benefit criterion to justify zoning, consider San Francisco's treatment of its Chinese population. In the 1880s, the city passed laws that explicitly segregated the Chinese. When explicit segregation was declared unconstitutional, the city passed a zoning law that banned laundries from certain neighborhoods. The zoning law did not violate the Constitution because it promoted public welfare by keeping an undesirable land use (laundries) out of some residential areas. Because the Chinese operated most of the city's laundries, the zoning law provided a legal means of ethnic segregation.

Equal Protection

The equal-protection clause of the Fourteenth Amendment requires that all laws be applied in an impersonal (nondiscriminatory) fashion. Zoning is exclusionary in the sense that it excludes some types of people from a city, for example, people who live in apartments instead of single-family dwellings. The plaintiffs in recent court cases have argued that zoning laws violate the equal-protection clause because they are not applied in an impersonal manner, but instead treat some people differently than others.

The federal courts have upheld the constitutionality of exclusionary zoning. In the *Euclid* v. *Ambler* decision, the Supreme Court suggested that although a zoning ordinance must generate some benefit for insiders (citizens of the community), the effects of zoning on outsiders are unimportant. In *Warth* v. *Selden* (1975), the court dismissed the claims of outsiders because they did not prove that the zoning ordinance caused specific personal damage. In *Village of Arlington Heights* v. *Metropolitan Housing Corporation* (1977), the court dismissed the claims of outsiders because they did not prove discriminatory intent on the part of zoning officials. In *Ybarra* v. *Town of Los Altos Hills,* the court ruled that although zoning laws that discriminate on the basis of race are unconstitutional, zoning laws that discriminate on the basis of income are legal. In general, the federal courts have adopted a noninterventionist approach to exclusionary zoning.

Some state courts have adopted a more activist role. In *Southern Burlington County NAACP* v. *Mount Laurel* (1975), the New Jersey Supreme Court ruled that Mount Laurel's exclusionary zoning harmed low-income outsiders. The court directed the city to develop a new zoning plan under which the city would accommodate its "fair share" of low-income residents. The court established quotas for communities to provide enough housing for low- and moderate-income workers to live within reasonable commuting distances of their jobs. The effects have been minor, in part because the state legislature modified the quotas and even allowed communities to buy and sell up to half their quotas (Mills and Lubuele, 1997).

Other states have also ruled on exclusionary zoning. The implication from *Associated Home Builders Inc.* v. *City of Livermore* (California Supreme Court, 1976) is that the courts will judge zoning on the basis of its effects on both insiders and outsiders. If a zoning ordinance does not represent a reasonable accommodation of the competing interests of insiders and outsiders, it may be declared unconstitutional. In Oregon, state law requires municipalities to plan and zone land for a diversity of housing types and income levels.

Just Compensation

The third criterion for the constitutionality of zoning is just compensation. The Fifth Amendment states ". . . nor shall private property be taken for public use, without just compensation." This is the taking clause: If the government converts land from private to public use, the landlord must be compensated. Most zoning ordinances do not actually convert land to public use, but merely restrict private use. For example, industrial zoning prevents a landowner from building a factory in a residential area, and minimum lot-size zoning prevents high-density housing. By restricting the use of private land, zoning decreases the market value of the property.

The policy issue is whether landowners should be compensated for the loss of property value caused by zoning. For example, if large-lot zoning decreases a landowner's property value by $5,000, should the local government pay $5,000 in

Not tested

compensation? According to Fischel (1985), the courts have provided mixed and confusing signals to local zoning authorities. The courts routinely uphold zoning laws that cause large losses in property values, suggesting that as long as the landowner is left with some profitable use of his land, compensation is not required. The courts have developed several rules to determine whether compensation is required;

1. **Physical invasion.** Compensation is required if the government physically occupies the land. The invasion rule is applicable only when the government actually occupies the land. It does not apply to most zoning actions in which the government merely restricts private land use.

2. **Diminution of value and reasonable beneficial use.** The origin of this rule is *Pennsylvania Coal* v. *Mahon* (1922), in which Justice Holmes states, ". . . while property may be regulated to a certain extent, if regulation goes too far it will be recognized as a taking." In other words, compensation is required if zoning decreases the property value by a sufficiently large amount. Unfortunately, the courts have not indicated how far zoning must go before compensation is required. A related rule is reasonable beneficial use: If zoning leaves the landowner with options that provide a reasonable rate of return, no compensation is required.

3. **Harm prevention.** According to this rule, compensation is not required if the zoning ordinance prevents a harmful use of the land. In other words, zoning is not a taking if it prevents the landowner from using land in ways that are detrimental to the general public. The harm-prevention rule suggests that a landowner, like a car owner, has limited property rights. The car owner has the right to drive her car, but she must stop at red lights. Should the driver be compensated for the opportunity cost of time spent waiting for the light to turn green? Since the traffic lights prevent a harmful use of the car, compensation is not required. Similarly, landowners have limited property rights: If zoning prevents the landlord from building a polluting factory in a residential district, compensation is unnecessary because zoning prevents a harmful use of the land. Most zoning ordinances are judged by a broad interpretation of the harm-prevention rule: If an ordinance promotes public health, safety, or welfare, compensation is usually not required.

A CITY WITHOUT ZONING?

What would an unzoned city look like? Would glue factories and pizza parlors invade quiet residential neighborhoods? Would land use be disorderly and ugly? Some tentative answers to these questions come from Siegan's (1972) analysis of Houston, the only metropolitan area in the United States without zoning. Land use in the city is controlled by restrictive covenants, voluntary agreements among landowners that limit land uses and structures. The covenants governing residential subdivisions (over 7,000 in number) are typically more strict than conventional zoning. They have detailed restrictions on architectural design, external appearance, and lot maintenance. The covenants for industrial parks limit the activities that can locate in the park.

How does Houston compare to zoned cities? Although a rigorous comparison of land-use patterns may be impossible, some tentative observations can be made:

1. **Dispersion of industry.** The spatial distribution of Houston's industrial firms is similar to that of zoned cities. As in other cities, Houston's industrial firms locate close to the transportation network (near railroads and highways) and tend to cluster to exploit localization economies.

2. **Retailers.** Few retailers locate in quiet residential neighborhoods. Like retailers in most cities, most retailers in Houston locate along major thoroughfares in strip developments and shopping centers to take advantage of large volumes of foot and auto traffic.

3. **Strip development.** Houston appears to have more strip development (retail and commercial establishments along arterial routes) than do zoned cities.

4. **Apartments.** Low-income housing is more plentiful and relatively inexpensive. There is a wide range of densities in apartment projects; the projects occupied by the wealthy have more open space and lower density, while the projects occupied by the poor have higher density.

There are two lessons from Houston's experience without zoning. First, in the absence of zoning, landowners have the incentive to negotiate restrictions on land use. It seems that neighborhood externalities are large enough to justify the cost of developing and enforcing restrictive covenants. This is the Coase solution to externalities (named after Ronald Coase): The parties affected by externalities negotiate a contract to solve the externality problem. Second, in the absence of zoning, most industrial firms cluster in locations accessible to the transportation network, and most retailers cluster in shopping centers and retail strips.

GROWTH CONTROL: URBAN GROWTH BOUNDARIES

Cities use a number of policies to restrict the amount of developed land and thus their population. A city can outlaw development beyond a growth boundary or restrict urban services such as roads, water, and sewers to certain areas. A survey completed in 1991 found that roughly a quarter of cities used urban service boundaries to limit their land areas. In this part of the chapter, we explore the consequences of these sorts of land restrictions.

We can use the utility curve developed in Chapter 4 to show the effects of growth boundaries on cities in a regional economy. We'll use the theoretical framework developed by Helsley and Strange (1995). Suppose we start with two identical cities in a regional economy. To simplify matters, we will assume that all city residents are renters, and land is owned by absentee landowners. Later in the chapter we'll explore the implications of changing this assumption. Figure 9–2 shows the initial utility curve for the typical city. Point i shows the initial equilibrium with 4 million workers in each city. The utility level is $72 in each city, so we have a locational equilibrium: No worker has an incentive to change cites.

FIGURE 9–2 Effects of Precise Growth Control in a Two-City Region

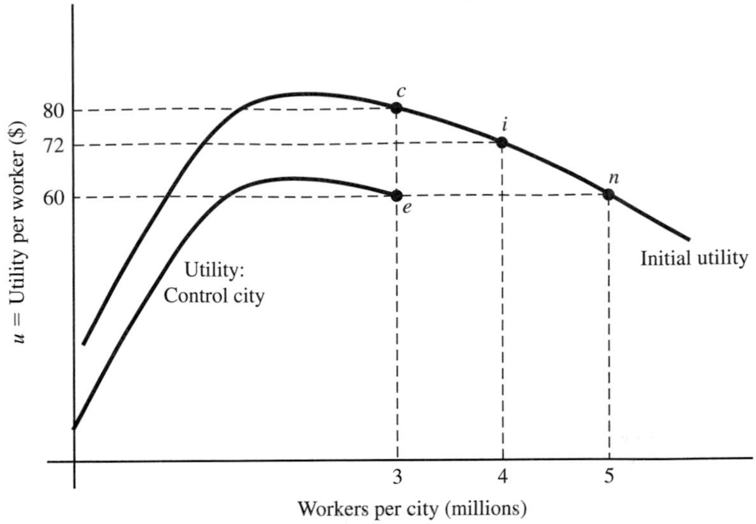

The initial equilibrium is shown by point *i*: Each of the two cities has a population of 4 million. A growth-control policy that reduces the population of the control city to 3 million (point *c*) and increases the population of the uncontrolled city to 5 million (point *n*), opens a utility gap of $20 (= $80 − $60). The resulting increase in the price of land in the control city shifts the city's utility curve downward until equilibrium is restored at points *e* and *n*.

Precise Growth Control: Limiting Land Area and Lot Size

Consider first the effects of precise growth control. Suppose one city caps the number of workers in the city by (a) specifying a minimum lot size per person and (b) fixing the total land area of the city. If the workforce of the controlled city is capped at 3 million, the workforce of the uncontrolled city must increase to 5 million to accommodate the fixed workforce of the region. Growth control in one city displaces workers to the other city.

The immediate effect of the policy is to generate a utility gap between the two cities. In Figure 9–2, utility in the control city rises from $72 (point *i*) to $80 (point *c*) as population decreases. In contrast, the increase in population in the other city decreases utility from $72 (point *i*) to $60 (point *n*). Workers are mobile between the two cities, so this utility gap will not persist. Recall the first axiom of urban economics:

Prices adjust to generate locational equilibrium

In this case, the workers of the region compete for a fixed number of lots in the control city, and the price of land in the control city will rise until the two cities have the same utility level, making workers indifferent between the two cities.

The increase in land rent in the control city shifts its utility curve downward. Recall that workers are renters, not property owners. An increase in land rent decreases the amount of money available to spend on consumer products, so the utility level drops. How low will utility go? Given the cap of 3 million workers in the control city, the uncontrolled city has a workforce of 5 million and a utility level of $60 (point *n*). In other words, the common (regionwide) utility level is anchored by point *n*. Land rent in the control city must rise to the point at which utility is $60. This is shown by point *e* on the lower utility curve for the control city. In the new locational equilibrium, the benefits of living in a smaller city (shorter commutes and less noise, dirt, and congestion) are fully offset by higher land rent.

Our analysis of growth control could be applied to a region with more cities. If the control city is one of 11 cities in a region rather than one of 2, the workers displaced by growth control would be spread among 10 other cities. Each uncontrolled city would experience a smaller increase in its workforce (100,000 instead of 1 million) and thus a smaller decrease in utility. Spreading out the displaced workers would mean a smaller utility loss per capita. This is sensible because when the control city is a small part of the regional economy, the per-capita effect of its policy will be relatively small.

Winners and Losers from Growth Boundaries

The growth-control policy decreases the utility of workers throughout the region. The workers in the uncontrolled city lose because their city grows, moving further downward along the negatively sloped utility curve. Both cities are initially too big, and the uncontrolled city moves even further from the optimum size. The workers in the controlled city lose too because locational equilibrium generates a common utility level, and utility in the control city is dragged down by the lower utility in the uncontrolled city.

The decrease in the common utility level reflects the basic inefficiency of replacing two identical cities with a large city and a small one. Recall that the immediate effect of the growth-control policy is shown by points *c* and *n*. Utility is higher in the smaller city ($80, compared to $60) so an efficient policy would move workers from the larger city to the smaller one. The growth-control policy prevents the efficient movement of workers so the common utility is lower than it would be with two cities of equal size.

Consider next the effects of the growth boundary on landowners in the control city. In Figure 9–3, the thin negatively sloped curve is the initial urban bid-rent curve, a composite of the residential and business bid-rent curves. The initial equilibrium is shown by point *i*, where the urban bid-rent curve intersects the horizontal agriculture bid-rent curve. The initial radius of the city is 12 miles. A growth boundary at 8 miles cuts off the last 4 miles from urban development so rent in this area drops to the agriculture rent (shown as the horizontal line between points *v* and *i*). Obviously, landowners who own land just outside the boundary are losers. In contrast, people who own land inside the boundary are winners. As we saw earlier, competition between workers for the fixed number of lots in the controlled city bids up lands rent. In Figure 9–3, the urban bid-rent curve shifts upward to the thick line, indicating higher rent on land inside the boundary.

FIGURE 9–3 Urban Growth Boundary and the Land Market

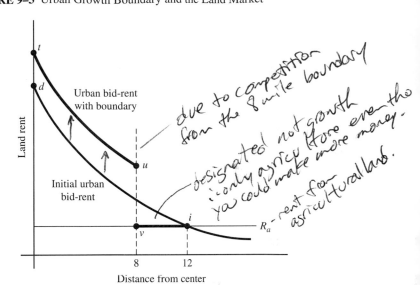

The initial equilibrium is shown by point i: The urban bid-rent curve intersects the agricultural bid-rent curve at 12 miles. An urban growth boundary at 8 miles from the center increases urban rent within 8 miles (the curve connecting points t and u) and decreases rent between 8 and 12 miles (the line connecting points v and i).

Urban Growth Boundary and Density

So far, we have considered a growth-control policy that precisely controls a city's population by limiting both the land area and lot size of the city. Suppose the city uses a growth boundary but does not restrict lot size. The immediate effects of a growth boundary are the same as the effects of the earlier policy, as shown in Figure 9–2 and reproduced in Figure 9–4 (page 198). We go from point i (4 million workers in each city) to points c in the growth-control city (3 million workers) and n in the other city (5 million workers). The utility gap is $20 (equal to $80 − $60). What happens next?

As before, the utility gap increases the price of land in the control city. When the price of land increases, density will increase as firms and people economize on land. Single-family homes will be built on smaller lots, and more people will live in high-density apartments and condominiums. Firms will occupy smaller lots and taller buildings. This increase in density weakens the growth boundary as a population-control policy: Higher density will partly offset the loss of urban land. In Figure 9–4, the new equilibrium is shown by points f and g, with 3.5 million workers in the growth-boundary city and 4.5 million in the other city. The new utility level is $67, compared to $60 with the earlier policy. Utility is higher with flexible density because the distortionary effects of growth control can be partially "undone" by increases in density.

FIGURE 9–4 Effects of an Urban Growth Boundary in a Two-City Region

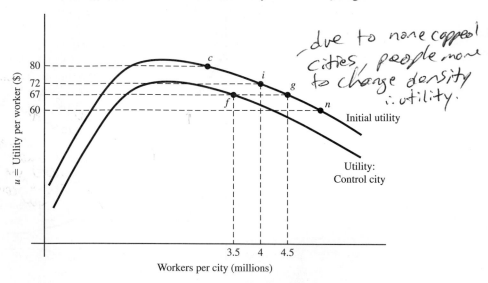

The initial equilibrium is shown by point *i*: Each of the two cities has a population of 4 million. If the control city does not limit lot size, the increase in the price of land resulting from a growth boundary will increase density, generating a population of 3.5 million (point *f*). Regional equilibrium is restored at points *f* and *g*, with a common utility level of $67 and a total of 8 million people in the two cities, with 3.5 million in the control city and 4.5 million in the other city.

Since an urban growth boundary increases density, is it an appropriate response to the problem of urban sprawl? As we saw earlier in the book, a number of public policies contribute to sprawl (low density) in U.S. cities, including the underpricing of travel and local public services, subsidies for housing, and exclusionary zoning. The efficient response to these distortions is to eliminate them directly, allowing individuals to make socially efficient location and density decisions. A growth boundary is a blunt tool to deal with the distortions for two reasons.

1. Although a growth boundary may change density in the correct direction, it may go too far or not far enough.
2. A growth boundary creates distortions of its own.

Portland's Urban Growth Boundary

The urban growth boundary in Portland, Oregon is a metropolitan boundary that is periodically expanded to accommodate growth. By law, there must be a 20-year supply of vacant land within the boundary, which was expanded by 4,000 acres in 1998 and by 1,940 acres in 2004. The recent expansion was implemented to increase the supply of land suitable for industrial development.

The Portland growth boundary differs from the growth-boundary policy we have discussed in two important respects. First, the Portland boundary is extended as the population of the metropolitan area increases. Second, the boundary is combined with a number of policies that promote rather than inhibit increases in density. The objective is to direct development to locations that promote the efficient utilization of public infrastructure such as schools, roads, and highways. In other words, the growth boundary is an integral part of urban planning, the set of policies that determines the spatial arrangement of activities in the metropolitan area.

Municipal versus Metropolitan Growth Boundaries

Our discussion of growth boundaries considers the case of a metropolitan boundary. The analysis is applicable to the two metropolitan areas in the United States—Portland and Minneapolis–St. Paul—that use growth and service boundaries to control the population of a metropolitan region. Urban service boundaries typically apply to individual municipalities rather than an entire metropolitan area. The basic logic of growth boundaries doesn't change with the level of geography. If one municipality adopts a growth boundary, it will displace households to other municipalities in the metropolitan area, triggering the same sort of changes in the common utility level and land rent.

There are two differences between a municipal and a metropolitan boundary. First, people are more mobile between municipalities than between metropolitan areas, so we would expect a quicker response to a municipal growth boundary. Second, some of the people displaced by a municipal boundary will relocate to other municipalities in the same metropolitan area, so some congestion and pollution will simply move to other parts of the metropolitan area. If the residents of the control city travel to neighboring municipalities to work, shop, or socialize, they will encounter some of the congestion and pollution displaced from their own municipality.

Trade-Offs with Growth Boundaries and Open Space

We've seen that a growth boundary decreases utility levels throughout a region and increases land rent in the control city. Renters are harmed by higher prices for land and housing, while landowners who own land within the boundary obviously benefit from higher land prices. This raises two questions.

How does a growth boundary affect homeowners? As land owners, homeowners benefit from higher land prices. So a policy that increases the price of land in a city benefits people who own homes at the time the growth control policy is implemented. In contrast, newcomers must pay higher housing prices, so they are harmed.

How do the benefits of growth compare to the cost? This question is very difficult to answer, and the answer is likely to vary from one city to another. A recent study suggests that in one English city, the cost outweighs the benefit (Cheshire and Sheppard, 2002). The key feature of a growth boundary—or a green belt or open space within the city—is that it provides public space at the expense of private space. The public open space in and around a city provides a bucolic atmosphere and opportunities for outdoor recreation and views. The trade-off is that the limited supply of developable land leads to higher prices and higher density—less private

space. The authors conclude that a modest relaxation of the open space and boundary policies of Reading, England would generate a net gain of $384 per household
per year, or about 2 percent of annual income.

OTHER GROWTH-CONTROL POLICIES

In addition to growth and service boundaries, cities use a number of policies to control their growth. In this part of the chapter, we explore the effects of two alternative
policies, limits on building permits and development taxes.

Limiting Building Permits

Consider a city that limits the number of building permits for new housing and business facilities. If the number of permits issued is less than the number demanded by
developers, the policy decreases the number of people who can live and work in the
city. Like a growth boundary, a limit on building permits displaces households from
one city to another, triggering changes in the two cities that generate lower utility in
both cities. This is shown by Figure 9–4, with a shift of 0.5 million people from the
control city to the other city.

Figure 9–5 shows the implications of a permit limit on the price of new housing.
The initial equilibrium is shown by point *i*, with a price of $200,000 and 120 new

FIGURE 9–5 Market Effects of Limit on Building Permits

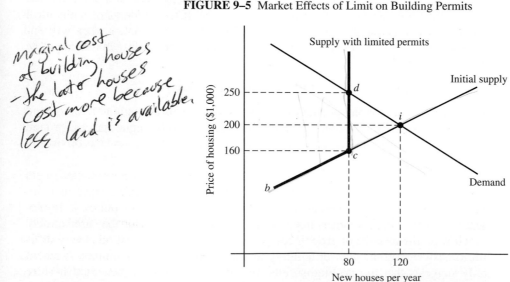

marginal cost
of building houses
- the later houses
cost more because
less land is available.

If the number of building permits is limited to 80, the supply curve for housing is
the kinked curve *bcd*. The new equilibrium is shown by point *d* (price of housing
= $250,000). Point *c* shows the marginal cost of production ($160,000). The
difference between the price and the marginal cost is the developer's willingness
to pay for the building permit ($90,000).

houses per year. If the city limits the number of building permits to 80 per year, the new supply curve for housing is the kinked curve that includes points *b, c,* and *d*: The maximum number of new houses is 80, so the supply curve goes vertical at 80 houses. The new supply curve intersects the demand curve at an equilibrium price of $250,000, meaning that the permit policy increases the price of housing by $50,000.

The permit policy also decreases the cost of producing housing. As reviewed in Section 2.2 of "Tools of Microeconomics," the appendix at the end of the book, a supply curve is also a marginal-cost curve. Like other supply curves, the housing supply curve shows the marginal cost of production. For example, at the initial equilibrium price of $200,000, firms supply 120 houses. The 120th house would not be supplied at a price of $199,000 because it costs more than $199,000 to produce; a price of $200,000 is just high enough to cover the production cost, so the marginal cost is just under $200,000. Farther down the supply curve at point *c*, the cost of supplying the 80th house is $160,000. The permit policy decreases the number of houses built from 120 to 80, so the marginal cost of production decreases.

The permit policy decreases the marginal cost of production because it decreases the demand for land and its price. For example, if houses are built on quarter-acre lots, the permit policy decreases the demand for vacant land from 30 acres per year (120 houses times 0.25 acres per house) to 20 acres per year. The decrease in the demand for land decreases the market price of land, decreasing the cost of producing housing. Comparing point *i* to point *c* in Figure 9–5, the permit policy decreases the marginal cost of production by $40,000.

The city must decide how to allocate its 80 building permits among its developers. One option is to auction the permits to the highest bidders. What is the monetary value of a building permit? A person with a building permit can make a profit equal to the difference between the market price of a house ($250,000, as shown by point *d*) and the cost of producing the house ($160,000, as shown by point *c*), so the monetary value of a permit is $90,000. If the city auctions the permits to the highest bidders, the market price would be $90,000. A second option is to allocate building permits to developers that promote the city's development objectives. A city could allocate its permits to high-density housing or to a project in an area targeted for development. Or a city could stage a "beauty contest," giving the permits to the development project that is most appealing to planning officials.

Development Fees

Another way to limit a city's population is to impose a development tax on new dwellings. As explained in detail later in the book, local governments use various taxes and fees to finance local public goods. When the taxes from a property owner fall short of the costs of providing public services, one response is to impose a one-time development fee to cover the gap. In this case, a development tax is simply solving a fiscal problem and is not really a growth-control policy.

Some cities impose impact fees on commercial and industrial developers, using the revenue from the fees to expand local transportation networks. For example, in the Westchester area of western Los Angeles, developers pay a one-time fee of

$2,010 for each additional rush-hour trip generated by new office buildings. The revenue from the impact fee is used to widen the roads used by the employees of the new office buildings. Impact fees can reduce the fiscal burden of new development, decreasing the opposition to development.

SUMMARY

This chapter describes the history of zoning and its legal foundations, and it also explores the effects of various growth-control policies. Here are the main points of the chapter.

1. Zoning is a blunt policy to control pollution because it just moves pollution around. An alternative policy is to combine pollution taxes with zoning.
2. Local governments can use minimum lot-size zoning to exclude land users who would generate a fiscal deficit—paying less in taxes than they get in public services.
3. The use of zoning to provide open space generates excessive amounts of open space because voters don't bear the full cost of the public good.
4. In a two-city region, an urban growth boundary in one city decreases utility in both cities and increases land rent in the city with the boundary.
5. A limit on building permits increases the equilibrium price of housing and decreases the price of vacant land.

APPLYING THE CONCEPTS

1. **Voting for Open Space**
   The city of Medianville has 100 citizens with income ranging from $20,000 to $70,000. The average income is $50,000 and the median income is $60,000. An individual's demand for open space depends only on income, and the individual demand curve has a vertical intercept equal to $1/1,000$ of income and a slope of $-\$0.50$ per acre of open space. The marginal cost of open space is $2,000.
   a. Suppose the city uses a head tax to finance open space and uses majority rule to determine how much open space to provide. Predict the amount of open space.
   b. How would your answer to (a) change if the city used zoning to provide open space without any compensation to landowners?
2. **Permit Queue with No Cuts**
   Consider the building-permit policy depicted in Figure 9–5. Suppose that the city announces on January 1 that 300 days later (October 28) it will give the 80 permits to the first 80 licensed building contractors through the planning office door. The police chief announces the following queuing rules:
   i. **No cuts:** When a person joins the queue, he or she goes to the end of the queue.
   ii. **No substitutions:** No one can reserve a place in line for anyone else.

To receive a permit, a licensed contractor must be one of the first 80 people in line and must remain in the line until October 28. Therefore, instead of an equilibrium price for the permits, there is an equilibrium waiting time (time spent in line). Suppose that 30 of the city's 120 licensed contractors have an opportunity cost of $300 per day, 30 have an opportunity cost of $500 per day, 30 have an opportunity cost of $1,000 per day, and 30 have an opportunity cost of $2,000 per day.

a. What is the equilibrium waiting time? Illustrate with a graph showing the vertical supply of permits and demand curve for permits, with the price measured as the days spent in line.

b. Suppose that the city eliminates the no-substitution rule. Would you expect the equilibrium waiting time to increase, decrease, or not change?

3. Madam Crystal and a Growth Boundary

In the city of Tarotown, there are 15 vacant lots, each with an initial market value of $20. Five of the lots are inside a proposed growth boundary and 10 are outside the boundary. Madame Crystal looked into her crystal ball and announced, "The growth boundary will reduce the price of vacant land outside the boundary to zero. The price of land within the boundary will either double or quadruple (the 2s in her fuzzy crystal ball look a lot like the 4s)." If the boundary is approved, the city will impose an 80 percent capital gains tax on land and distribute the tax revenue equally among the owners of the outside lots. For example, if the price of inside land increases from $20 to $30, the tax would be $8 per lot (80 percent of the $10 gain).

a. If everyone believes that the price of inside lots will quadruple, how many of the 15 lot owners will vote in favor of the growth boundary?

b. If the price of inside lots quadruples, is the boundary socially efficient?

c. How would your answers to (a) and (b) change if everyone believes correctly that the price of inside lots will double?

4. Revenue from Building Permits

Suppose a city auctions building permits for new housing to the highest bidders, and the city's objective is to maximize the total revenue from its building permits. The city's housing market is depicted in Figure 9–5.

a. Draw a curve showing the relationship between the price of permits (on the vertical axis) and the number of permits (on the horizontal axis) for the following numbers of permits: 40, 60, 80, 100. Explain why the relationship is positive or negative.

b. Of the four possible numbers of permits (40, 60, 80, 100), which generates the most total revenue?

REFERENCES AND ADDITIONAL READING

1. Brueckner, Jan K. "Strategic Control of Growth in a System of Cities." *Journal of Public Economics* 57 (1995), pp. 393–416.
2. Cheshire, Paul, and Stephen Sheppard. "The Welfare Economics of Land Use Planning." *Journal of Urban Economics* 52 (2002), pp. 242–69.

3. Engle, Robert, Peter Navarro, and Richard Carson. "On the Theory of Growth Controls." *Journal of Urban Economics* 32 (1992), pp. 269–83.
4. Evenson Bengte, and William C. Wheaton. "Local Variation in Land Use Regulations." *Brookings-Wharton Papers on Urban Affairs: 2003.* Washington DC: Brookings, 2003.
5. Fischel, William. *The Economics of Zoning Laws.* Baltimore: Johns Hopkins, 1985.
6. Fischel, William. "An Economic History of Zoning and a Cure for its Exclusionary Effects." *Urban Studies* 41 (2004), pp. 317–340.
7. Helsley, Robert W., and William C. Strange. "Strategic Growth Controls." *Regional Science and Urban Economics* 25 (1995), pp. 435–60.
8. Lillydahl, Jane H., Arthur C. Nelson, Timothy V. Ramis, Antero Rivasplata, and Steven R. Schell. "The Need for a Standard State Impact Fee Enabling Act." *Journal of the American Planning Association* 54 (Winter 1988), pp. 7–17.
9. Mills, Edwin S., and Luan Sende Lubuele. "Inner Cities." *Journal of Economic Literature* 35 (1997), pp. 727–56.
10. Siegan, Bernard. *Land Use without Zoning.* Lexington, MA: D.C. Heath, 1972.

PART THREE

Urban Transportation

One of the advantages of an urban location is its proximity to the many activities within a metropolitan area. This part of the book examines the two main components of the urban transportation system. Chapter 10 considers the automobile/highway system, focusing on three externalities caused by automobiles: congestion, environmental degradation, and collisions. The chapter explores various policy responses to these externalities. Chapter 11 explores the economics of urban mass transit, focusing on the commuter's choice of a mode of travel (e.g., automobile versus mass transit) and a city planner's choice of a mass-transit system (e.g., buses versus light rail versus heavy rail). The chapter explains why so few commuters in the United States use mass transit and why light-rail and heavy-rail transit systems are usually less efficient than bus systems.

CHAPTER 10

Externalities from Autos

The home is where part of the family waits until the others are through with the car.
—HERBERT PROCHNOW

I started to slow down but the traffic was more stationary than I thought.
—FROM AN AUTOMOBILE INSURANCE CLAIM FORM

*T*his first chapter on urban transportation discusses the automobile, the travel mode for 88 percent of commuting, and over 90 percent of all travel. We explore three externalities generated by the automobile—congestion, air pollution, and vehicle collisions—and discuss policy responses to the externalities. Recall the third axiom of urban economics:

Externalities cause inefficiency

The economic approach to externalities is to internalize them, imposing a tax equal to the marginal external cost. We also explore the merits of alternative policies to address the externalities, including subsidies for mass transit, mileage charges, and gasoline taxes.

Figure 10–1 (page 208) shows the distribution of travel modes for U.S. workers. About three-fourths drive alone, and another 12 percent carpool in private vehicles. The drive-alone shares are highest in cities in Ohio and Alabama, which together have 6 of the top 10 drive-alone cities. Carpooling rates are highest in California and Texas, which together have 8 of the top 10 carpooling cities, with rates between 18 percent and 20 percent. The share of commuting by automobile is highest among workers who commute within suburban areas and lowest among workers who commute within a central city.

At the national level, 5 percent of commuters use public transit, but the transit share varies substantially across cities. The transit share is above 10 percent in just two metropolitan areas, New York (25 percent) and Chicago (12 percent). Seven metropolitan areas have transit shares above 6 percent: San Francisco, Washington,

FIGURE 10–1 Modal Choice for U.S. Commuters

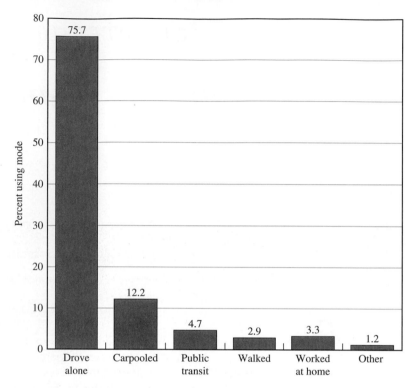

Source: U.S. Census Bureau. *Journey to Work: 2000.* Washington DC: U.S. Census Bureau, 2004.

TABLE 10–1 Purposes of Travel

	Share of Travel (percent)	Average Trip Length (miles)
Social and recreational	30	11.36
To/from work	19	12.11
All other family and personal business	19	7.84
Shopping	14	7.02
Work-related business	9	28.26
School/church	6	6.00
Other	4	43.08

Source: U.S. Department of Transportation. *Summary of Travel Trends, 2001 National Household Travel Survey* (2004).

Boston, Philadelphia, Honolulu, Seattle, and Pittsburgh. The rest of the U.S. metropolitan areas have transit shares less than 6 percent. The transit share is 11 percent for central-city residents, compared to 2 percent for suburban residents.

As shown in Table 10–1, commuting (driving to and from work) is responsible for only one-fifth of travel by private vehicles. Social and recreational travel is at

FIGURE 10–2 Commuting Distance, Time, and Speed

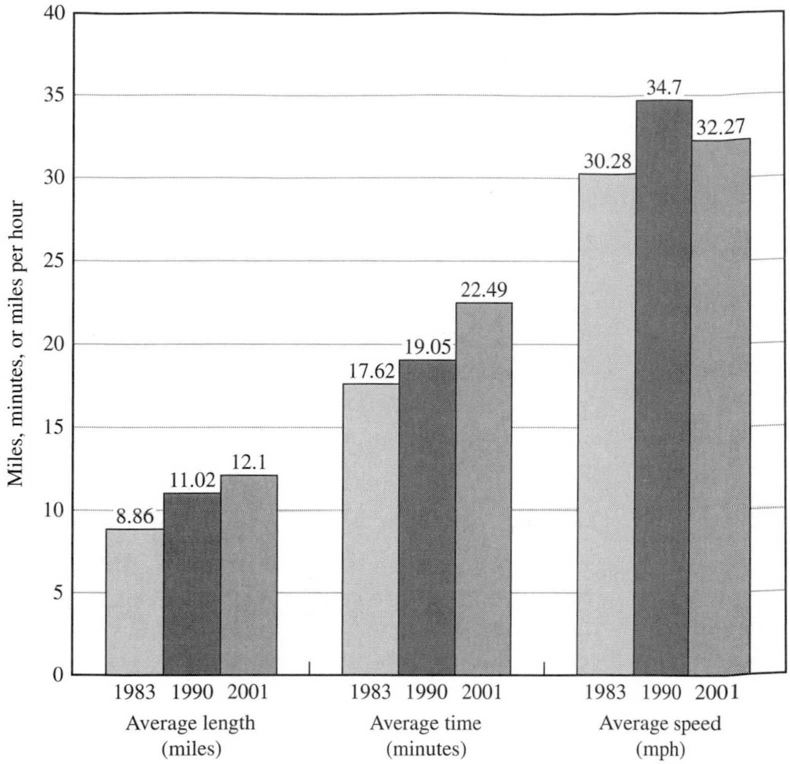

Source: U.S. Department of Transportation. *Summary of Travel Trends, 2001 National Household Travel Survey.* Washington, DC: U.S. Department of Transportation, 2004.

the top of the list, with a 30 percent share. The average annual mileage per household is over 35,000, with about 6,700 for commuting. Table 10–1 shows the average trip lengths: 12 miles for commuting and 11 miles for social and recreational trips.

Figure 10–2 shows trends in the length, time, and speed of commuting (the numbers are for one-way travel). Between 1983 and 2001, trip length increased by about 37 percent, while travel time increased by a smaller percentage (28 percent) because travel speed increased. Between 1990 and 2001, speed decreased while the trip length increased, so travel time increased by 18 percent.

CONGESTION EXTERNALITIES

According to the Texas Transportation Institute, the typical U.S. commuter in 2003 wasted about 47 hours because of traffic congestion. In some cities, the time lost by the typical commuter is much higher: 93 hours in Los Angeles, 72 hours in San Francisco, 69 hours in Washington DC, 67 hours in Atlanta, and 63 hours in

Houston. In addition to time lost, we also waste $5 billion worth of gasoline and diesel fuel each year because of delays and slow travel. Adding the value of lost time to the wasted fuel, the annual cost is $63 billion per year. This is about five times the congestion cost experienced in 1982.

We'll use a simple model to explain congestion externalities and evaluate some alternative public policies to deal with it. Consider a travel route within a metropolitan area with the following characteristics:

- **Distance.** The travel route is 10 miles long, and could be a radial highway into the city or a circumferential highway linking suburbs.
- **Monetary travel cost.** The monetary cost of auto travel is 20 cents per mile, or $2.00 for the 10-mile route.
- **Time cost.** The time cost of a trip is the time times the opportunity cost per minute ($0.10).

The total cost of a trip is the $2.00 monetary cost plus the time cost, which depends on how long the trip takes. There is one person per vehicle, so we can use "vehicles" and "drivers" interchangeably.

The Demand for Urban Travel

Consider first the demand side of urban travel. In Figure 10–3, the horizontal axis measures the number of vehicles per lane per hour and the vertical axis measures

FIGURE 10–3 Congestion Externalities and the Congestion Tax

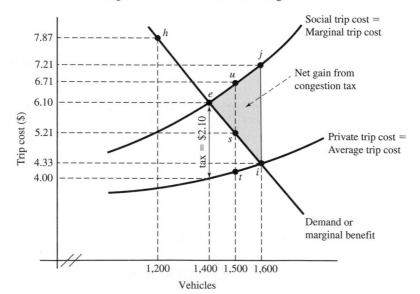

The equilibrium is shown by point *i*: When drivers pay the private trip cost, traffic volume is 1,600. The optimum is shown by point *e*, where the marginal benefit (shown by the demand curve) equals the marginal cost (the Social trip cost), generating a volume of 1,400 vehicles. The net gain from congestion tax is shown by the shaded area.

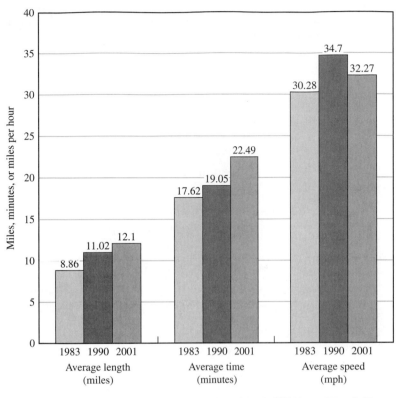

the cost of the commuting trip, the sum of the monetary and time costs. The demand curve shows the number of drivers who make the trip, which depends on its cost. For example, if the trip cost is $7.87, point *h* shows that there are 1,200 people for whom the benefit of the trip exceeds the cost, so the traffic volume is 1,200 vehicles per lane per hour. As the cost of the trip decreases, the benefit exceeds the cost for more people, so we move downward along the demand curve to 1,400 vehicles at a cost of $6.10 and 1,600 vehicles at a cost of $4.33.

As explained in Section 2.1 in "Tools of Microeconomics," the appendix at the end of the book, a demand curve is also a marginal-benefit curve. The demand curve in Figure 10–3 shows how much the marginal traveler is willing to pay for a trip. For example, at a price of $7.87, 1,200 people make the trip. The 1,200th traveler makes the trip if the cost is $7.87, but wouldn't make the trip if the cost were any higher, say $7.88. This tells us that the benefit of the 1,200th trip is just below $7.87. Similarly, the marginal benefit for the 1,400th traveler is $6.10 and the marginal benefit for the 1,600th vehicle is $4.33. As we move downward along the demand curve, people with progressively lower marginal benefits use the highway.

The Private and Social Costs of Travel

Table 10–2 shows the relationships between traffic volume and travel time. Column B lists the trip time for different volumes. For up to 400 vehicles, there is no congestion: Everyone travels at the legal speed limit of 50 miles per hour, and the trip takes 12 minutes. But after we cross the congestion threshold of 400 vehicles, the time required to make the trip increases. For example, the trip time increases to 12.48 minutes with 600 vehicles, to 17.28 minutes with 1,200 vehicles, to 27.12 minutes with 1,800 vehicles. As the highway becomes crowded, the space between vehicles decreases, and drivers slow down to maintain safe distances between cars.

TABLE 10–2 Traffic Volume, Travel Time, and the Congestion Externality

A	B	C	D	E	F	G	H
			Increase in	Increase in			
Volume		Private	Time per	Total Travel	External	Social	Marginal
(vehicles	Trip Time	Trip Cost	Vehicle	Time	Trip Cost	Trip Cost	Benefit
per lane)	(minutes)	($)	(minutes)	(minutes)	($)	($)	(demand)
200	12.000	3.20	0.000	0.00	0.00	3.20	16.73
400	12.000	3.20	0.000	0.00	0.00	3.20	14.96
599	12.476						
600	12.480	3.248	0.004	2.40	0.24	3.49	13.19
1,199	17.268						
1,200	17.280	3.728	0.012	14.40	1.44	5.17	7.87
1,399	19.985						
1,400	20.000	4.000	0.015	21.00	2.10	6.10	6.10
1,599	23.262						
1,600	23.280	4.328	0.018	28.80	2.88	7.21	4.33
1,799	27.100						
1,800	27.120	4.712	0.020	36.00	3.60	8.31	2.56

Column C shows the private trip cost, defined as the cost incurred by the typical driver. The time cost equals the trip time (shown in column B) times the opportunity cost ($0.10 per minute), for example, $1.20 for a volume of 400 vehicles, $1.248 for 600 vehicles, and so on. Adding the $2 monetary cost to this time cost, we get the numbers for the private trip cost in column C. The private trip cost increases from $3.20 for volume up to 400, to $3.248 for 600 vehicles, $3.728 for 1,200 vehicles, and so on up to $4.712 for 1,800 vehicles.

Columns D, E, and F show the numbers behind the congestion externality. Column D shows the increase in travel time per vehicle from one additional vehicle. For example, the travel time for 599 vehicles is 12.476 minutes, and the travel time for 600 vehicles is 0.004 minutes longer, 12.480 minutes. In other words, when the 600th vehicle enters the roadway, it slows down each other vehicle by 0.004 minutes. Multiplying this by the 600 vehicles, the increase in total travel time when the 600th vehicle enters is 2.40 minutes. Finally, multiplying the increase in travel time by the opportunity cost of travel time ($0.10 per minute), we get the external cost of the 600th vehicle, $0.24. This tells us that the 600th vehicle imposes a cost on other drivers of $0.24. Repeating the same calculations, we get an external cost of $1.44 for the 1,200th vehicle, $2.10 for the 1,400th vehicle, and so on. The external cost increases with traffic volume.

Column G shows the social trip cost, the sum of the private cost and the external cost. When there is no congestion (when the volume is less than 400 vehicles), the external cost is zero, so the social cost equals the private cost (column C). But once we pass the congestion threshold, the social cost of the trip exceeds the private cost. For example, at a volume of 1,400 vehicles, the social cost is $6.10 compared to a private cost of $4.00.

There are some alternative labels for the private trip cost and the social trip cost. The private trip cost is the cost per driver, so we could call it the average cost of travel. The social trip cost is the social cost associated with the last or marginal vehicle, so we could call it the marginal cost of travel.

Equilibrium versus Optimum Traffic Volume

What is the equilibrium number of vehicles? A person will use the road if his or her willingness to pay for the trip (the marginal benefit) exceeds the private trip cost. Figure 10–3 shows the demand curve and the private trip cost curve. The demand curve intersects the private-cost curve at point i, indicating that the equilibrium volume is 1,600 vehicles and the equilibrium trip cost is $4.33. For the first 1,600 people, the willingness to pay is greater than or equal to the private trip cost, so they use the roadway. The 1,601st vehicle does not use the roadway because the willingness to pay is less than the private trip cost.

What is the optimum number of vehicles? We can use the marginal principle to identify the socially efficient number of vehicles. The marginal principle is reviewed in Section 1.1 of "Tools of Microeconomics," the appendix at the end of the book. According to the marginal principle, we should increase the level of an activity until the marginal social benefit equals the marginal social cost. No positive externalities are associated with travel, so the demand curve shows the marginal social benefit of travel. The marginal social cost is shown by the social trip cost curve in Figure 10–3. The demand curve intersects the social-cost curve at point *e*, so the optimum volume is 1,400 vehicles. For the first 1,400 vehicles, the social benefit of travel (the willingness to pay) is greater than or equal to the social cost, so their use of the roadway is socially efficient. In contrast the social cost of the 1,401st vehicle exceeds the social benefit so its use of the highway is not socially efficient.

The equilibrium volume exceeds the optimum volume because each driver ignores the congestion cost imposed on others. An additional vehicle slows traffic, forcing other drivers to spend more time on the road. Suppose that Lois, the 1,500th driver, has a willingness to pay of $5.21 (shown by point *s*). With 1,500 vehicles, the private trip cost is $4.16 (shown by point *t*), and the social trip cost is $6.71 (shown by point *u*). She will use the road because her willingness to pay exceeds her private trip cost ($5.21 > $4.16). But her use of the road is inefficient because her willingness to pay is less than the social trip cost ($5.21 < $6.71). The burden she imposes on society equals the gap between the social benefit (her benefit) of $5.21 and the social cost of $6.71, or $1.50. Lois ignores the external cost of her decision, so she makes an inefficient choice.

THE CONGESTION TAX

The simple solution to the congestion problem is to use a congestion tax to internalize the externality. In Figure 10–3, a congestion tax of $2.10 per trip would shift the private trip cost curve upward by $2.10, decreasing the equilibrium number of vehicles from 1,600 to 1,400. For Lois (in vehicle 1,500), the benefit of the trip is still $5.21, but if 1,500 vehicles use the road, her cost is the sum of the private trip cost of $4.16 (point *t*) and a tax of $2.10, or $6.26. Her cost now exceeds her willingness to pay, so she doesn't use the highway. Similarly, for the 1,401st through the 1,600th vehicles, the willingness to pay is now less than the cost of making the trip, so they stay off the road. The congestion tax ensures that decision-makers face the full social cost of travel so highways will be used efficiently.

Benefits and Costs of the Congestion Tax

From the perspective of the individual traveler, the imposition of congestion taxes generates good news and bad news. Consider first the people who pay the tax and continue to use the highway. In Figure 10–3, Hiram is at point *h* on the demand curve. The bad news is that he pays a congestion tax of $2.10. There are two bits of good news:

- **Decrease in time cost.** The tax decreases traffic volume, so travel speed increases and travel time decreases. In Figure 10–3, the tax decreases the private trip cost from $4.33 to $4.00, a savings of $0.33 for Hiram and every other driver.
- **Lower income tax.** The government can use the revenue from the congestion tax to cut other local taxes. Suppose the government divides the congestion tax revenue equally among the 1,600 people who initially used the roadway, cutting each person's income tax by $1.84.

TABLE 10–3 Benefits and Costs of the Congestion Tax

| | Cost | | Benefit | | |
	Tax Paid	Lost Consumer Surplus	Decrease in Time Cost	Lower Income Tax	Net Benefit
Hiram	$2.10	—	$0.33	$1.84	$0.07
Lois	—	$0.88	—	$1.84	$0.96

As shown in the first row of Table 10–3, Hiram has a net benefit of $0.07 from the congestion tax, equal to a benefit of $2.17 minus the $2.10 congestion tax.

Consider next the people like Lois who don't use the roadway after the congestion tax is imposed. The good news is that her income tax is cut by $1.84, just like everyone else who initially used the road. The bad news is that she loses a consumer surplus. (For a review of the concept of consumer surplus see Section 2.5 of "Tools of Microeconomics," the appendix at the end of the book.) Before the tax, her consumer surplus from using the highway was the gap between her willingness to pay ($5.21) and the private trip cost when 1,600 vehicles use the road ($4.33), or $0.88. In the second row of Table 10–3, Lois's tax cut exceeds her loss of consumer surplus, so the congestion tax makes her better off too.

We can use the marginal approach to measure the welfare gain to society from moving from the market equilibrium to the optimum. The relevant concepts are reviewed in Section 1.2 of "Tools of Microeconomics," the appendix at the end of the book. The shaded area in Figure 10–3 shows the welfare gain to society. To explain the logic of the welfare gain, consider a small move from the equilibrium toward the optimum. If we persuade the 1,600th driver not to use the road, what are the benefits and costs?

- **Benefit:** The total travel cost for society decreases by the social trip cost associated with the 1,600th driver ($7.21 at point *j*).
- **Cost:** The driver loses the benefits of the highway trip; the willingness to pay for the trip is shown by the demand curve ($4.33 at point *i*).

By diverting this vehicle, society saves $7.21 in travel costs and sacrifices only $4.33 in forgone travel benefits, for a net gain of $2.88. This is shown in Figure 10–3 as the gap between the social trip cost curve and the demand curve at 1,600 vehicles.

To compute the welfare gain to society from moving to the optimum, we repeat this thought experiment for the 1,599th driver, the 1,598th driver, and so on down to the 1,401st driver. The net gain from diverting the 1,599th driver is slightly lower than the gain from diverting the 1,600th driver because the social trip cost is lower (we are lower on the cost curve) and the willingness to pay is higher (we are farther up the demand curve). As we decrease the number of vehicles, the net gain from diverting a vehicle decreases as the gap between the social trip cost and the demand curve shrinks. The gain to society (the welfare gain) from moving all the way to the optimum level is the sum of the net gains from the diverted vehicles, shown as the shaded area between the social cost curve and the demand curve.

FIGURE 10–4 A Congestion Tax Causes Urban Growth

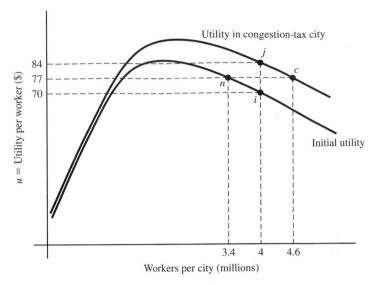

The initial equilibrium is shown by point i: Each of the two cities has a population of 4 million. Internalizing congestion externalities reduces the diseconomics of urban growth, shifting the utility curve upward and opening a utility gap (shown by points i and j) between the two cities. Migration to the congestion-tax city eliminates the utility gap, restoring equilibrium at points n (no congestion tax) and c (congestion tax). The congestion-tax city grows at the expense of the other city, and utility increases in both cities.

Congestion Taxes and Urban Growth

We've seen that because the congestion tax internalizes an externality, it improves the efficiency of the economy and generates a welfare gain to society. We can use the utility curves derived earlier in the book to show the implications of a congestion tax for urban growth. As we'll see, a city that implements a congestion tax will grow at the expense of other cities in the region.

Figure 10–4 shows the utility curves for a two-city region. Suppose that initially congestion is unpriced in both cities, generating point i as the initial equilibrium: Each city has a population of 4 million and a utility level of $70. Suppose one city implements a congestion tax and uses the revenue from the congestion tax to cut income taxes. In Figure 10–4, the congestion tax shifts the city's utility curve upward because the internalization of congestion externalities reduces the diseconomies of urban size. Recall that these diseconomies (more noise, pollution, and congestion as population increases) pull utility down as a city grows. The reduction of congestion affects the utility curve in two ways:

- The curve is positively sloped over a larger population range because agglomeration economies dominate diseconomies over a larger population range.
- For the negatively sloped portion of the utility curve, the curve is not as steep: Diseconomies are weaker, meaning that utility falls less rapidly as population increases.

The upward shift of the utility curve causes the congestion-tax city to grow at the expense of the other city. The immediate effect is a utility gap shown by points *i* and *j*: With a population of 4 million each, utility is $14 higher in the congestion-tax city, reflecting the efficiency gains of internalizing the externality. Workers will migrate to the congestion-tax city, causing movement downward along its utility curve (from point *j* toward point *c*). As workers leave the other city, we move upward along the initial utility curve (still relevant for the other city) from point *i* toward point *n*. Equilibrium is restored at points *n* and *c*: The congestion-tax city gains population at the expense of the other city. In addition, utility increases in both cities.

PRACTICALITIES OF THE CONGESTION TAX

We've seen that the congestion tax internalizes an externality, leading to efficiency gains and urban growth. In this part of the chapter, we'll discuss several practical issues concerning the implementation of a system of congestion taxes. We address three questions.

1. How would the perfect congestion tax vary by time of day?
2. How high would a congestion tax be?
3. What sort of experiences do cities have with pricing urban travel?

Peak versus Off-Peak Travel

The congestion tax equals the gap between the private and social cost of travel, and it varies across time and space. As shown in Figure 10–5, during peak travel times,

FIGURE 10–5 Congestion Tax in Peak versus Off-Peak Periods

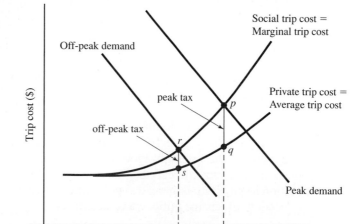

During the peak travel period, traffic volume is relatively high, generating a large gap between the private and social cost of travel (shown by points *p* and *q*) and thus a higher congestion tax. During the off-peak period, the gap between the social and private cost of travel is lower (points *r* and *s*), so the congestion tax is lower.

the demand curve is relatively high, generating a large gap between the private and social cost of travel and thus a large congestion tax. In contrast, during off-peak periods when demand is relatively low, the congestion tax is low as well. Historically, commuting trips have been concentrated during the morning peak period (6:30–8:30 a.m.) and the evening peak period (4:30–6:30 p.m.).

The term "rush hour" refers to peak travel periods, but the phrase is ironic rather than literal. Although people may be in a rush, they move slowly. In modern cities, traffic volume is high and traffic is slow for most of the work day, not just for a couple of hours. In cities with populations of at least 1 million, there is no midday break in congestion: Travel speeds start to drop early in the morning and continue to drop during the day until they rise after about 7 p.m. In medium-sized cities (populations of 500,000 to 1 million), there is a midafternoon lull in traffic (1 p.m. to 4 p.m.). The term "rush hour express" applies to subways, and in Japan, rush hour workers called "fanny pushers" (euphemistic translation) are hired to pack people into rush-hour trains.

Estimates of Congestion Taxes

What is the appropriate congestion tax? Studies of several metropolitan areas provide estimates of the socially efficient congestion tax:

- **San Francisco Bay Area.** Pozdena (1988) updated earlier estimates of Keeler and Small (1977). During the peak travel periods, the appropriate tax is $0.65 per mile on central urban highways, $0.21 per mile on suburban highways, and $0.17 per mile on fringe highways. During the off-peak periods, the appropriate tax is between $0.03 and $0.05 per mile at all locations.
- **Minneapolis–St. Paul.** Mohring (1999) shows that about 2,000 of 9,700 miles in the metropolitan area are congested during the peak periods. A congestion tax would average about $0.09 per mile, with a tax as high as $0.21 per mile on the most congested roads. The imposition of congestion taxes would decrease traffic volume by 12 percent on average and by 25 percent on the most congested roads.
- **Los Angeles.** Small (1992) shows that congestion occurs for about 28 percent of the total vehicle miles traveled. The peak-period congestion tax would average about $0.15 per mile. A congestion tax would decrease traffic volume during the peak period by about 26 percent, increasing travel speeds and reducing delays.

Implementing the Congestion Tax

Modern technology allows the efficient and convenient collection of congestion taxes. Under a vehicle identification system (VIS), each car is equipped with a transponder—an electronic device that allows sensors along the road to identify a car as it passes. The system records the number of times a vehicle uses a congested highway and sends a congestion bill to the driver at the end of the month. For example, a driver who travels 10 miles along a congested highway 20 times per month would pay a monthly congestion bill of $42.00 (20 times $2.10). The alternative approach, which avoids issues of privacy, is to use anonymous debit cards to charge for driving on congested roads.

Singapore was the first city to use prices to control the volume of traffic. Under the Area Licensing System (ALS) implemented in 1975, drivers were charged about $2 per day to travel in a toll zone in the central area of the city. The system decreased traffic volume by about 44 percent and increased travel speeds. In 1998, the city adopted Electronic Road Pricing (ERP), a debit-card system with charges that increase with the level of congestion. Vehicles that do not have an in-vehicle unit or sufficient value on their debit cards are photographed for what Singapore officials call "subsequent enforcement action."

In Toronto, the users of the Express Toll Road pay fees that depend on the distance traveled and time of day. The per-kilometer toll is $0.10 (Canadian) during peak periods, $0.07 during other weekday times, and $0.04 cents on the weekend. The system uses a VIS to compute the toll for each trip. For occasional users without in-vehicle transponders, the system photographs license plates and sends bills to the registered owners.

Pricing HOT Lanes

One approach that is gaining popularity is to allow drivers to buy into the use of high-occupancy vehicle (HOV) lanes. An HOV lane—sometimes known as a "diamond" lane or an express lane—is a lane designated for use by high-occupancy vehicles, typically defined as a vehicle with at least three passengers. A HOT lane is a lane that can be used both by high-occupancy vehicles and other vehicles that pay a toll (HOT stands for "high occupancy and toll").

The first HOT project was along Riverside Freeway (California State Route 91), which connects employment centers in Los Angeles and Orange Counties with rapidly growing areas to the east. Two HOV lanes that had been added in the median strip of the freeway were switched to HOT lanes. The toll varies by time of day, with the highest toll ($2.75 per trip) between 5 a.m. and 9 a.m. on weekdays. Each car has a transponder in its windshield for identification purposes and an account that is charged for using the lane. The conversion to a HOT lane increased traffic volume, with about 80 percent of users paying the toll. The conversion also decreased traffic volume and increased speeds along the regular lanes on Route 91, generating benefits for other commuters.

Another HOT project is along Interstate 15 in San Diego. The reversible facility consists of an eight-mile stretch of two lanes in the freeway median, which are accessible only at the endpoints of the facility. A fee is charged for each trip, with the toll varying in "real time" from $0.50 to $4.00, depending on the level of congestion. Each vehicle has a transponder and a prepaid account that is charged for using the lane. The toll is highest between 7 a.m. and 8 a.m. and between 4 p.m. and 5 p.m.

These recent experiences with congestion pricing are promising. Travelers respond to higher prices by changing their travel behavior in ways that decrease traffic volume and improve the efficiency of travel. The most frequent responses are: (1) forming carpools, (2) switching to mass transit, (3) switching to off-peak travel, (4) picking alternative routes, and (5) combining two or more trips into a single trip (Small and Gomez-Ibanez, 1998).

ALTERNATIVES TO A CONGESTION TAX

A number of alternative congestion policies have been proposed. To set the stage for a discussion of the alternatives, consider the four ways that a congestion tax decreases traffic volume:

1. **Modal substitution.** The tax increases the cost of single-driver travel relative to carpooling and mass transit (buses, subways, light rail), causing some travelers to switch to other travel modes.
2. **Time of travel.** The tax is highest during the peak travel periods, causing some travelers to travel at different times. Because work and school schedules are relatively inflexible, commuters and students would be less likely to change their travel times than other travelers (e.g., shoppers). Nonetheless, firms would have an incentive to change work schedules to allow their workers to avoid costly travel during the peak periods.
3. **Travel route.** The congestion tax is highest on the most congested routes, causing some travelers to switch to alternative routes.
4. **Location choices.** The congestion tax increases the unit cost of travel (travel cost per mile), causing some commuters to decrease their commuting distances. Some workers may move closer to their jobs, and others may switch to jobs closer to their residences.

These four responses cause us to move up the travel-demand curve as the cost of travel increases. In Figure 10–3, the congestion tax decreases traffic volume from 1,600 to 1,400 because it changes travel modes, times, routes, and distances.

Gasoline Tax

One alternative to the congestion tax is a gasoline tax. The simple idea is that if the cost per mile of travel increases, people will drive less. The problem is that a gas tax increases the cost of all automobile travel, not just travel along congested routes during peak periods. A gas tax decreases the relative cost of alternative travel modes, causing modal substitution in the right direction (#1 above). It also increases the cost per mile traveled, affecting location choice in the right direction (#4). But the gas tax fails to affect the time of travel or the travel route (#2 and #3), except to the extent that congestion generates lower gas mileage.

It may be tempting to conclude that getting two responses (mode and location) out of four isn't so bad. But consider the gasoline tax required to internalize congestion externality for peak-period congestion. If the appropriate congestion tax is $0.21 per mile and the average vehicle gets 20 miles per gallon of gasoline, the required gas tax would be $4.20 per gallon. The problem is that the tax would apply to all gasoline purchased, not just the gasoline used during the peak period on congested roads. As we'll see later in the chapter, there are some environmental benefits from taxing gasoline, but the appropriate tax is much less than $4.20 per gallon. It is worth noting that a tax of $4.20 would cause the price of gasoline in the United States to be close to the prices in several countries in Western Europe.

Subsidies for Transit

Another alternative to a congestion tax is to subsidize mass transit. The basic idea is to match the underpricing of car travel with equivalent underpricing of buses, subways, commuter trains, and light rail. Transit subsidies change modal choice (#1) in the right direction but don't directly affect travel time, travel routes, or location choice.

There are two basic problems with using transit subsidies to deal with congestion externalities. First, neither transit ridership nor auto use is very responsive to changes in the price of transit. Therefore, a decrease in the price of transit would not affect the volume of auto traffic very much. A classic study (Kraft and Domencich, 1972) suggests that making mass transit free would increase transit ridership by only one-third, and only a part of the increase in ridership would come from diverted auto drivers. The second problem is that matching the underpricing of auto travel with underpricing of transit travel leads to an underpricing of transportation in general, leading to excessive amounts of travel.

Eliminating Parking Subsidies

Shoup (1993) suggests that the subsidization of parking by employers contributes to the congestion problem. In 1990, about 95 percent of American commuters who drove to work benefited from free parking at their place of work. In Los Angeles, the average subsidy from free parking provided by employers was $3.87 per day. Shoup estimates that employer-paid parking shifts 25 percent of all commuters into solo driving and increases the number of cars driven to work by 19 percent. One possible response to this problem is to "cash out" the parking subsidy, giving workers the option of free parking or the cash equivalent of, say, $80 per month, for example. The elimination of subsidized parking would cause modal substitution away from solo driving, decreasing the demand for solo travel. In Figure 10–3, eliminating this distortion of travel behavior would shift the demand curve to the left, decreasing the equilibrium traffic volume and the costs associated with congestion.

There is evidence that commuters respond to changes in the price of parking. When the city of Ottawa, Canada, increased parking rates for government employees from zero to 70 percent of the commercial rate, the number of workers driving to work decreased by 23 percent, the automobile occupancy rate increased from 1.33 to 1.41, and bus ridership increased by 16 percent (DiRenzo, Cima, and Barber, 1981). When a Los Angeles firm increased its parking fee from zero to $28.75 per month, the number of solo drivers dropped by 44 percent (Small, 1992).

THE ROAD CAPACITY DECISION

How could a government determine the socially efficient capacity of a road? As we'll see, a government that imposes a congestion tax can use a simple rule to decide on road width: If the total revenue from the congestion tax exceeds the cost of building the road, the government should build a wider road. The optimum road width generates just enough congestion-tax revenue to pay for the road.

Interpreting the Spaghetti Cost Curves

The demonstration of this convenient rule requires some background on the different components of travel and road costs. Figure 10–6 shows two sets of cost curves, one for a two-lane road and a second for a four-lane road. At first glace, the figure looks like a pile of unruly spaghetti, but there is some logic to the curves.

The curves labeled ATC show the average total cost of travel. These curves include the cost of building the road and the private cost of travel (shown in earlier

FIGURE 10–6 Expand Capacity until Congestion Tax Revenue Equals Road Cost

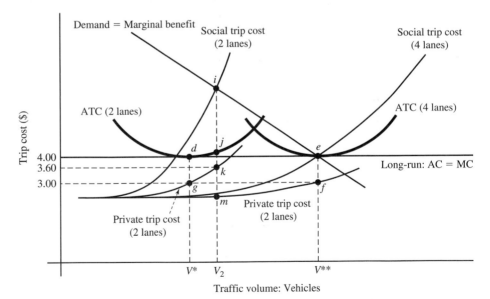

The congestion tax per vehicle is the gap between the private and social trip cost (the gap between points i and k for a two-lane road). The average road cost is the gap between the average total cost and the private trip cost (the gap between j and k for a two-lane road). For a two-lane road, tax revenue per vehicle exceeds the average road cost, so capacity should be expanded. For a four-lane road, the congestion tax is shown by the gap between points e and f, and so is the average road cost: Congestion taxes pay for the optimum road. The four-lane road is socially efficient because at point e, the long-run marginal cost ($4) equals the marginal benefit (from the demand curve).

figures). For example, ATC (two lanes) is a U-shaped curve that reaches a minimum at point d, with a volume of V^* and an average cost of \$4. As traffic volume increases, two conflicting forces affect average total cost:

- **Decrease in average road cost.** The cost of building a two-lane road is fixed, and the larger the volume, the lower the road cost per vehicle.
- **Increase in private trip cost.** Once the congestion threshold is passed, private trip cost increases.

The ATC curve is U-shaped because the decrease in the average road cost dominates for small volumes, but the rising trip cost dominates for large volumes. The other important feature of the ATC curve is that the gap between ATC and the private trip cost curve is the average road cost (average fixed cost).

The cost curves for the four-lane road show the benefits of building a road with a larger capacity. The average total cost curve reaches the minimum at twice the volume (V^{**} is twice as large as V^*). In addition, the private trip cost curve stays horizontal for twice the traffic volume and is lower for all volumes. Similarly, the social trip cost curve for the four-lane road is lower than the associated curve for the two-lane road. However, the four-lane road costs twice as much to build.

Let's start at the equilibrium with a two-lane road. If the government imposes a congestion tax, the equilibrium is shown by point i, with a traffic volume of V_2. The congestion tax is shown by the gap between the social trip cost (point i) and the private trip cost (point k). The average road cost is shown by the gap between the average total cost curve (point j) and the private trip cost (point k). The congestion tax per vehicle exceeds the road cost per vehicle, meaning that total congestion tax revenue exceeds the cost of building the road.

Widen the Road if Congestion Tax Revenue Exceeds the Cost

The excessive revenue from congestion tax is a signal to the government to build a wider road. To double the capacity, the government could add two lanes, making a four-lane road. The new equilibrium is shown by point e, where the social trip cost curve intersects the demand curve. Now the congestion tax is shown by the gap between points e and f. This is also the gap between the private trip cost and the average total cost, or the average road cost. In other words, for a four-lane road, the congestion tax equals the average road cost, so total tax revenue is just enough to pay for the road. The people who use the road pay the entire cost of building it.

The capacity rule tells the government to widen the road to the point where congestion tax revenue equals the cost of the road. In addition to its appeal in terms of fairness and equity (road users pay), this rule generates the socially efficient road width. Recall that the average cost curve for the four-lane road reaches the same minimum average cost (\$4) as the two-lane road but with twice the capacity: V^{**} is twice V^*. This is sensible if there are constant returns to scale in road building. If so, we can build twice as many lanes at twice the cost (the average road cost doesn't change) and handle twice as much traffic at the same private trip cost (the trip cost per vehicle doesn't change). In other words, the long-run average cost (including road cost and travel cost) is constant. If the average cost is constant, the average cost equals the marginal cost, as shown by the horizontal cost curve at $4.

Point e is the efficient outcome because it satisfies the marginal principle, equating the marginal benefit of travel to the marginal cost. At point e on the demand curve, the marginal benefit is $4. The marginal cost is shown by the horizontal long-run marginal-cost curve (equal to average cost), which is constant at $4. If the government were to build a wider road, the marginal cost would still be $4, but the demand curve tells us that for volume above V^{**}, the willingness to pay is less than $4. Additional travelers are not willing to pay the full cost of widening the road to accommodate them, so it would be inefficient to widen the road. In contrast, when we start with a two-lane road (at point i), widening the road is socially efficient because the willingness to pay for an additional vehicle exceeds the cost of expanding the road to accommodate the vehicle.

Capacity Expansion and Latent Demand

There are many anecdotes about roads that did not experience less congestion after they were widened. The reason is that the demand for peak-period travel is highly elastic. Many travelers avoid using congested roads because travel is so slow. But when a road is widened and travel initially moves faster, travelers who were deterred by slow speed start using the road. This is the phenomenon of "latent demand." In the language of Small (1992), there is a "reserve army of the unfulfilled" that will switch to a previously congested highway as soon as an increase in capacity increases travel speeds. This latent demand may fill most or all of the new capacity during peak periods.

In Figure 10–6, the widening of the road leads to a moderate reduction in the private trip cost. With an initial volume of V_2, point k tells us that the private trip cost is $3.60. Doubling the road width increases volume to V^{**} and, as shown by point f, the private trip cost is $3.00. If we ignored the demand side of road travel, we might imagine that a doubling of road capacity would lead to a larger reduction in travel time and private trip cost. For example if we assumed that demand was perfectly inelastic (it stays at V_2), we would go from point k to point m, with a much lower trip cost. But because consumers respond to lower travel costs by traveling in larger numbers, travel time and trip costs decrease by a smaller amount.

Who Pays for Roads?

The use of congestion taxes to pay for roads is appealing for reasons of equity and efficiency. In the United States, roads are actually financed by various user fees. Auto and truck drivers pay federal and state taxes on gas, oil, and auto parts. In addition, truck drivers also pay user fees based on the weight of the truck and the miles traveled. During the 1960s, revenue from user taxes exceeded the highway cost by about 25 percent, but since then gasoline taxes have not kept pace with inflation, so revenue from user fees no longer covers the cost of roads and highways.

Historically, urban road users have done better than rural travelers in covering the cost of roads.

AUTOS AND AIR POLLUTION

Automobile use causes two sorts of environmental externalities, air pollution and greenhouse gases. Motor vehicles emit volatile organic compounds (VOC), carbon monoxide (CO), nitrogen oxides (NOx), and sulfur dioxide (SO_2). VOCs react with NOx in the atmosphere to form ozone (O_3, aka smog) and also generate particulate matter. In the United States, transport activities are responsible for about two-thirds of CO emissions, about half of VOC emissions, and about two-fifths of NOx emissions (Small and Kazimi, 1995). Poor air quality can exacerbate respiratory problems and cause premature death. As we saw earlier in the book, urban air quality has generally improved in the last 20 years because lower emissions per mile driven have more than offset increases in mileage. Automobile travel also generates greenhouse gases, contributing to global climate change.

Internalizing the Externality

The economic approach to air pollution is to internalize the externality. A tax equal to the marginal external cost of pollution would cause drivers to incorporate the full costs of driving into their decisions, leading to the socially efficient level of pollution. A pollution tax would encourage people to buy cleaner cars and drive fewer miles. The direct approach would be to install a monitoring device in each car to measure its emissions and then charge the owner for the emissions.

An alternative approach is to impose a one-time pollution tax on each new car. The tax would vary by car model and would equal the estimated lifetime emissions times the external cost per unit of emissions. For example, if a particular model is expected to emit 5,000 units of pollutants over its lifetime and the external cost per unit of pollution is $0.20, the one-time pollution tax would be $1,000. Under this system, car buyers would have an incentive to buy cleaner cars, but would not have an incentive to drive less once they buy a car.

A Gasoline Tax

Another approach is to use a gasoline tax to increase the private cost of auto travel. The tax would increase the cost per mile driven, so it would decrease the total miles driven and decrease air pollution. The problem with a gas tax is that every driver would pay the same tax per gallon, regardless of how much pollution is generated per gallon of gasoline. So a gasoline tax would decrease pollution by decreasing miles driven but would not encourage people to drive cleaner cars. Of course, if government emissions standards generate relatively small differences in emissions per gallon across car models, the lack of incentives to buy clean cars would be less of an issue.

FIGURE 10–7 Market Effects of a Gasoline Tax

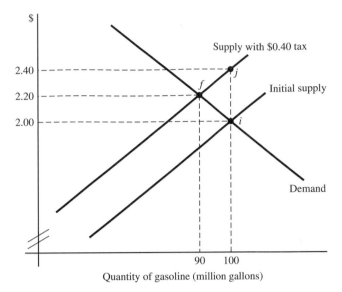

A tax of $0.40 per gallon of gasoline shifts the supply curve upward by $0.40, increasing the equilibrium price and decreasing the equilibrium quantity. Half the tax is borne by consumers, and half is shifted backward onto the people who supply the crude oil used to produce gasoline.

Figure 10–7 shows the effects of using a gasoline tax to internalize the externalities from air pollution. Point *i* shows the initial equilibrium, given a supply curve that does not include any pollution or greenhouse taxes. The equilibrium price is $2.00 and the quantity is 100 million gallons. Small and Kazimi (1995) estimate that the pollution-related external cost is about $0.02 per vehicle mile (or about $2,400 over the life of a car). With an average gas mileage of 20 miles per gallon, this translates into a gas tax of $0.40 per gallon. In Figure 10–7, this pollution tax shifts the supply curve upward by $0.40, increasing the equilibrium price from $2.00 to $2.20 and decreasing the equilibrium quantity from 100 to 90 million gallons.

In Figure 10–7, the increase in the equilibrium price is half the tax. This is consistent with studies of the effects of gasoline taxes on the price of gasoline (Chouinard and Perloff, 2004). Consumers pay half the tax, and the rest is paid by the people who supply the scarce input used to produce gasoline, crude oil. In Figure 10–7, the tax decreases the quantity of gasoline consumed by 10 percent, so it decreases the demand for crude oil. A decrease in the demand for crude oil decreases the equilibrium price, so part of the gasoline tax is shifted backward onto the people who own oil wells in Texas, Saudi Arabia, and other oil-producing areas.

An alternative approach for reducing auto pollution is to subsidize mass transit. A transit subsidy would encourage people to switch to buses and subways, which generate less pollution per passenger. As we saw earlier in the case of congestion externalities, using transit subsidies to reduce auto traffic presents some problems.

Travelers are not very responsive to changes in the price of transit, so a transit sub-sidy wouldn't reduce automobile pollution by very much. In addition, matching the underpricing of automobiles with underpricing of transit leads to a general under-pricing of transportation, which in turn leads to a misallocation of resources, with too much labor, capital, and energy allocated to transportation.

Greenhouse Gases and a Carbon Tax

The environmental and economic consequences of accumulating greenhouse gases remain uncertain. As carbon levels rise, scientists expect crop losses as well as substantial costs to protect coastal regions from rising waters, but quantifying these consequences is difficult. In terms of environmental policy, the key number is the ex-ternal cost per ton of carbon emitted, which determines the appropriate carbon tax. The current estimates are in the range of $25 to $100 per ton. A carbon tax of $50 per ton translates into a gasoline tax of $0.13 per gallon. We could extend Figure 10–7 to show the effects of carbon-based gasoline tax. A $0.13 tax would shift the supply curve upward by $0.13, increasing the equilibrium price and decreasing the equilib-rium quantity. The price would increase by about half the tax ($0.065), meaning that about half the tax would be shifted backward onto the suppliers of crude oil.

MOTOR VEHICLE ACCIDENTS

A third externality from the use of the automobile is motor-vehicle accidents—collisions with other vehicles, bicycles, and pedestrians. Collisions result in prop-erty damage, injuries (3.1 million per year in the United States), and deaths (about 40,000 per year in the United States). A recent study estimates that the annual cost of vehicle collisions is over $300 billion, or more than $1,000 per person (Miller, 1993). The externality occurs because when one person's driving decisions lead to a collision, roughly one-third of the costs are borne by someone else.

    The accident-related external cost of driving depends on the miles driven. The more you drive, the more likely you are to collide with someone else, generating costs for you and the other person. Of course, both the likelihood of a collision and the consequences depend on traffic conditions as well as how carefully people drive. Parry (2004) suggests that the accident-related external cost of travel is about 4.4 cents per mile driven. By way of comparison, the fuel cost per mile is about 10 cents. In this part of the chapter, we'll explore the effects of policies that improve vehicle safety. We'll also discuss a proposed policy under which people would pay for each mile they drive.

Vehicle Safety Policies: Bikers Beware

The Vehicle Safety Act of 1966 established safety standards for new cars, and sub-sequent legislation has extended the standards. Among the mandated features are head restraints, padded dashboards, seatbelts, shatterproof windshields, dual braking systems, collapsible steering columns, and air bags. These safety features add about $1,000 to the price of a car (Small, 1997).

Around the world, dozens of countries have laws that require car occupants to wear seat belts. Studies of these and other vehicle-safety laws uncover two puzzles:

1. Death rates among car occupants were predicted to drop significantly but instead decreased by a relatively small amount.
2. The death rates for pedestrians and bicyclists increased.

The theory of risk compensation (Peltzman, 1975) explains these puzzles. The idea is that in deciding how fast to drive, a person weighs the benefits and costs and chooses a speed that maximizes his or her utility. A mandated safety feature like seat belts decreases the cost of driving fast—crash injuries are less severe—so people drive faster and experience more collisions. The increase in the frequency of collisions partly offsets the fact that injuries are less severe. In addition, faster driving means higher death rates for pedestrians and bicyclists.

We can use a simple example of travel speed to explore the effects of mandated safety features on risk taking. Duke drives every Saturday night to a dance hall in Hazard City and must decide how fast to drive. The benefit of speed is that he spends less time on the road, leaving him more time to dance with Daisy. In Figure 10–8, the marginal benefit curve is negatively sloped, reflecting the diminishing marginal benefit of dancing time. For example, as shown by point s, traveling at

FIGURE 10–8 Speed and Safety Regulations

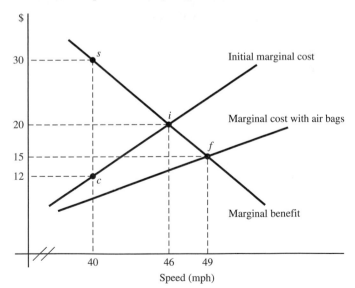

A traveler chooses the speed at which the marginal benefit (the value of time saved) equals the marginal cost (the expected accident costs). The introduction of a safety regulation such as air bags decreases the marginal cost and increases the speeed from 46 mph (point i) to 49 mph (point f).

40 miles per hour (mph) instead of 39 gives him additional dance time that he values at $30. Farther down the marginal-benefit curve, traveling at 46 mph instead of 45 mph gives him additional dance time that he values at only $20.

The cost of speed is that driving faster increases the likelihood of a collision and the severity of injuries. The positively sloped marginal-cost curve shows that the cost of speed rises at an increasing rate. When Duke speeds up from 39 to 40 mph, the likelihood and severity of injuries increases by a moderate amount, increasing the expected injury cost of the trip by $12 (shown by point c). When he speeds up from 45 to 46 mph, the likelihood and severity of injuries are larger, and the expected injury cost increases by $20 (point i).

The initial equilibrium is shown by point i, where the initial marginal-cost curve intersects the marginal-benefit curve. If Duke tentatively chooses a slower speed, say 39 mph, he could do better. As shown by points s and c, speeding up to 40 mph generates a bigger benefit ($30 worth of extra dance time) than a cost (an increase of $12 in expected injury costs). He will continue to speed up until he reaches point i, with a speed of 46 mph. He doesn't drive faster because the marginal benefit of additional speed is less than the marginal cost: The extra dance time is not worth the large increase in the expected injury cost.

How would mandated safety equipment affect Duke's choice of speed? Suppose the government requires air bags in all cars. The air bags reduce the severity of injuries from a collision, so the expected cost of driving fast decreases. In Figure 10–8, the marginal-cost curve shifts downward, and the marginal principle is now satisfied at point f. Without the air bag, the cost of going between 47 and 49 mph was higher than the benefits of the extra dance time; with the air bag, the cost is lower, so Duke drives faster. He compensates for the lower cost of risky behavior (driving fast) by driving faster, accepting a higher likelihood of a collision because he knows that the injuries suffered in a collision will be less severe.

There is evidence of risk compensation in response to mandated vehicle safety features. Peltzman (1975) notes that collision rates were higher than expected in the years following the implementation of safety regulations, and pedestrian death rates were higher too. Crandall et al. (1986) show that the death rates for pedestrians and bicyclists are positively related to an index of safety features, suggesting that drivers in safer cars take more risks and endanger others. Overall, the vehicle safety features have decreased traffic deaths because the decrease in driver deaths exceeds the increase in the deaths of pedestrians and bicyclists.

Pay to Drive Policies

In recent years, a new sort of policy has been proposed to deal with the problem of vehicle collisions. Since the external cost of driving depends on the miles driven, it is natural to consider imposing a per-mile tax on driving, known as a vehicle miles traveled (VMT) tax. Table 10–4 shows the marginal external cost for different types of vehicles and drivers of different ages. The external cost of young drivers is over three times as high as the external cost of middle-aged drivers. The external cost is highest for pick-up trucks and lowest for minivans. The relatively high external cost for small cars reflects the greater usage of small cars by young drivers.

TABLE 10–4 External Accident Costs for Different Vehicles and Driver Ages

	Small Car	Large Car	SUV	Minivan	Pickup	<25 years	25–70 years	>70 years
Cents per mile	4.8	3.94	3.59	3.04	5.76	10.87	3.42	5.43

Source: Parry, Ian W.H. "Comparing Alternative Policies to Reduce Traffic Accidents." *Journal of Urban Economics* 56 (2004), pp. 346–68.

FIGURE 10–9 Accident Costs and VMT Tax

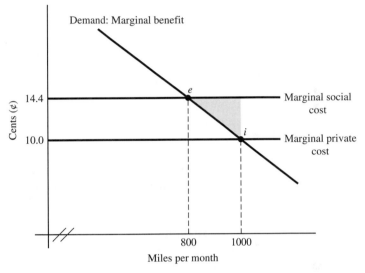

Automobile travel causes accidents, and the average external cost is 4.4 cents per mile. The individual decision about how many miles to drive is based on private costs, so the equilibrium number of miles (1,000 at point *i*) exceeds the socially efficient number (800 at point *e*). The shaded triangle shows the welfare loss from the accident-related underpricing of travel.

We can use the marginal approach to measure the inefficiency from accident externalities. The relevant concepts are reviewed in Section 1 of "Tools of Microeconomics," the appendix at the end of the book. In Figure 10–9, the demand curve for driving shows the marginal benefit of driving. The lower marginal-cost curve is the private cost of driving, assumed to be a constant 10 cents per mile driven. Among the private costs are the costs of fuel and other costs that depend on miles driven. This does not include insurance premiums, which are fixed on an annual basis and do not increase with mileage. The upper cost curve is the marginal social cost of driving, the sum of the marginal private cost and a marginal external cost of 4.4 cents per mile driven.

The initial equilibrium is shown by point *i*. People base their driving decisions on the costs they bear themselves—the private cost. According to the marginal principle, a driver will pick the number of miles where the marginal benefit equals the marginal private cost, generating 1,000 miles in this example (point *i*). The socially efficient outcome is shown by point e, where the marginal benefit equals the marginal *social* cost. For miles 801 through 1,000, the marginal benefit experienced by the driver (shown by the demand curve) is less than the marginal social cost, so driving these miles is socially inefficient.

The shaded triangle shows the welfare loss to society from the underpricing of driving. Starting from point i, the last mile driven (1,000) generates a benefit of 10 cents and a social cost of 14.4 cents, so the net loss to society is the difference, or 4.4 cents. Similarly, for mile number 900, the benefit is 12.2 cents and the cost is 14.4 cents, for a net loss of 2.2 cents. Adding up the losses for the 801st through the 1,000th miles, the cost of driving exceeds the benefit by the gap between the social-cost curve and the demand curve. The shaded triangle shows the welfare loss from collision externalities.

The obvious solution to the externality problem is to get drivers to pay for the accident costs they impose on society. A tax of 4.4 cents per mile would internalize the externality, moving us from point i to point e. The gain to society is the welfare loss averted, shown by the shaded triangle. As shown in Table 10–4, the external cost varies across vehicles and driver ages, and a precise driving-tax policy would involve higher taxes on the vehicles and drivers that generate the highest external cost. Specifically, the highest driving taxes would be imposed on young drivers and pickup drivers.

Parry (2004) estimates the welfare gains from alternative pricing schemes for accident externalities. A perfect VMT tax would be differentiated according to driver age (the young pay 10.87 cents per mile) and vehicle type (pickup drivers pay 5.76 cents; minivan drivers pay only 3.04 cents). In this case, the estimated welfare gain is 0.38 cents per mile driven, or $9.4 billion per year at the national level. Table 10–5 shows the welfare gains from tax schemes with different degrees of differentiation. A uniform tax (no differentiation) generates a welfare gain about three-fourths of the maximum gain of $9.4 billion.

Parry also considers two alternatives to the VMT tax. First, if insurance premiums were based strictly on mileage traveled, the effects on travel and efficiency would be about two-thirds of the effects from a perfect VMT tax. Second, a gasoline tax fares poorly as a way to internalize accident externalities, with welfare gains of about one-quarter of the gains generated by a differentiated VMT tax. The basic problem is that a person's gas-tax bill depends on the amount of gasoline consumed, not the number of miles driven. Gas mileage varies across vehicles, so a gas tax is a blunt policy instrument to reduce miles traveled. In addition, consumers would respond to a higher gas tax by purchasing more fuel-efficient cars, further weakening the connection between the tax and accident externalities.

TABLE 10–5 Imperfect VMT Taxes

Type of Differentiation	Percent of Maximum Welfare Gain
None: Uniform tax	76
Age	98
Vehicle Type	78

Accidents and Congestion

One of the external costs of traffic accidents is the congestion that results from blocked traffic. Parry (2004) estimates that traffic delays from accidents generate a cost of almost $5 billion per year in the United States. Although a VMT tax would decrease traffic volume and reduce traffic-snarling accidents, local governments would still need policies to respond to accidents that occur.

Cities have developed policies to respond quickly to accidents and clear disabled vehicles to restore traffic flow. Incident-response teams, equipped with strategically placed tow trucks, respond quickly to accidents. In some cities, tow trucks cruise the roads in anticipation of a radio call to clear up a nearby accident. Some cities have installed loop detectors in roadbeds that detect traffic slowdowns and alert officials immediately. Other cities use remote cameras to monitor traffic.

Some cities have developed special plans for dealing with congestion expected to occur during special events. In 1984, the city of Los Angeles anticipated severe congestion during the Olympics and developed a plan to use heavy-lift military helicopters to swoop in and remove disabled vehicles. An early fanciful report speculated that the helicopters would be equipped with large magnets, allowing them to pick up the disabled vehicles and transport them, dangling at the end of a cable, to the wrecking yard. It turns out that traffic was relatively light during the Olympics, so the helicopters were never actually used.

AUTOMOBILES AND POVERTY

In the chapter on neighborhood choice, we discussed the spatial mismatch between central-city workers and suburban jobs. The concentration of low-income workers in central cities, far from suburban jobs, leads to long commutes, low wages, and low employment rates. What is the possible role of automobiles in reducing the spatial mismatch?

Although many black central-city residents commute to suburban jobs, this sort of reverse commuting is costly and time-consuming because most low-income households don't own cars. About 27 percent of urban low-income families (with incomes less than $20,000) do not own a car, compared to 3 percent of urban households with incomes greater than $20,000. Among black workers living in central cities, 45 percent do not have access to a car. For low-skilled workers, having access to a car offers three benefits (O'Regan and Quigley, 1998):

- For a central-city worker who commutes to the suburbs by public transit, switching to an automobile would save about 19 minutes each day.
- Low-skilled workers with cars search for jobs over a much wider area and discover more job opportunities.
- Low-skilled workers with cars are more likely to complete job-training programs and get a job.

These studies have some important implications for welfare policy. In recent years, welfare policy has focused on moving people off welfare and into jobs.

O'Regan and Quigley (1998) summarize the possible role of automobiles:

> If potential commute patterns of people coming off public assistance are similar to those of people currently in poor working households, government policy must pay more attention to auto ownership opportunities. . . . So programs that help job takers obtain a used car—a secured loan for purchase, a leasing scheme, a revolving credit arrangement—may offer real promise, particularly in less dense and less centralized urban areas.

SUMMARY

Automobile travel generates externalities from congestion, pollution, carbon emissions, and accidents. Here are the main points of the chapter.

1. Automobile drivers base their travel decisions on private costs rather than social costs, so the equilibrium traffic volume exceeds the socially efficient volume.
2. A congestion tax internalizes the congestion externality.
3. Internalizing the environmental externalities from automobiles would require a tax of about $0.53 per gallon of gasoline.
4. People in safer vehicles drive less carefully, putting bicyclists and pedestrians at greater risk.
5. On average, the external cost of accidents is 4.4 cents per mile driven. The external cost is highest for young drivers and pickup trucks.

APPLYING THE CONCEPTS

1. **Using Thump-Thump Data**
   Cities lay cables (plastic-coated sensors) in roadways to gather data on traffic volume and speeds. Drivers know when they drive over the cables by the thump-thump sound. Based on thump-thump data, you have concluded that at a volume of 1,500 vehicles, the time required for a 10-mile trip is 24 minutes, compared to 23.98 minutes with 1,499 vehicles. The monetary cost of the trip is $1 and the opportunity cost of time is $0.10.
   a. Compute the external trip cost at a level of 1,500 vehicles.
   b. Suppose the initial volume (equilibrium without a congestion tax) is 1,500 vehicles. Use a graph like Figure 10–3 to show this situation, providing as many numbers as possible.
   c. Use your graph to identify the initial external trip cost and the optimum tax (in force once people have fully adjusted to a congestion tax). Is the optimum tax higher or lower than the initial external trip cost? Why?
2. **Bikers against Seat Belts**
   In a column of *The State Paper* (Columbia, South Carolina) on April 5, 2004, columnist John Monk describes the efforts of motorcycle riders to defeat a proposed law that would allow police to issue $25 tickets to automobile drivers and passengers who are not wearing seat belts. The law would not apply to motorcycles, yet the bikers showed up in groups of a dozen or more, some dressed in full biker regalia, to urge legislators to reject the law. Why?

3. **Vaporville: Ma'am, Step Away from the Car**

    Vaporville is evaluating the merits of using a vaporizer to clear up highway accidents. Helicopters could deliver a vaporizing beam to instantly vaporize any vehicles involved in an accident, clearing the roadway instantly. This is an alternative to a tow-truck system that takes 20 minutes to clear away vehicles. To simplify matters, assume the following:

    i.   An accident simply stops traffic until the disabled vehicles are removed. The opportunity cost of travel time is $0.10 per minute.

    ii. During peak periods, the typical accident stops 4,000 cars.

    iii. The cost of the tow-truck system is $200 per accident and the cost of the vaporizer is $1,200 per accident.

    As the vapo-gunner on the helicopter, your job is to decide when to use the vaporizer and when to wait for the tow truck. Describe a decision-making rule.

4. **Speed, Makeup Violations, and the Invisible Hands**

    Using Figure 10–8 as a starting point, show the effects of the following changes on the speed chosen by Duke of Hazard City.

    a. Daisy is grounded for makeup violations, leaving Duke without his favorite dance partner.

    b. The normal country band is replaced by the punk group Adam Smith and the Invisible Hands. For Duke, slam-dancing generates twice the utility as country-western dancing.

    c. The legal speed limit is set at 40 mph, and the fine on a speeding ticket increases with the gap between the driver's speed and 40 mph. Specifically, the fine equals the speed gap times $100. The probability of being caught and fined is 0.10.

5. **Youngsters Pay to Drive**

    The demand for automobile travel by the typical young driver (25 years or younger) has a vertical intercept of $1.00 per mile and a horizontal intercept of 200 miles per week. Initially, the cost of automobile insurance is a fixed weekly sum, independent of mileage. The average cost of driving (for gasoline, oil, maintenance, and repair) is constant at $0.20.

    a. Use a completely labeled graph to show the market equilibrium with "i."

    b. Use the data in Table 10–4 to show the socially efficient outcome on your graph with "e."

    c. Suppose the insurance company switches to a per-mile fee equal to the marginal external accident cost. Compute the net gain to society from the switch.

REFERENCES AND ADDITIONAL READING

1. Adams J.G.U. *Risk and Freedom: The Record of Road Safety Regulation.* Transport Publishing Projects, 1985.

2. Adams J.G.U. *Risk.* London: UCL Press, 1995.

3. Chouinard, Hayley, and Jeffrey M. Perloff. "Incidence of Federal and State Gasoline Taxes." *Economics Letters* 83 (2004), pp. 55–60.

4. Crandall, Robert W., Howard K. Gruenspecht, Theodore E. Keeler, and Lester B. Lave. *Regulating the Automobile.* Washington DC: Brookings Institution, 1986.

5. DiRenzo, J.; B. Cima; and E. Barber. "Parking Management Tactics." Vol. 3, *Reference Guide.* Washington, DC: U.S. Department of Transportation, 1981.

6. Harvey A.C., and J. Durbin. "The Effects of Seat Belt Legislation on British Road Casualties: A Case Study in Structural Time Series Modeling." *Journal of the Royal Statistical Society* 149 (1986), pp. 187–227.

7. Keeler, Theodore E., and Kenneth A. Small. "Optimal Peak-Load Pricing, Investment and Service Levels on Urban Expressways." *Journal of Political Economy* 85 (1977), pp. 1–25.

8. Meyer, John R., and Jose A. Gomez-Ibanez. *Autos, Transit and Cities.* Cambridge, MA: Harvard University Press, 1981. Chapter 11, pp. 185–229.

9. Miller, T.R. "Costs and Functional Consequences of U.S. Roadway Crashes." *Accident Analysis and Prevention* 25 (1993), pp. 593–607.

10. Mohring, Herbert. "Congestion." Chapter 6 in *Essays in Transportation Economics and Policy,* eds. Jose A. Gomez-Ibanez, William B. Tye, and Clifford Winston. Washington DC: Brookings, 1999.

11. Kraft, Gerald, and Thomas Domencich. "Free Transit." In *Readings in Urban Economics,* ed. Matthew Edel and Jerome Rothenberg. New York: Macmillan, 1972, pp. 459–80.

12. O'Regan, Katherine M., and John M. Quigley. "Cars for the Poor." *Access* 12 (Spring 1998), pp. 20–25.

13. Parry, Ian W.H. "Comparing Alternative Policies to Reduce Traffic Accidents." *Journal of Urban Economics* 56 (2004), pp. 346–68.

14. Peltzman, Sam. *Regulation of Automobile Safety.* Washington DC: American Enterprise Institute, 1975.

15. Pozdena, Randall J. "Unlocking Gridlock." *Federal Reserve Bank of San Francisco Weekly Letter,* December 1988, pp. 1–5.

16. Shoup, Donald C. "Cashing Out Employer-Paid Parking." *Access* (1993), pp. 3–9.

17. Small, Kenneth A. *Urban Transportation Economics.* Philadelphia: Harwood Academic Publishers, 1992.

18. Small, Kenneth A. "Urban Economics and Urban Transportation Policy in the United States." *Regional Science and Urban Economics* 27 (1997), pp. 671–91.

19. Small, Kenneth A., and Jose A. Gomez-Ibanez. "Road Pricing for Congestion Management: The Transition from Theory to Policy." In *Road Pricing, Traffic Congestion, and the Environment,* eds. Kenneth J. Button and Erik T. Verhoef. Cheltenham, UK: Edward Elfar, 1998.

20. Small, Kenneth A., and Camilla Kazimi. "On the Costs of Air Pollution from Motor Vehicles." *Journal of Transport Economics and Policy* (1995).

21. Texas Transportation Institute. *2002 Urban Mobility Study.* mobility.tamu.edu/ums.

22. U.S. Department of Transportation. *Summary of Travel Trends, 2001 National Household Travel Survey.* Washington DC: U.S. Department of Transportation, 2004.

CHAPTER 11

Mass Transit

While real trolleys in Newark, Philadelphia, Pittsburgh, and Boston languish for lack of patronage and government support, millions of people flock to Disneyland to ride fake trains that don't go anywhere.

—KENNETH T. JACKSON

*I*n this second chapter on urban transportation, we explore the role of mass transit—buses, light rail, and heavy rail. We will look at the modal-choice decision from two perspectives: individual travelers and transportation planners. At the national level, fewer than 5 percent of commuters use mass transit, but transit ridership is higher in many large cities and is relatively high among low-income commuters. Transit ridership is also much higher in most European cities.

In addition to looking at the present state of urban mass transit, we will explore the prospects for deregulation of the urban transit system. Here are some of the questions answered in the chapter.

1. Why do so few commuters use mass transit?
2. Under what circumstances is a bus system superior to a rail system—light rail (streetcars) or heavy rail (subways)?
3. What is the minimum population density required to efficiently utilize a bus system, light rail system, or subway?
4. How does the revenue from transit fares compare to the cost of operating the system?
5. How would deregulation affect the mix of transit options available to commuters?

MASS TRANSIT FACTS

Table 11–1 (page 236) shows the means of transportation to work in 2000 for the U.S. workforce. Overall, 4.7 percent of commuters use mass transit, and the share for central-city residents (11 percent) exceeds the share for suburban residents (2 percent). Transit usage is highest among workers who commute within the

TABLE 11–1 Means of Transportation to Work, 2000

Travel Mode	Number of Commuters	Percent
Workers 16 years and over	128,279,228	100
Car, truck, or van	112,736,101	87.9
Drove alone	97,102,050	75.7
Carpooled	15,634,051	12.2
Public transportation	6,067,703	4.7
Bus or trolley bus	3,206,682	2.5
Streetcar or trolley car	72,713	0.1
Subway or elevated train	1,885,961	1.5
Railroad	658,097	0.5
Ferryboat	44,106	
Taxicab	200,144	0.2
Motorcycle	142,424	0.1
Bicycle	488,497	0.4
Walked	3,758,982	2.9
Other means	901,298	0.7
Worked at home	4,184,223	3.3

Source: U.S. Bureau of the Census. *Journey to Work 2000.* Washington DC: U.S. Government Printing Office, 2004.

TABLE 11–2 Public Transit Ridership, 1940–2000 (in millions)

Year	Heavy Rail	Light Rail	Trolley Coach	Motor Bus	Total
1940	2,382	5,943	534	4,239	13,098
1950	2,264	3,904	1,658	9,420	17,246
1960	1,850	463	657	6,425	9,395
1970	1,881	235	182	5,034	7,332
1980	2,388	133	142	5,837	8,500
1990	2,346	176	126	5,677	8,325
2000	2,632	320	122	5,678	8,752

Source: American Public Transit Association. *Transit Fact Book 1991; Transit Fact Book 2005.* Washington, DC, 1994, 2005.

central city (16 percent). The shares of central-city workers who use public transit are 47 percent in New York, 26 percent in Chicago, and 25 percent in Philadelphia.

Table 11–2 shows the time trends in transit ridership. Total ridership in 2000 was about half of the ridership in 1950. Ridership reached a low point in 1970, recovered a bit between 1970 and 1980, and has been relatively steady since then. The trolley coach (a bus powered by overhead electric wires) reached its peak in 1950 and has declined since then. Light rail (streetcars) was the top mode in 1940 but declined through 1980 before again gaining riders. Light-rail systems have been built or restored in many cities, including Portland, San Jose, Sacramento, Buffalo, San Diego, and Pittsburgh. In Canada, there are new light-rail systems in Edmonton and Calgary.

Variation in Ridership across Metropolitan Areas and Income

Transit ridership varies substantially across metropolitan areas. In the New York metropolitan area, about 25 percent of workers use public transit. Three metropolitan areas have transit shares between 10 and 14 percent: Chicago, Washington DC, and Philadelphia. Eight metropolitan areas are in what we could call the trillion-mile club—areas where the annual passenger mileage is at least 1 trillion miles. At the top of the list is New York (18.4 trillion), followed by Chicago (3.7), Los Angeles (2.8), Washington DC (2.2), San Francisco (2.1), Boston (1.9), Philadelphia (1.5), and Seattle (1.0). Together these eight metropolitan areas are responsible for four-fifths of the transit passenger miles among the 38 metropolitan areas with populations of at least 1 million.

Transit ridership is relatively high among low-income families. Figure 11–1 shows the shares of transit riders that come from different income groups. For metropolitan areas with populations less than 1 million, over half of transit riders come from families with incomes of less than $15,000. At the national level, only about 10 percent of families are in this income range. About two-fifths of transit riders come from families with incomes between $15,000 and $50,000, which is roughly equal to the share of the nation's families in this income interval. For the largest metropolitan areas (with populations greater than 1 million), low-income households are overrepresented in transit, but to a lesser extent. As we saw in the previous chapter, low-income families have relatively low car ownership.

FIGURE 11–1 Shares of Transit Riders by Income and Metropolitan Population

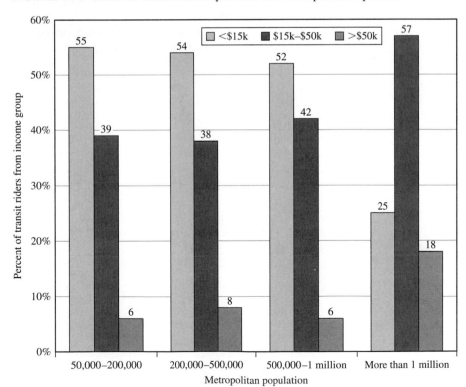

Source: American Public Transit Association. *Transit Fact Book 2005.* Washington, DC: American Public Transit Association, 2005.

Elasticities of Demand for Transit

A number of studies have measured the responsiveness of transit ridership to changes in prices and service. They present four main conclusions:

1. **Price elasticity.** A common rule of thumb is that a 10 percent increase in fares decreases ridership by about 3.3 percent, meaning that the price elasticity is −0.33. According to Small (1992), the price elasticity is relatively large for off-peak trips and trips by high-income commuters.
2. **Time elasticities.** The demand for transit is more responsive to changes in travel time. For the line-haul portion of the trip (time spent in the vehicle), Kraft and Domencich (1972) report an elasticity of −0.39: A 10 percent increase in line-haul time decreases ridership by about 3.9 percent. For access time (time spent getting to the bus stop or transit station), they report an elasticity of −0.71.
3. **Value of travel time.** According to Small (1992), the average commuter values the time spent in transit vehicles at about half the wage: The typical commuter would be willing to pay half the hourly wage to avoid an hour on the bus or train. The value of time spent walking and waiting is two to three times larger, meaning that the typical commuter would be willing to pay up to 1.5 times the hourly wage to avoid an hour of walking or waiting. As income increases, the value of travel time increases less than proportionately.
4. **Noncommuting trips.** The elasticities of demand for noncommuting travel are higher than the elasticities for commuting trips.

These empirical results have three principal implications. First, an increase in transit fares will increase total fare revenue. A fare increase decreases ridership by a relatively small amount, so total revenue (fare times ridership) increases. Kraft and Domencich (1972) suggest that dropping the price of mass transit to zero—making transit free—would increase ridership by only about a third. Second, a simultaneous improvement in service and fares may increase ridership. Suppose that a transit authority increases the frequency and speed of buses, and finances the improved service with higher fares. Because people are more sensitive to changes in time cost than changes in fares, ridership may increase. Third, service improvements that decrease walking and waiting time (more frequent service, shorter distances between stops) generate larger increases in ridership than improvements that decrease line-haul time.

CHOOSING A TRAVEL MODE: COMMUTER CHOICES

How does a commuter choose a travel mode? The objective of the commuter is to minimize the full cost of travel, including both the monetary and time costs. To illustrate a worker's modal choice, consider Carla, a commuter who travels 10 miles from her suburban home to a job in the central city. She has three travel options: the automobile, the bus, and a fixed-rail transit system such as BART (San Francisco), Metro (Washington DC), or MARTA (Atlanta).

TABLE 11–3 Modal Choice: Auto, Bus, or Heavy Rail?

	Auto	Bus	BART
Collection Time Cost			
Collection time (minutes)	0	10	15
Cost per minute ($)	0.30	0.30	0.30
Collection time cost ($)	0	3.00	4.50
Line-haul Time Cost			
Line-haul time (minutes)	40	50	30
Cost per minute ($)	0.10	0.10	0.10
Line-haul time cost ($)	4.00	5.00	3.00
Distribution Time Cost			
Distribution time (minutes)	0	5	9
Cost per minute ($)	0.3	0.3	0.3
Distribution time cost ($)	0	1.50	2.70
Total Time Cost ($)	4.00	9.50	10.20
Monetary Cost			
Operating cost or fare ($)	2.00	1.00	1.50
Parking cost ($)	3.00	0	0
Total Cost: Time + Monetary ($)	9.00	10.50	11.70

An Example of Modal Choice

Table 11–3 shows the monetary and time costs of Carla's one-way commute. We assume that Carla values in-vehicle time at half her $12 hourly wage (or $0.10 per minute) and walking and waiting time at 1.5 times her wage ($0.30 per minute). We can divide the commuting trip into three parts.

1. **Collection:** Travel from the home to the main travel vehicle. Carla walks 10 minutes to the bus stop or 15 minutes to a BART station. Getting to a BART station takes longer because the stations are more widely spaced than bus stops.
2. **Line-haul.** Time spent on the main travel vehicle. At 30 minutes, BART is the fastest mode because it operates on an exclusive right-of-way. Next at 40 minutes is the automobile, which travels on congested roads. Finally the bus, which travels on congested streets and stops to pick up passengers, takes 50 minutes.
3. **Distribution:** Travel from the end of the vehicle trip (transit station, bus stop, or parking garage) to the workplace. If parking is available near the workplace, the auto has the shortest distribution time, followed by the bus and the fixed-rail system. Carla parks her car in a parking lot under her office building, so the distribution time of the auto trip is zero. The distribution time for the bus (five minutes) is less than the time for BART (nine minutes) because bus stops are spaced closer than BART stations.

Adding up the time costs of all three parts of the trip, we get $4.00 for the auto, $9.50 for the bus, and $10.20 for BART. The time costs for the auto are lower because the opportunity cost of collection and distribution time are so high.

Table 11–3 also shows the monetary costs of the three travel modes. The monetary cost of the auto trip is $3.00 for parking ($6.00 per day) plus $2.00 for gas and other costs that vary with distance traveled. The bus fare is assumed to be $1.00, and the BART fare is $1.50. It's worth noting that the monetary costs for the two transit modes are small relative to the time costs.

In this example, the least costly travel mode is the automobile. As shown in the last row of Table 11–3, auto commuting is $1.50 less costly than bus commuting and $2.70 less costly than BART. Although driving has a higher monetary cost, this disadvantage is more than offset by its lower collection and distribution costs. The automobile has a collection and distribution advantage of $4.50 over the bus and $7.20 over BART. As a result, the rational choice for Carla is to drive to work.

What would it take to get Carla to switch from driving to riding the bus? The cost gap for the two modes is $1.50, so one possibility is to increase the cost of driving by $1.50. This could be accomplished with two sorts of taxes:

- **Congestion tax.** A tax of $0.15 per mile would close the cost gap, and such a tax would be in the range of the estimated peak-period congestion taxes noted in the previous chapter.
- **Gasoline tax.** The per-gallon tax would have to be $3.00 (assuming gas mileage of 20 miles per gallon).

An alternative approach is to improve bus service:

- **Collection and distribution time.** Cutting access time by five minutes would close the cost gap (5 minutes times $0.30 per minute = $1.50).
- **Line-haul time.** Cutting the line-haul time by 15 minutes would close the gap (15 minutes times $0.10 = $1.50). The change in line-haul time is relatively large because the opportunity cost of time spent in the bus is relatively low.

What about cutting the bus fare? This would not work because even if the bus were free, Carla would still drive herself.

The same logic applies to the task of getting Carla to switch to BART. The cost gap between driving and BART is larger, so it would take a larger congestion tax or gasoline tax to get her to switch. Similarly, it would take larger improvements in BART service to get Carla to switch, and a reduction in access time would be more effective than a reduction line-haul time.

The Role of Density

In an earlier chapter on land-use patterns, we briefly discussed the role of population density in supporting mass transit. Mass transit is feasible only if density around bus stops or transit stations is high enough to attract a sufficient number of riders. For most people, the maximum walking time to a transit stop is about 10 minutes, so a transit stop can serve households within an 800-meter radius.

Table 11–4 shows the minimum densities required to support various types of transit. The built-up density of a metropolitan area is defined as total population

TABLE 11–4 Minimum Densities to Support Mass Transit

	Built-up Density: People per Hectare	Residential Density: People per Hectare
One bus per hour	21	30
Two buses per hour	31	44
Light rail	37	53
Heavy rail	50	71

Notes: Hectare = 2.5 acres; intermediate service = 40 buses per day; high service = 120 buses per day.
Source: Holtzclaw, J. *Using Residential Patterns and Transit to Decrease Auto Dependence and Costs.* Washington DC: Natural Resources Defense Council, June 1994.

divided by the amount of land in urban use, including residential areas, industrial districts, commercial areas, roads, schools, and city parks. In contrast, residential density is defined as population divided by the residential area. The minimum density for hourly bus service is 21 people per built-up hectare and 30 people per residential hectare. Moving down the table, the minimum densities increase as we move to more frequent bus service, light rail, and heavy rail. As Bertaud (2003) noted, a minimum average density is at best an approximation because it is based on average density and ignores variation in density within a metropolitan area.

As we saw in an earlier chapter, few U.S. metropolitan areas meet these minimum density thresholds. New York (40 people per hectare) meets the threshold for light rail and bus service, and Honolulu (31) meets the threshold for intermediate bus service (two buses per hour). The 10 most dense metropolitan areas, with densities of 18 or more people per hectare, come close to the low-level threshold of bus service. Of course, these are average densities, and parts of some of these metropolitan areas have population densities high enough to support transit. For example, the density in New York City is 80 people per hectare. In contrast, European cities such as Barcelona (with a density of 171 people per hectare) and Paris (88 per hectare) have high enough densities to support the highest level of transit service.

Trade-offs in Transit Service

How do changes in transit design and scheduling affect ridership? Service improvements that decrease the time cost of transit will increase ridership. As we saw earlier, travelers are most responsive to changes in the walking and waiting time associated with the collection and distribution parts of the trip.

The designer of a bus system has two key choices. The first is the bus headway, the period of time between buses on the bus route. As the headway decreases, riders spend less time waiting at the bus stop, so their time cost decreases. The second is the space between bus stops, which affects line-haul time as well as collection and distribution time. The shorter the distance between stops, the shorter the distance travelers must walk, but also the longer the line-haul time because more time is spent picking up and dropping off passengers.

Consider next the design of a fixed-rail system. San Francisco's BART provides a nice illustration of the design trade-offs:

1. **Mainline versus integrated system.** BART is a mainline system because it relies on other modes to collect its riders from residential neighborhoods. Riders must walk, drive, or ride a bus to the BART station. The alternative is an integrated system, under which a commuter makes the entire trip in a single vehicle.

2. **Spacing between stations.** BART has widely spaced stations (about 2.5 miles apart), and the small number of stops means that line-haul time is relatively low. In contrast, access time is relatively high because commuters must travel long distances to get to the widely spaced stations.

BART was designed to compete with the line-haul portion of the automobile trip. It achieves this objective, providing comfortable, speedy service from the suburban stations to the city center. The trade-off is that collection cost is relatively high because BART is a mainline system with widely spaced stations. Because walking and waiting time is more costly than in-vehicle time, the negative attribute (high collection cost) dominates the positive one (comfortable, speedy line-haul travel), so the full cost of a BART trip is relatively high and BART has diverted a relatively small number of auto commuters.

High-Occupancy Vehicle Lanes and Busways

Many cities have established exclusive rights of way for buses, vans, and carpools, allowing these high-occupancy vehicles (HOV) to bypass congested roadways. At one extreme is a separate roadway for buses, sometimes called a busway. At the other extreme is simply designating a single lane on an existing highway for use by carpools and buses, sometimes called a diamond lane. Some cities use HOV facilities as a core element in their transportation plans (Giuliano and Small, 1994). HOV facilities improve bus service in two ways:

- Line-haul times decrease because buses bypass congestion. Pittsburgh's East Busway has faster travel speeds than similar light-rail lines.
- An increase in bus ridership means that buses can run more frequently, generating lower collection and distribution costs. Miami's South Dade Busway has increased bus ridership by 50 percent, in large part because it offers more frequent service.

What are the effects of diamond lanes on commuters who continue to drive? The good news is that some auto drivers switch to buses and car pools, so there is less car traffic. The bad news is that there are fewer lanes for the remaining cars. The ill-fated diamond lane on the Santa Monica Freeway in Los Angeles shifted a relatively small number of commuters to car pools, so 25 percent of the freeway's capacity was used by only 6 percent of the vehicles. After the resulting public outcry, the lane was returned to general use. In contrast, Houston's HOV system caused large increases in carpooling and bus ridership, diverting large volumes of traffic from general-purpose lanes. As a result, congestion dropped by 4 percent (Richmond, 1998).

FIGURE 11–2 Average Cost of Alternative Transportation Systems

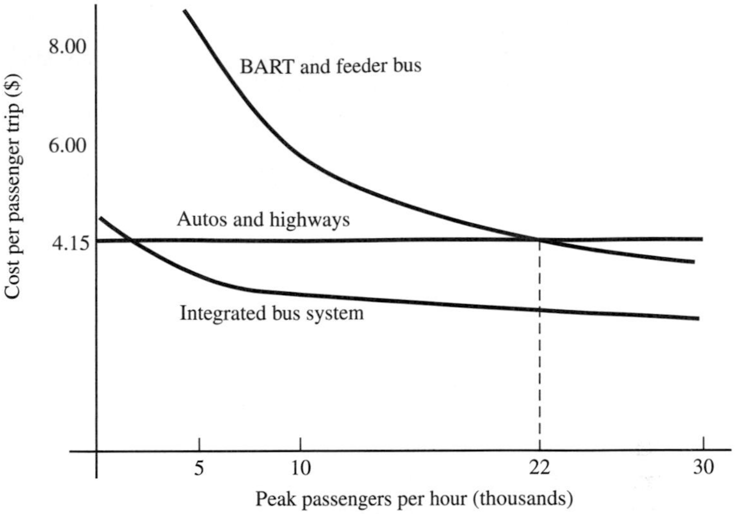

The average cost of an automobile system is constant, but the average cost of a bus system or BART decrease as volume increases. The bus system is more efficient than BART for all volumes studied and more efficient than an automobile system for volumes exceeding 1,100.

DESIGNING A TRANSIT SYSTEM

This part of the chapter discusses the costs of alternative transportation systems from the perspective of a transportation planner. The classic study of system choices considers three options: an auto-based highway system, an integrated bus system, and a fixed-rail system like BART (Keeler, Merewitz, Fisher, and Small, 1975).

The principal conclusions of their study are shown in Figure 11–2. The horizontal axis measures the number of commuters traveling through a transportation corridor during the one-hour peak period. The vertical axis measures the long-run average cost of a "typical" commuting trip—a six-mile line haul and additional time spent in residential collection and downtown distribution. The cost curves show that the bus system is more efficient than the auto system for volumes above 1,100 passengers per hour and is more efficient than BART for all traffic volumes. The auto system is more efficient than BART for volumes up to about 22,000 passengers per hour.

Cost of the Auto System

The cost of the auto system is the sum of the driver's time and operating cost and the public cost of auto traffic. The public cost includes the cost of building the optimum road system. As explained in the previous chapter, the revenue from the optimum congestion tax equals the cost of building the optimum road, so congestion taxes can be used to both internalize congestion externalities and pay for the roads. The public cost also includes the cost of air and noise pollution. It does not include the external costs of greenhouse gases or traffic accidents.

The average cost curve is horizontal for two reasons. First, Keeler et al. (1975) assumed that the unit operating cost and pollution cost do not depend on traffic volume. Second, in the long run, the highway is widened to accommodate any increase in traffic without any reduction of travel speeds. As we saw in the previous chapter, if there are constant returns to scale in building highways, doubling highway capacity doubles traffic volume without changing the trip time. Using data for 1972, Keeler et al. estimate that the full cost of an auto trip with a six-mile line haul is $4.15.

Cost of the Bus System and BART

The cost of the integrated bus system is the sum of capital cost, operating cost, pollution cost, and the time cost of riders. Included in the capital cost is the cost of modifying the roadway to accommodate buses. In Figure 11–2, the average-cost curve for the bus system is negatively sloped because an increase in the ridership spreads the fixed cost over more riders. In addition, an increase in ridership decreases the collection and distribution time of riders. A larger volume of riders allows shorter headways (time between buses) and shorter distances between bus stops. As a result, riders will spend less time walking to bus stops and less time waiting for buses. If the traffic volume along the corridor exceeds 1,100 passengers, the integrated bus system is less costly than the auto system.

The BART option is a mainline heavy-rail system combined with feeder buses to bring commuters to and from the BART stations. The BART system has the same basic cost structure as the bus and experiences the same sort of economies of volume. In Figure 11–2, the BART curve is negatively sloped because a larger volume spreads the fixed cost over more riders and decreases collection and distribution time. BART is more costly than the bus system for three reasons:

- **Higher collection and distribution cost.** BART is a mainline system, and it has relatively high costs for travel to and from the widely spaced stations.
- **Higher capital cost.** According to Webber (1976), BART could have purchased enough buses to carry its passengers for only $40 million (2.5 percent of BART's capital cost).
- **Higher operating cost.** BART average operating cost was about 15 percent higher than the bus.

System Choice

The Keeler study provides important information for transit planners. For all corridor volumes studied (up to 30,000 passengers per hour), BART was more costly than an integrated bus system. At a peak volume of 30,000 passengers per hour, BART is 50 percent more costly than the bus system. BART's peak ridership through most corridors is well below this threshold. The lesson for planners is clear: With the possible exceptions of New York City and Chicago, which have corridor volumes exceeding 30,000 passengers per hour, an integrated bus system is likely to be more efficient than a modern fixed-rail system like BART. Recent experience with new heavy-rail systems in other metropolitan areas confirm the results of the earlier study. Ridership on the new systems in Washington, D.C., Atlanta, Miami, and Baltimore has fallen well short of levels required to make heavy rail less costly than bus systems.

Light Rail

In recent years, many medium-size cities have built light-rail transit systems. Light rail is the modern version of the trolley and streetcar systems that were built in the late 1800s and early 1900s. The first modern light-rail system opened in Edmonton in 1978. Richmond (1998) examines light-rail systems in 11 cities (Baltimore, Buffalo, Dallas, Denver, Los Angeles, Pittsburgh, Portland, Sacramento, San Diego, San Jose, and St. Louis) and compares their performance to bus systems. Here are some of his conclusions:

1. **Light rail has higher capital costs.** For example, the capital cost of the Long Beach light-rail system was $881 million, compared to the $168 million in capital costs that would have been required for an equivalent bus system.
2. **Light rail has higher operating costs.** Most data reported on the operating costs of light rail omit the costs of the feeder buses that bring riders to light-rail stations. Ignoring these costs, the average operating cost for light rail is somewhat higher or perhaps slightly lower than that for equivalent bus lines. For example, the cost per passenger mile for Portland's MAX is $0.38, compared to $0.32 for one equivalent bus line, and $0.39 for another. Once the cost of feeder buses is included, light rail is more expensive than equivalent bus lines.
3. **Light rail diverts passengers from buses.** For the Blue Line in Los Angeles, 63 percent of riders were previously bus riders. In Portland, about 55 percent of MAX's riders switched from buses to light rail.

A light-rail system requires feeder buses to collect passengers, and this is expensive for transit authorities and bothersome for potential riders. In the modern metropolitan area with dispersed employment and retail activities, it is difficult to attract enough riders to make light rail less costly than a well-designed bus system. In many cases, busways and other HOV systems would be less expensive—and more effective—in increasing transit ridership (Richmond, 1998). In other cases, simple and inexpensive changes in regular bus service (adding buses, changing routes or schedules, or decreasing fares) may be more efficient than big projects.

SUBSIDIES FOR PUBLIC TRANSIT

Taxpayers provide large subsidies for mass transit. In 2002, the total value of the subsidies from federal, state, and local governments was $23.2 billion, with $13.8 billion in subsidies for operating costs and another $9.4 billion in capital subsidies. The federal government provided about 30 percent of the subsidies, while state

FIGURE 11–3 Fare-Box Ratios for Public Transit, 2002

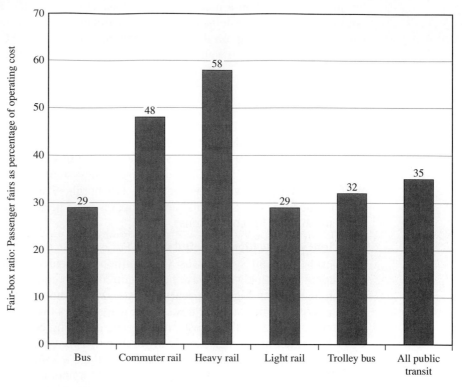

Source: Author's calculations based on data from American Public Transit Association. *Transit Fact Book 2005.* Washington DC: American Public Transit Association. 2005. Fare-box ratio: Passenger fares as percentage of operating cost.

governments provided 36 percent and local governments provided the remaining 34 percent. These subsidies are necessary because transit fare revenue falls short of operating and capital costs. Figure 11–3 shows the fare-box ratios, defined as the percentage of operating costs covered by fares. Overall, passenger fares covered 35 percent of the operating costs (and none of the capital costs).

Justification for Transit Subsidies

The subsidization of mass transit can be justified on efficiency grounds. Recall the fourth axiom of urban economics:

Production is subject to scale economies

In the case of rail transit, the indivisible inputs are the tracks and transit vehicles. Once a city has laid out the system of tracks and tunnels, traffic volume can range between one vehicle per day and hundreds. The substantial capital cost of the transit network leads to declining long-run average cost, as shown in Figure 11–4. An added factor discussed earlier in the chapter is the economies associated with higher

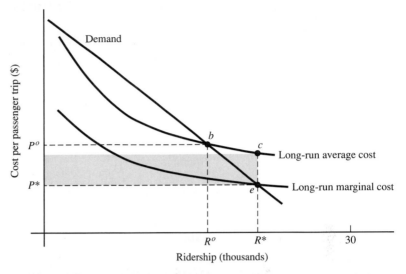

FIGURE 11–4 Scale Economies and Transit Subsidies

Because of scale economies, the long-run average cost curve for transit is negatively sloped. Point e is the socially efficient point where the marginal benefit (shown by the demand curve) equals the marginal cost. At the efficient quantity, price is less than average cost, so a subsidy (shown by the shaded area) is necessary.

traffic volume: the larger the number of riders, the more frequent the service and the lower the time cost of riders. In Figure 11–4, the long-run average cost is negatively sloped, and the long-run marginal cost lies below the average curve.

What is the socially efficient level of transit ridership? We can use the marginal principle to determine the optimum ridership. The marginal principle is reviewed in Section 1.1 of "Tools of Microeconomics," the appendix at the end of the book. Using the marginal principle, the socially efficient level is where the marginal cost equals the marginal benefit. The marginal benefit is shown by the market demand. Point e is the socially efficient point, with a price of $P*$ and a ridership level of $R*$. Because of economies of scale, the average cost of $R*$ (shown by point c) exceeds the price $P*$, and the shaded area shows the transit deficit associated with the socially efficient level of ridership.

The government could require the transit authority to cover all of its costs, including both operating and capital costs. In Figure 11–4, this would lead us to point b, with a price of P^0 and a ridership of R^0. This is socially inefficient because the willingness to pay for an additional rider exceeds the marginal cost of serving the rider. In other words, an additional rider values a trip more than it costs society to provide it, so stopping at R' riders is inefficient.

Reasons for Transit Deficits

The fare-box ratio is one measure of the fiscal health of mass transit. The lower the ratio, the larger the shortfall between fare revenue and operating costs. Between

1960 and 2002, the fare-box ratio decreased from 102 percent to 35 percent. There were several factors behind the decrease in the fare-box ratio (Pickerell, 1983; Small, 1997):

1. **Low fares.** Transit fares have been kept relatively low, in part to attract riders. Because demand for transit is price inelastic, lower fares mean lower total revenue.
2. **Higher wages.** Wages for transit workers have increased rapidly over the last few decades.
3. **Increase in transit mileage.** Transit service was extended into low-density suburban areas, where ridership is relatively low.
4. **Decrease in labor productivity.** Between 1970 and 1995, total transit ridership increased slightly (by 6 percent), while total transit employment more than doubled, meaning that productivity (rides per worker) was cut in half.
5. **Increase in peak traffic.** The fraction of rides during the peak periods increased, requiring transit organizations to hire more workers, some of whom are idle during the off-peak periods.

DEREGULATION: CONTRACTING AND PARATRANSIT

In most cities in the United States, urban transportation is heavily regulated. Firms are prohibited from providing services that compete with the local transit authority, so the transit authority has a monopoly. In addition, a taxi cannot pick up additional passengers en route to one passenger's destination and cannot pick up customers along routes chosen by the driver. In other words, a taxi cannot serve as a common carrier.

One rationale for restricting entry is to prevent cream-skimming by private firms. A public transit authority covers a large number of routes, even the ones with low ridership and thus revenue that falls well short of the cost of service. The revenue from more lucrative routes helps cover the losses on the less lucrative ones. If firms were free to enter the transit market, they would take business away from public transit on the profitable routes (skimming the cream) and hamper the cross-subsidization efforts. The result could be higher fares or reduced service on the low-volume routes. Alternatively, the government could continue to subsidize low-volume routes, but the subsidies would be explicit and transparent.

Contracting for Transit Services

One option for deregulation is to write contracts to have private firms provide specific transit services. The local government can specify the service characteristics of the transit system (e.g., headways, travel times, location of bus stops, fares) and then accept bids from private firms for the transit service. The Federal Transit Administration estimates that this sort of contracting would generate savings in operating costs between 25 and 30 percent. When the city of Tidewater, Virginia, contracted for bus service to low-density areas, a private transit company provided the same transit service at a cost per passenger of about $3 lower. Other cities using transit contracts have experienced similar cost savings. Cities also use contracting for subsidized dial-a-ride services.

Private firms provide transit services for a lower cost for three reasons. First, they pay lower wages. When BART accepted bids for feeder-bus service to serve transit stations, the average hourly wage among bidders was $2 below the wage of public transit workers. Second, private companies have more flexible work rules. They use split shifts and part-time workers, so they don't pay idle workers during the off-peak periods. Third, private companies use minibuses on low-density routes, saving on operating and capital costs.

Paratransit

A second option for deregulation is to allow private firms to compete for transit consumers. Deregulation would change the mix of transportation services available in most cities. The current system has two extremes—solo-rider taxis and large transit vehicles (large buses and rail cars)—and would be replaced by a system that provides travelers with a wider variety of services in a variety of vehicles.

The term *paratransit* was adopted in the 1970s to describe a wide variety of services that fall between the private automobile and the conventional bus.

- **Shared-ride taxis (three to four passengers).** During World War II, shared-ride taxis thrived in Washington DC. Cab drivers displayed destination signs, allowing people along the route to hail cabs going their way. Currently a number of cities allow the sharing of taxis.
- **Jitneys (6 to 15 passengers).** Compared to a large bus, a jitney has a lower cost per passenger and can provide more frequent service. Jitneys also have the flexibility to change routes, pickup points, and schedules. Several cities allow jitney service, resulting in lower fares and profits for the provider. Atlantic City restricts the number of jitneys, and the market value of a jitney license was $160,000 in 1995.
- **Subscription commuter vans and buses (10 to 60 passengers).** Riders pay in advance for commuter bus service. In San Francisco, Golden Gate Transit established 22 commuter routes between suburban communities and the downtown financial district. In New York City, private bus lines carry about 60,000 workers per day to jobs in Manhattan. The private operators have lower costs than public buses in part because they pay lower wages.

Paratransit can fill the gap in the urban transportation system between solo-rider taxis and large public buses. In contrast to subsidized public buses, paratransit operations actually earn profits. In summarizing the prospects for paratransit, Cervero (1996) notes that:

> Given the fiscal cutbacks facing America's public transit industry today, the expansion of more entrepreneurial, commercial transportation services seems unavoidable. While critics charge that the poor will suffer as a result, other remedies—like user-side subsidies—are available for redressing inequities. Moreover the history of commercial paratransit is certainly not one of ignoring poor neighborhoods. For jitneys and neighborhood car services, low-income areas have traditionally been their market base.

The British Experience with Deregulation

In Britain, the transit industry was deregulated under the British Transport Act of 1985. The act relaxed controls on entry into the transit industry, reorganized most public transit authorities as for-profit organizations, and introduced competitive bidding for some transit services. In addition, transit subsidies were cut significantly, leading to higher fares and service cuts. Deregulation led to an increased use of minivans, lower production costs as wages fell and work rules were relaxed, and the elimination of service on some low-volume routes.

Gomez-Ibanez and Meyer (1990) discuss three lessons from the British deregulation experience. First, it is possible to have both competition in the local bus industry and subsidies for unprofitable services. Cities can use competitive bidding to pick low-cost private providers. Second, deregulation causes service innovation and lower costs. Third, because most of the benefits from deregulation come from competition among transit firms, the public sector must develop policies to ensure competition.

TRANSIT AND LAND-USE PATTERNS

As we saw in Chapter 7, urban transportation technology determines urban form. The monocentric city of the early 20th century resulted from the combination of streetcars for the transportation of workers and primitive technology for the transportation of goods (the horse-drawn wagon) and the transmission of information (nonelectronic). The development of the truck and the interstate highway system allowed the decentralization of manufacturing jobs, while the development of electronic transmission allowed the decentralization of information (office) jobs. The automobile freed workers from their dependence on walking and streetcars, causing suburbanization and lower residential density.

In this part of the chapter, we explore the effect of modern mass-transit systems on land-use patterns. Do systems like BART and MARTA increase the density of employment and residence near transit stations?

The experience of Atlanta shows that supplying mass transit does not create demand for it. In the last two decades, there have been substantial investments in mass transit, including the building of a heavy-rail system with 74 kilometers of tracks. Although the transport network runs smoothly and safely (it won the award for "Safest Transit System in America in 17 out of 20 years), it has failed to attract jobs and people. Between 1990 and 1999, nearly 700,000 people were added to the Atlanta metropolitan area, but only a small fraction of the new residents lived or worked at locations accessible to the transit system.

Table 11–5 shows how few of the new residents are accessible to mass transit. As shown in the first column, only 2 percent of the additional residents chose locations that are accessible to a MARTA station, and only 13 percent chose locations accessible to a bus line. Over the same period, over 400,000 jobs were added to the metropolitan area, but as shown in the second column of Table 11–5, only 1 percent were accessible to MARTA and 22 percent were accessible to a bus line. The fact

TABLE 11–5 Transit Accessibility of Additional Residents and Jobs in Atlanta

	Residence	Jobs
Percent within 800 meters of MARTA station	2	1
Percent within 800 meters of bus line	13	22
Percent inaccessible to mass transit	85	77

Source: Alain Bertaud. "Clearing the Air in Atlanta: Transit and Smart Growth or Conventional Economics?" *Journal of Urban Economics* 54 (2003), pp. 379–400.

that so few people chose locations accessible to mass transit suggests a weak connection between transit design and urban form, at least in Atlanta.

One of the objectives of San Francisco's BART was to increase employment opportunities in the areas near transit stations. Studies of BART suggest that BART had a moderately positive effect on employment near stations in downtown San Francisco, but not much of an effect elsewhere (Cervero and Landis, 1995). This is consistent with studies of other rail systems, which support two conclusions (Altshuler, 1979):

1. In a growing economy, rail transit contributes to the clustering of activities near downtown stations. These clustering effects are usually negligible outside the central business district.
2. Investment in rail transit is sensible only if it is used in concert with more powerful land-use instruments such as zoning and property taxation. If the government uses its zoning and tax policies to generate high-density development, rail transit provides an efficient means of delivering a large number of workers to the dense central area.

MASS TRANSIT AND POVERTY

In the chapter on neighborhood choice, we discussed the spatial mismatch between central-city workers and suburban jobs. The concentration of low-income workers in central cities, far from suburban jobs, leads to long commutes, low wages, and low employment rates. In the previous chapter, we discussed the virtues of promoting automobile ownership among low-income households. What is the role of mass transit in the spatial mismatch?

As shown in Figure 11–1, low-income workers rely more on mass transit. Although many low-income, central-city residents commute to suburban jobs, this sort of reverse commuting is costly and time-consuming. Most mass-transit systems are designed to deliver suburban residents to city centers and are ill-suited for bringing central-city residents to suburban jobs.

A recent modification of BART in the San Francisco Bay Area illustrates the potential of mass transit to improve employment prospects for central-city residents (Holzer, Quigley, and Raphael, 2003). The system was extended to link a suburban area that has experienced rapid job growth with central-city areas that have large concentrations of minority workers. The new link increased Latino employment in suburban jobs close to the new transit route. In contrast, the new link had little effect on the employment of black workers because the transit route was less accessible to black households.

SUMMARY

Transit ridership is relatively low in most U.S. metropolitan areas because population densities are relatively low. Here are the main points of the chapter.

1. Overall, 4.7 percent of commuters use mass transit. Transit ridership is higher for central-city residents and low-income workers.
2. The price elasticity of demand for transit is –0.33, and ridership is more unresponsive to changes in waiting and walking times. The disutility of walking and waiting is two to three times the disutility of time in transit vehicles.
3. Only a few U.S. metropolitan areas meet the minimum density requirements for self-supporting transit service.
4. A study of alternative transport systems for the San Francisco Bay area concluded that an integrated bus system was superior to an auto-based system for corridor volumes exceeding 1,100 per hour and superior to a heavy-rail system like BART for all corridor volumes studied.
5. Light rail has higher capital and operating costs than a bus system.
6. In 2000, passenger fares covered only about 35 percent of the operating cost of transit. Transit deficits have increased over the last few decades, a result of lower fares and worker productivity and the extension of service to low-density areas.
7. Transit systems have modest effects on land-use patterns.

APPLYING THE CONCEPTS

1. **Distance between Bus Stops**
   Consider a city that decreases the distances between bus stops, which decreases the walking time of bus riders by 20 percent, increases the in-vehicle (line-haul) time by 10 percent, and increases operating cost by 10 percent.
   a. Use the estimates of the relevant elasticities to predict the percentage change in ridership.
   b. How would your answer to (*a*) change if the transit authority passes on the higher operating cost in the form of an increased fare?
2. **Internalizing Automobile Externalities**
   Consider a city where the fixed cost of a transit system is $1,400 per hour. The marginal cost is constant at $1 per rider. The demand curve is linear, with a vertical intercept of $11 and a slope of $-\$0.01$ per rider.
   a. Compute the socially efficient price, ridership, and deficit per rider. Illustrate with a graph.
   b. Suppose the city internalizes the externalities from automobiles (from environmental effects, congestion, and accidents). The willingness to pay for transit increases by $4 at each ridership level. Use your graph to show the effects on ridership and the deficit per rider.

3. **Disney Transit**

   Consider the chapter opening quote. Suppose your city hires the entire team of workers that designed the most popular Disneyland rides and asks them to redesign the city's transit system. The objective is to increase ridership and eliminate the transit subsidy: Fares will cover the full cost of the system.

   a. Predict the features of the Disney-inspired transit system.

   b. Would you expect the new system to meet the city's objectives?

4. **Personal Transporter in a Briefcase**

   Consider a large city with severe congestion on highways and exclusive busways. Suppose the city gives each of its citizens a human transporter, a self-balancing personal transportation vehicle. As the latest marvel of miniaturization, the transporter can be collapsed into a package the size of a briefcase and carried onto buses. The transporter allows travel at four times the speed of walking and, with a special bubble accessory, can be used for comfortable transport even in nasty weather.

   Use a figure like Figure 11–4 to show the effects of the transporter on transit ridership and the transit deficit per transit passenger.

5. **A Planner's Bomb in Atlanta**

   Consider the effects of dropping a planner's bomb on the Atlanta metropolitan area. A planner's bomb doesn't hurt any people, but destroys everything except the MARTA infrastructure (tracks, vehicles, and stations). Most important, it destroys all buildings, so the metropolitan area must be completely rebuilt. To simplify the geography, imagine that the MARTA tracks are radial, with two lines intersecting at the center.

   a. The planner's objective is to generate transit ridership equal to the levels observed in Barcelona while accommodating Atlanta's prebomb population. Describe the features of the plan for rebuilding the city.

   b. If the plan is implemented, would you expect the population of the metropolitan area to change?

REFERENCES AND ADDITIONAL READING

1. Altshuler, Alan A. *The Urban Transportation System.* Cambridge, MA: Joint Center for Urban Studies of MIT and Harvard, 1979.
2. American Public Transit Association. *Transit Fact Book 2005.* Washington DC, 2005.
3. Beesley, Michael E., and Michael A. Kemp. "Urban Transportation." In *Handbook of Regional and Urban Economics* Vol. 2, ed. Edwin S. Mills. Amsterdam: North Holland, 1987.
4. Bertaud, Alain. "Clearing the Air in Atlanta: Transit and Smart Growth or Conventional Economics?" *Journal of Urban Economics* 54 (2003), pp. 379–400.
5. Bollinger, Christopher, and Keith Ihlanfeldt. "The Impact of Rapid Rail Transit on Economic Development: The Case of Atlanta's MARTA." *Journal of Urban Economics* 42 (1997), pp. 179–204.

6. Cervero, Robert. "Commercial Paratransit in the United States: Service Options, Markets, and Performance." Working Paper No. 299, University of California Transportation Center, 1996.

7. Cervero, Robert, and John Landis. "The Transportation-Land Use Connection Still Matters." *Access* 7 (Fall, 1995), pp. 2–10.

8. Dahlgren, Joy. "Are HOV Lanes Really Better?" *Access* 6 (Spring 1995), pp. 25–29.

9. Fielding, Gordon J. *Managing Public Transit Strategically: A Comprehensive Approach to Strengthening Service and Monitoring Performance.* San Francisco: Jossey-Bass, 1987.

10. Giuliano, Genevieve, and Kenneth A. Small. "Alternative Strategies for Coping with Traffic Congestion." University of California Transportation Center, Working Paper No. 188. Berkeley: University of California Transportation Center, 1994.

11. Gomez-Ibanez, Jose A. "A Dark Side to Light Rail?" *Journal of the American Planning Association* 51 (Summer 1985), pp. 337–51.

12. Gomez-Ibanez, Jose A., and John R. Meyer. "Privatizing and Deregulating Local Public Services: Lessons from Britain's Buses." *Journal of the American Planning Association* 56 (Winter 1990), pp. 9–21.

13. J. Holtzclaw. *Using Residential Patterns and Transit to Decrease Auto Dependence and Costs.* Natural Resources Defense Council, June 1994.

14. Holzer, Harry J., John M. Quigley, and Steven Raphael. "Public Transit and the Spatial Distribution of Minority Employment: Evidence from a Natural Experiment." *Journal of Policy Analysis and Management* 22 (2003), pp. 415–41.

15. Keeler, Theodore E., L. Merewitz, P. Fisher, and K. Small. *The Full Costs of Urban Transport.* Monograph 21, part 3. Institute of Urban and Regional Development. Berkeley: University of California, 1975.

16. Kraft, Gerald, and Thomas Domencich. "Free Transit." In *Readings in Urban Economics,* ed. Matthew Edel and Jerome Rothenberg. New York: Macmillan, 1972, pp. 459–80.

17. Lave, Charles A. *Urban Transit: The Private Challenge to Public Transportation.* Cambridge, MA: Ballinger, 1985.

18. Pickerell, Don H. "The Causes of Rising Transit Operating Deficits." *Transportation Research Record* 915 (1983), pp. 18–24.

19. Richmond, Jonathan E. "New Rail Transit Investments—A Review." Taubman Center for State and Local Government, 1998.

20. Small, Kenneth A. *Urban Transportation Economics.* Philadelphia: Harwood, 1992.

21. Small, Kenneth A. "Economics and Urban Transportation Policy in the United States." *Regional Science and Urban Economics* 27 (1997), pp. 671–91.

22. Webber, Melvin W. "The BART Experience—What Have We Learned?" *The Public Interest,* Fall 1976, pp. 79–108.

PART FOUR

Urban Crime

*U*rban crime generates large costs to victims and to society as a whole, and affects the location decisions of households and firms. This part of the book develops a model of a rational, utility-maximizing criminal and uses the model to explore the causes of urban crime and various policy responses to crime. We'll explore the role of education as a crime-fighting tool. In addition, we'll examine the reasons for higher crime in big cities and the reasons for the dramatic reduction in urban crime in the 1990s.

CHAPTER 12

Crime

Erle Gardner, the writer of detective stories, was paid by the word, and his villains were always killed by the last bullet in the gun. When asked why his heroes were so careless with their first five shots, he responded, "Every time I say bang in the story, I get three cents. If you think I'm going to finish the gun battle while my hero has fifteen cents worth of unexploded ammunition in his gun, you're nuts."
—BARTLETT'S BOOK OF ANECDOTES (2000)

The economic approach to crime is based on the notion that criminals base their decisions on the costs and benefits of crime and respond to incentives. As a society, we can reduce crime by adding police officers, prosecutors, and prison cells to increase the certainty of severe penalties for crime. We can also reduce crime by adding teachers and other school resources that transform dropouts into high-school graduates who are less likely to commit crime because they have better lawful opportunities. As a society, we make the difficult choice of how much crime to allow. Although a crime-free environment sounds appealing, what would we sacrifice to get it? Some crimes are more costly to prevent than to experience, so the socially efficient level of crime is positive.

CRIME FACTS

The Federal Bureau of Investigation (FBI) collects data from local police departments on seven index crimes, divided into personal and property crimes:

- **Personal crime.** The victim of a personal crime is placed in physical danger. For some crimes, the objective is to injure the victim (homicide, rape, aggravated assault). For other crimes, the objective is to steal property, but the criminal uses a show of force to coerce the victim (robbery).

TABLE 12–1 FBI Index Crimes, 1960–2003

	Number of Crimes per 100,000 People					
	1960	1970	1980	1990	1995	2003
Personal Crime						
Murder	5.0	7.8	10.2	9.4	8.2	5.7
Rape	9.5	18.6	36.8	41.2	37.1	32.1
Aggravated assault	85	177	299	424	418	295
Robbery	60	187	251	257	221	142
Property Crime						
Auto theft	182	457	502	658	561	433
Larceny	1,024	2,124	3,167	3,184	3,045	2,415
Burglary	504	1,152	1,684	1,236	988	741
Total Index Crimes	1,870	3,949	5,950	5,820	5,278	4,064

Source: U.S. Federal Bureau of Investigation. *Crime in the United States, Various Years.* Washington DC: U.S. Government Printing Office.

- **Property crime.** These are crimes of stealth rather than force and include burglary (illegal entry of a building), larceny (purse snatching, pocket picking, and bicycle theft), and auto theft.

The FBI data provide only a partial picture of the crime scene. Among the crimes omitted in the *Uniform Crime Reports* are disorderly conduct, shoplifting, arson, employee theft, and drug-related offenses.

Table 12–1 lists the crime rates for the period 1960 to 2003, expressed as the number of crimes per 100,000 people. The total crime rate rose from 1960 to 1980, fell slowly between 1980 and 1995, and then dropped rapidly between 1995 and 2003. Later in the chapter, we'll explore the reasons for the dramatic drop in crime in the 1990s. The FBI data include only the crimes that are reported to the police—38 percent of all property crimes and 48 percent of personal crimes. A more complete picture comes from the victimization surveys of the Department of Justice. The surveys indicate that the overall level of crime has decreased since its peak in 1981.

The Victims of Crime

Who are the victims of crime? As Table 12–2 shows, victimization rates vary with income and place of residence. Another factor is race.

- **Income.** Victimization rates for violent crime decrease as income increases. For example, a person in a household with an income less than $7,500 is nearly three times as likely to be victimized as a person in a household with an income above $75,000. Differences in victimization rates for property crime are not so clear-cut. Although the lowest income group has a relatively high victimization rate, the differences between other income groups are relatively small.

TABLE 12–2 Criminal Victimization Rates, 2003

	Population (million)	Violent (per 1,000 people)			Property (per 1,000 households)			
		Total	Robbery	Assault	Total	Burglary	Motor Vehicle Theft	Theft
Household Income								
Less than $7,500	8	49.9	9	39.3	204.6	58	6.3	140.3
$7,500–$14,999	16	30.8	4	25	167.7	42.2	7.3	118.3
$15,000–$24,999	25	26.3	4	21.5	179.2	38.4	8.9	131.9
$25,000–$34,999	24	24.9	2.2	21.8	180.7	35.3	12.3	133.1
$35,000–$49,999	32	21.4	2.1	18.3	177.1	27.6	9.5	140
$50,000–$74,999	35	22.9	2	20.4	168.1	24.9	8.4	134.7
$75,000 or more	48	17.5	1.7	15.4	176.4	20.8	11.9	143.7
Region								
Northeast	45	21	2.7	18.1	122.1	20.5	7.2	94.4
Midwest	56	23.6	2.7	19.4	160.2	32.5	6.9	120.9
South	86	21.1	2.5	17.8	160.5	32.2	7.8	120.4
West	52	25.2	2.1	22.5	207.4	30.6	15.2	161.6
Residence								
Central city	66	28.2	3.7	23.8	216.3	38.7	13	164.7
Suburban	116	21.3	2.3	18.1	144.8	24	9.3	111.6
Rural	57	18.6	1.6	16.4	136.6	30.5	4	102.1

Source: U.S. Bureau of Justice. Criminal Victimization in the United States, 2003. Washington DC, 2005.

- **Place of residence.** Victimization rates are lowest in rural areas and highest in central cities. The suburbs fall between the two extremes.
- **Race.** For violent crime, the victimization rate is 29.1 for blacks and 21.5 for whites. Blacks are also more frequently the victims of property crime.

The Costs of Crime

Figure 12–1 (page 260) shows the estimated costs of crime in 1992. The costs incurred by victims include the value of lost property, medical expenses for injuries, the opportunity cost of lost work time, pain and suffering, and the value of lives cut short. The costs of the criminal justice system include the costs of police, the courts, and correction facilities. Citizens spent about $39 billion on their own prevention measures, including locks and hired guards. The opportunity cost of having 1.35 million people in jails and prisons instead of working was $46 billion. Altogether, the cost of crime was $250 billion per year, or 3.8 percent of GDP.

THE RATIONAL CRIMINAL

The economic approach to crime is based on the notion that criminals are rational like everyone else and commit a crime if the benefit exceeds the cost. Of course, crime is an uncertain enterprise, and potential criminals must consider the likelihood

FIGURE 12–1 The Costs of Crime

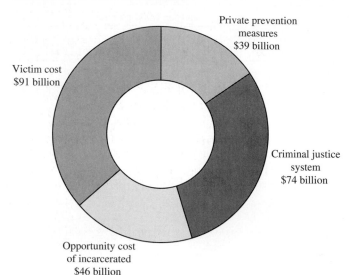

Source: Based on Richard Freeman. "Why Do So Many Young American Men Commit Crimes and What Might We Do About It?" *Journal of Economic Perspectives* 10, no. 1 (1996), pp. 25–42.

of different outcomes. We'll start our discussion of the rational criminal with a simple crime that most of us have at least considered, double parking.

The Economics of Double Parking

Suppose you have an opportunity to buy the last ticket to a concert, but to get it, you must double park your car, violating the law. If your consumer surplus from getting the concert ticket is $44, that's your benefit from the crime of double parking. Suppose you have a 50 percent chance of getting caught and paying a fine of $36. Is the risk of double parking—a 50–50 chance of getting $44 or losing $36—worth taking?

People differ in their willingness to take the risks associated with crimes. Some people, given an equal chance of either getting $44 or losing $36, will take the risk. Other people won't, but they might take the risk if the benefits were higher or the costs were lower. For example, if the consumer surplus from the ticket were $200, more people would commit the crime. Similarly, if the fine and the probability of getting caught were low enough, more people would break the law. In other words, as the benefit of the crime increases relative to the cost, more people will commit the parking crime.

What if you believe that violating the law is simply wrong? Most people have an underlying aversion to engaging in antisocial behavior such as crime and experience an anguish cost when they commit a crime. We will incorporate anguish cost into the economic approach to crime and see what happens when people have different anguish costs.

Expected Utility and the Decision to Commit Crime

We'll use a numerical example to illustrate the decision to commit a burglary. To keep the example simple and transparent, we'll keep the numbers small. One way to interpret the numbers in our example is to imagine that they are in thousands of dollars and apply to a 10-year period. Suppose a person can earn $100 in a lawful occupation and can supplement this income with money earned in weekly burglaries. His objective is to maximize his expected utility, and he will choose either a lawful or a criminal life, whichever generates the highest expected utility.

The crime decision is based on utility maximization, so we must translate monetary amounts into a measure of utility or satisfaction. In Figure 12–2, the utility curve shows the relationship between income (on the horizontal axis) and utility (on the vertical axis, measured in utils). The utility curve is concave, reflecting the assumption of diminishing marginal utility of income: As income increases, utility increases, but at a decreasing rate. This means that the first dollar of income is worth more in utility terms than the second, which is worth more than the third, and so on. We will use the following simple utility function:

$$Utility = (Income)^{1/2}$$

In words, utility is the square root of income.

FIGURE 12–2 Expected Utility from Crime

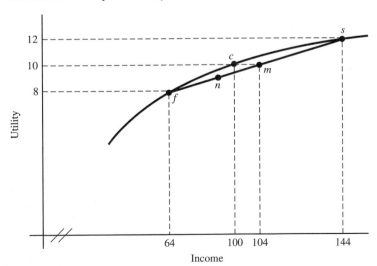

The utility curve is concave because of diminishing marginal utility of income. Point c shows the certain lawful outcome, with utility = 10. Point s shows the outcome with successful crime. Point f shows the outcome with a failed attempt at crime. With a probability of prison = 0.50, the expected utility from crime is the average of 12 utils (point s) and 8 utils (point f), or 10 utils, shown by point m (halfway between s and f).

TABLE 12–3 The Expected Utility of Crime

	Baseline	Higher Probability of Prison	Longer Prison Term	Less Loot	Higher Income	Lower Probability of Prison
Lawful income ($)	100	100	100	100	400	100
Loot ($)	44	44	44	21	44	44
Probability of prison	0.5	0.75	0.5	0.5	0.5	0.25
Prison time	0.36	0.36	0.51	0.36	0.36	0.36
Lawful utility = (lawful income)$^{1/2}$	**10**	**10**	**10**	**10**	**20**	**10**
Utility from successful crime						
Net income = Legal income + Loot	144	144	144	121	444	144
Utility = (Net income)$^{1/2}$	12	12	12	11	21	12
Utility from failed crime						
Prison cost = prison time · legal income	36	36	51	36	144	36
Net income = Legal income − prison cost	64	64	49	64	256	64
Utility = (Net income)$^{1/2}$	8	8	7	8	16	8
Expected utility from crime (utils)	**10**	**9**	**9.5**	**9.5**	**18.5**	**11**

The first column of numbers in Table 12–3 shows how to compute the utility associated with the lawful and criminal options. The first four numbers are the values of key parameters. The lawful income is $100, and a program of weekly burglaries generates $44 worth of loot over the time period considered. If a person commits crime, the probability of eventually being caught and sent to prison is 0.50. The prison term for a criminal who is caught is 0.36 units of time in prison (e.g., 3.6 years over a decade). A criminal who is caught also loses any loot stolen, and supervision after being released from prison prevents a return to crime.

We can compute the utility levels associated with three possible outcomes. First, the lawful option generates an income of $100 and thus a certain utility of 10 utils (the square root of $100). This is shown as point c in Figure 12–2. Second, a successful criminal earns a net income of $144 (equal to $100 + $44 in loot) and receives utility = 12 utils (point s). An unsuccessful criminal spends 0.36 units of time in prison, leaving only 0.64 units of time to earn lawful income. The net income for the failed criminal is $64 (0.64 times $100) and utility = 8 utils (point f).

A potential criminal doesn't know ahead of time whether he will succeed or fail at crime. But since we know the utilities of success and failure and the probability of each, we can compute the expected utility of crime, equal to a weighted average of the two values, with the probabilities as the weights:

$$EU\{U_1, U_2; p_1, p_2\} = p_1 \cdot U_1 + p_2 \cdot U_2$$

p_1 is the probability of an outcome that generates a utility of U_1 utils. In our example, the expected value of crime is 10 utils:

$$EU\{12, 8; 0.50, 0.50\} = 0.50 \cdot 12 + 0.50 \cdot 8 = 10 \text{ utils}$$

In graphical terms, the utility is shown by the midpoint of the line connecting the two utility points (point m is midway between s and f). It is the midpoint because each outcome is equally likely.

The person will choose crime if the expected utility of crime exceeds the certain utility of remaining lawful. In the example shown in the first column of Table 12–3, the lawful utility equals the expected utility of crime, so the person is indifferent between the two options. The person is just as well off with either a certain lawful utility of 10 utils or a risky crime career, with equal chances of either 12 or 8 utils.

If we look at the monetary payoffs from crime and lawful activity, there is a puzzle. The person is indifferent about taking a risk that will either generate a gain of $44 (the loot) or a loss of $36 (net income of $64 instead of $100). The two possibilities are equally likely, so why not accept a risk that could either earn $44 or lose $36? The reason is diminishing marginal utility of income. The pleasure of getting more income (moving upward along the utility curve) is small compared to the displeasure of losing income (moving downward along the utility curve). The pleasure from getting $44 more income exactly offsets the displeasure from losing only $36, so the person is indifferent between a lawful and a criminal life.

Preventing Crime

Our example shows that our potential criminal is indifferent between crime and a lawful life. We can tip the balance away from crime by changing the values of the key parameters. In the second column of Table 12–3, the probability of imprisonment increases to 0.75, meaning that a criminal is more likely to lose the loot and go to prison. This change doesn't affect the utility levels associated with criminal success and failure but simply changes the probability of each outcome—and the expected utility of crime:

$$EU\{12, 8; 0.25, 0.75\} = 0.25 \cdot 12 + 0.75 \cdot 8 = 9 \text{ utils}$$

The expected utility from crime is now less than the lawful utility, so the person will not commit crime. In other words, an increase in the certainty of punishment decreases crime.

In Figure 12–2, the increase in the probability of imprisonment moves the crime outcome from point m to point n. Point m is the midpoint between points s (success) and f (failure), showing what happens with a 50 percent chance of failure. As the probability of failure (prison) increases, we move closer to point f and farther from point s. Point n is three-fourths of the distance between s and f, showing what happens when the probability of failure is 0.75.

We can also tip the balance away from crime by increasing the penalty for crime. In the third column of Table 12–3, the prison time for a failed criminal increases to 0.51. This change affects only the failed criminal, increasing the prison cost to $51 and decreasing the net income to $49. As a result, the utility for a failed criminal decreases to 7 utils. The expected utility of crime decreases to 9.5 utils:

$$EU\{12, 7; 0.50, 0.50\} = 0.50 \cdot 12 + 0.50 \cdot 7 = 9.5 \text{ utils}$$

The utility from crime is now less than the lawful utility, so the person will not commit crime. An increase in the severity of punishment reduces crime.

We can also tip the balance away from crime by decreasing the value of the loot. In the fourth column of Table 12–3, the loot is $21 instead of $44. The decrease in loot affects only the successful criminal: The net income drops to $121 and the utility drops to 11 utils. As a result, the expected utility from crime drops to 9.5 utils (the average of 11 utils and 8 utils), which is less than the lawful utility. Less loot means less crime.

Would a person with higher income be more or less inclined to commit crime? The fifth column of Table 12–3 shows the calculations for a person with four times as much income. The higher-income person gets the same loot, but has four times the opportunity cost of prison time. As a result, the lawful utility (20 utils) exceeds the expected utility from crime (18.5 utils), and the high-income person will not commit crime. Because the opportunity cost of crime increases with income while the benefits do not, we expect less crime among high-income people.

Morality and Anguish Costs

So far we have assumed that people do not consider the moral consequences of crime. In fact, most people have an aversion to committing antisocial acts, and they won't commit crime even if the expected payoff is positive. Of course, some people are less troubled by committing antisocial acts, and they are more likely to commit crime. We can incorporate morality by introducing an anguish cost, defined as the cost of committing an antisocial act. For example, suppose a person's anguish cost for a life of crime is 2 utils. In Table 12–3, the numbers for the expected utility of crime would drop by 2 utils.

The sixth column of Table 12–3 shows an example of a person whose anguish cost prevents crime. The probability of prison is relatively low (0.25), so the expected utility of crime before considering anguish cost (11 utils) exceeds the lawful utility (10 utils). If the anguish cost is 2 utils, however, the expected utility from crime would drop to 9 utils, below the lawful utility. Of course, this person would commit crime if the payoff were high enough to offset his 2-util anguish cost. For example, if the certainty or severity of punishment were low enough, the person would commit crime.

Incorporating morality and anguish costs helps explain why most people don't commit crime even when it appears that the payoff from crime is positive. In the sixth column of Table 12–3, before we include anguish cost, the expected utility of crime exceeds the lawful utility by 1 util. A person with an anguish cost of 2 utils will not commit crime, but a person with an aguish cost of only 0.50 utils will. In other words, morality explains why two people who face the same benefits and costs of crime may make different choices.

THE EQUILIBRIUM QUANTITY OF CRIME

We can use the insights from the model of the rational criminal to discuss the equilibrium quantity of crime. We'll take the perspective of criminals, using their benefit and cost curves to show how much crime rational criminals commit. As we'll see, we can use various crime policies to shift the benefit and cost curves and thus reduce crime. To simplify matters, we will switch from units of utility to dollars, allowing us to measure the costs and benefits of crime in monetary terms.

Drawing the Supply Curve

Like any other supply curve, the supply curve for crime shows the relationship between the price of crime and the number of crimes supplied (committed). The price is the benefit experienced by the criminal, equal to the loot or booty captured in the crime. The crime supply curve shows how the number of crimes committed increases with the loot. In Figure 12–3, the vertical intercept at point *m* indicates that the first crime is committed when the loot reaches $400. For a lower level of loot, say $399, no crimes would be committed because the benefit of a crime is less than the cost of committing it. As the value of loot increases, the quantity of crime supplied increases: If the loot is $600 per crime, 30 crimes will be committed; if the loot is $800, there will be 60 crimes.

FIGURE 12–3 Equilibrium Quantity of Crime

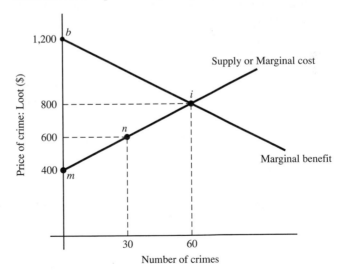

The supply curve shows the marginal cost of crime, which is positively sloped because potential criminals vary in their opportunity costs and anguish costs. The marginal benefit curve is negatively sloped because targets vary in their loot, and the most lucrative targets are victimized first. The equilibrium occurs at point *i*, where the marginal benefit equals the marginal cost.

A supply curve is also a marginal-cost curve, as explained in Section 2.2 in "Tools of Microeconomics," the appendix to the book. The crime supply curve shows, for each quantity of crime, the cost incurred for the marginal crime. For example, point n shows that with a loot of $600, 30 burglaries are committed. If the value of loot were only $599, the 30th burglary would not be committed, indicating that the benefit of the 30th burglary ($599) is less than its cost. When the loot rises to $600, the 30th crime is committed because now the benefit exceeds the cost. Therefore the cost of the 30th crime is just below $600. Similarly, the 60th crime is committed when the loot rises to $800, so the marginal cost of that crime is just below $800.

We know from the model of the rational criminal that the cost of crime to the criminal is determined by four variables:

- The probability of being caught and imprisoned.
- The length of the prison term.
- The opportunity cost of time spent in prison, which varies with income.
- The anguish cost of crime, which varies across individuals.

Let's assume for the moment that all potential criminals face the same probability of prison and the same prison term.

The vertical intercept of the supply curve shows the cost of crime for the criminal with the lowest crime cost. Point m indicates that the lowest-cost criminal has a crime cost of $400. This cost includes the opportunity cost of prison time and the anguish cost, both of which vary across potential criminals. If everyone faces the same probability of prison, the same prison term, and the same anguish cost, then the first crime will be committed by the person with the lowest opportunity cost— the lowest lawful income. Alternatively if everyone has the same lawful income, the first crime would be committed by the person with the lowest anguish cost. In general, criminals on the lower end of the supply curve are people with relatively low income and low anguish costs.

The supply curve is positively sloped because potential criminals vary in their opportunity costs and anguish costs. As we move upward along the supply curve, a larger loot induces people with higher opportunity and anguish costs to enter the crime market. For example, at point n a total of 30 crimes are committed by people whose cost of committing a crime is less than $600. A bigger loot persuades people with higher opportunity cost and anguish cost to commit crime.

The Marginal-Benefit Curve and the Equilibrium Quantity of Crime

Figure 12–3 also shows the marginal benefit curve for crime from the criminal's perspective. The marginal benefit of a crime is the loot taken. The marginal-benefit curve is negatively sloped because crime targets vary in the amount of loot available and the difficulty in grabbing it. At the top of the marginal-benefit curve at point b, the most lucrative and easy target, with a loot of $1,200, is targeted first, so the marginal benefit of the first crime is $1,200. As we move downward along the marginal-benefit curve, criminals turn to progressively less lucrative targets, with less loot and greater difficulty in grabbing it.

Point *i* in Figure 12–3 shows the initial equilibrium in the market for crime. The equilibrium price (loot) is $800 per crime and 60 crimes are committed. For the first 60 crimes, the criminal's marginal benefit (the loot) exceeds his marginal cost, so the equilibrium quantity of crime is 60. Criminals stop at 60 crimes because for the 61st crime the marginal cost exceeds the loot, so additional crime does not pay.

Increasing the Certainty of Punishment

We as a society can shift the crime supply curve by increasing the certainty of punishment. An increase in the probability of prison increases the cost of committing crime and shifts the supply curve upward. In Figure 12–4, the marginal-cost curve shifts upward by $240. For example, the cost of the 60th crime is now $1,040, up from $800. Of course, to increase the probability of imprisonment, we must use more resources (police and judges) to capture and convict criminals.

The upward shift of the supply curve decreases the equilibrium number of crimes. The new equilibrium is shown by point *f*. The equilibrium number of crimes drops from 60 to 42. This is a deterrent effect of the criminal-justice system: When the probability of prison increases, potential criminals respond to the higher cost by committing fewer crimes.

How responsive are criminals to increases in the certainty of punishment? The estimated elasticity of crime with respect to the probability of imprisonment is −0.30: A 10 percent increase in the probability decreases crime by about 3 percent.

FIGURE 12–4 Public Policy Shifts the Supply Curve and Decreases Crime

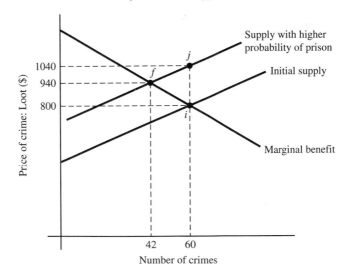

An increase in the probability of imprisonment increases the marginal cost of committing crime, shifting the supply curve upward by $240. The equilibrium quantity of crime decreases to 42 and the equilibrium price (loot) increases to $940.

The elasticity of crime with respect to the arrest ratio (the number of arrests divided by the number of crimes committed) is -0.30 as well. The elasticity of the crime rate with respect to the number of police officers is between -0.40 and -0.50. In general, there is convincing evidence that an increase in the certainty of punishment decreases crime.

Increasing the Severity of Punishment

We can also shift the supply curve by changing the length of the prison term. Like a higher probability of imprisonment, a longer prison term means a higher marginal cost of crime, resulting in an upward shift of the supply curve. If nothing else changed, we would expect the equilibrium crime rate to decrease.

Studies of criminal behavior suggest that longer prison sentences do not have much of an effect on crime rates. The estimated elasticity of crime with respect to the length of prison terms is close to zero. Longer prison terms cause other changes in the criminal environment that offset the higher costs associated with more time in prison:

1. **Hardening the criminal.** Criminals have a relatively low aversion to committing antisocial acts and a longer prison term may reduce their aversion further, making crime more likely when they are released. A decrease in crime anguish costs shifts the supply curve downward, at least partly offsetting the deterrent effect of a longer prison term.
2. **Prison schooling.** If prison allows a criminal to learn the tricks of the trade from other criminals—or at least to learn from their mistakes—a longer prison term means a more skillful criminal. This leads to a lower probability of being caught, and thus a lower cost of committing crime. In other words, prison schooling shifts the supply curve downward, at least partly offsetting the deterrent effect of a longer prison term.

LEGAL OPPORTUNITIES AND EDUCATION

So far we have focused on the obvious strategies to reduce crime. Increasing the certainty or severity of punishment increases the cost of committing crime. In this part of the chapter, we'll look at more subtle strategies that reduce crime by increasing the value of lawful activities. As we saw in Table 12–3, an increase in wages increases the opportunity cost of crime. One way to increase wages is to increase educational attainment, especially the rate of high-school graduation.

Lawful Opportunities and Crime

An increase in the wage for lawful employment increases the opportunity cost of crime and decreases the supply of crime. In graphical terms, the effect of an increase in the wage is similar to the effect of increasing the probability of imprisonment, as shown in Figure 12–4: An increase in the wage from lawful activity shifts the crime supply curve upward, decreasing the equilibrium level of crime.

How responsive is the crime rate to the opportunities for lawful work? Consider first the connection between the unemployment rate and the crime rate. Although there is a positive relationship between unemployment and crime, the overall relationship is relatively weak. In contrast, the crime rates of first offenders are relatively sensitive to the unemployment rate. Specifically, teenage crime rates are lower in cities with more legal opportunities.

Consider next the connection between wages and crime. A recent study concludes that the elasticity of crime with respect to the wages of low-skilled workers is relatively large, between -1.0 and -2.0 (Gould, Weinberg, Mustard, 2002). In other words, a 10 percent increase in wages decreases crime by between 10 percent and 20 percent. Grogger (1991, 2000) shows that the wages of low-skilled workers and crime rates move in opposite directions. The recent trend of lower wages for low-skilled labor presents a policy challenge Freeman (1995):

> How to improve the job market for less skilled young American men, and reverse the huge decline in their earnings and employment opportunities is the problem of our times, with implications for both crime and many other social ills.

Education as Crime-Fighting Policy

Education reduces crime by increasing the opportunities for lawful work. College graduates earn almost twice as much high-school graduates and high-school graduates earn almost 1.5 times as much as dropouts. So the link between education and crime is the graduation premium: Graduation increases wages, and higher wages decrease crime. Given the large graduation premium (50 percent) and the large elasticity of crime with respect to wages (-1.0 to -2.0), education policy has the potential to be a powerful anticrime policy.

A recent study suggests that investment in high-school education is an effective tool for reducing crime (Lochner and Moretti, 2004). The effects of high school education are measured in two ways:

1. **An additional year of high school.** Each additional year decreases the crime participation rate by about 0.10 percentage points for white males and by 0.40 percentage points for black males.
2. **Graduation.** High-school graduation decreases the crime participation rates of white males, with reductions of 9 percent for violent crime, 5 percent for drug crime, and 10 percent for property crime. The elasticity of arrest rates with respect to high-school graduation rates is -2.0 for violent crime and -1.3 for motor-vehicle theft.

The authors compute the benefits and costs of a small increase in the high-school graduation rate. Each year of schooling has a per-pupil cost of $6,000, so if getting a student from dropout status to graduation takes one more year of schooling, the additional cost per graduate is $6,000. Given the 50 percent graduation premium, the typical graduate benefits by earning $8,400 more per year for the rest of his working life. In addition, the resulting reduction in crime generates external benefits for the rest of society, about $1,600 per year for the rest of the graduate's working life. For a one-time expense of $6,000, society gets a crime-reduction benefit of $1,600 per year for 30 or 40 years.

APPLICATIONS: BIG-CITY CRIME AND THE CRIME DROP

We can use the insights from the model of the rational criminal to explain two observations. First, big cities experience higher crime rates than small cities. Second, during the 1990s, crime rates for both violent and property crime decreased by about a third.

Why Are Crime Rates Higher in Big Cities?

Crime rates increase with city size. Large cities (population at least 250,000) have twice as much violent crime as small cities (population less than 10,000). For property crime, the big-city crime rate is about 30 percent higher. Overall, the elasticity of crime with respect to city size is 0.15: A 10 percent increase in population increases the crime rate by about 1.5 percent (Glaeser and Sacerdote, 1996).

Why are crime rates so much higher in big cities? Glaeser and Sacerdote provide three reasons:

1. **More loot (25 percent of difference).** Big cities have more lucrative targets: The average value per crime is about $900 in a city of 1 million, compared to a value of about $550 in a small city.
2. **Lower probability of arrest (15 percent of difference).** As shown in Table 12–4, bigger cities have lower arrest rates. Arrest rates are lower in big cities because (a) the pool of suspects is larger and (b) lawful citizens in impersonal big cities are less inclined to help their neighbors and the police in crime-control efforts.
3. **More female-headed households (50 percent of difference).** It's not clear why higher rates of single parenthood have such a powerful influence on crime. The authors speculate that children raised in single-parent families may have fewer job skills and less powerful ethical restraints on criminal behavior.

Since 1970, the correlation between city size and crime has weakened, and in recent years crime rates in big cities have dropped.

Figure 12–5 illustrates the reasons for higher crime rates in big cities. A big city has a lower arrest rate, so the cost of committing crime is lower. The lower cost generates a lower supply (marginal cost) curve. In addition, there is more loot in big

TABLE 12–4 Arrest Rates and City Size

Population (1,000)	25–50	50–100	100–250	250–500	500–1 Million	More than 1 Million
Arrest rate (%)	12	11	11	10	8	7

Source: Edward L. Glaeser, and B. Sacerdote. "Why Is There More Crime in Cities?" NBER Working Paper #5430, 1996.

FIGURE 12–5 More Crime in Big Cities

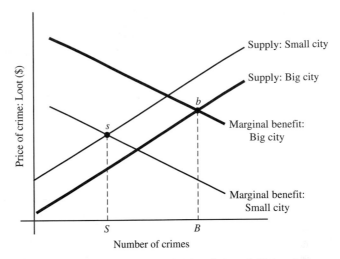

A big city has more loot, so the marginal benefit curve is higher. A big city has a lower probability of arrest, so the marginal cost (supply curve) is lower. The equilibrium in the big city (point *b*, with *B* crimes) generates a higher crime rate than a small city (point *s*, with *S* crimes).

cities, so the marginal benefit curve is higher. The equilibrium in the big city is shown by point *b*, and the equilibrium in the small city is shown by point *s*. The combination of lower marginal cost and higher marginal benefit leads to a higher crime rate in the big city.

Why Did Crime Rates Decrease in the 1990s?

During the 1990s, crime rates for both violent and property crime decreased by about a third. As shown in Figure 12–6 (page 272), both violent crime and property crime peaked in 1991 and decreased steadily through the rest of the decade.

A recent study explores the factors that reduced crime during the 1990s (Levitt, 2004), and Figure 12–7 (page 273) summarizes the conclusions:

- **Strong economy.** There were more jobs and higher wages, causing a 2 percent reduction in property crime.
- **Demographics.** A decrease in the share of the population in the crime-prone years of 16–24 decreased violent crime by 2 percent and property crime by 5 percent.
- **Police techniques.** A number of innovative police policies, including community policing and more aggressive control of public nuisances, reduced crime by a relatively small amount.

FIGURE 12–6 Crime Rates, 1980–1999

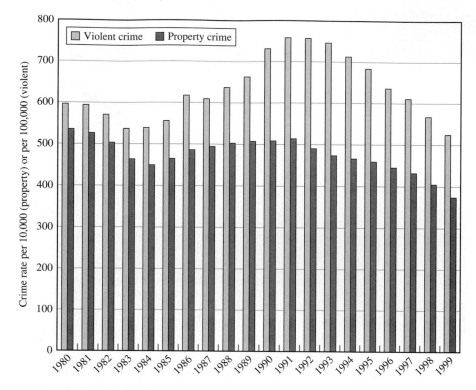

Source: FBI Uniform Crime Reports.

- **Increase in police.** Over the decade, the number of police officers per capita increased by 14 percent (at a cost of $8.4 billion per year), decreasing crime by 5.5 percent.
- **Increase in prisoners.** The national prison population doubled over this period, decreasing violent crime by 12 percent and property crime by 8 percent.
- **Decrease in crack cocaine sales.** In the 1980s, there was lucrative trade in crack cocaine, and rival drug sellers battled over market areas in central cities. These turf battles generated a lot of violent crime in cities. As crack cocaine sales dropped over the 1990s, so did the violent turf battles, reducing violent crime by about 3 percent.

A subtle and surprising factor in lower crime is legalized abortion. The legalization of abortion in 1974 decreased the number of unwanted births. There is evidence that crime rates are higher among children born to reluctant parents. The wider availability of abortion starting in the 1970s reduced the number of children born in such circumstances, and thus decreased the number of crime-prone people maturing in the 1990s. As shown in Figure 12–7, the legalization of abortion cut crime rates by 10 percent.

FIGURE 12–7 Why Did Crime Drop in the 1990s?

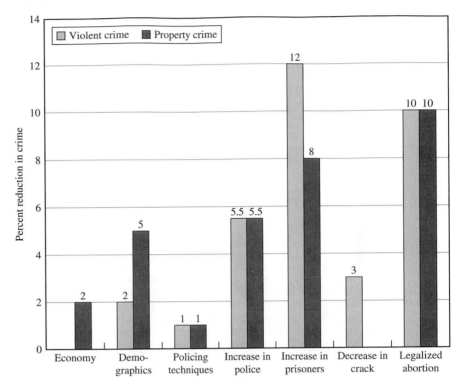

Source: Data from Steven Levitt, "Understanding Why Crime Fell in the 1990s: Four Factors That Explain the Decline, and Six That Do Not." *Journal of Economic Perspectives* 18 (2004), pp. 163–190.

HOW MUCH CRIME?

A society can use its resources—labor, capital, and land—in different ways to promote economic well-being. The problem of crime presents society with some stark choices about how much crime to experience. It would be possible, in principle, to cut the crime rate to one-tenth or one-hundredth of its current level. The question is whether such a dramatic reduction in crime would be socially efficient. As we'll see, the reason we tolerate so much crime is that some crimes are more costly to prevent than to experience.

The Optimal Amount of Crime

Consider a society's choice of how much burglary to allow. As we saw earlier in the chapter, the public sector can decrease crime by using resources to increase the certainty and severity of punishment. In addition, potential victims can deter crime by investing in security measures such as locks, guards, and alarms. We can combine these two sorts of prevention efforts into a single measure of crime-prevention costs.

FIGURE 12–8 The Socially Efficient Amount of Crime

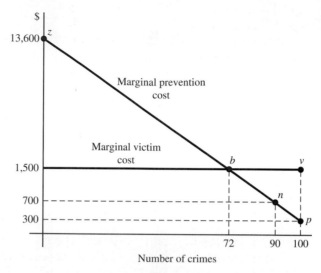

The socially efficient quantity of crime is where the marginal victim cost equals the marginal prevention cost, shown by point *b* with 72 crimes. Going beyond that point, crimes are more costly to prevent than to experience.

We will use the marginal principle to determine the optimum level of crime. The marginal principle is reviewed in Section 1.1 of "Tools of Microeconomics," the appendix at the end of the book. In Figure 12–8, the horizontal axis measures the number of crimes committed, which ranges from zero to 100. The negatively sloped curve is the marginal cost of crime prevention. Starting at point *p*, if we don't allocate any resources to crime prevention, there will be 100 crimes. The marginal-cost curve indicates that the cost of preventing a single crime (reducing crime from 100 to 99) is $300. As we prevent more and more crimes, the marginal cost of prevention increases, and we move upward along the marginal prevention cost curve. For example, the marginal cost of preventing crime number 90 is $700 (shown by point *n*), and the marginal cost continues to increase, reaching $13,600 to prevent the last crime (at point *z*). In other words, it is relatively easy to go from 100 to 90 crimes, but the lower the crime rate, the more costly it is to prevent another crime.

The other cost of crime is experienced by the victim. As we saw earlier in the book, victim costs include the opportunity cost of lost work time, monetary losses, and the costs of injuries. Miller, Cohen, and Wiersema (1996) estimate the following costs for different crimes: $370 for larceny, $1,500 for burglary, $4,000 for auto theft, $13,000 for armed robbery, and $15,000 for assault. In Figure 12–8, we assume that each burglary imposes a cost on society of $1,500, so the marginal victim cost is constant at $1,500.

The socially efficient quantity of crime minimizes the sum of prevention and victim costs. The total cost is minimized where the two marginal-cost curves intersect, which happens at point *b*, with 72 burglaries. If we start with 100 burglaries (point *p*), the 100th burglary has a victim cost of $1,500 but costs only $300 to prevent. We can spend $300 to save $1,500, so the total cost of crime decreases by $1,200. Moving upward along the prevention-cost curve, the marginal prevention cost is less than the marginal victim cost down to a crime rate of 72, so that's the place to stop. If we were to move beyond point *b* to fewer crimes, the cost of preventing each crime would exceed the cost of experiencing it, so we would be better off at point *b*.

Differences in victim costs generate differences in the socially efficient level of crime. As we saw earlier in the chapter, robbery has a higher victim cost. If it has the same marginal prevention cost as burglary, the socially efficient number of robberies will be smaller. This means that it is sensible for the government to use more resources in the prevention of more serious crime, in part by imposing longer prison terms. So there is some economic logic behind the notion of making the punishment fit the crime.

Crime Substitution and the Principle of Marginal Deterrence

Criminals have options too. We, as a society, pick a set of crime penalties, one for each type of crime (e.g., one year for burglary, three years for armed robbery), providing criminals with a menu of crime penalties. Criminals respond by picking the most lucrative crime, given the penalty menu and the payoffs from different crimes. This has important implication for policies that "get tough" on one crime or another. For example, if we triple the prison term for burglary to make it the same as the penalty for robbery, how would that affect the number of burglaries and armed robberies?

Figure 12–9 shows the implications of a longer prison term for burglary. A group of 60 people choose between burglary, armed robbery, and a lawful job. The net return from an activity equals the expected benefit (loot or wages) minus the

FIGURE 12–9 Equalizing Penalties and Crime Substitution

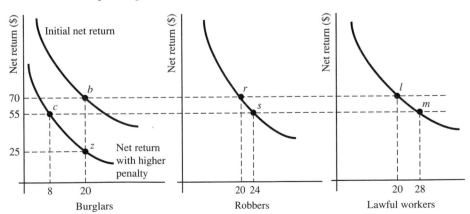

In equilibrium, the net return of burglary, robbery, and lawful work are equal. An increase in the penalty for burglary shifts the burglary return curve downward. Equilibrium is restored with a lower common net return ($55, down from $70), fewer burglars (8 instead of 20), more robbers (24 instead of 20) and more lawful workers (28 instead of 20).

expected cost, which includes the expected penalty for crime. In equilibrium, the net returns of the three alternative activities will be equal, making the marginal person indifferent among the three activities. For each of the three options, the net return curve is negatively sloped, indicating that the larger the number of people in an activity, the lower the net return. The initial equilibrium is shown by points b (burglary), r (robbery), and l (lawful), with 20 people in each activity. The net return for each activity is $70 per day.

Suppose we increase the penalty for burglary. In the left panel of Figure 12–9, the increase in the expected cost of crime shifts the net-return curve for burglary downward. If the number of burglars remained at 20, the net return would drop to $25 (shown by point z). The net return is now higher in the other activities, so people will switch to robbery and lawful work. As they do, we move upward along the new curve for burglary (from point z to point c), downward along the curve for robbery (from r to s) and downward along the curve for lawful work (from l to m).

In the new equilibrium, there are fewer burglars, but more robbers and lawful workers. The equilibrium is shown by points c, s, and m: The net return of each activity is $55, and the number of people in the three activities adds up to 60. Of the 12 people who stop committing burglary, 4 switch to robbery and 8 choose lawful work.

How does the larger penalty for burglary affect the victim cost of crime? It depends on the change in the mix of crime and the victim cost of each crime. The victim cost of armed robbery is almost nine times the victim cost of burglary, so we would break even in terms of total victim cost if, for each additional robbery, the number of burglaries decreased by nine. In our simple example, there are 4 additional robberies and only 12 fewer burglaries, so the total victim cost increases. Of course, this is just an example; if the increase in robberies were smaller and the reduction in burglaries were larger, the total victim cost would decrease.

The principle of marginal deterrence is that penalties should increase with the victim cost of crime. For example, the penalty for burglary should be less than the penalty for armed robbery, with almost nine times the victim cost. Although equalizing penalties for the two crimes would decrease burglary, it would also cause some criminals to switch to more costly armed robberies. The challenge for crime policy is to develop a penalty menu that generates the mix of crimes that minimizes the social cost of crime.

THE ROLE OF PRISONS

Earlier in the chapter we saw that putting people in prison decreases crime rates. The elasticity of crime with respect to the prison population is about –0.25 for property crime and about −0.40 for violent crime. In this part of the chapter, we explore why incarceration reduces crime. Specifically, we look at three ways that prisons decrease crime:

- **Deterrence.** The threat of being locked up in prison persuades some people not to commit crime.

- **Incapacitation.** Isolating criminals from potential victims prevents crime.
- **Rehabilitation.** Prisons may improve the attitudes or skill level of convicts, making them less likely to commit crimes after they leave.

We discussed deterrence earlier in the chapter. Recall that an increase in the certainty of punishment is more effective than an increase in severity. According to a recent study (Levitt, 1998), each burglary arrest deters 2.3 burglaries and each arrest for car theft deters 0.50 car thefts.

Incapacitation

The second function of the prison system is to take criminals out of circulation. The benefit of keeping a criminal locked up equals the number of crimes prevented times the social cost per crime. Studies of the incapacitation effects generate mixed results. DiIluio (1996) suggests that incapacitating the typical criminal prevents between 17 and 21 crimes per year, while Levitt (1998) suggests that the number of crimes prevented is much smaller.

A recent study of the prison system in Texas quantifies the trade-offs with prisons (Spelman, 2005). The author computes the benefit of incapacitation as the victim cost avoided by holding an inmate in prison. In 2000, the marginal benefit of incapacitation was $15,000 per inmate. The authors estimate that the marginal cost of holding an inmate in prison is about $36,000, a figure that includes the cost of building and operating prisons as well as the opportunity cost of having a person in prison rather than working. These numbers indicate that the marginal cost of incarceration exceeds the marginal benefit, meaning that the number of inmates exceeds the socially efficient number.

The authors of the Texas study note that their figure of a marginal benefit of $15,000 excludes some potential benefits from incarceration. They do not include the benefits associated with a reduced fear of crime or the savings on protective measures such as locks and guard dogs. If these nonvictim costs are high enough, the marginal benefit of incarceration could be greater than or equal to the marginal cost. In that case, the current level of incarceration in Texas could be justified on efficiency grounds.

Rehabilitation

The third function of prisons is to rehabilitate criminals by providing them with the skills and attitudes required for success in lawful employment after their release. About one-third of inmates participate in education and vocational training programs, and about one-third participate in drug and alcohol programs. If we add participation in programs that provide training in life skills, about two-thirds of inmates participate in some type of rehabilitation program.

The simple facts on rehabilitation are not encouraging. Roughly two-thirds of former inmates are rearrested within three years of release, and roughly half return to prison within three years. Released inmates account for between 10 percent and 12 percent of property and violent crimes. Dozens of studies have measured the effects of rehabilitation programs for adults, and the consensus is that they are ineffective for three reasons.

1. It is difficult to change the antisocial attitudes that make certain people receptive to crime.
2. By the time the typical criminal reaches the prison rehabilitation stage, he or she has committed dozens of crimes, and is entrenched in the criminal world.
3. It is difficult to make legal opportunities more profitable than crime: Crime pays, and it is difficult to increase the job skills of an adult criminal.

There is evidence that anticrime programs targeted at youths pass the benefit-cost test. The high cost of crime means that even a relatively expensive program that reduces crime rates by a small amount will pass the test. The average juvenile-delinquent program reduces crime rates by a small amount (Lipsey, 1992). Some early-intervention programs help reduce crime among youths, again by modest amounts (Mendel, 1995).

SUMMARY

The model of the rational criminal suggests that like other people, criminals respond to incentives. Here are the main points of the chapter:

1. Crime is risky because there is a chance of being caught and paying a large penalty. A potential criminal compares the certain utility of lawful work to the expected utility of criminal activity.
2. An increase in the probability of punishment has a larger deterrent effect than an increase in the severity of punishment.
3. The optimum amount of crime is the level at which the marginal victim cost equals the marginal prevention cost.
4. Education reduces crime by increasing the opportunities for lawful work. High-school graduation decreases crime participation rates by 9–10 percent.
5. The dramatic reductions in crime during the 1990s resulted from more police and prisoners, more favorable demographics (caused in part by legalized abortion), a decline in crack cocaine, and a stronger economy.

APPLYING THE CONCEPTS

1. **Women and Crime**
   During the 1970s, the crime rate for women increased five times faster than the crime rate for men. Make a list of the possible reasons for the more rapid increase for women. Then check the conclusions of the article "Women and Crime" by Ann Bartel (see the list of references at the end of the chapter). Do the key factors identified by Bartel appear on your list?
2. **Why Doesn't a More Severe Penalty Work?**
   Using the first column of Table 12–3 as a starting point, modify the numbers to make the loot $156 and the anguish cost from crime 1 util.

a. How does the payoff from crime (the expected utility minus anguish cost) compare to the payoff (utility) from lawful activity?

b. Now suppose the length of the prison term increases to 0.91 units of time and nothing else changes. How do the two payoffs compare?

c. Now suppose that extra schooling from the longer prison term increases criminal productivity, decreasing the probability of being caught and imprisoned from 0.50 to 0.40 (and no other numbers change from [b]). How do the two payoffs compare?

d. Now suppose that a longer prison term reduces anguish cost to zero (and no other numbers change from [c]). How do the two payoffs compare?

3. Budget-Balancing Prison Change

Consider a state with a prison capacity of 1,000. When a law is passed establishing a minimum term of 10 years (twice the current average term), the state cuts the number of prisoners in half, cutting the probability of imprisonment for crime in half. Predict the effect of these changes on the crime rate. Illustrate your answer with a graph like Figure 12–3.

4. Allocation of Crime Fighting Resources

Consider a city where the burglary rate in the low-income neighborhood is 15, compared to 5 in a high-income neighborhood. The two neighborhoods have the same victim costs per burglary ($1,500).

a. Depict graphically a situation in which a higher crime rate in the low-income neighborhood is socially efficient. Explain the logic of your graph.

b. Use a second graph to show a situation in which the socially efficient crime rate is the same in the two neighborhoods. What are the implications for the allocation of crime-fighting resources between the two neighborhoods?

5. Birthday Conversion

Consider two states that have the same crime penalties for adults (18 years or older), but Juviland has lighter penalties for juveniles (16–18 years). For each state, draw a curve that shows the crime participation rate as a function of age for ages 16–24. Explain any differences between the two curves.

REFERENCES AND ADDITIONAL READING

1. Bartel, Ann P. "Women and Crime: An Economic Analysis." *Economic Inquiry* 42 (1979), pp. 29–51.
2. Blumstein, Alfred, and Joel Wallman. *The Crime Drop in America.* New York: Cambridge University Press, 2000.
3. DiIulio, John J., Jr. "Help Wanted: Economists, Crime, and Public Policy." *Journal of Economic Perspectives* 10 (1996), pp. 3–24.
4. Freeman, Richard B. "The Labor Market." In *Crime,* eds. J.Q. Wilson and Joan Petersilia. San Francisco: Institute for Contemporary Policies, 1995.
5. Freeman, Richard B., and Harry J. Holzer. "The Black Youth Employment Crisis: Summary of Findings." In *The Black Youth Employment Crisis,* ed. Richard B. Freeman and Harry J. Holzer. Chicago: University of Chicago Press, 1986.

6. Glaeser, Edward L., and B. Sacerdote. "Why Is There More Crime in Cities?" NBER Working Paper no. 5430, 1996.

7. Gould, Eric D, Bruce A. Weinberg, and David B. Mustard. "Crime Rates and Local Labor Market Opportunities in the United States: 1979–1997." *Review of Economics and Statistics* 84 (2002), pp. 45–61.

8. Grogger, Jeffrey. "An Economic Model of Recent Trends in Violence." Chapter 8 in *The Crime Drop in America,* eds. Alfred Blumstein and Joel Wallman. New York: Cambridge University Press, 2000.

9. Grogger, Jeffrey. "Certainty vs. Severity of Punishment." *Economic Inquiry* 29 (1991), pp. 297–309.

10. Levitt, Steven D. "Juvenile Crime and Punishment." *Journal of Political Economy* 106 (1998), pp. 1156–85.

11. Levitt, Steven D. "The Effect of Prison Population Size on Crime Rates: Evidence from Prison Overcrowding Litigation." *Quarterly Journal of Economics* 111 (1996), pp. 319–52.

12. Levitt, Steven D. "Understanding Why Crime Fell in the 1990s: Four Factors That Explain the Decline, and Six That Do Not." *Journal of Economic Perspectives* 18 (2004), pp. 163–190.

13. Levitt, Steven D. "Why Do Increased Arrest Rates Appear to Reduce Crime: Deterrence, Incapacitation, or Measurement Error?" *Economic Inquiry* 36 (1998), pp. 353–72.

14. Lipsey, Mark. "Juvenile Delinquency Treatment: A Meta-Analysis Inquiry into the Variability of Effects." In *Meta-Analysis for Explanation: A Casebook,* ed. Thomas D. Cook et al. Beverly Hills, CA: Sage Foundation, 1992.

15. Lochner, Lance and Enrico Moretti. *American Economic Review* 94 (2004), pp. 155–89.

16. Marvel, Thomas B., and Carlisle E. Moody. "Prison Population Growth and Crime Reduction." *Journal of Quantitative Criminology* 10 (1994), pp. 109–40.

17. Mendel, Richard A. "Prevention or Pork? A Hard-Headed Look at Youth-Oriented Anti-Crime Programs." Washington DC: American Youth Policy Forum, 1995.

18. Raphael, Steven, and Michael Stoll. "The Effects of Prison Releases on Regional Crime Rate." Brookings-Wharton Papers on Urban Affairs 2004 (2004), pp. 207–243.

19. Spellman, William. "Jobs or Jails? The Crime Drop in Texas." *Journal of Policy Analysis and Management* 24 (2005), pp. 133–65.

20. Tauchen, Helen, Ann Dryden Witte, and Harriet Griesinger. "Criminal Deterrence: Revisiting the Issue with a Birth Cohort." *Review of Economics and Statistics* 76 (1994), pp. 399–412.

21. Thaler, Richard. "Econometric Analysis of Property Crime—Interaction between Police and Criminals." *Journal of Public Economics* 8 (1977), pp. 37–51.

22. Wilson, James Q. *Crime and Public Policy.* San Francisco: Institute for Contemporary Studies, 1983.

23. Wilson, James Q. *Thinking about Crime.* New York: Basic Books, 1975.

24. Witte, Ann D. "Estimating the Economic Model of Crime with Individual Data." *Quarterly Journal of Economics* 94 (1980), pp. 57–84.

PART FIVE

Housing

*T*his part of the book explores the economics of the urban housing market and evaluates the merits of various housing policies. Chapter 13 explains why housing is different from other products: housing is heterogeneous (dwellings differ in size, age, design, and location) and durable, and moving from one house to another is very costly. The filtering model of the housing market explains the economic forces that cause dwellings to move down the quality ladder to households with progressively lower incomes. As we'll see in Chapter 14, the federal government spends about $30 billion per year to assist low-income households, with the money spent on public housing, subsidized private housing, and vouchers issued to low-income households. In addition, the federal government sacrifices about $66 billion in tax revenue per year to subsidize mortgage interest, and most of the benefits go to high-income households.

CHAPTER 13

Why Is Housing Different?

The fellow that owns his own house is always just coming out of a hardware store.

—KEN HUBBARD

Last week I helped my friend stay put. It's a lot easier than helping someone move. I just went over to his house and made sure that he did not start to load his stuff into a truck.

—MITCH HEDBERG

*H*ousing has three features that make it different from other products. First, the housing stock is heterogeneous, with dwellings that differ in size, age, style, interior features, utilities, and location. Second, housing is durable and can deteriorate over time at a fast rate or a slow one, depending on the maintenance and repair decisions of its owner. Third, moving is costly, so when income or housing preferences change, consumers don't instantly adjust their housing consumption. Instead, they wait until the gap between the ideal house and their actual house is large enough to justify the large cost of moving. In this chapter, we explore the implications of these unusual features of the housing market.

HETEROGENEITY AND HEDONICS

The housing stock is heterogeneous, with each dwelling offering a different bundle of housing services. Dwellings differ in size, layout, style, utilities (heating and electrical), and the quality of the interior and the exterior. As we saw in the chapter on neighborhood choice, when you choose an apartment or house, you also choose a neighborhood, with its own bundle of housing services. Neighborhoods differ in accessibility to jobs and social opportunities, local public goods and taxes, and environmental quality.

What determines the equilibrium price of a dwelling? Under the hedonic approach, we determine the price of each part of the housing bundle. A hedonic study of the market might generate the following information:

1. **Base price.** The average house, with a price of $200,000, has three bedrooms, is five miles from the city center, and its roof is six years old.
2. **Access price.** The price drops by $2,000 for every additional mile from the city center.
3. **Size.** The price increases by $30,000 for every additional bedroom.
4. **Roof age.** The price of housing decreases by $500 for every year of roof age.
5. **Air quality.** The price decreases by $1,000 for every additional unit of air pollution.
6. **Schools.** The price increases by $2,000 for every one-unit increase in the average test score of students in the local elementary school.

To predict the price of a particular dwelling, we add to the base price to reflect differences between the average dwelling and a particular dwelling. For example, a fourth bedroom adds $30,000 to the price, while a new roof adds another $3,000 and a four-unit difference in air pollution adds $4,000. If the average test scores in the local school are three points higher than the city average, that adds another $6,000. Adding up these adjustments, the predicted price of the dwelling is $243,000.

The classic hedonic study is by Kain and Quigley (1970). They used data from the St. Louis housing market in the 1960s to estimate the dollar values of different housing attributes. Figure 13–1 shows the percentage changes in monthly rent and house value for one-unit changes in each of various housing features. For example, a one-unit increase in interior quality increases monthly rent by 2.1 percent and market value by 5.6 percent. The exterior quality of nearby dwellings was measured on a scale of 1 (bad) to 5 (excellent). A one-unit increase in the quality of adjacent dwellings increased rent by 3 percent and market value by 5.3 percent. A one-unit increase in the quality of dwellings on the block increased rent by 6 percent and market value by 2.9 percent.

Other hedonic studies have explored the effects of amenities on housing prices. Among the neighborhood characteristics with positive effects on housing prices are proximity to jobs, high-performing schools, transit stations, and churches. In contrast, property values are lower in neighborhoods close to areas with high crime rates, toxic waste facilities, and noisy highways.

How does a household choose among alternative dwellings, each of which provides a different bundle of characteristics? Most consumers do not have access to a hedonic study of their housing market. As they shop, they gather their own information about the implicit prices of location, size, and design features. The household then chooses the best affordable bundle.

DURABILITY, DETERIORATION, AND MAINTENANCE

Housing is durable in the sense that with proper maintenance, a dwelling can provide housing services for 100 years or more. But in the absence of routine maintenance and repair, a dwelling deteriorates, and the quality of the dwelling decreases

FIGURE 13–1 Results of Hedonic Study

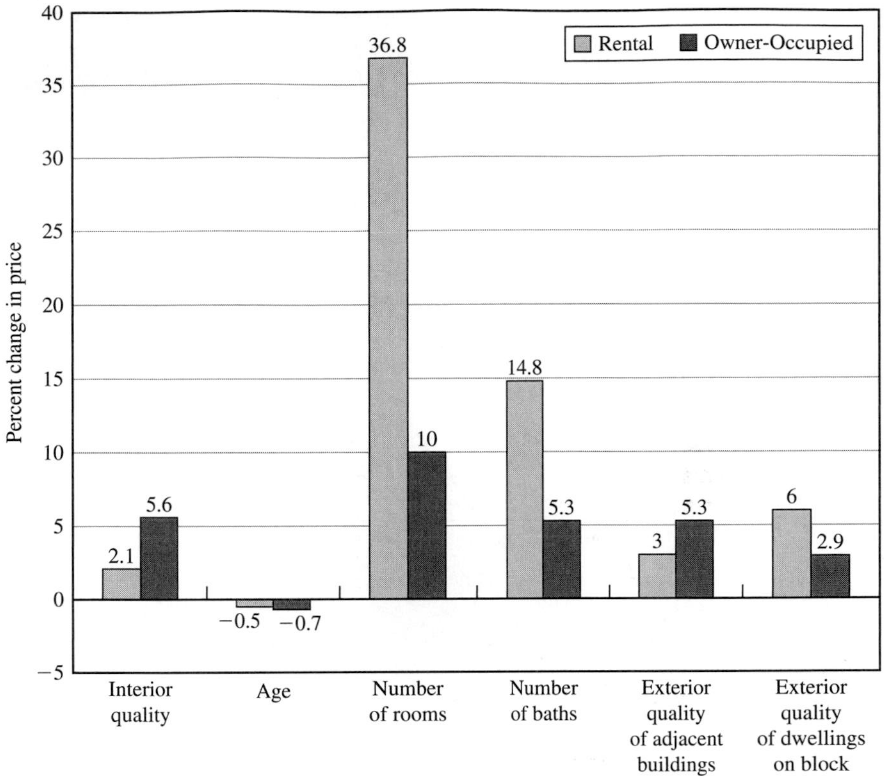

Source: Based on John Kain, and John Quigley. "Measuring the Value of Housing Quality." *Journal of the American Statistical Association* 65 (1970), pp. 532–48.

over time. Imagine a quality ladder for housing, with the highest quality dwellings at the top of the ladder and progressively lower quality as we move down the ladder. Each year, a property owner must decide where on the quality ladder to position his or her dwelling. If the owner does nothing, the dwelling will drop one or more rungs on the ladder. With a moderate expenditure on maintenance and repair, the owner can keep the dwelling at the same level. To raise the quality of the dwelling, the owner must spend a substantial amount of money to renovate or remodel.

Picking the Quality Level

We can use Figure 13–2 (page 286) to explore a property owner's decision about where on the quality ladder to position an existing dwelling. The horizontal axis measures the quality level, a general representation of the quantity of housing services generated by a dwelling. As shown in the upper panel, the cost of managing and maintaining a dwelling increases with its quality. This is sensible because

FIGURE 13–2   Picking a Position on the Quality Ladder

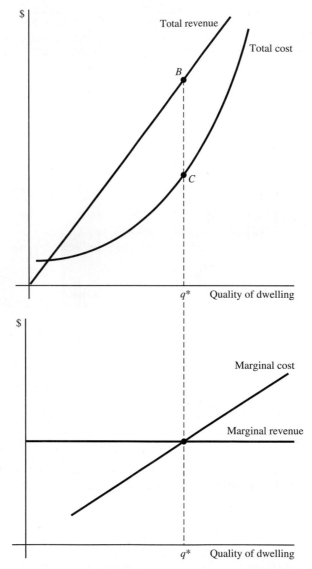

The owner's objective is to maximize profit, the gap between total revenue and total cost. Profit is maximized at the quality level where the marginal benefit (the price of quality) equals the marginal cost: q^*.

maintenance and repair costs are required to offset physical deterioration. The higher the quality, the greater the expense required to keep the dwelling at that quality level. The total-cost curve is convex, reflecting diminishing returns to maintenance: As the quality increases, it becomes progressively more costly to maintain the dwelling at the given quality level.

Consumers are willing to pay more for higher quality dwellings. For a rental dwelling, the price of quality is the change in the monthly rent for a one-unit increase in quality. In the upper panel of Figure 13–2, the linear curve shows the total revenue (monthly rent) on a dwelling as a function of the quality level. The total-revenue curve is linear, reflecting the assumption that consumers' willingness to pay for a dwelling increases linearly with quality. For example, doubling the quality doubles a consumer's willingness to pay for a dwelling, allowing the owner to double the rent.

The owner's objective is to maximize profit, equal to the gap between total revenue and total cost. In the upper panel of Figure 13–2, the gap is maximized at a quality level q^*. The lower panel uses the marginal principle, reviewed in Section 1.1 of "Tools of Microeconomics," the appendix at the end of the book. The profit-maximizing quality is where the marginal benefit of quality equals the marginal cost. The marginal benefit is the marginal revenue, the change in monthly rent per unit, change in quality (the slope of the total-revenue curve, the price of quality), and the marginal cost is the slope of the total-cost curve. To maximize profit (the gap between total revenue and total cost), the owner picks the quality where marginal revenue equals marginal cost.

Changes in Quality and Retirement

Figure 13–2 shows the quality choice with a particular set of revenue and cost curves. The profit-maximizing quality level is affected by changes in revenue or costs. As a dwelling ages, the cost of maintaining a given quality level increases, shifting the marginal-cost curve upward, as shown in Figure 13–3 (page 288). As a result, if the price hasn't changed (the marginal-revenue curve hasn't shifted), the profit-maximizing quality decreases. In Figure 13–3, this is shown as a move from point i to point j. If the marginal cost continues to increase as the dwelling ages, the owner's chosen quality level will continue to decrease. Eventually, the marginal-cost curve will lie entirely above the marginal-revenue curve. At that point, the cost of keeping the dwelling on the market exceeds the revenue that can be earned, so the property is retired—withdrawn from the market.

The profit-maximizing quality level is also affected by changes in price. An increase in price shifts the marginal-revenue curve upward, increasing the profit-maximizing quality, as shown by the move from point i to point k. In this case, the owner spends money to upgrade the dwelling because the extra revenue from a higher quality dwelling exceeds the extra cost of upgrading. In the opposite direction, a decrease in the price will shift the marginal-revenue curve downward, decreasing the quality. If the price reduction is large enough that the marginal-revenue curve lies entirely below the marginal-cost curve, the property will be retired.

When a dwelling is retired from the housing market, there are three possible scenarios:

1. **Boarding up.** A dwelling can be boarded up and taken off the market temporarily. This will be the best option if (a) the price is expected to increase sometime in the future and (b) the opportunity cost of holding wealth in housing

FIGURE 13–3 Dwelling Age and Quality Level

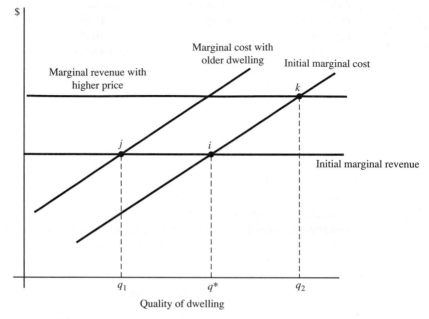

As a dwelling ages, the marginal cost of maintenance increases, decreasing the profit-maximizing quality level (point *i* to point *j*). An increase in the price of quality increases the profit-maximizing quality (point *i* to point *k*).

instead of another asset, such as a bank account, is relatively low. This sort of temporary retirement was common during the Great Depression.

2. **Conversion.** A dwelling can be converted to nonresidential use such as an office, a store, or a parking lot. Conversion is profitable if the alternative activity generates enough profit to offset the cost of conversion.
3. **Abandonment.** The owner will disown the dwelling if the best alternative use does not generate enough profit to cover the cost of conversion.

Abandonment and Public Policy

We've seen that a dwelling will be abandoned if it cannot be profitably used for housing or any alternative use. Local tax policy can contribute to the abandonment problem if the property tax is inflexible. As a dwelling moves down the quality ladder over time, profit decreases. For example, suppose the annual profit from a dwelling is initially $4,000 and the annual tax is $3,000. If the profit drops to $2,000 per year and the property tax is fixed at $3,000, the owner will abandon the property because the tax exceeds the profit. In contrast, if the property tax were flexible, it would be cut in half from $3,000 to $1,500, and the owner would have an incentive to keep the property because the profit ($2,000) still exceeds the tax.

White (1986) showed that during the 1980s the property tax was the most important factor in abandonment in New York City. The elasticity of abandonment with respect to the property tax was 1.65: a 10 percent increase in the property tax increased the frequency of abandonment by 16.5 percent. For example, if the average assessed value of properties in the Brownsville section of Brooklyn were cut by $1,000 (a 6 percent reduction) the resulting decreases in property taxes would lower the abandonment rate from 17 percent per year to 14.8 percent. Given this large elasticity, a tax cut would generate a fiscal surplus for the city. Although the tax liability per property would decrease, the direct revenue loss would be offset by (1) an increase in the number of properties on the tax rolls and (2) a decrease in the number of properties that the city must either take over or demolish.

There are external costs associated with abandonment. Recall the third axiom of urban economics:

Externalities cause inefficiency

Abandoned buildings provide targets for vandals and graffiti artists, and they quickly become eyesores. They often become the temporary homes and retail outlets for transients and drug dealers, so they contribute to crime. For these reasons, abandonment decreases the relative attractiveness of a neighborhood, decreasing the rent that other landlords can charge for their properties. The decrease in profit on other properties encourages more abandonment, so the process can be self-reinforcing.

Durability and Supply Elasticity

The durability of housing has important implications for the market supply curve and the price elasticity of supply. An increase in the price of housing increases the quantity supplied in three ways:

1. **Build more new dwellings.** An increase in price increases the profitability of new housing, so more will be built.
2. **Increase maintenance on used dwellings.** A higher price gives owners a greater incentive to spend money on maintenance and repair to slow the movement of dwellings down the quality ladder.
3. **Upgrade used dwellings.** A higher price provides owners an incentive to move their dwellings up the quality ladder by renovation and remodeling.

The bulk of housing on the market at any particular time is used housing. The general rule of thumb is that in a given year, new construction is between 2 percent and 3 percent of the total housing stock. So the supply response to a price hike is determined in large part by the response of used housing. The supply of used housing is relatively inelastic for relatively long periods of time for two reasons. First, the rate of deterioration is relatively low, so even if an increase in maintenance halts the movement of dwellings down the quality ladder, the response is relatively small. Second, remodeling and renovation are relatively expensive, so it takes a relatively large price hike to make upgrading worthwhile.

The same logic applies to a decrease in the market price. If lower prices halt new construction altogether, the quantity supplied decreases by only 2 to 3 percent per year. A lower price decreases maintenance spending and speeds the movement down the quality ladder, but even the fastest deterioration rate is relatively slow. In general, supply is relatively inelastic for long periods.

What is the price elasticity of the supply of housing? The existing studies of housing supply suffer from a number of statistical problems, so their results must be interpreted with caution (see Olsen, 1969 and Quigley, 1979). Ozanne and Struyk (1978) estimate that the 10-year supply elasticity of used housing is between 0.20 and 0.30. In other words, a 10 percent increase in the market price, sustained over a 10-year period, increases the quantity of used housing by between 2 and 3 percent. Over a 10-year period, new construction provides only about 30 percent of the housing stock, so their estimate applies to 70 percent of the housing stock. De Leeuw and Ekanem (1971) estimate that the long-run supply elasticity for rental housing is between 0.30 to 0.70.

MOVING COSTS AND CONSUMER DISEQUILIBRIUM

For most households, a change in housing consumption requires a move to a different dwelling, and the cost of moving is substantial. In addition to the large cost of moving furniture and other possessions, there is also a large personal cost associated with leaving a neighborhood, with its familiar people, schools, and stores. The notion of neighborhood attachment captures the idea that a move to a new neighborhood disrupts social and consumption patterns, imposing a substantial cost on the household.

Consider first a household whose income is increasing over time. Like many other goods, the utility-maximizing housing consumption increases with income. Specifically, the income elasticity of demand for housing is about 0.75 (Ellwood and Polinski, 1979): A 10 percent increase in income increases housing consumption by about 7.5 percent. As income increases, the gap between the household's ideal dwelling and its actual dwelling will grow, and it eventually may become large enough to justify moving.

We can use the consumer choice model to represent the household's options. The choice model is reviewed in Section 4 of "Tools of Microeconomics," the appendix at the end of the book. In Panel A of Figure 13–4, the starting point is i: Given an initial income level represented by the lower budget line, utility is maximized at point i, with a housing quality level q^* and A^* of other goods. An increase in income shifts the budget line to the northeast. If the household remains in its original dwelling, housing consumption doesn't change and the household goes to point j. All the additional income is spent on other goods, and utility increases from U_0 to U_1. A move to a different dwelling with quality = q_2 (point k) would generate a higher utility level (U_2). If moving cost were zero, the household would instantly move from point i to point k. But with large moving costs, the increase in utility ($U_2 - U_1$) must be large enough to offset moving costs. If the household's

FIGURE 13–4 Moving Costs and Consumer Decisions

A: Increase in Income   B: Decrease in Quality

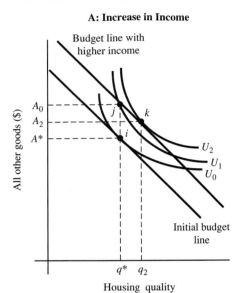

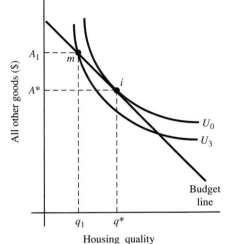

An increase in income shifts the budget line outward. If the consumer doesn't move, she goes from point *i* to *j* and utility increases from U_0 to U_1. If she moves, she gets to point *k* with utility level U_2. Moving is sensible if the difference in utility $(U_2 - U_1)$ is large enough to offset the cost of moving.

A decrease in the quality of the dwelling moves the consumer upward along the budget line from *i* to *j* and decreases utility from U_0 to U_3. The owner will move to a different dwelling with quality = q^* if the difference in utility $(U_0 - U_3)$ is large enough to offset the cost of moving.

income continues to increase, the utility gap will eventually be large enough to trigger a move.

Consider next a household that occupies a dwelling that moves down the quality ladder over time. As shown in Panel B of Figure 13–4, as quality decreases, so does the monthly rent (the price per unit of quality times quality), so the household moves upward along the original budget line from point *i* to point *m*. As the household moves away from its utility-maximizing point, its utility decreases, and at point *m*, the utility level is shown by the indifference curve U_3. To restore the original utility level U_0, the household must move, but moving generates a moving cost. The household will continue to move upward along its budget line until the utility gap $(U_0 - U_3)$ is large enough to offset the cost of moving.

There are two lessons from Figure 13–4. First, households do not instantly respond to a change in circumstances, such as an increase in income or a decrease in the quality of housing, but instead tolerate a gap between the ideal and actual consumption levels. Second, when a household moves, it eliminates the housing gap, so the change in housing consumption is likely to be large. In fact, if a household anticipates future changes in the utility-maximizing consumption level, it may overshoot its current ideal level to reduce the size of a future gap between the ideal and actual consumption.

THE FILTERING MODEL OF THE HOUSING MARKET

The filtering model of the housing market shows how a dwelling changes over time in quality and in the income of its occupants. The filtering process has two basic features:

1. **Decrease in quality.** The quantity of housing services generated by a dwelling (summarized in "quality") decreases over time because of physical deterioration, technological obsolescence, and changes in housing fashion.
2. **Decrease in occupant income.** As a dwelling moves down the quality ladder, it is occupied by households with progressively lower incomes.

Filtering and the Housing Stepladder

Figure 13–5 represents the essential features of the filtering model. The horizontal axis shows household income, with three types of households, low-income ($100), medium-income ($200), and high income ($300). The vertical axis shows the

FIGURE 13–5 Filtering and the Quality Stepladder

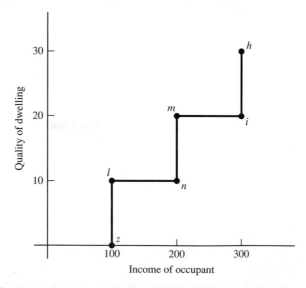

Housing quality is assumed to be proportional to income, and quality decreases by 10 units over the decade. A dwelling occupied by a high-income household moves from point *h* to *i* (quality decreases), and then from point *i* to *m* (vacated by the high-income household after it moves to new housing and then occupied by the middle-income household). Similarly, a dwelling initially occupied by a middle-income household goes from *m* to *n* to *l*, and the dwelling occupied by a low-income household goes from *l* to *z* (retirement).

quality of housing, with three levels, low (10 units), medium (20), and high (30). Suppose the demand for housing is proportional to income, with each household occupying a dwelling with a quality level equal to 10 percent of its income. At the start of a decade, the chosen points are h for the high-income household, m for the medium-income household, and l for the low-income household.

We will make a few assumptions to simplify matters and make the filtering process transparent. First, suppose that regular maintenance activity by the property owner means that each dwelling loses one unit of quality per year. Second, this underlying movement down the quality ladder can be reversed, but only at a substantial cost for remodeling and renovation. Third, each household has a maximum gap between its ideal and actual housing quality. Once the gap reaches 10 units, the household closes the gap by either upgrading its existing dwelling or moving to a different dwelling.

These assumptions mean that all the action happens at the end of each decade. Each household experiences a growing mismatch between the ideal and the actual quality of housing. The high-income household starts at point h, but by the end of the decade is at point i, with a 10-unit gap between the ideal and the actual quality. Similarly, the middle-income household goes from point m to point n, and the low-income household goes from l to z. At the end of the decade, each household has to choose between the house to restore the original quality, upgrading and moving to a different house.

Consider first the choice of the high-income household. The decrease in quality could be reversed by replacing old pipes and leaky windows, repairing dinged woodwork and walls, and retrofitting the house with the latest communications technology. In most cases, this sort of upgrading is costly relative to the price of a new house, which is built from scratch with new materials and modern technology. Therefore, most high-income households move rather than upgrade. Moving to a new house gets them back to point h, with a quality level $q = 30$. They vacate their old house with $q = 20$, selling it to the highest bidder.

The middle-income household has a similar problem, with a twist. An alternative to upgrading the original house (moving it from n back to m) is to buy a used house from a high-income household. If the supply of used housing with quality level 20 is relatively large (if a large number of high-income households sell their old houses), the price will be low enough that moving is less costly than upgrading the old house. So the dwelling formerly occupied by the high-income household moves from point i to point m. To summarize, the filtering process is shown by the movement of a dwelling down the housing stepladder, from point h to i (decrease in quality) and then from point i to m (decrease in occupant income).

The final step involves low-income households that can either upgrade or move into the dwellings vacated by the middle-income households. If the supply of used housing of quality level 10 is relatively large, the price will be low enough that it is more efficient to move rather than upgrade. So the household moves from point z back to point l by moving to a dwelling that has moved down the stepladder from point m to n (decrease in quality) and then from point n to l (decrease in occupant income). The houses vacated by the low-income households with quality $= 0$ are then retired from the housing market.

The filtering process allows each household to restore its desired quality level and get back to its original position on the quality ladder. This occurs even though each dwelling moves down the ladder over the decade. The production of new housing offsets the decline in the quality level of old housing in two ways. First, for each dwelling retired at the low end, one new house is built at the high end. Second, high-income households are accommodated in new housing, freeing up used dwellings and thus allowing other households to reach their ideal quality level.

This little housing model generates tidy results, with a perfect matching of dwellings and households. Of course, things don't operate so smoothly in real markets, but the model captures the essential features of the filtering process. One realistic complication worth mentioning is that the housing occupied by the wealthiest households does not typically filter down to lower-income households. Much of the housing occupied by the wealthy has luxury features (e.g., 10-foot ceilings, fancy fixtures, spa-like bathrooms, and open space) that middle-income and low-income households don't demand. As a result, there is a greater incentive to maintain these dwellings to prevent their movement down the quality ladder.

Subsidies for New Housing

We can use the filtering model to explore the effects of government subsidies on new housing. Although new housing is typically occupied by high-income households, the subsidies hasten the filtering of used housing to lower income households, so everyone benefits from the subsidies.

Suppose the government subsidizes new housing, which we assume is occupied exclusively by high-income households. The subsidy decreases the price of new housing to high-income consumers, and they demand higher quality houses. Figure 13–6 has the same starting points as Figure 13–5, with the high-income household starting at point h. Suppose the ideal point for high-income households shifts from point h to point j (quality level 35). Suppose as before that a household tolerates up to a 10-unit mismatch between its ideal and actual quality level. Given the higher ideal quality level (35), a household will move once the quality level of its original house has dropped from 30 to 25. So the household will move after 5 years instead of 10, and vacate a dwelling with quality level 25 instead of 20. When households are given the option of subsidized new housing, they move sooner and the quality level of housing available for filtering increases.

What are the implications for middle-income and low-income households? Now a middle-income household chooses between moving to a house with quality level 25 (point p) and upgrading its old house with quality level 15 (point r). The excess supply of $q = 25$ houses will decrease their prices, providing households with an incentive to move and thus vacate their $q = 15$ houses (a move from point r to p). Similarly, low-income households will have an incentive to move into the $q = 15$ houses vacated by middle-income households (going from point x to point y).

The filtering process transmits the benefits of housing subsidies throughout the housing market. In this simple example, each type of household experiences a five-unit increase in housing quality. The subsidies shift the quality stepladder up by five

FIGURE 13–6 The Effects of Subsidies for New Housing

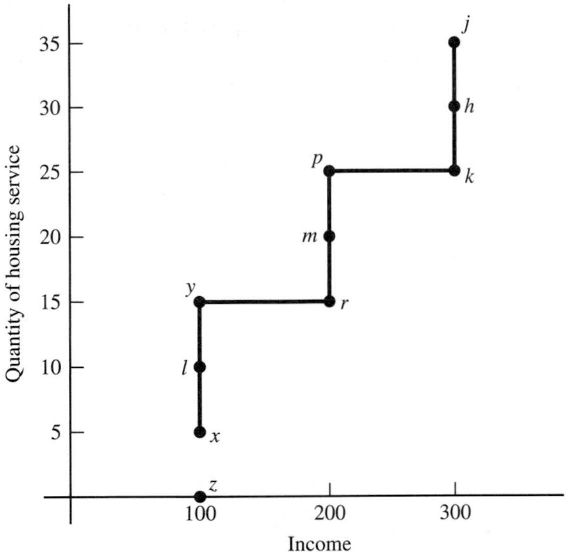

A subsidy for new housing increases the ideal quality for the high-income household, and it vacates its original dwelling earlier, leaving a higher quality dwelling for filtering down to middle-income households. In general, a housing subsidy shifts the quality stepladder up, so everyone in the housing market gets higher quality housing.

units: Once everyone has adjusted to the subsidy, the high-income household reaches point *j* instead of point *h*, while the middle-income household reaches *p* instead of *m*, and the low-income household reaches *y* instead of *l*.

The Effects of Growth Controls

Consider next the implications of growth controls that decrease the number of new houses that can be built. To simplify matters, suppose a city outlaws new housing, all of which would have been occupied by high-income households. The building ban will affect the filtering process, leading to higher prices and lower quality housing.

   The building ban has a direct effect on high-income households, the potential occupants of new housing. Looking back at Figure 13–5, moving to a new house is no longer an option, so at the end of the decade when the house has deteriorated from quality level 30 to 20, the household must either bear the relatively high cost of upgrading, or tolerate a growing mismatch. In either case, the lack of new housing means that no houses will be vacated for filtering to middle-income households. As a result, middle-income households will either upgrade at a high cost or tolerate a mismatch, meaning that no houses will be vacated for filtering to low-income households.

In our simple model, the imposition of a building ban causes a switch from a market in which everyone moves to a market in which no one moves. Growth control is costly because it causes costly upgrading for some households and forces other households to tolerate bigger housing mismatches. In both cases, the costs of the building ban are borne by everyone in the housing market, not just those who are prevented from buying new houses at the top of the quality ladder.

In a more complex model of the housing market, people enter and leave the market, so some houses will change hands. Nonetheless, growth controls will generate higher prices for two reasons. First, the elimination of new housing will decrease the supply of housing in general, leading to higher prices for new and used housing. Second, prices will reflect the higher costs of upgrading houses to offset deterioration.

Filtering with Rising Income

Our simple model of the filtering process assumes constant income over time for each income group. In a model with rising income, rising demand for housing means that filtering is even more beneficial. For example, suppose the ideal quality level for a high-income household increases from 30 to 40. To meet its greater demand by modifying its old house, the household would be forced to not only restore the original quality level, but also to increase it with substantial remodeling. As a result, the advantage of new housing over used housing would be even greater. Similarly, if the incomes of middle-income households are rising over time, they would find the houses vacated by high-income households more attractive relative to upgrading their old houses. The same logic applies to low-income households. In general, when income increases over time, filtering is more advantageous, reflecting the high cost of moving dwellings up the quality ladder.

The Price Effects of Growth Controls

Figure 13–7 provides a closer look at the price effects of a growth-control policy. Consider the market for rental dwellings, and imagine that there are three quality submarkets: high, medium, and low. The number of renters and the number of dwellings are fixed. Each property owner chooses a submarket for the dwelling. The owner of a high-quality dwelling has two options: (1) do nothing, and the dwelling moves down the quality ladder to medium quality, or (2) spend money on maintenance to keep the dwelling at the high quality level. The owner of a medium-quality dwelling has three options: (1) do nothing, and the quality drops to the low level, (2) spend a moderate amount on maintenance to keep the medium quality level, and (3) spend a large amount on maintenance to move the dwelling up quality ladder to the high level.

Panel A of Figure 13–7 shows the high-quality submarket, which includes new dwellings. If a growth-control policy outlaws new housing, the supply curve will shift to the left, with fewer dwellings supplied at each price. Comparing point i to

FIGURE 13–7 The Price Effects of a Building Ban

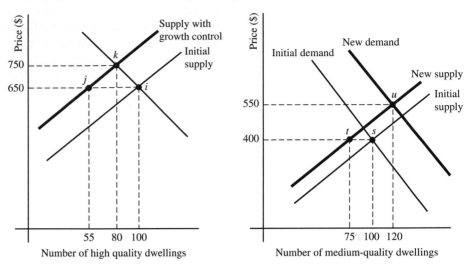

A: A ban on new housing shifts the supply curve for high-quality dwellings to the left, increasing the equilibrium price.
B: An increase in the price of high-quality dwellings (1) decreases the supply of medium quality dwellings as fewer filter down from the high-quality market and (2) increases demand as consumers switch from the high-quality submarket to the medium-quality market. The equilibrium price rises.

point j, 45 new dwellings that would have been built at the original price of $650 are not built. The new supply curve intersects the demand curve at point k, with a higher price ($750) and a smaller quantity of dwellings (80 instead of 100). The net loss in dwellings is 20, which is less than the loss of 45 new dwellings. The higher price of high-quality housing gives property owners a greater incentive to spend money on maintenance to keep the dwellings at the high quality level. In other words, in-creased maintenance means fewer dwellings move down the quality ladder, partly offsetting the loss of new housing from the building ban.

Panel B of Figure 13–7 shows the implications for the medium-quality sub-market. The increase in the price of high-quality dwellings has two effects. First, as we saw in Panel A, fewer dwellings filter down to the medium-quality market. This is shown as a leftward shift of the market supply curve. Comparing point t to point s, 25 dwellings that would have filtered down stay at the high-quality level. On the demand side, the two types of dwellings are imperfect substitutes, and consumers move between the two submarkets. The increase in the price of high-quality dwellings (from $650 to $750), causes some consumers to switch to medium-quality dwellings. The demand curve for medium-quality dwellings shifts to the right, with a larger quantity demanded at each price. At the new equi-librium shown by point u, the price of medium-quality dwellings is $550, up from $400.

The general lesson from Figure 13–7 is that a supply restriction in the high-quality market causes higher prices in both markets. A growth control policy that restricts the supply of new housing reduces filtering, so its effects are transmitted to the medium-quality submarket. In addition, consumers fleeing higher prices in the high-quality market increase the demand for medium-quality housing. The combination of decreased supply (less filtering) and increased demand (fleeing consumers) generates higher prices in the medium-quality market. The same logic applies to the low-quality submarket. The increase in the price in the medium-quality submarket reduces the flow of apartments downward along the quality ladder and causes some consumers to flee to the low-quality market. The result is higher prices for low-quality housing.

SUMMARY

This chapter explores three characteristics that distinguish housing from other markets. Housing is heterogeneous and durable, and moving costs make it costly to change consumption. Here are the main points from the chapter.

1. The hedonic approach is based on the notion that a dwelling is composed of a bundle of housing services, each with an implicit price.
2. Housing is durable and the owner controls its position on the quality ladder by spending on maintenance, repair, renovation, and remodeling.
3. The supply of housing is relatively inelastic for long periods of time because the bulk of the housing stock is used.
4. The cost of moving is relatively large, so households change their housing consumption infrequently and make large changes when they move.
5. The filtering model explains how a dwelling moves down the quality ladder to households with progressively lower income.
6. Dwellings at different quality levels are related on the supply side because of filtering and related on the demand side because of consumer substitution. A policy that reduces the quantity of new, high-quality dwellings increases the equilibrium prices of all quality levels.

APPLYING THE CONCEPTS

1. Picking a Quality Level
Suppose dwelling quality is measured on a scale of 1 to 10, and the monthly cost of producing a particular quality equals the square of the quality level: for quality = 1, the cost is $1; for quality = 2, the cost is $4, and so on. The monthly rent equals the price per unit of quality (P) times the quality level.
  a. If the price is $9, what's the profit-maximizing quality level? Illustrate with a graph like Figure 13–3.

    b. Suppose the price of quality increases to $13. Show the new profit-maximizing quality on your graph.

2. **Stay or Move?**

   Consider a household with income of $100 and housing consumption equal to 40 units of quality. The income elasticity of demand for housing is 0.75.

   a. Use a graph like the one shown in Figure 13–4 to show the household's initial utility-maximizing choice (labeled as point *i*).

   b. Suppose the household's income increases to $120. Show the household's new choice in the absence of moving costs (labeled as point *m* for "move") and in the presence of moving costs high enough that the household will not move (labeled as point *s* for "stay").

   c. Suppose that given its moving cost, the household will move if the gap between its actual housing consumption and its ideal consumption (with moving cost = 0) is at least 30 percent. Will the household choose point *m* or point *s*?

   d. What is the threshold income level, the income just high enough to cause the household to move?

3. **Stepladder versus Ramp**

   The real estate agents in Rampville are baffled. Although dwellings are subject to the normal decrease in quality over time, there is no filtering: No resident has changed houses in the last 10 years. Provide an explanation for this phenomenon. Use a figure like Figure 13–5 to depict the housing market in Rampville.

4. **Subsidies for Middle-Income Households**

   Suppose the government implements a new subsidy program that pays 20 percent of the housing expenses of middle-income households. The price elasticity of demand for housing is −1.0. As before, assume that each household tolerates up to a 10-unit difference between the ideal and actual quality of housing. All new housing is built for high-income households. Upgrading housing to a higher quality level is prohibitively expensive.

   a. Use Figure 13–5 as a starting point, with points *l*, *m*, and *h*. After how many years will dwellings change occupants? What types of dwellings are put on the market, and what types of households buy them?

   b. Draw a graph like Figure 13–5 to show the long-run effects of the subsidy program on the housing stepladder.

5. **Mandated Energy Conservation**

   Consider a city where each year 10 households move from old houses (energy consumption = 20 units per year) into modern (new) houses (energy consumption = 12 units per year). Suppose a new law requires that all houses built in the future include an energy-saving device that adds $5,000 to construction cost and cuts energy consumption from 12 to 9 units.

   a. Use a figure like Figure 13–7 to show the effects of the new law on the markets for new and used housing.

   b. According to Ms. Wizard, "I predict that the new law will actually harm our energy-conservation efforts." Describe the circumstances under which Ms. Wizard is correct.

REFERENCES AND ADDITIONAL READING

1. De Leeuw, Frank, and Nkanta Ekanem. "The Supply of Rental Housing." *American Economic Review* 61 (1971), pp. 806–17.

2. Ellwood, David, and Mitchell Polinski. "An Empirical Reconciliation of Micro and Grouped Estimates of the Demand for Housing." *Review of Economics and Statistics* 61 (1979), pp. 199–205.

3. Follain, James R., and Emmanuel Jiminez. "Estimating the Demand for Housing Characteristics." *Regional Science and Urban Economics* 15 (1985), pp. 77–107.

4. Kain, John, and John Quigley. "Measuring the Value of Housing Quality." *Journal of the American Statistical Association* 65 (1970), pp. 532–48.

5. Olsen, Edgar O. "A Competitive Theory of the Housing Market." *American Economic Review* 59 (1969), pp. 612–22.

6. Ozanne, L., and Raymond Struyk. "The Price Elasticity of Supply of Housing Services." In *Urban Housing Markets: Recent Directions in Research and Policy,* eds. L.S. Bourne and J.R. Hitchcock. Toronto: University of Toronto Press, 1978.

7. Quigley, John M. "What Have We Learned about Housing Markets?" In *Current Issues in Urban Economics,* eds. Peter Mieszkowski and Mahlon Straszheim. Baltimore: Johns Hopkins University Press, 1979.

8. White, Michelle. "Property Taxes and Urban Housing Abandonment." *Journal of Urban Economics* 20 (1986), pp. 312–30.

CHAPTER 14

Housing Policy

Fools build houses, and wise men buy them.

—PROVERB

Almost any man worthy of his salt would fight to defend his home, but no one ever heard of a man going to war for his boarding house.

—MARK TWAIN

*T*his chapter discusses housing policies that assist low-income as well as high-income households. For low-income households, the federal government spends about $30 billion per year to provide public housing, subsidize privately produced housing, and provide vouchers that households use to help pay for housing they choose themselves. The federal government also uses a number of community development programs to support local efforts to improve housing conditions and revitalize neighborhoods. For middle-income and high-income households, the government sacrifices about $66 billion in tax revenue per year to subsidize home ownership through the tax deduction for mortgage interest.

Figure 14–1 (page 302) shows the number of renter households with inadequate housing or a relatively high rent burden. Between 1980 and 1997, the number of renter households in "severely inadequate housing" dropped significantly, while the number paying more than 30 percent of income for rent increased to 14.6 million. Only about 30 percent of the households that are eligible for public housing, subsidized housing, or vouchers actually receive assistance. There are long waiting lists for households to get into public housing, and voucher programs are not funded at a level necessary to serve all the eligible households.

PUBLIC HOUSING

In 1998, about 1.3 million households lived in public housing. In terms of budgetary costs, the federal government's outlays for public housing included $3.1 billion for operating subsidies (to cover the gap between the rent collected from tenants and

FIGURE 14–1 Number of Households in Inadequate or Unaffordable Housing

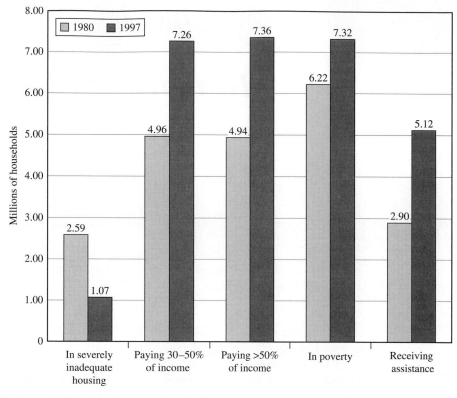

Source: Based on John Quigley. "A Decent Home: Housing Policy in Perspective." *Brookings-Wharton Papers on Urban Affairs* (2000), pp. 53–99.

the costs of operating the project) and $3.8 billion for capital expenditures (for repair, upgrading, and demolition). Public housing is managed by local housing authorities, subject to rules adopted by the federal government. The rent charged to a particular tenant can be no more than 30 percent of the household's income. In recent years, there has been no investment in new public housing, but funds have been allocated for the repair and renovation of decaying public housing.

Public Housing and Recipient Welfare

Figure 14–2 uses the consumer choice model to represent the housing choices of a low-income household. The choice model is reviewed in Section 4 of "Tools of Microeconomics," the appendix at the end of the book. The horizontal axis measures housing consumption (the quantity of housing service from a dwelling), and the vertical axis measures the monthly consumption of all other goods (in dollars). Suppose the household has a monthly income of $800 and the price of housing is $1 per unit of service. The initial budget line shows the household's options, with a one-for-one trade-off between housing and other goods. The household maximizes

FIGURE 14–2 Utility Maximization with Public Housing

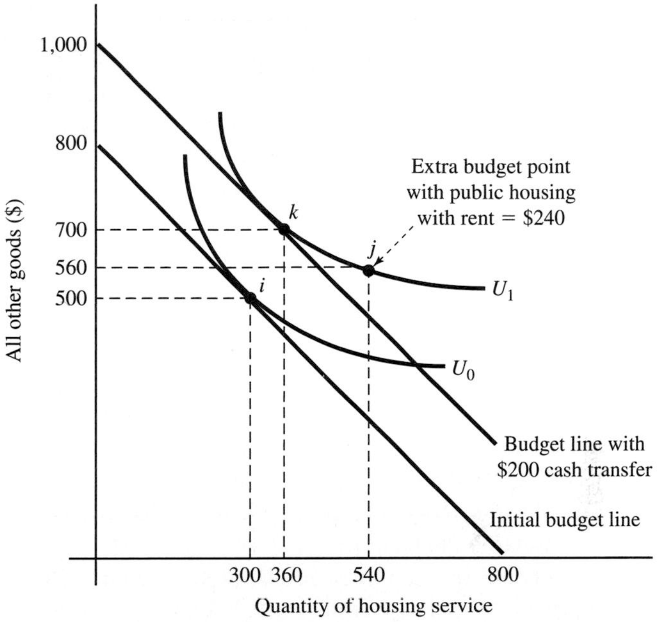

The government charges public housing tenants 30% of income ($240) for a dwelling with 540 units of service, so point j is added to the budget set and the recipient's utility level increases from U_0 to U_1. The recipient would reach the same utility level with a cash transfer of $200. The subsidy is $300 ($540 − $240 rent) so the value of public housing is two-thirds of the subsidy.

utility at point i, where the indifference curve is tangent to the budget line. At this point, the marginal rate of substitution of housing and other goods equals the price ratio, so the household is doing the best it can. The household occupies a dwelling that generates 300 units of housing service at a cost of $300, leaving $500 to spend on other goods.

Suppose the typical dwelling in public housing generates 540 units of housing service. The government charges rent equal to 30 percent of the tenant's income, or $240 for our hypothetical household (0.30 times $800). Public housing adds point j to the household's budget set. In addition to all the points on or below the initial budget line, the household also has the option of 540 units of service for only $240, leaving $560 to spend on other goods. By accepting the offer of public housing, the household gets more of both goods and reaches a higher utility level (U_1 instead of U_0).

How much is public housing worth to the tenant? The value of public housing can be measured by answering the following question: What cash payment would make the household indifferent between the cash and the public housing offer (a 540-unit dwelling at a price of $240)? In other words, what cash payment would move the household to the indifference curve associated with public housing (U_1)?

In Figure 14–2, a $200 payment shifts the budget line upward in a parallel fashion, and the household maximizes utility at point k, reaching the indifference curve U_1. In other words, the household is indifferent between $200 in cash and a housing subsidy of $300 (equal to the dollar value of the 540-unit dwelling ($540) minus the rent paid ($240). The value of public housing is two-thirds of the subsidy. This is consistent with the results of studies that measure the value of public housing to recipients (Green and Malpezzi, 2003).

How does the cost of new public housing compare to the cost of private housing? Public housing is more expensive for two reasons. First, the private sector can build new low-income housing more efficiently than the public sector. Second, there is a plentiful supply of used low-quality housing, so even the least costly new housing costs more than used housing. Economists measure the production efficiency of public housing by the ratio of the market value of the dwelling divided by the production cost. According to Green and Malpezzi (2003), the production efficiency of public housing is 0.50, meaning that the production cost is twice the market value. In our example, if it costs the government $1,080 to produce a dwelling worth $540, the budgetary cost of getting to the public-housing point (point j in Figure 14–2) is $840 ($1,080 minus the $240 rent paid by tenants).

What is the bang per buck of public housing? In other words, what is the recipient benefit per taxpayer dollar spent on public housing? As shown in Figure 14–2, recipients would be indifferent between $200 in cash and public housing, so the bang from each public-housing dwelling is $200. If the government subsidy per dwelling is $840, the bang per buck is $0.24 (equal to $200/$840).

Subsidies for Private Housing

One alternative to public housing is a system of subsidies to encourage the private sector to build and manage low-income housing. Under two programs, Section 236 and Section 8—Project Based, the government pays a property owner the difference between the household's rent and the "fair market rent." In most cases, the household's contribution is 30 percent of its income. The fair market rent is determined by either the cost of building and managing the property or the prevailing rent in the area. For example, suppose the fair market rent of an apartment is $500, and an eligible household's income is $800. In this case, the household would pay $240 (30 percent of $800) and the government would pay $260, for a total payment of $500.

Under these subsidy programs, the federal government signs long-term contracts to provide annual payments to property owners. The owner is guaranteed the fair market rent on all units occupied by eligible households. In 1998, 1.4 million households were assisted under the Section 8 program, and just under half a million were assisted under Section 236 (Quigley, 2000).

Although subsidies for private housing are more efficient than public housing, they still produce dwellings with market values less than their production cost. As reported by Green and Malpezzi (2003), estimates of the production efficiency of subsidized new private housing range from 0.61 to 0.85, with a median of about 0.75.

Low Income Housing Tax Credit

The Tax Reform Act of 1986 instituted a program of tax credits for investment in affordable housing for low-income households. To qualify for tax credits, a project must set aside a fraction of the dwellings to be "rent restricted" (a maximum rent for the dwelling) and "occupant restricted" (a maximum income for tenants). There are two tests for these set-asides:

1. **The 20/50 test:** At least 20 percent of the rental dwellings must be occupied by households with income no greater than 50 percent of the median area income.
2. **The 40/60 test:** At least 40 percent of the rental dwellings must be occupied by households with income no greater than 60 percent of the median area income.

In both cases, the maximum rent is 30 percent of the qualifying income. A builder of low-income housing earns an annual credit of 9 percent of the project cost attributable to low-income housing. For example, a project with a $10 million cost for low-income housing generates an annual tax credit of $900,000, and the builder's federal tax liability drops by that amount. The builder can get the annual credit for up to 10 years, although the set-aside restrictions apply for 15 years.

The tax-credit program has been used in projects that had produced 700,000 low-income dwellings by 1999. The credits are allocated by state housing authorities, subject to restrictions established by the federal government. In 2002, each state was allowed to grant credits totaling $1.50 per capita, and the allocation rose to $1.75 per capita in 2003. In 2003, the cost of this tax expenditure in terms of lost revenue was about $3.5 billion (Office of Management and Budget, 2002).

The revenue loss from the tax-credit program is large relative to the amount of housing produced. The complexity and riskiness of the program mean that investors demand relatively high rates of return on funds invested. In 1996, each dollar of federal subsidy produced only about $0.62 worth of housing, so the efficiency of the tax-credit program is not much different from that of public housing (Quigley, 2000). DiPasquale, Fricke, and Garcia-Diaz (2003) estimate that the cost of providing a one-bedroom rental unit under the tax-credit program is 19 percent higher than an equivalent unsubsidized unit, and the cost gap for a two-bedroom unit is 14 percent.

The Market Effects of Subsidized Housing

Government subsidies for privately produced housing currently support about 2.6 million dwellings. Does this mean that housing subsidies have increased the total housing stock by 2.6 million units? As we'll see, housing subsidies displace unsubsidized housing, so the net effect of the subsidies on the housing stock is relatively small.

Figure 14–3 (page 306) shows the effects of housing subsidies on the unsubsidized market. At the initial equilibrium before subsidies (shown by point *i*) the price is $500 and the quantity is 300 unsubsidized dwellings. If government subsidies generate 100 new housing units, 100 households leave the unsubsidized market, so

FIGURE 14–3 The Displacement Effect of Housing Subsidies

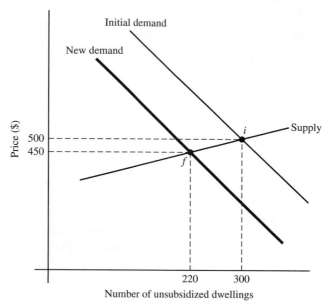

Housing subsidies decrease the demand for unsubsidized low-quality dwellings. The resulting excess supply decreases the equilibrium price from $500 to $450. The number of unsubsidized dwellings decreases from 300 to 220.

the demand curve shifts to the left by 100 dwellings. The resulting excess supply will cause the price to drop, and equilibrium is restored at point *f*, with a price of $450 and a quantity of 220. In other words, the number of unsubsidized dwellings decreases by 80, partly offsetting the effects of housing subsidies.

Let's take a closer look at the movement downward along the supply curve for unsubsidized housing as the price drops. This is low-income housing, so we are at the low end of the housing quality ladder. The quantity of low-quality unsubsidized dwellings decreases for two reasons.

- **More retirement.** A decrease in the price of low-quality dwellings reduces the profit on unsubsidized dwellings, so more dwellings are retired from the housing market, either converted to another use or abandoned.
- **Slower downward filtering.** A decrease in the price of low-quality housing relative to the price of medium-quality housing causes property owners to slow the movement of dwellings downward along the quality ladder. Owners spend more on maintenance and repair to hold their dwellings in the medium-quality submarket.

What are the facts on the displacement or "crowding out" of unsubsidized housing by subsidized housing? Murray (1999) estimates that in the long run, the reduction in the number of unsubsidized dwellings is at least one-third of the increase in subsidized dwellings. His "best estimate" is that there is a one-for-one crowding out, implying that housing subsidies do not increase the total housing stock in the long run. Similarly, a study of the low-income tax credit program by Malpezzi and Vandell (2002) found no evidence that the program increased the total housing stock.

HOUSING VOUCHERS

So far we have considered policies that help low-income households by increasing the supply of housing. Under a demand-side policy, low-income households are given housing coupons or vouchers that can be redeemed for housing. Like food stamps, housing vouchers allow recipients to make their own consumption choices. In 1999, about 1.6 million households received housing vouchers at a budgetary cost of $7 billion. (Some of the vouchers are called "rent certificates.") A voucher household must occupy a dwelling that meets minimum quality standards. The face value of a voucher is based on household income and the fair market rent in the metropolitan area. The formula is

Face value = Fair market rent − 0.30 · Income

The fair market rent is defined as the 45th percentile of rents in the metropolitan area (45 percent of dwellings rent for less).

Vouchers and Consumer Welfare

We can use the consumer choice model to show the effects of a voucher on a recipient's budget decisions and utility. As in the example of public housing, income is $800 and the price of housing is $1 per unit of housing service. Suppose the fair market rent is $540 (a dwelling with 540 units of housing service). The face value of the voucher is $300 (equal to $540 − 0.30 · $800).

Figure 14–4 (page 308) shows the recipient's response to a housing voucher. The voucher program shifts the household's budget line to the right by $300. Point *m* is in the new budget set because the household could use the voucher to get $300 worth of housing (assuming the minimum standard is met) and spend all of its own income ($800) on other goods. As spending on housing rises above $300, there is a dollar-for-dollar trade-off between housing and other goods. We are assuming for the moment that vouchers do not affect the market price of housing.

The voucher increases housing consumption and household utility. The new utility-maximizing point is *v*, compared to the initial point *i*. Housing consumption increases from $300 to $400, and spending on other goods increases to $700. In other words, the household spends one-third of the voucher on housing, leaving two-thirds to spend on other goods. Comparing point *v* to the public-housing point (*j*), we see that utility is higher under the voucher program. From the recipient's perspective, vouchers are better because they provide more options, letting the recipient pick the utility-maximizing consumption bundle. In fact, if the utility-maximizing spending on housing is at least $300, the voucher is equivalent to a cash transfer of $300.

FIGURE 14–4 Utility Maximization with Housing Voucher

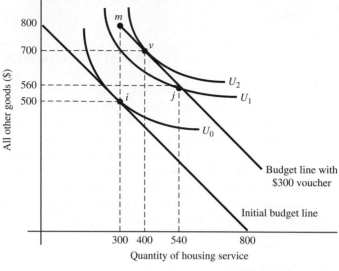

A $300 voucher shifts the budget line to the right by $300 and the recipient chooses point v, with 400 units of housing service and $700 of other goods. The voucher generates higher utility than public housing because the voucher gives the recipient more options.

Market Effects of Vouchers

What are the market effects of housing vouchers? In Figure 14–4, vouchers increase the housing consumption from 300 to 400 units of housing service. What are the implications for housing prices and the welfare of recipients and other households? Consider a city with two income groups (low-income and middle-income) and three levels of housing quality (low, moderate, and medium). All low-income households live in low-quality (300 units of housing service) or moderate-quality (400 units of housing service) housing. All middle-income households live in medium-quality housing.

Figure 14–5 shows the market effects of the voucher program. In Panel A, the initial equilibrium in the moderate-quality submarket is shown by point i, with a price of $400 and a quantity of 100 dwellings. The voucher program shifts the demand curve for moderate-quality housing to the right as most recipients switch from the low-quality submarket to the moderate submarket. The resulting excess demand for housing raises the price until equilibrium is restored at point f, with a price of $480. The quantity of moderate-quality dwellings supplied increases by 40 dwellings for two reasons:

1. **More rapid filtering from medium-quality submarket.** The price of moderate-quality dwellings increases relative to the price of medium-quality dwellings, so dwellings move down the quality ladder more rapidly.

FIGURE 14–5 The Market Effects of Housing Vouchers

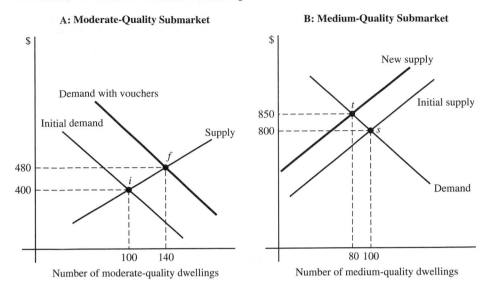

A: A voucher program increases the demand for moderate-quality housing and increases the equilibrium price (from $400 to $480).
B: The increase in the price of moderate-quality dwellings decreases the supply of medium-quality dwellings as more dwellings filter down to the moderate-quality submarket. The equilibrium price rises from $800 to $850.

2. **Slower filtering to low-quality submarket.** The higher price of moderate-quality dwellings gives owners a greater incentive to keep their dwellings at the moderate level, so fewer dwellings filter down to the low level.

Panel B of Figure 14–5 shows the implications of housing vouchers for the medium-quality submarket. By speeding up the filtering process, vouchers decrease the supply of medium-quality housing, shifting the supply curve to the left. As a result, the equilibrium price increases from $800 (point *s*) to $850 (point *t*). In other words, medium-income households are hurt by the housing vouchers given to low-income households. Although the two types of households do not compete directly for housing in the medium-quality market, they compete indirectly through the filtering process.

What about the low-quality and high-quality submarkets? At the high end, the increase in the price of medium-quality housing increases the filtering rate from higher quality levels, and the resulting decrease in supply of high-quality dwellings increases the price. At the low end, an increase in the price of moderate-quality dwellings slows the filtering down to the low-quality submarket, and the decrease in supply of low-quality dwellings increases the price. This means that low-income households that do not get vouchers are hurt by higher housing prices. In general, the filtering process means that the increase in demand for housing triggered by the vouchers increases the prices of housing of all quality levels.

A recent study of the 90 largest metropolitan areas estimates the effects of housing vouchers on the prices in different submarkets (Susin, 2003). The results suggest that vouchers increased the price of low-income housing by about 16 percent. This implies that the price elasticity of supply of low-income housing is low— between zero and 0.38. The estimated price effect on middle-income housing was smaller (3.2 percent), and the effect for high-income housing was close to zero.

Portable Vouchers: Moving to Opportunity

A social experiment called Moving to Opportunity (MTO) was designed to test whether low-income households would fare better in neighborhoods with relatively low poverty rates. A group of public-housing tenants and other low-income households receiving rental assistance were randomly assigned to one of three groups:

1. **The MTO treatment group:** Received rent vouchers that initially could be used only in neighborhoods with poverty rates less than 10 percent. After one year, the vouchers could be used anywhere.
2. **A comparison group:** Received vouchers with no restrictions.
3. **A control group:** Received assistance tied to a specific public housing project.

The results from the first stage of research suggest that mobility improves the outcomes of low-income children (Goering, 2003). The mobile families (groups 1 and 2) moved into neighborhoods that had less poverty (15 percentage points lower on average), less segregation, less crime, and better schools. The children in the mobile groups had fewer behavioral problems, better school performance, and less juvenile crime. The adults in the mobile group reported better health and less stress and fear of crime. In contrast, there was no significant difference between the mobile groups and the control group (3) in terms of adult employment, hours worked, or use of public assistance.

COMMUNITY DEVELOPMENT AND URBAN RENEWAL

Dozens of programs and policies fit under the term *community development*. The mandate for federally supported community development calls for "systematic and sustained action by the federal, state, and local governments to eliminate blight, to conserve and renew older areas, to improve the living environment of low- and moderate-income families, and to develop new centers of population growth and economic activity." The two principal purposes of community development policies are to revitalize declining areas of the city and improve the housing of low-income households.

Urban Renewal

Urban renewal, the original community development program in the United States, was established under the Housing Act of 1949 and was eventually dropped in 1973. The national government provided local governments with the power and the money to demolish and rebuild parts of their cities. Local agencies acquired property under the right of eminent domain, cleared the site of "undesirable" uses (such as low-income housing and small businesses), and then either built a public facility or sold the site to a private developer at a discount. The federal government covered two-thirds of the loss incurred by local government. The private developer built housing, government buildings, or commercial establishments.

The urban renewal program displaced low-income households in favor of higher income residents, public facilities, and commercial operations. A total of 600,000 dwellings were demolished and were replaced by 250,000 new dwellings, 120 million square feet of public facilities, and 224 million square feet of commercial space. The assessed value of property on the renewed sites increased by a factor of 4.6. The critics of urban renewal focus on its demolition aspects, pointing out that 2 million low-income people were displaced. The defenders of the program focus on its rebuilding aspects, pointing out that the new commercial developments provided jobs for the poor residents of the central city.

Recent Community Development Programs

More recent federal community-development programs have avoided many of the problems of the urban renewal program. The newer programs are executed on a smaller scale, so they displace fewer households. In addition, the modern programs place a greater emphasis on providing housing for low-income households.

The bulk of federal funding for community development is for Community Development Block Grants (CDBG). In 1997, the CDBG budget was $4.7 billion, with about 70 percent of the funds going to central cities and urban counties. The allocation formula for fund distribution favors cities with relatively old and overcrowded housing, high poverty rates, and slow economic growth. The funds are used to improve housing, support public services, promote economic development, and clear land for new development. As Connerly and Liou (1998) report, about 40 percent of CDBG funds are spent on housing programs, with the remainder divided into public works (20 percent), economic development (13 percent), and public services (10 percent) and other programs. The CBDG program is a relatively small part of the system of intergovernmental grants—funding never reaches 8 percent of the total grant budget.

Several recently developed grant programs provide flexibility to local governments (Quigley, 2000). Under the McKinney Act, funds are provided to address homelessness, with funds for emergency shelters and the rehabilitation of single-room occupancy dwellings. Under the HOPE IV program, local governments receive funds to renovate or demolish obsolete public housing projects. The HOME program provides funds to produce and preserve low-income housing. These three programs allow most of the decisions to be made at the local level, by local officials and members of nonprofit community organizations.

Homelessness

As we've seen, the federal government provides grants to local governments to address homelessness. The McKinney Homeless Assistance Act of 1987 defines a homeless person as someone who sleeps (a) outside, (b) inside in places not intended for sleeping (e.g., the lobby of a public building), or (c) in housing shelters (places providing temporary housing).

Studies of the homeless indicate that about three-fourths of the homeless are single men. One survey (Burt, 1992) computed the percentages of the adult homeless population as follows:

- Single men: 73 percent.
- Single women: 9 percent.
- Married couples with children: 1 percent.
- Married couples without children: 2 percent.

Children make up the remaining 15 percent of the homeless population.

The background and experiences of many of the homeless are not conducive to economic success. As shown in Table 14–1, nearly half of homeless people are high school dropouts and more than half have spent time in jail. A relatively large fraction of the homeless population has problems with drugs and mental health.

What causes homelessness? From an economic perspective, a person will be homeless if his or her income is low enough relative to the price of housing that it is not sensible—or not even possible—to purchase housing services. This simple theory is supported by studies of homelessness, which show that homeless rates are higher in areas with relatively high rent on low-quality housing (Honig and Filer, 1993; Green and Malpezzi, 2003). Honig and Flier estimate an elasticity of homelessness with respect to rent on low-quality housing of 1.25, meaning that a 10 percent increase in rent increases the homeless rate by 12.5 percent.

Several other factors contribute to homelessness. The homeless population is higher in areas with weak labor markets (slow employment growth), low levels of public assistance, and low institutionalization rates for the mentally ill. These other factors suggest that homelessness is not simply a housing problem, but a complex problem with many causes. Although it appears that current housing policies have little effect on homelessness (Early, 1998, 1999), there is evidence that the problem could be mitigated by policies that improve the functioning of the low end of the housing market (O'Flaherty, 1996; Green and Malpezzi, 2003).

TABLE 14–1 Background of the Homeless Population

Outcome	High School Dropout	Spent Time in Mental Hospital	Treated for Chemical Dependency	Spent Time in Jail	Spent Time in Prison	Attempted Suicide
Percent of homeless	49	19	33	53	24	21

Source: Author's calculations based on Martha R. Burt. *Over the Edge: The Growth of Homelessness in the 1980s.* New York: Sage, 1992.

WHICH HOUSING POLICY IS BEST?

Economists and policy makers have an ongoing debate about the relative merits of supply-side and demand-side housing policies. As we've seen, public and subsidized housing is more costly than unsubsidized housing, and it gives recipients fewer options. On the other side of the market, vouchers give recipients more options and generate housing at a relatively low cost, but they increase housing demand and housing prices. The higher prices are especially problematic for the 70 percent of low-income households who are eligible for housing assistance but don't receive any.

Which policy is best? Analyses by Apgar (1990) and Struyk (1990) suggest that this question is misguided. The "best" policy varies across metropolitan areas and within metropolitan areas, depending on market conditions. In areas with a plentiful supply of low-income housing and a relatively large elasticity of supply, the price effects of vouchers will be relatively small. In contrast, in areas with a relatively inelastic supply of low-income housing, vouchers will generate large price hikes, and carefully crafted supply-side policies could play an important role. Given the large cost of new low-income housing, Struyk (1990) advocates policies that preserve the existing supply of low-income housing, for example, rehabilitation grants and property-tax abatements. He also argues for replacing the tax-credit program with direct grants to local governments. The direct grants would give local officials the flexibility to decide the best policy mix of supply subsidies and vouchers.

SUBSIDIES FOR MORTGAGE INTEREST

In 2002, the federal government provided tax breaks to homeowners that reduced total tax revenue by $66 billion (Office of Management and Budget, 2002). Homeowners can deduct mortgage-interest payments from their gross income, so every dollar of mortgage interest decreases the tax liability by the household's marginal tax rate. For example, if the marginal tax rate is 28 percent, every dollar spent on mortgage interest decreases the tax liability by $0.28. This is an example of a "tax expenditure." Instead of giving money directly to homeowners (an expenditure), the government cuts their taxes. The budgetary consequence of a tax expenditure is the same as an explicit expenditure: In both cases, the government either spends less on other programs or increases other taxes.

The household's benefit from the mortgage tax break increases with household income for two reasons. First, under a progressive tax system, the marginal tax rate increases with income, so the tax benefit per dollar of mortgage interest increases with income. Second, because the demand for housing increases with income, wealthier households have larger mortgage payments and thus larger deductions. In 2002, about 62 percent of the benefits of this tax break went to households with income above $100,000.

Mortgage Subsidy and Efficiency

We can use the marginal principle to explore the efficiency effects of the mortgage subsidy. The marginal principle is reviewed in Section 1.1 of "Tools of Microeconomics," the appendix at the end of the book. In Figure 14–6, the demand curve shows a household's willingness to pay for housing, or the marginal benefit of housing. The horizontal line at $1 shows the marginal social cost (the opportunity cost) of housing: By spending $1 on housing, society sacrifices $1 worth of investment in other capital (e.g., factories, machines, schools). As shown by point e, the marginal social cost equals the marginal benefit at 2,000 square feet, so that's the socially efficient quantity of housing. For housing consumption above this level, the marginal benefit is less than the opportunity cost, meaning that the money would be more efficiently spent on factories, machines, or schools.

The mortgage subsidy causes inefficiency because it creates a gap between the private and social cost of housing. Suppose the marginal tax rate for the household is 28 percent, so each dollar spent on housing cuts taxes by $0.28 and thus has a net cost to the consumer of only $0.72. In Figure 14–6, the marginal private cost is $0.72, and housing consumption increases to 2,420 square feet. This is socially inefficient because it violates the marginal principle: The marginal benefit from the extra housing is less than the opportunity cost ($1). By spending more on housing,

FIGURE 14–6 The Mortgage Subsidy Increases Housing Consumption

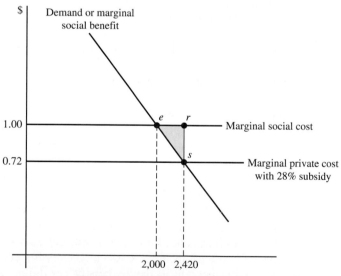

The socially efficient level of housing consumption is shown by point e, where the marginal social benefit equals the marginal social cost. The mortgage subsidy reduces the private cost, leading to excessive consumption. The shaded triangle shows the social loss.

society has less to spend on factories, machines, and schools. The shaded triangle shows the loss resulting from excessive housing consumption. The computation of market surplus is reviewed in Section 1.2 of "Tools of Microeconomics," the appendix at the end of the book.

Mortgage Subsidy and Home Ownership

The mortgage subsidy also creates a bias toward home ownership as opposed to renting. Consider Bedrock, a town where everyone lives in identical rock houses, each of which has a market value of $100,000. There are no maintenance or repair expenses, so the only cost for a property owner is the interest payment on the money borrowed to purchase the house. If the interest rate is 8 percent per year, the annual interest cost is $8,000, so in a competitive market with zero economic profit, the annual rent on housing would be $8,000. Barney owns rental property and makes zero economic profit, with $8,000 rent matching his $8,000 interest expense. If the government allows him to deduct interest payments from his gross income, his taxable income will be zero, so he will pay no taxes.

The mortgage subsidy creates a bias toward ownership because homeowners can deduct their interest expenses even though they don't declare any income from the property. For example, suppose Wilma moves out of rental housing and buys a house for $100,000. She pays $8,000 interest per year and she can deduct her interest costs, so her taxable income is $8,000 less than it was when she rented. With a 28 percent marginal tax rate, her tax bill will decrease by $2,240, so the benefit of owning rather than renting an identical dwelling is $2,240. As Green and Vandell (1999) show, the mortgage subsidy has been an important factor in rising home-ownership rates in the last several decades—from about half of households in 1945 to about two-thirds today.

The government could eliminate the tax bias toward homeownership in one of two ways. The simple and obvious response is to eliminate the mortgage-interest deduction for homeowners. An alternative is to change how homeowners calculate their income. A homeowner's imputed rental income is defined as the income earned from owning a dwelling and renting it to yourself. Alternatively, it is the money you could earn if you rented your dwelling to someone else. In our example, Wilma's imputed rental income is $8,000 per year. Suppose she declared $8,000 of imputed rental income as part of her income, and then deducted her $8,000 mortgage cost. The two items would cancel one another, and the ownership bias would disappear. Her taxable income would be the same with renting and owning, so she would be indifferent between renting and owning.

What is the rationale for the mortgage subsidy? One possibility is that it could internalize a neighborhood externality. When I paint my peeling house or weed my lawn or otherwise improve the external appearance of my house, the neighborhood looks better, and the market values of neighboring houses increase. The problem with this line of reasoning is that the mortgage subsidy applies to all elements of housing consumption, not just the elements such as exterior painting and weeding that generate neighborhood externalities. A second possible rationale is to encourage ownership to promote stable communities. But the tax breaks are concentrated among high-income households, so the subsidy provides relatively small ownership incentives for households with below-average income.

RENT CONTROL AND RENT REGULATION

During World War II, the federal government instituted a national system of rent controls, establishing maximum rents for rental properties. New York City was the only city to retain rent controls after the war. During the 1970s, rent regulations were introduced in many cities, including Boston, Washington DC, San Francisco, and Los Angeles. In contrast with pure rent control (a fixed maximum price), a policy of rent regulation provides for annual rent increases tied to inflation, and it often allows larger price hikes to offset higher costs and guarantee a "fair" or "reasonable" rate of return on investment (Arnott, 1995). Some types of rental housing are commonly exempted from regulation, including new housing and high-rent housing. Some regulation policies permit the deregulation of prices once they reach a certain level, and others allow unrestricted price increases when tenants change.

Figure 14–7 shows the market effects of pure rent control. In the initial equilibrium shown by point *i*, the price is $500 and the quantity is 100 dwellings. If the maximum rent is set at $400, the quantity supplied decreases to 70 dwellings and

FIGURE 14–7 The Market Effects of Pure Rent Control

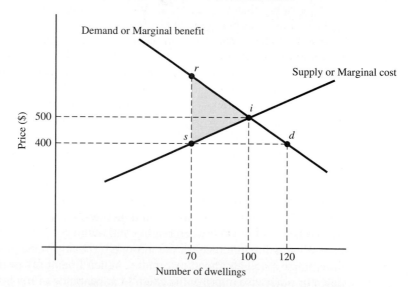

Pure rent control (a maximum rent at $400) decreases the quantity of housing supplied from 100 to 70 and causes permanent excess demand for housing at the maximum price: The quantity demanded (point *d*) exceeds the quantity supplied (point *s*). The lost surplus is shown by the shaded triangle *ris*.

the market moves to point *s*. The quantity demanded is 120 (shown by point *d*), so the excess demand is 50 dwellings. The equilibrium quantity of housing drops from 100 to 70 dwellings.

We can use the notion of market surplus to measure the inefficiency of rent control. The concept of market surplus is reviewed in Section 2.5 of "Tools of Microeconomics," the appendix at the end of the book. Rent control decreases the quantity of housing below the equilibrium quantity and reduces the surplus of the housing market. The loss in value is shown by the area between the demand (marginal benefit) curve and the supply (marginal cost) curve from the rent-control quantity of 70 to the market-equilibrium quantity of 100 (the shaded triangle).

The winners from rent control are the consumers who manage to get one of the rent-controlled dwellings at the artificially low price. The gains of the occupants are diminished by three responses to rent control:

- **Search costs.** Given the excess demand for housing, vacancy rates will be relatively low, and it will take a longer time to find a dwelling. The higher search cost at least partly offsets the benefit of a lower price.
- **Key money.** Competition among consumers may increase the effective price above the controlled price. In some rent-control cities, property owners charge tenants a large sum of money for the keys to the dwelling, and others impose nonrefundable deposits. In the city of Cairo, payments of key money increase the effective rent from about 38 percent of the market price to about 71 percent (Malpezzi, 1998).
- **Reduced quality.** The lower price of rental housing decreases the owners' incentives to maintain and repair property, so the quality of housing decreases.

Among the losers from rent control are households that are displaced by the policy. Rent control decreases the quantity of housing supplied as rental properties are converted to other uses (condominiums or commercial property) or retired from the housing market. In addition, households displaced by rent control in one municipality bid up the price of housing in other municipalities, generating costs for people outside the rent-control city.

Property owners lose under rent control. A decrease in the allowable rent decreases the profit that can be earned on a property, decreasing the market value of the property. In a study of New York City's rent-control program, Olson (1972) concluded that the loss of property owners was about twice as large as the gain to consumers. Toronto's rent-control program decreased the market value of apartment buildings by about 40 percent over a five-year period (Smith and Tomlinson, 1981).

How does the analysis of rent regulation differ from the analysis of pure rent control shown in Figure 14–7? The key difference between control and regulation is the flexibility of the regulated price, which increases with inflation and may increase with production cost. In addition, the price regulations may apply only while a particular tenant occupies the dwelling, allowing the owner to adjust the price with each new tenant. As a result, the price gap (the equilibrium price minus the regulated price) is likely to be smaller under regulation, so the effects on the quantity and quality of housing are likely to be smaller.

SUMMARY

This chapter explores the effects of housing policies that assist low-income house-holds and subsidize the mortgage costs of middle-income and high-income house-holds. Here are the main points of the chapter:

1. Public housing is more costly to produce than private housing and limits the choices of recipients.
2. Housing vouchers give recipients more options, but they increase the demand for housing, increasing prices for recipients and nonrecipients.
3. The mortgage subsidy increases housing consumption beyond the socially efficient level, and the bulk of the benefits go to high-income households.
4. In contrast with rent control (a fixed maximum price), a policy of rent regulation allows greater flexibility in the regulated price of housing.

APPLYING THE CONCEPTS

1. **Bang Per Buck of Low-Income Housing Tax Credits?**
   Suppose you build a low-income house that qualifies for the low-income housing tax credit. The cost of building the house is $100,000.
   a. Over a 10-year period, what is your tax credit?
   b. Based on Quigley's results, predict the market value of the house.
   c. Why is the market value less than the building cost?
2. **The Price Effects of Vouchers and Recipient Welfare**
   Using Figure 14–4 as a starting point (v is the voucher point and j is the public-housing point), consider the implications of higher prices under a voucher program. Suppose the voucher program increases the price of housing by 50 percent to $1.50 per unit of housing.
   a. Draw the voucher budget line with a housing price of $1.50. For example, 300 units of housing service costs $450, leaving the recipient how much to spend on other goods?
   b. Show that the recipient would prefer public housing (point j) to a $300 voucher.
3. **Filtering and Price Effects**
   The study by Susin (2002) suggests that vouchers increase the price of low-income housing by about 16 percent and increase the price of middle-income housing by about 3 percent. Suppose that her results for "low-income housing" apply to moderate quality housing and her result for "middle-income housing" applies to medium-quality housing. The initial price of moderate quality is $500, and the initial price of medium quality is $1,000. Use graph like Figure 14–5 to represent these effects.
4. **Deadweight Loss from the Mortgage Subsidy**
   Suppose the marginal value of a square foot of factory space is constant at $1.00. The marginal benefit of a square foot of housing space is $1.00 for 1,000 square feet and $0.80 for 1,200 square feet. Suppose the government provides

a 20 percent mortgage subsidy, cutting the net price of housing to consumers from \$1.00 to \$0.80 per square foot.

a. Use a graph like Figure 14–6 to depict graphically the welfare loss resulting from the mortgage subsidy.

b. Compute the welfare loss.

c. Use the notion of consumer surplus to compute the benefit of the subsidy for the typical consumer. How does the consumer benefit compare to the tax revenue loss to the government?

REFERENCES AND ADDITIONAL READING

1. Apgar, William. "Which Housing Policy Is Best?" *Housing Policy Debate* 1 (1990), pp. 1–32.

2. Arnott, Richard. "Time for Revisionism on Rent Control?" *Journal of Economic Perspectives* 9 (1995), pp. 99–120.

3. Burman, Leonard. "Low Income Housing Credit." In *Encyclopedia of Taxation and Tax Policy,* eds. Joseph Cordes, Robert Ebel, Jane Gravelle. Washington DC: Urban Institute Press, 1999, pp. 263–65.

4. Burt, Martha R. *Over the Edge: The Growth of Homelessness in the 1980s.* New York: Sage, 1992.

5. Connerly, Charles E., and Y. Thomas Liou. "Community Development Block Grants." In *The Encyclopedia of Housing,* ed. Willem Van Vliet. Thousand Oaks, CA: Sage Publications, 1998.

6. DiPasquale, Denise, Dennis Fricke, and Daniel Garcia-Diaz. "Comparing the Costs of Federal Housing Assistance Programs." *Federal Reserve Bank of New York Policy Review* (June 2003), pp. 147–66.

7. Early, Dirk. "The Role of Subsidized Housing in Reducing Homelessness: An Empirical Investigation Using Micro-data." *Journal of Policy Analysis and Management* 17 (1998), pp. 687–96.

8. Early, Dirk. "A Microeconomic Analysis of Homelessness: *An Empirical Investigation Using Choice-Based Sampling*" *Journal of Housing Economics* 8 (1999), pp. 312–27.

9. Goering, John. "The Impacts of New Neighborhoods on Poor Families: Evaluating the Policy Implications of the Moving to Opportunity Demonstration." *Federal Reserve Bank of New York Policy Review* (June 2003), pp. 113–40.

10. Green, Richard K., and Stephen Malpezzi. *A Primer on U.S. Housing Markets and Housing Policy.* Washington DC: Urban Institute Press, 2003.

11. Green, Richard K., and Kerry D. Vandell. "Giving Households Credit: How Changes in the U.S. Tax Code Could Promote Homeownership." *Regional Science and Urban Economics* 29 (1999), pp. 419–44.

12. Gyourko, Joseph, and Peter Linneman. "Equity and Efficiency Aspects of Rent Control: An Empirical Study of New York City." *Journal of Urban Economics* 26 (1989), pp. 54–74.

13. Honig, Marjorie, and Randall K. Filer. "Causes of Intercity Variation in Homelessness." *American Economic Review* 83 (1993), pp. 248–55.

14. Malpezzi, Stephen, and Kerry Vandell. "Does the Low-Income Housing Tax Credit Increase the Supply of Housing?" *Journal of Housing Economics* 11 (2002), pp. 360–80.

15. Malpezzi, Stephen. "Welfare Analysis of Rent Control with Side Payments: A Natural Experiment in Cairo, Egypt." *Regional Science and Urban Economics* 28 (1998), pp. 773–95.

16. Murray, Michael. "Subsidized and Unsubsidized Housing Stocks 1935–1987: Crowding Out and Cointegration." *Journal of Real Estate Finance and Economics* 18 (1999), pp. 107–24.

17. Office of Management and Budget. *Budget of the United States Government Fiscal Year 2002,* Table 8–1. Washington DC: 2002.

18. O'Flaherty, Brendan. *Making Room: The Economics of Homelessness.* Cambridge, Mass: Harvard University Press (1996).

19. Ohls, James C. "Public Policy toward Low-Income Housing and Filtering in Housing Markets." *Journal of Urban Economics* 2 (1975), pp. 144–71.

20. Olson, Edgar. "An Econometric Analysis of Rent Control." *Journal of Political Economy* 80 (1972), pp. 1081–1100.

21. Poterba, James M. "Taxation and Housing: Old Questions, New Answers." *American Economic Review* 82 (1992), pp. 237–42.

22. Quigley, John. "A Decent Home: Housing Policy in Perspective." *Brookings-Wharton Papers on Urban Affairs* (2000), pp. 53–99.

23. Smeeding, Timothy M. "Alternative Methods for Evaluating Selected In-Kind Transfer Benefits and Measuring Their Effect on Poverty." Technical Paper no. 50. Washington DC: U.S. Bureau of the Census, 1982.

24. Smith, Lawrence, and Peter Tomlinson. "Rent Control in Ontario: Roofs or Ceilings." *American Real Estate and Urban Economics Journal* 9 (1981), pp. 93–114.

25. Stegman, Michael A. "The Excessive Costs of Creative Finance: Growing Inefficiencies in the Production of Low-Income Housing." *Housing Policy Debate* 2 (1991), pp. 357–73.

26. Struyk, Raymond J. "Comment on William Apgar's 'Which Housing Policy Is Best?'" *Housing Policy Debate* 1 (1990), pp. 41–51.

27. Susin, Scott. "Rent Vouchers and the Price of Low-Income Housing." *Journal of Public Economics* 83 (2002), pp. 109–52.

PART SIX

Local Government

*T*he final part of the book explains the role of local government and explores how citizens respond to local taxes and intergovernmental grants. As explained in Chapter 15, local governments provide local public goods, deal with natural monopolies, and respond to externalities. The chapter also explores local decision-making through elections and explains why majority rule is unlikely to generate socially efficient choices. Chapter 16 looks at the revenue side of local government, focusing on the two largest revenue sources: the property tax and intergovernmental grants. As we'll see, the person who pays the property tax in a legal sense may shift the tax onto other people, so the economic burden is different from the legal burden. Local governments respond to intergovernmental grants by cutting taxes and shifting resources into other programs, so part of a grant is spent on other public goods and private goods.

CHAPTER 15

The Role of Local Government

Pedro: Do you think people will vote for me?
Napoleon Dynamite: Heck yes! I'd vote for you.
Pedro: Like what are my skills?
*Napoleon Dynamite: Well, you have a sweet bike. And you're
really good at hooking up with chicks. Plus you're like the
only guy at school who has a mustache.*
　　　　—FROM THE MOVIE NAPOLEON DYNAMITE (2004)

*Democracy is the worst form of government except all the
others that have been tried.*
　　　　　　　　　—WINSTON CHURCHILL

*T*his chapter provides an overview of the local public sector. After presenting the facts on local government, we explore the role of local government in a federal system of government. We'll see why products such as public schooling, public safety, parks, and transit systems are produced by local governments rather than private firms or higher levels of government. We'll also see why voting with majority rule is unlikely to generate socially efficient decisions and explore different responses to the inefficiency of majority rule.

As shown in Table 15–1 (page 324), there are more than 87,000 local governments in the United States. In terms of total expenditures, the most important types of local governments are municipalities and school districts (each about a third of local government expenditures) and counties (about a quarter of expenditures). A special district serves a single function, such as fire protection, natural-resource management, or the administration of housing or community-development programs.

Table 15–2 (page 324) shows the per-capita spending for local government in general and municipalities. Education is the dominant program for local government, with nearly half of total expenditures, 90 percent of which goes to elementary and secondary education. The spending of municipalities is more evenly divided, with the largest expenditures on police, education, highways, sewerage, and fire protection.

TABLE 15–1 Types of Local Governments in 2002

Type of Local Government	Number
County	3,034
Municipal	19,429
Township and town	16,504
School	13,506
Special	35,052
Total	87,525

Source: U.S. Bureau of the Census. *2002 Census of Governments.*

TABLE 15–2 Expenditures Per Capita for Local Government, 2002

	Local Government	Municipalities
Education	$1,537	$125
Police protection	196	129
Governmental administration	188	76
Hospitals	179	35
Highways	157	78
Interest on general debt	156	56
Public welfare	141	35
Sewerage	107	66
Health	104	21
Housing and community development	99	44
Fire protection	92	63
Parks and recreation	89	55
Correction	65	11
Solid waste management	58	34
Natural resources	19	1
Protective inspection and regulation	13	9
Parking facilities	4	4
Transit subsidies	1	1
Total	3,206	843

Source: U.S. Bureau of the Census. *2002 Census of Governments.*

THE ROLE OF LOCAL GOVERNMENT

What is the role of local government in the market economy? Musgrave and Musgrave (1980) distinguish between three roles for government:

1. **Stabilization.** The government uses monetary and fiscal policy to control unemployment and inflation.
2. **Income redistribution.** The government uses taxes and transfers to alter the distributions of income and wealth.
3. **Resource allocation.** The government makes decisions about what to produce and how to produce it. When the government actually produces a particular good or service, it makes these resource allocation decisions directly. When the government subsidizes or taxes private activities, it influences the resource allocation decisions of the private sector.

How do local governments fit into this three-part scheme of governmental activity?

The national government has assumed the responsibility for stabilization policy for two reasons. First, although each local government could print its own money and execute its own monetary policy, such a system would be chaotic. Instead, the national government prints the money and manages a national monetary policy. Second, because a large fraction of local income is spent on goods produced outside the local area, local monetary and fiscal policies would be relatively weak and ineffective. Fiscal policy is more effective at the national level because a relatively small fraction of national income is spent on imports.

Consider next the distribution role of government. Local attempts to redistribute income will be frustrated by the mobility of taxpayers and transfer recipients. Suppose that a city imposes a tax on its wealthy citizens and provides transfer payments to the poor. To escape the tax, some wealthy households will leave the city, causing a decrease in total tax revenue. At the same time, some poor households will migrate to the relatively generous city, causing a decrease in the transfer payment per recipient. In combination, the flight of the wealthy and the migration of the poor will weaken the city's redistribution program. A national redistribution program is more effective because there is less mobility between nations than between cities.

The third role of government is resource allocation, which involves decisions that determine how an economy's resources are allocated to different goods and services. As Table 15–2 shows, local governments are responsible for providing several goods and services, including education, highways, police and fire protection, parks, and sewers. In the next three parts of the chapter, we explore three sorts of resource allocation by local government: providing local public goods, dealing with natural monopoly, and internalizing externalities.

LOCAL PUBLIC GOODS: EQUILIBRIUM VERSUS OPTIMUM

A local public good has three characteristics. First, it is nonrivalrous: The fact that one person benefits from a public good doesn't reduce the benefit for someone else. In contrast, a private good such as a hot dog is rivalrous because only one person can consume it. Many of the goods provided by local governments are impure or congestible in the sense that if enough people use the good, each person reduces the benefit to others. One example of an impure public good is a city park; if enough people use the park, they get in each others' way, with frisbees flying into birthday cakes. As we saw earlier in the book, streets and highways are subject to congestion during peak travel periods.

The second characteristic of a local public good is that it is nonexcludable. In other words, it is impossible or impractical to exclude people who do not pay for the good. Consider the park example. Although it may be possible to charge everyone for using a park and exclude people who don't pay, it would be costly to fence off the parks, install turnstiles and monitor their use. Although it might be possible to bill people for fire and safety services, a system of user fees for the fire department and police would violate most people's notions of equity and fairness.

The third characteristic of a local public good is that its benefits are confined to a relatively small geographical area—a municipality or a metropolitan area. Unlike national defense, which generates benefits for the entire nation, most of the benefits of the local police force and local fire department go to local citizens. Similarly, local citizens get most of the benefits from local streets and highways. The appropriate size of the jurisdiction is determined by the "localness" of the public good—the geographical extent of the benefits from the good. The more widespread the benefits, the larger the jurisdiction required to contain all the beneficiaries.

The Efficient Quantity of Local Public Goods

In the chapter on neighborhood choice, we discussed the provision of city parks in a three-person city. Figure 15–1 uses Figure 8–2 as a starting point. We have three citizens who vary in their demand for park acres: Lois has a low demand (with marginal-benefit curve MB_L); Marian has medium demand (MB_M); Hiram has high demand (MB_H).

The optimum level of the local public good is the quantity at which the marginal social benefit equals the marginal social cost. The social benefit of a city park is the sum of the benefits going to the citizens, and the marginal social benefit is the sum of the individual marginal benefits. In Figure 15–1, the marginal social benefit

FIGURE 15–1 Optimum versus Equilibrium Local Public Good

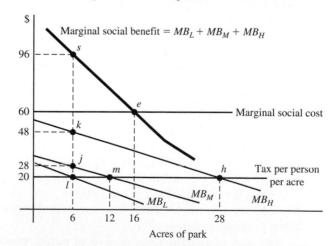

The marginal social benefit is the sum of the marginal private benefits of the three citizens. The optimum acreage is 16 acres shown by the intersection of the marginal social benefit curve and the marginal social cost curve (point e). Under majority rule, the equilibrium is the preferred choice of the median voter (12 acres, shown by point m).

of the sixth acre is $96 (point *s*), equal to the sum of the marginal benefits of $20 for Lois, $28 for Marian, and $48 for Hiram. Similarly, for other park sizes, we add the individual marginal benefits to get the marginal social benefit. The marginal social-benefit curve is the vertical sum of the individual marginal-benefit curves.

We can use the marginal principle to identify the socially efficient park size. The marginal principle is reviewed in Section 1.1 of "Tools of Microeconomics," the appendix at the end of the book. At the efficient level, the marginal social benefit of park acreage equals its marginal social cost. In Figure 15–1, the marginal cost is $60 per acre, so the optimum acreage is 16 acres. For any amount less than this, citizens in the city would collectively be willing to pay more than $60 per additional acre, so an increase in size would increase social welfare. For example, suppose the city starts at six acres. At this point, the willingness to pay for parks (from the social-benefit curve) is $96 and the cost is only $60, so another acre of park would generate a net gain. In contrast, for any amount exceeding 16 acres, the aggregate willingness to pay for another acre would be less than the social cost, so a smaller park would be more efficient.

The Median Voter Picks the Equilibrium Quantity

As we saw in the chapter on neighborhood choice, the equilibrium quantity under majority rule is the preferred quantity of the median voter. If the government imposes a common head tax of $20 per person per acre of parks, each citizen faces a marginal cost of $20 per acre, and Marian the median voter prefers 12 acres of parks (point *m*). If the government holds a series of pair-wise elections between the preferred quantities of the three citizens, the median voter will win. The median voter always wins because she can get one other person to vote against any other option.

In Figure 15–1, the voting equilibrium is not the same as the optimum. The median voter prefers a quantity less than the optimum, and so the city chooses an inefficiently small park. If the city had a direct election of the median preference versus the optimum, the median preference would win because Lois would join Marian to defeat the optimum. The power and inefficiency of the median-voter result can be seen clearly by imagining that the marginal benefit of the high-demand consumer doubles. Such a change would increase the optimum park acreage but would not affect the voting equilibrium because the preference of the median voter hasn't changed.

Tiebout Model: Voting with Feet

Most metropolitan areas in the United States have dozens of municipalities, school districts, and other local governments. When citizens disagree about how much of a local good to provide, they can "vote with their feet," moving to jurisdictions with like-minded people. One of the implications of the Tiebout model is that interjurisdictional mobility (voting with feet) may prevent the inefficiencies associated with majority voting.

The simple version of the Tiebout model is based on five assumptions about local government and location choices:

1. **Municipal choice.** A household chooses the municipality (or school district or other local jurisdiction) that provides the ideal level of local public goods. There are enough municipalities to ensure that every household finds the perfect jurisdiction.
2. **Perfect information and mobility.** All citizens have access to all relevant information about the alternative municipalities, and moving is costless.
3. **No interjurisdictional spillovers.** There are no spillovers (externalities) associated with local public goods: All the benefits from local public goods accrue to citizens within the municipality.
4. **No scale economies.** The average cost of production is independent of output.
5. **Head taxes.** A municipality pays for its public goods with a head tax: If you have a head, you pay the head tax.

Under the Tiebout process, households will sort themselves into municipalities according to their demand for parks. Suppose three low-demand citizens form a municipality called Loisville. The marginal social benefit of 6 acres is three times $20, or $60, the same as the marginal social cost of park acreage. When each voter pays a tax of $20 per acre, they will all prefer 6 acres, so they will vote unanimously for the optimum. Similarly, if three Marians form a municipality, they will choose the optimum for medium demanders—12 acres. This type of sorting eliminates the inefficiencies of majority rule because everyone in a homogeneous municipality has the same preferred level of the local public good.

There is evidence that citizens sort themselves with respect to the demand for local public goods. Heikkila (1996) shows that communities in Los Angeles are relatively homogeneous with respect to the demand for local public goods. Fisher and Wassmer (1998) show that the greater the variation across households in the underlying demand for local public goods in a metropolitan area, the larger the number of municipalities and school districts in the metropolitan area. At the international level, the greater the ethnic diversity of a nation, the more decentralized its public sector (Panizza, 1999).

Benefit Taxation

The Tiebout response to diversity in demand for local public goods is to eliminate diversity by forming homogeneous municipalities. An alternative response is to match the diversity in demand with diversity in tax liabilities. Under the Lindahl approach (named after economist Erik Lindahl), taxes are proportional to the willingness to pay for local public goods.

Figure 15–2 shows how Lindahl or benefit taxes work. Suppose the government knows the marginal-benefit curves of its citizens and can determine the optimum level of the public good—equal to 16 acres of parks in our example. The government allocates the cost of the public good to its citizens according to their willingness to pay (marginal benefit). Hiram's tax liability is $38 per acre, while Marian's is $16,

FIGURE 15–2 Lindahl or Benefit Taxation

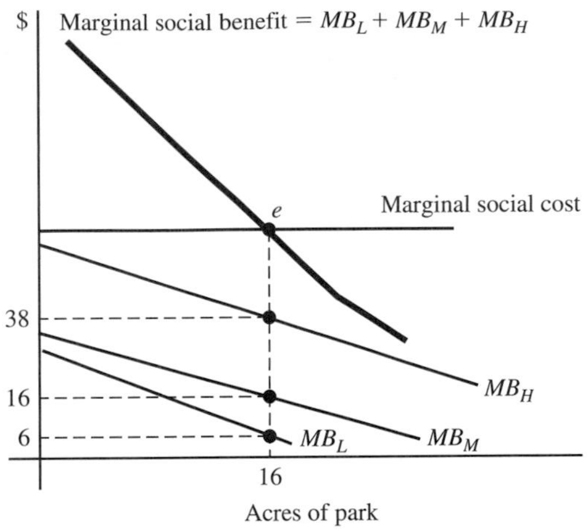

Under benefit taxation, each household pays a per-acre tax equal to its marginal private benefit for the socially efficient part size (16 acres), and everyone prefers the efficient size. The benefit tax is $6 per acre for Lois, $16 for Marian, and $38 for Hiram.

and Lois's is $6. Faced with a marginal cost per acre of $38, Hiram's preferred park size is 16 acres, the optimum size. Similarly, Lois has a marginal cost of $6, and prefers the optimum size too. Under benefit taxation, citizens with larger benefits pay higher taxes, and diversity in demand is matched by diversity in tax liabilities.

Is the benefit principle practical? One problem is the government doesn't know its citizens' marginal-benefit curves, so it can't precisely determine the appropriate taxes. The government can't simply ask its citizens to reveal their willingness to pay because each citizen has an incentive to understate their willingness to pay—and thus pay lower taxes. But for some public goods such as fire protection or public safety, the benefit from local public goods may be roughly proportional to property value, so a property tax could serve as a rough benefit tax. Similarly, if the benefits from local public goods increase with income, an income tax could serve as a rough benefit tax.

NATURAL MONOPOLY

Local governments operate natural monopolies such as water systems and waste-disposal systems. A natural monopoly occurs if the increasing returns to scale in production are large relative to the demand for the product. Recall the fourth principle of urban economics:

Production occurs with increasing returns to scale

FIGURE 15–3 Natural Monopoly in Sewage Services

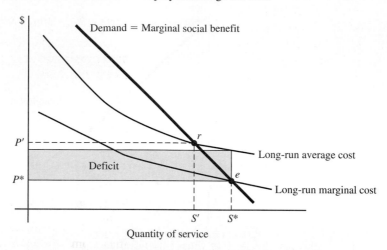

Sewage service is a natural monopoly, with a negatively sloped long-run average cost curve. The socially efficient output occurs where the marginal social benefit equals the marginal cost (point *e*). At this quantity, the price is less than the average cost, generating a deficit. The government can provide the services and cover the deficit with general tax revenue. Alternatively, the government could regulate a private firm.

The provision of sewage services involves a large network of pipes and a large treatment plants, so the indivisible inputs are large and expensive. In Figure 15–3, the long-run average-cost curve for sewage services is negatively sloped over a wide range of output, reflecting the substantial costs of these indivisible inputs. As output increases, the average cost decreases as the cost of these indivisible inputs is spread over larger quantities.

We can use the marginal principle to identify the socially efficient level of sewage service. The marginal principle is reviewed in Section 1.1 of "Tools of Microeconomics," the appendix at the end of the book. The efficient output is the quantity at which the marginal benefit of service equals the marginal cost. The demand curve is a marginal-benefit curve, so the efficient point is where the demand curve intersects the marginal-cost curve (point *e*), and the efficient quantity is S^* units of service. One problem is that a firm producing the efficient output will lose money. To get consumers to purchase S^* units of sewage service, the firm must charge a price of P^*, which is less than the average cost of producing S^*. The shaded area shows the deficit that occurs at the socially efficient quantity of output.

The government has several options in responding to the deficit problem. First, the government could produce the service itself, charging a price of P^* and covering the deficit with general tax revenue. Second, the government could subsidize a private firm to provide sewage service: The firm would charge the efficient price (P^*) and the city would cover the firm's deficit with tax revenue. Third, the government could allow the private firm to charge P' instead of P^*. At the higher price, the quantity sold would be S' and the average cost would equal the price, so the firm would cover all of its cost. Under this scheme, the output (S') is less than the socially efficient output.

Local governments have the same options for other natural monopolies. In the chapter on mass transit, we explored the pricing and regulation of mass transit and discussed transit deficits. For other natural monopolies such as water systems and solid-waste disposal, a local government can either produce the service itself or regulate a private producer.

EXTERNALITIES

Another role for government is to internalize externalities. Recall the third axiom of urban economics:

Externalities cause inefficiency

In earlier chapters, we have seen several sorts of externalities and explored ways to internalize them. The three externalities from driving—congestion, pollution, and traffic accidents—can be internalized with taxes on driving. A tax on peak-period driving internalizes the congestion externality, while a tax on pollution internalizes pollution externalities. A per-mile tax that depends on the age of the driver can internalize accident externalities. In this chapter, we consider externalities that come from education and public safety (police and fire protection).

Public Education Externalities and Vouchers

As we saw earlier in the book, education generates external benefits because it makes people better team workers, improves the democratic process, and decreases crime. One option for government is to take responsibility for providing education. A system of free compulsory education could encourage citizens to consume more education. An alternative approach is to subsidize private education, using tax credits or education vouchers to cover part or all the costs associated with private education.

Under a pure education-voucher system, each child is issued a voucher or coupon that can be used to pay for either public or private schooling. The face value of the voucher would be equal to the current cost per pupil for public schools (for example, $6,000), allowing a family to choose either the public school or a private school charging up to $6,000. The school would collect vouchers from its patrons and redeem them from the state government. To qualify for the voucher program, a school would be required to teach basic cognitive skills and civics, and admit students without regard to race, sex, or religion.

What are the possible consequences of education vouchers? If vouchers force public schools to compete with private schools for students, this competition could make public schools more efficient and more responsive to parental concerns. If so, achievement could increase, even for the students who remain in public schools. The opponents of vouchers suggest that wider school choice is likely to increase segregation with respect to income, race, and academic ability. Although a parent who receives a voucher can pick any school—public or private—not all parents will exercise this option. It appears that parents with the most education and the highest incomes are more likely to switch schools (Levin, 1997), so the peer environment— and achievement level—of students from low-income families may deteriorate.

Most proposals for education vouchers would provide vouchers for low-income families only. In recent years, there have been experiments with income-targeted vouchers in Milwaukee, Cleveland, New York, Dayton, and Washington DC. By targeting low-income families, the voucher programs do not cause the sort of income segregation that would occur with a universal program. In fact, if the face value of the voucher is high enough, it would encourage private schools to accept more low-income students, promoting integration rather than segregation.

How do targeted vouchers affect achievement? Using data from Milwaukee, Rouse (1998) shows that students in the voucher program had higher math test scores but about the same reading scores. In addition, low-income students attending special public schools with reduced classes did just as well or better than the students who used vouchers to attend private schools. This suggests that the achievement advantage of voucher (private) schools comes in part from their smaller classes.

As we saw in our earlier discussion of the education production function, the teacher is a key factor in student achievement. As shown by Rivkin, Hanushek, and Kain (1998), most of the differences between schools are explained by differences in the quality of teachers, not by differences in school organization or other education resources. What really matters are teachers, so vouchers could increase achievement if the greater competition for students causes schools to hire better teachers.

Externalities from Public Safety Programs

Consider next the externalities that result from public safety. Spending on police services generates positive and negative externalities. Both externalities result from the fact that criminals are mobile: They can move from one jurisdiction to another.

- **Capturing externality.** The positive externality occurs when one municipality uses resources to capture a criminal. By getting a criminal off the street, the municipality generates benefits for surrounding municipalities: The marginal social benefit of police spending exceeds the marginal local (municipal) benefit.
- **Chasing externality.** The negative externality occurs when a municipality's crime-fighting activities cause a criminal to move to another jurisdiction. In this case, police spending just moves crime around, so the marginal local benefit of police spending exceeds the marginal social benefit.

The greater the mobility of criminals, the larger the jurisdiction required to contain all the people who are affected by crime fighting activities. In the United States, the typical response to these positive and negative externalities is to provide police services through municipal governments.

The other public safety service, fire protection, also generates externalities. Fires can spread from one house to another, so the marginal social benefit of fire protection exceeds the marginal private benefit. In most metropolitan areas, fire protection is provided by local governments, while some municipalities contract with private firms to provide fire protection.

FEDERALISM AND METROPOLITAN GOVERNMENT

Under the federal system of government, the responsibility for providing public goods is divided between the national, state, and local governments. Some goods, such as defense and space exploration, are provided at the national level. Others, such as education and police protection, are provided at the local level. Oates (1972) discusses the advantages and disadvantages of the local provision of public goods.

1. **Diversity in demand.** As we saw in the discussion of the Tiebout model, local governments can accommodate diverse demands for local public goods and thus promote efficiency.
2. **Externalities.** For some locally provided products, benefits spill over to people outside the municipality or school district. In this case, local voters will ignore the benefits of outsiders, so they will make inefficient choices.
3. **Scale economies.** If there are scale economies in the provision of public goods, a system of small local governments has a relatively high production cost.

The local provision of a public good is efficient if the advantages outweigh the disadvantages. In other words, local provision is efficient if (1) diversity in demand is relatively large, (2) externalities are relatively small in a geographic sense, and (3) scale economies are relatively small.

What are the facts on scale economies in the provision of local public goods? There have been dozens of studies of the relationship between production costs and jurisdiction sizes. The evidence suggests that there are moderate scale economies in the provision of water and sewage services. Because these services are capital intensive, average cost decreases as population increases. In contrast, studies of other local public goods (police protection, fire protection, schools) suggest that scale economies are exhausted with a relatively small population—about 100,000. Many small cities use intergovernmental contracts and joint service contracts to join forces and exploit scale economies in the provision of public services.

The most important trade-off associated with local service provision is between diversity of demand and externalities. Metropolitan government will be more efficient than municipal government if interjurisdictional spillovers are large relative to diversity in demand. In this case, the advantages of a small local government (the ability to accommodate diverse demands for local public goods) are relatively small, and the disadvantages (the inefficiencies associated with externalities that cross municipal boundaries) are relatively large. Therefore, a metropolitan system of government will be more efficient.

One solution to the spillover problem is a system of subsidies from a higher level of government. If the municipality receives a subsidy equal to the marginal external benefit of the public good, it bases its spending decisions on the marginal social benefit of the good. In the next chapter, we'll explore the effects of intergovernmental grants on local spending.

Another response to spillovers is to grant governmental bodies the power to deal with specific urban problems that cross municipal boundaries. Many economists and geographers believe that metropolitan areas—not municipalities or states—are the most important spatial units in today's economy. In the words of Anthony Downs (1998), it would be sensible to establish policy-making organizations for the entire metropolitan area

> because the various spatial sections of each metropolitan area are linked together in a series of densely interlocking networks. These networks transcend the boundaries of most individual communities but are not as intensive at the larger state level.

Among these networks are streets and highways, water systems, sewage-disposal systems, school systems, airsheds, and watersheds. Some of the problems that cross jurisdictional boundaries are highway congestion, air pollution, crime, and low educational achievement. In the current political system, the power to deal with these problems is divided among many small jurisdictions, most of which contain only a small fraction of the people affected by the problems. Two metropolitan areas— Portland, Oregon, and the Twin Cities in Minnesota—have governmental bodies with the power to deal with problems that cross municipal boundaries.

A CLOSER LOOK AT THE MEDIAN VOTER RESULT

Earlier in the book we explained the median-voter result in the context of a direct election with three citizens. In this part of the chapter, we'll take a closer look at voting, showing the general applicability of the median-voter result and its limitations. Many local jurisdictions—including most central cities—have large and heterogeneous populations, and decisions about local public goods are determined by voting with ballots, not by voting with feet.

A Series of Budget Elections

The median-voter result is applicable to a wide variety of election formats. Consider a school district that holds a series of elections to determine its budget. The district proposes a budget and holds an election in which citizens vote yes or no. If a particular budget proposal fails to receive a majority of votes, the school board decreases its proposed budget by $10 and then holds another election. This process continues until a majority of citizens vote in favor of the proposed budget. Under this election system, the school district chooses the largest budget that receives majority support.

Table 15–3 shows the preferences of the voters in the school district. The preferred budget of voter A is $49, while B's is $56, and so on. Suppose the district

TABLE 15–3 The Median Voter in a Series of School Budget Elections

Voter	Preferred Budget	Vote with $90 Budget	Vote with $80 Budget	Vote with $70 Budget
A	$49	N	N	N
B	56	N	N	N
C	63	N	N	N
D	70	N	N	Y
E	77	N	Y	Y
F	84	N	Y	Y
G	91	Y	Y	Y

starts with a proposed budget of $90. The voters know that if the $90 budget fails to get majority support, the next proposed budget will be $80. A citizen will vote yes if the $90 budget is better than an $80 budget, that is, if the citizen's preferred budget is greater than $85. For example, voter F, with a preferred budget of $84, will vote against the $90 budget because an $80 budget is closer to his preferred budget. Voter G is the only person who votes for the $90 budget, so the first budget proposal loses by a vote of 6 to 1. The second proposal ($80) fails by a vote of 4 to 3 because voters A through D, with preferred budgets less than $75, would prefer a $70 budget. In contrast, the preferred budget of the median voter ($70) wins by a vote of 4 – 3. The median voter is joined by voters with higher preferred budgets to approve the median voter's preferred budget.

In this example, the school district decreased its proposed budget in $10 increments, from $90 down to the preferred budget of the median voter. The same result would occur if the board decreased the proposed budget in increments of $1. Similarly, the same result occurs if the school district reverses the direction of the budget sequence. If it starts out with a low budget and works its way upward, the median voter still wins.

The Median Voter in a Representative Democracy

In a representative democracy, decisions about budgets are made by elected officials. Citizens make budgetary decisions indirectly, by electing people whose budget philosophies are consistent with their own preferences. Consider a city that provides a single local public good (police services). There are two candidates for mayor, Penny (a low spender) and Buck (a big spender). The only issue in the election is the police budget, which is set by the mayor. Each citizen votes for the candidate whose proposed police budget is closest to the citizen's preferred budget.

Figure 15–4 (page 336) shows the voters' distribution of budget preferences. The horizontal axis measures the police budget, and the vertical axis measures the number of votes for a given budget. For example, 6 citizens have a preferred budget of $2, while 12 have a preferred budget of $3, and so on. The distribution of budget preferences is symmetric, and the median budget (the budget that splits the rest of the voters into two equal halves) is $6.

FIGURE 15–4 The Median Voter in Representative Democracy

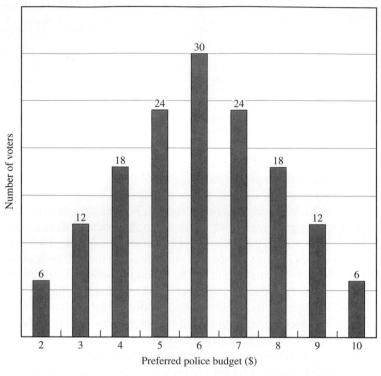

If Penny proposes a police budget of $4 and Buck proposes a budget of $8, the election will result in a tie: The two candidates split the votes of people with a preferred budget of $6, while Penny gets voters with lower preferred budgets and Buck gets voters with larger preferred budgets. By moving toward the median budget, Penny can increase her chance of being elected. In equilibrium, both candidates propose the budget of the median voter ($6).

If the candidates take a natural approach and stake out different budget territories, the result could be a tie vote. Suppose Penny starts with a proposed budget of $4 and Buck proposes $8. Penny will get a total of 75 votes:

- 60 votes from people with preferred budgets less than or equal to $5.
- 15 of the 30 voters with a preferred budget of $6. This is halfway between the candidates' proposed budgets, so the two candidates split the votes.

The distribution of voters is symmetric, so Buck gets 75 votes too (60 from voters with preferred budgets greater than or equal to $7 and 15 from voters who prefer $6). In other words, the election results in a tie vote.

This is not an equilibrium because each candidate has an incentive to move toward the median budget. Penny could increase her chance of being elected by increasing her proposed budget to $5. If she does, she will get all 30 votes of the citizens with a $6 preferred budget because her $5 proposal is now closer than Buck's $8. Penny will win by a vote of 90 (equal to 6 + 12 + 18 + 24 + 30) to 60 (equal to 24 + 18 + 12 + 6). If Buck responds by decreasing his proposed budget to $7, the election results in a tie vote again. Penny and Buck will continue to revise their proposed budgets until each candidate's budget is close to the preferred budget of the median voter ($6).

This example shows that the median-voter result occurs in a representative democracy. In equilibrium, both candidates propose a budget equal to the preferred budget of the median voter. Since both candidates propose the same budget, it doesn't matter which candidate actually wins the election. In either case, the median voter determines the size of the police budget.

Implications of the Median-Voter Rule

The median-voter rule has some important implications. First, as we saw earlier, there is no reason to expect voting to generate the socially efficient level of a local public good. The second implication concerns our ability to predict the outcome of an election. To predict the outcome, we need to first identify the median voter and then estimate his or her preferred budget. As a practical matter, it may be difficult to identify the median voter. One approach is to assume that the desired spending depends on income, so the person with the median income is the median voter. Of course, if the desired spending depends on other variables (household size, age, political philosophy), the predictions from this approach will be a rough approximation.

The third implication of the median-voter rule is that we can use the results of elections to estimate the elasticities of demand for local public goods. Consider two cities, one with a small police budget ($100 per capita) and a low median income ($1,000), and a second with a large police budget ($125 per capita) and high median income ($1,200). Assume that the "price" of police services (the opportunity cost of money spent on police) is the same in the two cities. The income elasticity of demand for police services is defined as the percentage change in the police budget divided by the percentage change in income. City L, with 20 percent higher income, has a 25 percent larger police budget, so the income elasticity of demand is 1.25 (25 percent divided by 20 percent). Table 15–4 summarizes the results of empirical

TABLE 15–4 Income and Price Elasticities of Demand for Local Public Goods

Public Good or Service	Price Elasticity	Income Elasticity
Total expenditures	−0.23 to −0.56	0.34 to 0.89
Education	−0.07 to −0.51	0.24 to 0.85
Parks and recreation	−0.19 to −0.92	0.99 to 1.32
Public safety (police and fire)	−0.19 to −1.0	0.52 to 0.71
Public works	−0.92 to −1.0	0.79

Source: Robert Inman. "The Fiscal Performance of Local Governments." In *Current Issues in Urban Economics,* eds. Peter Mieszkowski and Mahlon Straszheim. Baltimore: Johns Hopkins University Press, 1979.

studies based on the median-voter model. The income elasticities for most local public goods are less than 1.0.

If the price of local public goods varies across municipalities, we can use the median-voter model to draw the demand curve for local public goods and compute the price elasticity of demand. To plot the demand curve for local spending, we need information on price (the opportunity cost of local spending) and quantity (the local spending level). As shown in Table 15–4, the demands for local public goods are price-inelastic; the price elasticities are all less than or equal to 1.0 in absolute value.

Limitations of the Median-Voter Model

The median-voter model has a number of unrealistic assumptions. Although it provides a useful framework for thinking about local government decisions, three assumptions limit the model's applicability:

1. **No ideology.** Politicians care only about winning elections, so they slavishly adhere to voter preferences. Alternatively, a candidate could base her positions on ideology and use election campaigns to persuade voters that her position is the correct one, playing the role of a leader, not a follower.
2. **Single issue.** If there are several election issues (e.g., the police budget, the park budget, policies for the homeless), candidates will offer bundles or package deals to voters, and the notion of a median voter disappears.
3. **All citizens vote.** In real elections, only a fraction of eligible voters actually cast ballots. The benefit of voting will be relatively small if (a) the candidates are so close to one another that it makes little difference who wins (voter indifference), or (b) the best candidate is so far from the citizen's position that the citizen is alienated from the election process (voter alienation). If some citizens abstain from voting, the median-voter result will not necessarily occur.

SUMMARY

This chapter explores the role of local governement in a federal system of government. Here are the main points of the chapter:

1. The role of local government is resource allocation—providing local public goods, operating natural monopolies, and internalizing local externalities.
2. The inefficiency of majority rule encourages citizens to vote with their feet, forming municipalities with citizens who share their preferences for local public goods.
3. An alternative to foot voting is benefit taxation, under which tax liabilities are proportional to the benefit of a local public good.
4. The local provision of a public good is efficient if (a) diversity in demand for local public goods is relatively large, (b) externalities are relatively small, and (c) scale economies are relatively small.
5. The median-voter model is applicable to sequential budget elections as well as voting for representative government.

APPLYING THE CONCEPTS

1. **Hattie Hates Parks**

   Consider the example shown in Figure 15–1. Suppose Lois leaves town and is replaced by Hattie, whose marginal benefit of park acreage is negative: $-\$16$ per acre.

   a. Modify Figure 15–1 to show the socially efficient park size.

   b. Predict the outcome of a series of pair-wise elections between different park sizes: 0 acres (Hattie's favorite), 12 acres (Marian's favorite), and 28 acres (Hiram's favorite). Is the equilibrium park with majority rule too big or too small?

   c. Design a Lindahl tax scheme that will generate unanimous support for the socially efficient park size.

2. **Paying for Flood Protection**

   Suppose a city could spend $2,100 on a dike that would decrease the probability of flooding in a three-house neighborhood from 0.03 to 0.02. A flood would destroy all three houses, and flood insurance is not available. The market values of the three houses are $60,000, $120,000, and $240,000.

   a. Is the dike socially efficient? What is the benefit:cost ratio?

   b. Design a taxing scheme that would generate unanimous support for the dike.

3. **Cops: Chasing Criminals**

   Consider a metropolitan area with many municipalities. In Chaseville, the marginal social (municipal) benefit curve for police has a vertical intercept of $140 and a slope of $-\$10$ per police officer. The marginal cost (to the municipality) of a police officer is constant at $60.

   a. Suppose Chaseville uses the marginal principle to pick the number of police officers. How many police officers will the municipality hire?

   b. Suppose police officers chases criminals to other municipalities, increasing the cost of crime elsewhere by $30 for each police officer. Compute the socially efficient number of officers in Chaseville.

   c. You have been hired by the other municipalities to negotiate an agreement with Chaseville to hire the socially efficient number of police officers. What is the maximum amount other municipalities are willing to pay for an agreement? What is the minimum amount that Chaseville is willing to accept in exchange for agreeing? Is there room to cut a deal?

4. **Alienated Voters**

   Consider the example of voting in a representative democracy shown in Figure 15–4. Suppose a citizen abstains from voting if the best candidate has a budget position that is too far from the citizen's preferred budget. Specifically, a citizen abstains if the gap is greater than $2. If the gap is less than or equal to $2, the citizen votes.

   a. If we start with the median-voter outcome, does Buck have an incentive to increase his budget position to $8? Predict the outcome of the election if he does.

   b. Suppose we change the distribution of voters to a uniform distribution from $3 through $9, with 10 voters for each preferred budget level. For the two extremes ($2 and $10), there are 12 voters at each budget. The median budget remains the same ($6). If we start with the median-voter outcome, will Buck have an incentive to increase his budget position to $8? Predict the outcome of the election if he does.

5. Torn by Indifference?

Consider the example of voting in a representative democracy shown in Figure 15–4. Suppose half of all voters abstain from voting if the difference between the two candidates is too small. Specifically, half of voters of each type will abstain if the difference between the two candidates is less than $2. If the difference is greater than or equal to $2, everyone votes. If we start with the median-voter outcome, will Buck have an incentive to increase his police budget to $8? Explain.

REFERENCES AND ADDITIONAL READING

1. Downs, Anthony. "The Devolution Revolution: Why Congress Is Shifting a Lot of Power to the Wrong Levels." *Brookings Policy Brief* no. 18. Washington DC: Brookings Institution, 1998.
2. Fisher, Ronald C., and Robert W. Wassmer. "Economic Influences on the Structure of Local Government in U.S. Metropolitan Areas." *Journal of Urban Economics* 43 (1998), pp. 444–70.
3. Heikkila, Eric J. "Are Municipalities Tieboutian Clubs?" *Regional Science and Urban Economics* 26 (1996), pp. 203–26.
4. Inman, Robert P. "The Fiscal Performance of Local Governments: An Interpretive Review." In *Current Issues in Urban Economics,* eds. Peter Mieszkowski and Mahlon Straszheim. Baltimore: Johns Hopkins University Press, 1979, pp. 270–321.
5. Levin, Henry. "Educational Vouchers: Effectiveness, Choice and Costs." *Journal of Policy Analysis and Management* 17, no. 3 (1997). pp. 373–92.
6. Musgrave, Richard A., and Peggy B. Musgrave. *Public Finance in Theory and Practice.* New York: McGraw-Hill, 1980.
7. Oates, Wallace E. *Fiscal Federalism.* New York: Harcourt Brace Jovanovich, 1972.
8. Panizza, Ugo. "On the Determinants of Fiscal Centralization: Theory and Evidence." *Journal of Public Economics* 74 (1999), pp. 97–140.
9. Rivkin, Steven G., Eric A. Hanushek, and John F. Kain. "Teachers, Schools, and Academic Achievement." NBER Working Paper Number 6691 (1998).
10. Rouse, Cecilia. "Schools and Student Achievement: More Evidence from the Milwaukee Parental Choice Program." *Federal Reserve Bank of New York Economic Policy Review* (March, 1998), pp. 61–76.
11. U.S. Bureau of the Census. *Census of Government 2002.*

CHAPTER 16

Local Government Revenue

Sonja: What are you suggesting, passive resistance?
Boris: No, I'm suggesting active fleeing.
— FROM THE MOVIE *LOVE AND DEATH* (1975)

*T*his chapter explores the economics of the two most important revenue sources of local government, the property tax and intergovernmental grants. We address two key questions about these revenue sources:

1. **Who bears the cost of the property tax?**

We'll use the model of supply and demand to show that the person who pays the tax in a legal sense shifts the tax to landowners, capital owners, and consumers.

2. **How does a local government respond to a grant for a particular program such as special education?**

We'll use the model of the median voter to show that a local government will use part of a grant to cut taxes and increase spending on other local public goods. Figure 16–1 (page 342) shows the distribution of revenue for different types of local governments. For local governments as a whole, 41 percent of revenue comes from intergovernmental grants, 36 percent comes from local taxes, and the remaining 22 percent comes from charges and general revenue. School districts are heavily dependent on intergovernmental grants, while special districts are heavily dependent on charges and general revenue.

Figure 16–2 (page 343) shows the distribution of local government revenue from different taxes. The property tax generates about three-fourths of local tax revenue and about half of municipal revenue. The sales tax generates roughly three times as much revenue as the individual income tax. Taxes on corporate income generate a small fraction of local tax revenue.

FIGURE 16–1 Revenue Shares of Local Government

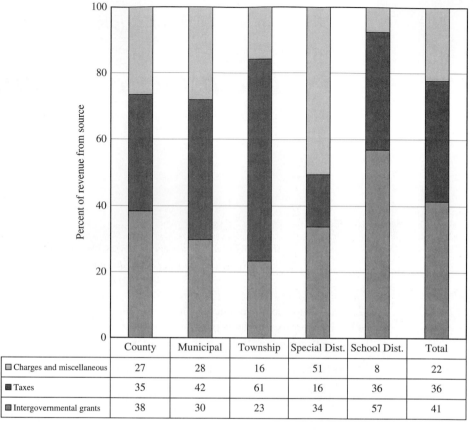

	County	Municipal	Township	Special Dist.	School Dist.	Total
☐ Charges and miscellaneous	27	28	16	51	8	22
■ Taxes	35	42	61	16	36	36
■ Intergovernmental grants	38	30	23	34	57	41

Source: U.S. Bureau of Census. *Census of Governments 2002.*

WHO PAYS THE RESIDENTIAL PROPERTY TAX?

No one likes to pay taxes, and once a tax is imposed, people change their behavior to try to avoid paying the tax. As a result, most taxes are at least partly shifted onto someone else. As we'll see, the property tax is shifted onto landowners, capital owners, and consumers.

Table 16–1 shows the tax rates on residential property for selected cities, each of which is the largest city in its state. The effective tax rate is defined as the tax liability of a property divided by its market value. Because many local governments assess property at less than its full market value, the effective tax rate is typically less than the nominal tax rate (tax divided by the assessed value). As shown in the table, the effective tax rate ranges from 0.37 percent of market value per year in Honolulu to 3.86 percent in Bridgeport, Connecticut.

FIGURE 16–2 Revenues from Different Taxes

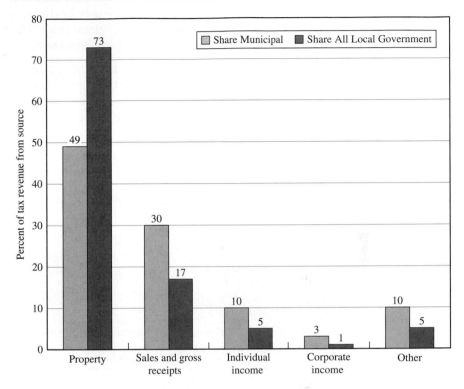

TABLE 16–1 Effective Property Tax Rates in Selected Cities, 2002

City	Effective Tax Rate	City	Effective Tax Rate
Bridgeport, CT	3.86%	Boston	1.10
Newark	2.95	Minneapolis	1.27
Milwaukee	2.67	Los Angeles	1.08
Des Moines	2.28	Phoenix	1.82
Houston	2.62	Chicago	1.69
Philadelphia	2.64	New York	0.93
Jacksonville	1.96	Denver	0.56
Memphis	1.76	Honolulu	0.37
Portland	1.46		

Source: U.S. Census Bureau. *Statistical Abstract of the United States.* Washington DC (2004).

The property tax is an annual tax on residential, commercial, and industrial property. The total value of a particular property is the value of the structure plus the value of land. For example, suppose a property has a market value of $100,000, with $80,000 for the structure and $20,000 for the land. With a 1 percent property tax, the annual tax liability will be $1,000, equal to $800 for the structure plus $200 for the land.

Consider the residential city of Taxton, where all land is used for rental housing in the form of mobile homes. The rental housing industry is perfectly competitive, and in equilibrium, each firm makes zero economic profit. Housing firms produce rental housing with two inputs, structure (capital) and land:

- **Structures.** A mobile home is a form of physical capital that housing firms rent from capital owners who live elsewhere. A mobile home can be moved cost-lessly from one city to another.
- **Land.** Housing firms rent the land under the mobile homes from absentee landowners. The lot size is fixed.

The housing firm rents housing (mobile home and land) to consumers. The initial (pretax) housing rent is $5,000 per year, equal to $4,000 for the structure rent and $1,000 for land rent.

We assume that the property tax is paid in a legal sense by housing firms. To simplify matters, suppose the property tax is $800 per mobile home and $200 per standard lot. In other words, the property tax is a unit tax rather than a tax based on value. We are interested in the effect of the property tax on four types of people: owners of housing firms, housing consumers, landowners, and capital owners.

The Land Portion of the Property Tax

Consider first the land portion of the property tax. In Figure 16–3, the supply of land is perfectly inelastic, with a fixed supply of 900 lots. The demand for land comes from housing firms, who use it as an input to rental housing. The demand curve intersects the supply curve at point *i*, generating an initial land rent of $1,000 per lot.

The demand curve shows how much a housing firm is willing to pay to landowners for one lot. If the firm pays a tax of $200 per lot, it is willing to pay $200 less to the landowner. In Figure 16–3, the $200 land tax shifts the demand curve downward by $200, and the new equilibrium is shown by point *t*, with a rent of $800. The tax decreases land rent paid to landowners by the full amount of the tax. In other words, housing firms shift the entire land tax backwards onto landowners. This happens because the supply of land is perfectly inelastic. If landowners refused to cut land rent by $200, the net price of land to housing firms (rent plus the tax) would rise above $1,000. As a result, the quantity of land demanded would be less than the fixed supply of 900 lots. The resulting excess supply would cause rent to decrease until it reached $800.

Structure Portion: A Partial Equilibrium Approach

Consider next the structure portion of the property tax. We will start with partial-equilibrium analysis, looking at the effect of the tax in one input market (structures) in once city (Taxton). The analysis is partial because it ignores the effects of the tax on other markets and other cities.

Figure 16–4 (page 346) shows the initial equilibrium in the structure market. The initial supply curve for mobile homes is horizontal at $4,000 per structure. As

FIGURE 16–3 Market Effects of the Land Portion of the Property Tax

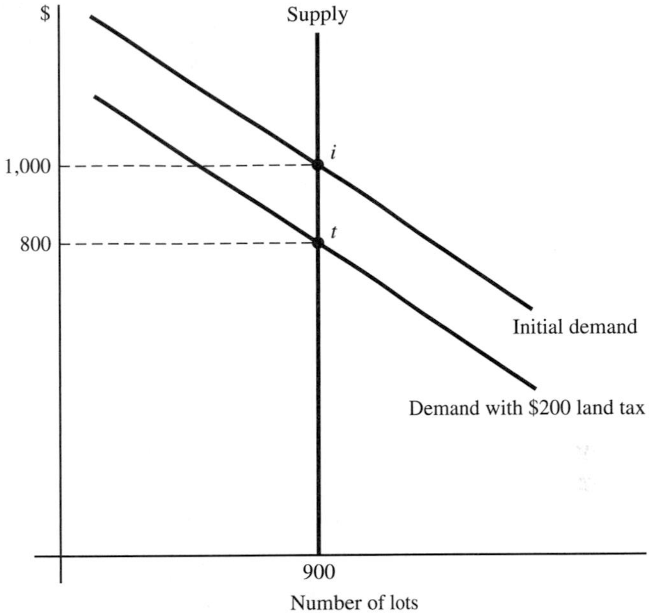

A land tax of $200 per lot decreases the amount a housing firm is willing
to pay to a landowner by $200. Because the supply is perfectly inelastic,
the equilibrium rent drops by $200, meaning that the landowner pays the
entire tax.

explained in Section 2.2 in the appendix "Tools of Microeconomics," a supply
curve is also a marginal-cost curve. Recall that a housing firm rents mobile homes
from capital owners, and the annual payment—the return to capital—is the firm's
only cost of providing a structure to consumers. Therefore, the structure supply
curve shows the housing firm's cost per mobile home. The horizontal supply curve
indicates that the return to capital (the firm's cost per mobile home) is fixed at
$4,000. To get a mobile home, a housing firm must pay the capital owner $4,000,
regardless of how many mobile homes are used in Taxton. The initial supply curve
intersects the demand curve at point i, with a quantity of 900 structures and a structure rent of $4,000.

In Figure 16–4, a structure tax of $800 shifts the supply curve upward by the
amount of the tax. The tax increases the housing firm's marginal cost by the amount
of the tax. For each structure, the housing firm pays $4,000 to the capital owner and
$800 to the government, so the firm's marginal cost of a structure is now $4,800.
The new equilibrium is shown by point t, with a price of $4,800 and a quantity
of 700 dwellings. In other words, the entire structure tax is passed forward onto
consumers, who pay $800 more for housing.

So housing firms don't pay *any* of the property tax? They shift the land portion
backward onto landowners, and shift the structure portion forward to consumers.

FIGURE 16–4 The Partial-Equilibrium Effects of the Structure Tax

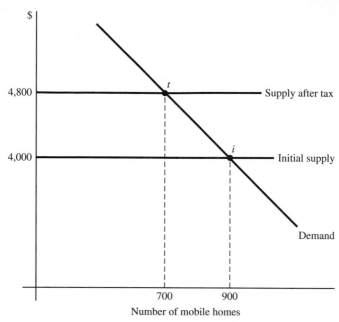

The supply curve for structures shows the firm's cost per mobile home, the cost of renting a mobile home from a capital owner. The structure tax shifts the supply curve upward by the amount of the tax. If the return to capital is fixed, the supply curve for structures is horizontal, and the tax increases the structure rent by the full amount of the tax.

They get the money to pay the $1,000 tax by paying $200 less for land and charging $800 more to consumers. This of course is not unique to the housing market, but is the normal consequence of a tax on a competitive industry. A tax is shifted backward onto input suppliers and forward onto consumers, leaving producers with zero economic profit, just as they had before the tax.

Structure Portion: A General-Equilibrium Approach

So far we have looked at the effects of the structure tax in the taxing city. The partial-equilibrium analysis ignores the effects of the tax on people outside the city. Figure 16–4 shows the need for a more general approach. The tax decreases the quantity of structures in Taxton from 900 to 700. Where do the mobile homes go? What are the economic consequences? A general-equilibrium approach answers these questions.

   We can extend our example by introducing a second city in the region, one without a property tax. Before Taxton imposes its property tax, the two cities are identical: Each city has 900 mobile homes and the equilibrium rent is $4,000.

FIGURE 16–5 General-Equilibrium Effects of the Structure Tax

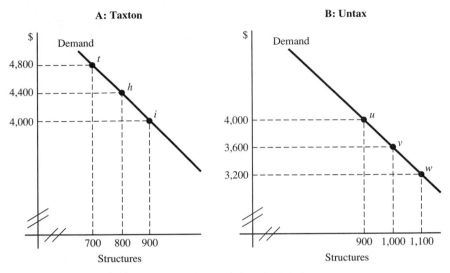

The partial-equilibrium outcome is shown by point *t* in Taxton. Consumers pay a structure rent of $4,800, including $4,000 return to structure capital and a $800 structure tax. The 200 structures that flee Taxton increase the number of structures in Untax (point *w*), decreasing the return to capital to $3,200. General equilibrium requires equal capital returns in the two cities, shown by points *h* in Taxton (structure rent = $4,400; return to structure capital = $3,600) and *v* in Untax (structure rent = return to structure capital = $3,600). The structure tax decreases the common return to capital from $4,000 to $3,600.

We assume that mobile homes can be moved costlessly between the two cities but cannot leave the region. In other words, the regional supply of structures (capital) is fixed.

Our general-equilibrium analysis must account for the 200 mobile homes that flee the tax in Taxton. In Figure 16–5, the partial-equilibrium outcome is shown as point *t* in Panel A. There are 700 structures in Taxton (down from 900 at point *i*), and consumers pay $4,800 per structure, enough to cover a return to capital of $4,000 and an $800 tax. In Panel B, if 200 structures flee to the untaxed city (Untax), we move downward along the demand curve from point *u* to point *w*, and the return to capital decreases from $4,000 to $3,200. The return to capital decreases because to get consumers in Untax to rent the additional mobile homes, the housing firm must cut the structure rent. Otherwise, some mobile homes will be vacant and generate zero rent.

The flight of the mobile homes from Taxton to Untax generates a gap between the return to capital in the two cities. In Taxton, the return is $4,000: Housing firms collect $4,800 from consumers, pay the $800 tax, and pay $4,000 to capital owners. In Untax, the increased supply of mobile homes decreases the return to $3,200. This is not an equilibrium because capital owners have an incentive to move their mobile homes to Taxton. Equilibrium requires the same return to capital in the two cities.

The second flight of the mobile homes—from Untax to Taxton—is shown by the movement upward along the Untax demand curve and downward along the Taxton demand curve. If 100 mobile homes make the trip, we go from point w to point v in Untax, and the return increases to $3,600. In Taxton, we go from point t to point h, and the return decreases to $3,600 (the $4,400 rent charged to consumers minus the $800 tax). With points v and h, the return to capital is equalized, so we have an equilibrium, with 800 structures in Taxton and 1,000 structures in Untax.

Our conclusion is that the structure tax is paid by capital owners throughout the region. A tax of $800 per structure in one city decreases the return on capital by $400 per structure throughout the region. The tax is fully shifted backward onto capital owners because the regional supply of capital is assumed to be fixed. Recall that the land tax is fully shifted backward to landowners because the supply of land is fixed. The same basic logic applies to the structure tax: If an input is fixed in supply, owners of the input will bear the tax.

What about consumers? Let's assume that consumers can move costlessly between the two cities. Housing firms make zero economic profit, so the housing rent is just high enough to pay the firm's cost:

Housing rent = Return to capital + structure tax + land rent

Assume for the moment that land rent is fixed at $1,000, as shown in the second row of Table 16–2. As a result, housing rent is $5,400 in Taxton ($3,600 + $800 + $1,000) compared to only $4,600 in Untax ($3,600 + $1,000). As a result, consumers have an incentive to move from Taxton to Untax.

Locational equilibrium for consumers requires the same housing rent in the two cities. Recall the first axiom of urban economics:

Prices adjust to generate locational equilibrium

In this case, the price of land will adjust to equalize housing rent and make consumers indifferent between the two cities. In the third row of Table 16–2, the gap in housing rent can be closed if land rent decreases to $600 in Taxton and increases to $1,400 in Untax. With these changes in land rent, housing rent is $5,000 in each city, so consumers will be indifferent between the two cities. This means that the structure tax causes landowners in Taxton to lose $400 per lot, while landowners in Untax gain $400 per lot.

TABLE 16–2 General Equilibrium Effects of the Structure Tax with Two Cities

	Taxton				Untax		
	Return to Capital	Structure Tax	Land Rent	Housing Rent	Return to Capital	Land Rent	Housing Rent
Initial	$4,000	$ 0	$1,000	**$5,000**	$4,000	$1,000	**$5,000**
Before change in land rent	$3,600	$800	$1,000	**$5,400**	$3,600	$1,000	**$4,600**
After change in land rent	$3,600	$800	$600	**$5,000**	$3,600	$1,400	**$5,000**

So who bears the cost of the structure portion of the property tax? Recall that for the moment we are assuming the supply of capital (structures) in the region is fixed.

- Capital owners bear the tax. The return to capital falls by $400 per structure in both cities.
- Landowners in the region experience zero-sum changes in rent, with landowners in the untaxed city gaining at the expense of landowners in the taxed city.
- Consumers pay the same price for housing, so they do not bear any part of the tax.
- Housing firms make zero economic profit. In the taxed city, they get the money to pay the $800 tax by paying $400 less to capital owners and $400 less to landowners. In the untaxed city, they pay $400 less to capital owners but pay $400 more to landowners.

Changing the Assumptions

The simple general-equilibrium model uses a number of assumptions to make the basic results transparent and clear-cut. If we modify some of these assumptions, things are not so tidy.

One of the key assumptions is that the total supply of capital (structures) is fixed. In fact, we expect that a lower return on capital will reduce the quantity of capital supplied. For example, some of the structures that flee the tax could be withdrawn from the market rather than simply moving to the untaxed city. If so, the initial excess supply of structures in the untaxed city won't be as large, so the return on capital won't drop as far. In equilibrium, housing rent will be greater than $5,000, meaning that part of the structure tax will be shifted to consumers, leaving a smaller burden on capital owners.

A second key assumption is that consumers are perfectly mobile between the two cities. As a result, any intercity differences in housing rent are eliminated by changes in land rent. If instead residents are immobile, the gap in housing rent will persist. Looking back at Table 16–2, with perfectly immobile consumers, we will be stuck in the second row, with consumers in Taxton paying $800 more for housing. To summarize, when consumers are perfectly mobile, there will be zero-sum changes in land rent; when consumers are perfectly immobile, there will be zero-sum changes in housing rent. Between these two extremes, when consumers are mobile but not perfectly mobile, both housing rent and land rent will change.

A third key assumption is that there are only 2 cities in the region. If there were 10 cities instead, the effects of Taxton's structure tax would be spread over five times as much capital. As a result, the decrease in the return to capital would be one-fifth as large: The return to capital would drop by $80 instead of $400. Table 16–3 (page 350) shows the implications for shifting the structure tax. To equalize housing rent between the cities, the price of land would increase by $80 in the untaxed cities and decrease by $720 in the taxing city. Notice that the changes in land rent in the region sum to zero: Nine cities experience an $80 rise and one experiences a $720 decline.

TABLE 16–3 The Structure Tax with 10 Cities

	Taxton				Untaxed cities		
	Return to Capital	Structure Tax	Land Rent	Housing Rent	Return to Capital	Land Rent	Housing Rent
Initial	$4,000	$ 0	$1,000	$5,000	$4,000	$1,000	$5,000
Before change in land rent	$3,920	$800	$1,000	$5,720	$3,920	$1,000	$4,920
After change in land rent	$3,920	$800	$280	$5,000	$3,920	$1,080	$5,000

FROM MODELS TO REALITY

To explain the effects of the property tax on different sorts of people, we have used a number of modeling artifices that may seem to limit the applicability of the results. But in fact we can easily apply the lessons from the artificial model to real markets. Consider the lessons for property owners and policy makers.

What about Rental Property Owners and Homeowners?

Our model of the housing market has four economic actors: consumers, owners of housing firms, landowners, and capital owners. In a real rental housing market, these roles are merged into two: Housing firms own property (land and structures), and consumers rent housing from the firm. In the homeowner market, the roles are merged into one, with consumers as property owners. What does the general-equilibrium model say about the burden of the property tax for rental property owners and homeowners?

Property owners in a taxing city lose as owners of land and capital. They lose as landowners because (1) the land portion of the tax decreases land rent and (2) part of the structure portion is shifted onto land. In addition, like other capital owners in the region, they lose because the return to capital decreases. In general, the property tax decreases the market value of property. This is sensible because the property now carries a tax liability, so potential buyers are willing to pay less for it.

Although property owners in other cities don't pay the tax in a legal sense, they are affected by it. They gain as landowners because land rent in their city rises to equalize housing rents. Like other capital owners, they lose as the regionwide return on capital decreases. So the net effect on their income and the market value of their properties is ambiguous.

A Practical Guide for Policy Makers

We've explored the effects of the residential property tax with different models and assumptions. Suppose an elected official asks, Who actually pays the property tax? The appropriate response depends on the official's perspective. We'll consider a city perspective and a national perspective.

TABLE 16–4 Who Pays the Structure Portion of the Property Tax?

Tax Imposed by a Single City

Effects in the taxing city
    1. Mobile households: Landowners receive lower land rent.
    2. Immobile households: Consumers pay higher housing rent.

Effects in an untaxed city
    1. Mobile households: Landowners receive higher land rent.
    2. Immobile households: Consumers pay lower housing rent.

Regional effects
    1. Capital owners receive lower return on capital.
    2. Mobile households and fixed capital: zero-sum changes in land rent.
    3. Immobile households and fixed capital: zero-sum changes in housing rent.
    4. Mobile households and variable supply of capital: Consumers pay higher housing rent; the reduction in the return on capital is smaller.

Tax Imposed by All Cities (a National Property Tax)
    1. Fixed supply of capital: Entire tax borne by capital owners.
    2. Variable supply of capital: Part of tax shifted to housing consumers.

Consider a mayor who wants to predict the effect of her city's structure tax on citizens in her city. Her city is one of 50 cities in a regional economy. As we saw in Table 16–3, in a 10-city region, the regionwide return to capital decreases by 1/10 of the tax ($80) and land rent in the taxing city decreases by 9/10 of the tax ($720/$800). For a region with 50 cities, the return to capital will decrease by 1/50 of the tax, leaving 49/50 for land. So the mayor can assume that most of the tax will be borne by local landowners. Of course, if households are not perfectly mobile, housing consumers will share the burden of the structure tax with local landowners, as explained earlier.

Consider next a president who wants to predict the effect of a uniform property tax across cities in the nation. With the same tax rate in all cities, structures have nowhere to flee from one city's property tax. If the national supply of capital is fixed, the entire tax will be borne by the owners of capital. In this case, capital owners cannot shift the tax to anyone else because they don't respond to the tax: They don't move their capital between cities, and they don't decrease the total amount of capital in the nation. Of course, if the supply of capital is variable rather than fixed, capital owners can shift the tax to households in the form of higher housing rent throughout the region.

Table 16–4 summarizes our analysis of the structure portion of the property tax. It shows who bears the burden of the tax under different assumptions about the type of tax, household mobility, and the supply of capital. The table also distinguishes between the taxing city and other cities.

What about the Business Property Tax?

The basic logic we have used to examine the residential property tax applies to the property tax on business property (commercial and industrial). Of course, instead of housing services as the output of the taxed industry, we have products such as books, haircuts, clothing, and manufactured goods. When a single city imposes a business property tax, the general-equilibrium approach shows that the structure portion of the tax will be borne by the owners of capital throughout the region as capital flees the taxing city. As in the case of the residential property tax, the effect on consumers depends on their mobility—their ability to switch to sellers in untaxed municipalities.

Tax exporting is the process of getting people outside the municipality to pay taxes. A city can use the business property tax to shift taxes to outsiders if they consume some of the city's products. There are limits, of course. As the price of a city's export goods increases, the quantity demanded decreases, decreasing the tax base. In addition, firms have an incentive to move to cities with lower property taxes. Tax exporting is more lucrative when a city has a unique production advantage that makes it a superior location for export firms.

THE TIEBOUT MODEL AND THE PROPERTY TAX

As we saw earlier in the book in the chapter on neighborhood choice, citizens sort themselves with respect to their demands for local public goods. If local public goods are financed with a property tax, households will also sort themselves with respect to housing consumption. This has important implications for the property tax, as Table 16–5 demonstrates.

Consider a metropolitan area where households have the same preferred level of local public goods ($6,000), but live in houses with different market values. The first row of Table 16–5 shows what happens in a mixed municipality with a tax rate of 0.02 (2 percent of value). Juan, who lives in a $100,000 house, pays a property tax of $2,000. At the other extreme, Thurl lives in a $500,000 house and pays five times as much. Thurl is paying more than her share of taxes, and has an incentive to form a municipality with other people in expensive houses.

The last three rows in the table show what happens when citizens sort themselves into municipalities according to house value. A municipality full of expensive houses needs a tax rate of only 0.012 to generate the $6,000 necessary to support $6,000 worth of public services per household. With Juan-type households in one municipality (second row) and Tupak types in another municipality (third row),

TABLE 16–5 Municipality Formation for Tax Purposes

		Tax bill for		
Outcome	Tax Rate	Juan ($100k house)	Tupak ($300k house)	Thurl ($500k house)
Mixed municipality	0.02	$2,000	$6,000	$10,000
All $100k houses	0.06	$6,000	—	—
All $300k houses	0.02	—	$6,000	—
All $500k houses	0.012	—	—	$6,000

everyone has the same tax liability, even though they have different house values. People in less expensive houses have higher tax rates, allowing them to pay $6,000 in taxes.

Because households sort themselves into homogeneous communities, the property tax is a user fee, not a conventional tax. A household's property tax liability is determined by its consumption of the local public good, not by its property value. In the Tiebout world, households get what they pay for, and the question of who pays the property tax is simple: Just as a consumer pays $2 to get a hot dog, a household pays a property tax of $6,000 to get $6,000 worth of local public goods. There is no tax shifting because the tax is a user fee.

How realistic is the Tiebout model and the user-fee view of the property tax? Given the large number of municipalities in the typical metropolitan area, households can choose from a wide variety of municipalities and local governments. But the sorting process is by no means perfect, even in suburban areas. The Tiebout model is clearly inapplicable to central cities, where a single municipality serves a large and diverse population. In large central cities, the property tax is not a user fee, but a conventional tax.

LIMITS ON PROPERTY TAXES

Limits on property taxes started in the 1870s and are currently in force in 44 states. About two-thirds of states limit the tax rate for specific types of local government, and about a quarter limit the tax rate for local government as a whole. Most of the rate limits fall in the range of 10 to 20 mills (1 to 2 percent of assessed value). About half of the states limit the annual growth rate of property tax revenue, with most limits in the range of 4 to 6 percent. Some states peg the growth rate to the inflation rate. In many states, local governments have the option to override a state limit with voter approval.

The first property tax revolt came during the Great Depression, a result of a mismatch between property tax liabilities and citizens' willingness to pay for local public services. As shown in Figure 16–6 (page 354), the share of income absorbed by the property tax doubled between 1929 and 1932, reaching 11.3 percent in 1932. During this three-year period, personal income was cut in half while property tax revenue decreased by only 9 percent. The decrease in citizens' ability to pay property taxes nearly tripled the delinquency rate. Fearing massive defaults on municipal bonds, the business community supported protax campaigns by paying for lapel buttons, mass mailings, and parades. The parades featured the descendants of canine war heroes, who barked and carried signboards urging people to pay their taxes.

In 1933, over 3,000 local tax leagues were agitating for tax reform. The clear message was that local government should scale back its operations to reflect lower income during the Great Depression. In the words of one agitator, "I buy less food, less tobacco, less recreation, and I'd like to buy less government." (Beito, 1989, page 18). In mass meetings organized by the tax leagues, citizens demanded the elimination of local services, including weed inspectors and county nurses.

FIGURE 16–6 Property Tax Revenue as a Share of Income

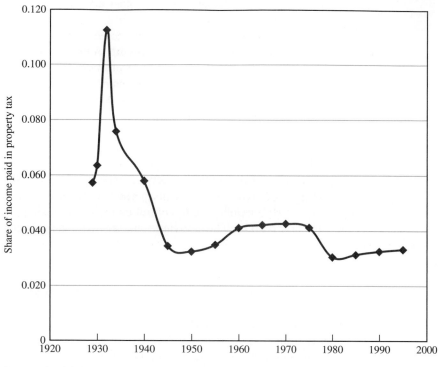

Source: Arthur O'Sullivan. "Limits on Local Property Taxation." Chapter 7 in *Property Taxation and Local Government Finance,* ed. Wallace E. Oates. Cambridge MA: Lincoln Institute, 2001.

   The tax revolt of the 1930s resulted in the passage of tax limits that reduced the tax burden. In 1932 and 1933, a total of 16 states passed tax limits, with most of the measures setting a maximum overall rate for local property taxes. As shown in Figure 16–6, the share of income absorbed by property taxes dropped between 1932 and 1940. The decrease in the tax share resulted from a combination of income growth and the tax limits. By 1940, personal income had almost reached the level observed in 1930, while the share of income absorbed by the property tax was 5.8 percent, compared to 6.3 percent in 1930.

   The modern tax revolt started in 1978 with the passage of Proposition 13 in California. As shown in Figure 16–6, during the period 1960 to 1975, the share of national income absorbed by the property tax was high by recent historical standards, about 4.2 percent, compared to 3.4 percent during the late 1940s and 1950s. By 1995, dozens of states had enacted new tax limits, and the share of income absorbed by property taxes dropped to 3.3 percent, the level observed in the 1940s and 1950s.

   In contrast with the earlier tax revolt, the supporters of modern tax limits expected local governments to provide the same level of service with less money. In California, 38 percent of the citizens believed that state and local governments could absorb a 40 percent cut in tax revenue without cutting services. In Massachusetts, 82 percent of the supporters of Proposition 2 1/2 believed that the proposition would cut taxes without reducing the quality of local public services. In Michigan, three-fourths of the supporters of the Headlee Amendment expected the government to absorb the revenue cut by simply becoming more efficient.

In the 1990s, two states changed their property-tax systems. Illinois established limits on the growth rate of property tax revenues in the Chicago metropolitan area. The maximum growth rate is the maximum of the inflation rate or 5 percent per year. In 1995, Michigan reformed its entire education finance system. The state cut, property tax revenue in half and offset the revenue loss by increasing sales taxes, tobacco taxes, and real estate transfer taxes.

There is evidence that modern tax limits reduce property taxes. As shown in Figure 16–6, the share of income paid in property taxes has fallen since the onset of the modern revolt in 1978. Property tax limits reduce real per-capita tax revenue by 3 percent to 6 percent (Advisory Committee on Intergovernmental Relations, 1995; Shadbegian, 1998). There is also some evidence of revenue substitution, with revenue from other sources at least partly offsetting the loss of property taxes. One response is to increase intergovernmental grants from state government. A second response is to increase nontax revenue from fees and charges. Shadbegian (1999) estimates that for each $1 reduction in county tax revenue, there is a $0.27 increase in miscellaneous revenue.

INTERGOVERNMENTAL GRANTS

This part of the chapter explores the economics of intergovernmental grants, examining how local governments respond to transfers of funds from higher levels of government. As we saw earlier in the chapter, intergovernmental grants provide about two-fifths of the revenue of local government and about one-fourth of the revenue of municipalities. Over half of this grant money goes to education, and the rest supports other local programs such as public welfare, housing and community development, highways, and health and hospitals. At the municipal level, about one-fifth of grant money supports the general operations of local government, and another fifth supports education. The two redistributional programs—public welfare and housing and community development—together get about a quarter of the grant money received by municipalities.

Why don't local governments pay their own way, supporting their spending programs with local taxes? First, intergovernmental grants can be used to internalize interjurisdictional spillovers, as discussed in the previous chapter. Second, if the desired spending on local public goods rises faster than the local tax base (e.g. property values and retail sales), there will be a mismatch between desired spending and local revenue. At the national level, tax revenue increases more rapidly with income, providing an opportunity to transfer surplus funds to local governments. Of course, a more straightforward response to the mismatch problem would be to increase local tax rates.

We will explore the responses of local government to two types of grants. A lump-sum grant is a fixed grant, independent of a local government's spending on a local public good. In contrast, under a matching grant, a higher level of government matches local spending, for example $1 of grant money for every $1 spent locally.

Lump-Sum Grants

Most lump-sum intergovernmental grants come with strings attached. The money from a conditional or categorical grant must be spent on a specific program. Conditional grants are provided for education, public welfare, health and hospitals, highways, housing, and community development. Within each expenditure group are program-specific grants. For example, education grants to local governments include specific grants for remedial reading, school libraries, special education, and other programs. We will use a grant for special education as an example.

We can use the consumer choice model to explore the effects of grants. The choice model is reviewed in Section 4 of "Tools of Microeconomics," the appendix at the end of the book. Figure 16–7 shows the budget line for Marian, the median voter in Grantburg. For every dollar spent on special education, there is one less dollar to spend on other goods, including local public goods and private goods. The indifference curves show Marian's trade-off between special education and other

FIGURE 16–7 Local Government Response to a Lump-Sum Grant

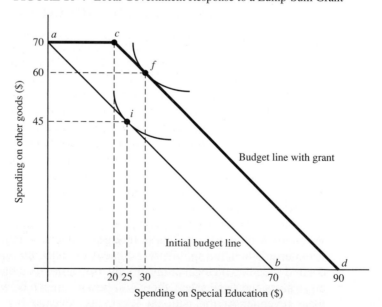

A lump-sum grant of $20 per capita shifts the budget line of the median voter from *ab* to *acd*, and the utility maximization point moves from point *i* to point *f*. The grant increases the spending on the target program (special education) by $5 and increases spending on other goods by $15.

goods. Given the initial budget line (*ab*) and her indifference curves, Marian's utility is maximized at point *i*. We know from earlier chapters that under majority rule, the city will choose the preferred budget of the median voter. In this case, the city spends $25 per household on special education, leaving Marian $45 for other goods.

Suppose the state gives the city a lump-sum grant of $20 per capita for special-education programs. The grant shifts the budget line from *ab* to *acd*. Point *c* is in the new budget set because Marian could spend all of her own money on other goods and use the $20 grant to support special education. For spending on special education above $20, there is a dollar-for-dollar trade-off between special education and other goods. The new utility-maximizing point is point *f*, meaning that the grant increases Marian's desired spending on special education to $30 (up by $5) and her desired spending on other goods to $60 (up by $15). In other words, one-fourth of the grant is spent on special education, and the rest is spent on other goods.

Why does a conditional grant of $20 increase spending on the target program by less than $20? The city can spend part of the grant on other goods because it decreases its own contribution to special education. Before the grant, $25 of local tax money was spent on special education. After the grant, total spending on special education is $30, and the city can combine the $20 grant with just $10 of local tax money. The grant frees up $15 worth of local tax money, which can be spent on other local public goods and private goods.

Matching Grants

Under a matching grant, the government contributes some amount for every dollar of local spending on a particular local public good. For example, under a one-for-one matching grant, the higher level of government gives one dollar in grant money for every dollar spent by local government. A matching grant decreases the opportunity cost of local public goods: With a one-for-one match, local citizens sacrifice only $0.50 in private goods to get a dollar's worth of local public goods ($0.50 of local spending plus a grant of $0.50).

Figure 16–8 (page 358) shows the effect of a one-for-one matching grant for special education. The grant decreases the slope of Marian's budget line, from $1 worth of other goods per dollar on special education to $0.50. Given the new budget line, Marian's utility-maximizing point moves from *i* to point *g*, and spending on special education increases from $25 to $40. Under the one-for-one grant, $20 of the city's $40 special-education budget comes from the state government.

The matching grant provides a greater stimulus to special education than an equivalent lump-sum grant. Although the state transfers the same amount for each type of grant ($20), the matching grant increases spending on special education to $40, while the lump-sum grant increases spending to only $30 (Figure 16–7). Both grants increase Marian's real income by $20, increasing her demand for special education and other goods. The matching grant also has a substitution effect because it cuts the opportunity cost (price) of special education in half. The decrease in the relative price of special education causes consumer substitution of special education for other goods.

FIGURE 16–8 Local Government Response to a Matching Grant

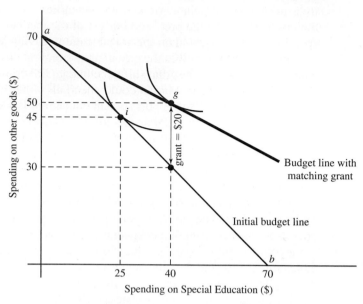

A one-for-one matching grant tilts the budget line of the median voter outward, and the utility maximization point moves from point *i* to point *g*. The grant increases the spending on the target program (special education) by $15 and increases spending on other goods by $5. The matching grant provides a bigger stimulus than a lump-sum grant because it decreases the opportunity cost of spending on the target program.

What about spending on other goods? Under a one-for-one matching grant, the local contribution to a $40 special-education budget is $20. This leaves $50 to spend on other goods, including other public goods and private goods, up from $45 before the grant. In other words, the city spends one-fourth of the $20 matching grant on other goods. Like a lump-sum grant, a matching grant increases spending on other goods as the local government cuts its own contribution to the program covered by the grant.

Up to this point, we have assumed that there is no upper limit on the matching grant. In many cases, the government specifies a maximum grant amount, and this type of grant is called a closed-ended matching grant. If the desired spending after the grant is less than the limit, the limit is irrelevant and the closed grant is equivalent to the open grant. If however, the desired spending exceeds the limit, the constraint is binding, and a closed grant generates a lower level of spending than an open grant.

Summary: The Stimulative Effects of Grants

As explained earlier in the chapter, local governments use intergovernmental grants to increase spending on local public goods and other goods, including private goods. Spending on private goods can increase because the local government can cut taxes. What fraction of grant money is used for additional local spending, and how much is left over to increase the consumption of private goods? Empirical studies of the local response to grants conclude that each dollar from a nonmatching grant increases local government spending by roughly $0.40 Oates (1999). In contrast, an additional dollar of household income increases local spending by about $0.10. In other words, a local grant provides a bigger stimulus for local spending. This is known as the flypaper effect: The grant money sticks where it first hits (the local government) rather than being passed on to households in the form of lower taxes.

What explains the flypaper effect? The most prominent theory assumes that government bureaucrats want to maximize their budgets (Filimon, Romer, Rosenthal, 1982). If the bureaucrats hide grant money from citizens, voters are more likely to approve larger budgets. In states that have direct votes on local budgets, ballots often have information about the tax base, but rarely have information about intergovernmental grants.

APPLICATIONS: WELFARE AND EDUCATION GRANTS

In this part of the chapter, we look at two intergovernmental grant programs. First, under a recent change in national welfare policy, matching grants were replaced by lump-sum grants. How will this affect state spending on welfare programs? Second, many states use intergovernmental grants to reduce inequalities in education spending across school districts.

Welfare Reform: Matching Grants to Lump-Sum Grants

A key component of the welfare-reform plan adopted in 1996 is the replacement of federal matching grants with lump-sum grants (also known as block grants). Under the old system, each state picked a level of welfare spending, and the federal government used matching grants to support local efforts. For low-income states, the federal rebate per dollar spent on welfare was $0.78, so from a state's perspective, each dollar spent on welfare cost the state only $0.22. The rebate was lower for high-income states, with a one-for-one match for the highest income states. Under the new grant system, the federal grant no longer depends on how much the state spends on welfare. There are no matching funds, so the state's price of a dollar spent on welfare is $1.00.

Figure 16–9 (page 360) uses the consumer choice model to show the effects of welfare reform on the budget choices of a low-income state. The budget line for the median voter under the matching grant is relatively flat, reflecting the low local price of welfare spending. The voter's initial preference (and thus the state's initial choice) is shown as point *i*, with $210 million on welfare and $260 million on other goods. The new lump-sum grant is $140 million, so the new budget line is shown by the line connecting points *g*, *m*, and *i*. The lump-sum grant is large enough that the median voter has the option of picking its initial point *i*. If the initial point is possible, will the state choose it?

FIGURE 16–9 A Switch from a Matching Grant to a Lump-Sum Grant Decreases Spending

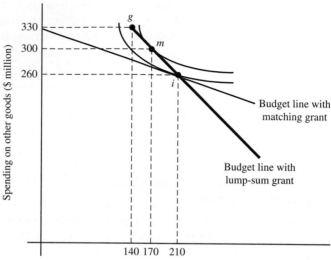

The replacement of a matching grant with a $140 lump-sum grant moves the utility maximizing point from point *i* to point *m*. The policy change reduces spending on the target program (welfare) because the opportunity cost of spending on welfare increases from $0.22 to $1.00.

Under the lump-sum grant, the state will actually spend less on welfare programs. To maximize the utility of the median voter, the state picks the point where the slope of the indifference curve (the marginal rate of substitution) equals the slope of the budget line (the price ratio):

Utility-maximizing rule: Marginal rate of substitution = Price ratio

For the initial choice (point *i*), the marginal rate of substitution equals the price ratio, $0.22. The switch to the lump-sum grant increases the price of welfare spending to $1, so to maximize utility, the median voter moves to point *m*, where the marginal rate of substitution is 1.0. In other words, the median voter chooses to spend less on welfare programs and more on other goods. Comparing point *m* to point *i*, the state will spend $40 million less on welfare programs and $40 million more on other goods (other public goods and private goods). The switch to a lump-sum grant increases the price of welfare spending, causing a substitution effect that decreases welfare spending.

The predicted changes in welfare spending are large. For a low-income state, the price hike from $0.22 to $1.00 is projected to decrease welfare spending by 40 to 66 percent (Inman and Rubinfeld, 1997). For a high-income state, the price hike is smaller (from $0.50 to $1.00), and the switch to lump-sum grants is projected to decrease welfare spending by 1 to 18 percent. Congress was apparently aware that welfare reform would cause states to cut their welfare spending. The law requires states to continue to spend at least 80 percent of the amount spent under the old matching-grant policy.

Intergovernmental Grants for Education

As we saw earlier in the chapter, a large share of funding for local schools comes from intergovernmental grants. Courts in many states have adopted the principle of fiscal neutrality:

Spending on education may not be a function of the
wealth of the local community

The courts have directed states to eliminate spending inequalities across school districts by supplementing local tax revenue. Most states use one of two types of grants to reduce spending inequalities.

A *foundation grant* is a lump-sum grant, the level of which is determined by the property wealth of the school district. The grant per pupil is computed as follows:

Grant = Foundation level − Foundation tax rate · Local tax base per pupil

For example, suppose a state specifies a foundation level of $5,000 and a foundation tax rate of 0.015 (1.5 percent). For a school district with a tax base (property value) per pupil of $200,000, the grant per pupil is

Grant = $5,000 − 0.015 · $200,000 = $2,000

If the district adopts the foundation tax rate of 1.5 percent, it will raise $3,000 per pupil. Adding this local revenue to the grant, the district reaches the foundation level of $5,000. The foundation grant is larger for school districts with lower tax bases. For example, for a district with a tax base of $100,000 per pupil, the grant is $3,500.

As we saw earlier in the chapter, a matching grant provides a bigger stimulus than a lump-sum grant. A guaranteed tax base plan (GTB) is a system of matching grants for school districts. The state specifies a guaranteed tax base per pupil, giving each school district the same revenue-generating capacity. The grant is computed as follows:

Grant = Local tax rate · (Guaranteed tax base per pupil − Local tax
base per pupil)

For example, suppose the guaranteed tax base is $300,000 and the local tax base is $200,000. The school district chooses its tax rate, and Table 16–6 shows the consequences of different rates. The grant increases with the local tax rate (local tax

TABLE 16–6 Grants Under a Guaranteed Tax Base Plan

Tax Rate	Local Revenue	Grant	Total
0.02	$4,000	$2,000	$6,000
0.025	$5,000	$2,500	$7,500

effort), rising from $2,000 for a tax rate of 2 percent to $2,500 for a tax rate of 2.5 percent.

As a matching grant, a GTB decreases the opportunity cost of local spending, stimulating spending on education. The matching feature is apparent from comparing the first two rows in Table 16–6. Increasing the tax rate from 0.02 to 0.025 increases local revenue by $1,000 but also increases the grant by $500, so total spending increases by $1,500. In this example, the GTB plan is equivalent to a matching grant with a match of $0.50 per dollar of local spending. The grant decreases the opportunity cost of spending on education from $1 to $0.67 (the local community sacrifices $1,000 to get an additional $1,500 in education).

A recent study explored the changes in spending inequalities in K–12 education between 1972 and 1992 (Evans, Murray, Schwab, 1997). During this period, a total of 37 states reformed their school finance systems, 16 of them under court order. In states implementing court-ordered reform, spending inequalities decreased significantly, with spending "leveling up" as spending in low-spending school districts increased by relatively large amounts. For example, for a school district in the 25th percentile (25 percent of districts spent less per pupil), education spending increased by 27 percent. In contrast, spending in the median district increased by only 15 percent, and spending in the district in the 75th percentile did not change.

It appears that in most cases, education finance reform requires a court order to reduce inequalities. In the states that were not subject to court orders for equalization, reform plans did not have any significant effects on spending inequalities. The one exception is Michigan. The state assumed responsibility for determining educational spending in all but the 28 wealthiest school districts. Spending per pupil increased in small rural districts and decreased in urban areas—in both poor central areas and rich suburban areas.

How have central-city schools fared under the reform of the education finance system? Central-city schools have relatively high costs because a large fraction of their students come from poor families. City schools devote more resources to deal with security measures, family crises, and medical problems. In addition, they use more resources to teach children who do not speak standard English and children with weak educational backgrounds. Because these schools have relatively high costs, they have above-average spending levels and do not benefit from equalization programs. In fact, some high-cost, high-spending districts actually do worse under equalization programs (Courant and Loeb, 1997; Duncombe and Yinger, 1997). If the formulas were modified to incorporate cost differences, some central-city school districts would receive two or three times as much grant money.

SUMMARY

The two largest sources of local government revenue are the property tax and intergovernmental grants.

1. The supply of land is fixed, so the land portion of the property tax is borne by landowners.

2. Under the general-equilibrium analysis of the structure portion of the property tax, if the supply of capital (structures) is fixed at the regional level, the tax is borne by capital owners throughout the region.

3. The structure tax generates zero-sum changes in land rent or housing rent across cities. If consumers are perfectly mobile between cities, they are unaffected by the structure tax, but landowners in the untaxed city gain at the expense of landowners in the taxing city.

4. In the Tiebout world of household sorting, a household's property tax bill is independent of its housing consumption, so the property tax is a user fee.

5. The model of the median voter predicts that part of a categorical grant is spent on other local public goods and private goods.

6. A matching grant decreases the opportunity cost of spending on the targeted good, so it provides a greater stimulus than a lump-sum grant.

APPLYING THE CONCEPTS

1. **A Tax on Mobile Home Pads**
   The residents of mobile home parks own their dwellings and rent pads (the land under the mobile home) from landowners. In Padville all land is initially occupied by mobile home parks, and each household rents one padacre (a standard pad). Each landowner owns one padacre. The city initially has 100 residents on 100 padacres, and the price of land is $200 per month. The demand curve for land has a slope of −$2 per padacre. Suppose the city imposes a tax of $40 per padacre, to be paid in legal terms by the occupant (resident). The tax is a fixed amount per padacre, regardless of how the land is used.
   a. Predict the effects of the land tax on the welfare of mobile home residents.
   b. Suppose landowners refuse to accept a rent less than $200 per padacre. Is this behavior consistent with equilibrium in the land market? What happens next?

2. **Tax Revenue versus Total Burden**
   Consider the analysis of the land tax (Figure 16–3) and the partial-equilibrium analysis of the structure tax (Figure 16–4). For each tax, compute the losses experienced by landowners or consumers.
   a. For the land tax, how does the total loss compare to the tax revenue generated?
   b. For the structure tax, how does the total loss compare to the tax revenue generated?
   c. Why do the two taxes differ in terms of the gap between the total loss (the total burden) and the tax revenue?

3. **Passive Resistance or Active Fleeing?**
   The motto for this chapter comes from a famous movie scene in which Boris is about to be forced into fighting in a war. After the exchange with his friend Sonja, Boris scrambles out the door and tries to outrun military recruiters. How is this scene related to the issue of who bears the burdent of a tax?

4. **Catatonia versus Fleetland**

   In the state of Catatonia, there are two cities (Cat1 and Cat2), and people don't move from one city to another. In the state of Fleetland, residents are perfectly mobile between the state's two cities (Flee1 and Flee2). You just discovered that one city in each state (Cat1 and Flee1) will impose a structure tax next week, and you are the only person who knows about the upcoming taxes. You currently own 10 acres of land in each of the four cities.

   a. If you want to keep a total of 20 acres in Catatonia, what if anything should you do?

   b. If you want to keep a total of 20 acres in Fleetland, what if anything should you do?

5. **Education Lottery**

   Consider a city that initially spends $20 million of its $100 million budget on public schools, a choice consistent with the preferences of the median voter. Suppose the city sets up a new lottery and by law must spend all the net revenue from the lottery ($15 million) on public schools. Use a completely labeled graph to predict the effects of the lottery money on the state government's spending on public education and other public goods.

6. **Librarian Grant**

   Consider a state that provides grants to cities for librarians. The daily cost of a librarian is $100, and the initial grant program is a categorical lump-sum grant of $500 per day. Under this program, the city hires a total of 10 librarians and spends $2,000 on all other goods. Suppose the state switches to dollar-for-dollar matching grant for librarians. Will the city hire more librarians, fewer librarians, or the same number? Illustrate with a completely labeled graph.

REFERENCES AND ADDITIONAL READING

1. Advisor Commission on Intergovernmental Relations. *Tax and Expenditure Limitations on Local Government.* Washington DC: U.S. Government Printing Office (1995).
2. Beito, David T. *Taxpayers in Revolt.* Chapel Hill, NC: University of North Carolina Press, 1989.
3. Citrin, Jack. "Do People Want Something for Nothing: Public Opinion on Taxes and Spending." *National Tax Journal* 32 (1979), pp. 113–30.
4. Courant, Paul, Edward Gramlich, and Daniel Rubinfeld. "Why Voters Support Tax Limitations: The Michigan Case." *National Tax Journal* 38 No. 1 (1980), pp. 1–20.
5. Courant, Paul N., and Susanna Loeb. "Centralization of School Finance in Michigan." *Journal of Policy Analysis and Management* 16 (1997), pp. 114–35.
6. Duncombe, William, and John Yinger. "Why Is It So Hard to Help Central-City Schools?" *Journal of Policy Analysis and Management* 16 (1997), pp. 85–113.

7. Dye, Richard, and Therese McGuire. "The Effect of Property Tax Limitation Measures on Local Government Fiscal Behavior." *Journal of Public Economics* 66 (1997), pp. 469–87.

8. Early, Dirk. "An Empirical Investigation of the Determinants of Street Homelessness." Journal of Housing Economics 14 (2005), pp. 27–47.

9. Early, Dirk. "The Determinants of Homelessness and the Targeting of Housing Assistance." Journal of Urban Economics 55 (2004), pp. 195–214.

10. Evans, William N., Sheila E. Murray, and Robert M. Schwab. "Schoolhouses, Courthouses, and Statehouses after *Serrano*." *Journal of Policy Analysis and Management* 16 (1997), pp. 10–31.

11. Filimon, R., T. Romer, and H. Rosenthal. "Asymmetric Information and Agenda Control: The Bases of Monopoly Power and Public Spending." *Journal of Public Economics* 17 (1982), pp. 51–70.

12. Inman, Robert P., and Daniel L. Rubinfeld. "Rethinking Federalism." *Journal of Economic Perspectives* 11:4 (Fall 1997), pp. 43–65.

13. Oates, Wallace. "An Essay on Fiscal Federalism." *Journal of Economic Literature* 37 (1999), pp. 1120–149.

14. O'Sullivan, Arthur. "Limits on Local Property Taxation." Chapter 7 in *Property Taxation and Local Government Finance,* ed. Wallace E. Oates. Cambridge MA: Lincoln Institute, 2001.

15. Sexton, Terri, Steven M. Sheffrin, and Arthur O'Sullivan. "Proposition 13: Unintended Effects and Feasible Reforms." *National Tax Journal* 52 (1999), pp. 99–112.

16. Shadbegian, Ronald. "Do Tax and Expenditure Limitations Affect Local Government Budgets? Evidence from Panel Data." *Public Finance Review* 26 (1998), pp. 218–36.

17. Shadbegian, Ronald. "The Effect of Tax and Expenditure Limitations on the Revenue Structure of Local Government, 1962–87." *National Tax Journal* 52 (1999), pp. 221–36.

18. Zodrow, George R. "The Property Tax as a Capital Tax: A Room with Three Views." *National Tax Journal* 54 (2001), pp. 139–56.

Tools of Microeconomics

This appendix reviews some of the basic tools of microeconomics used in various parts of the book. The appendix is divided into five sections:

1. **Marginal decision making.** The marginal principle tells us to pick the level of an activity where the marginal benefit equals the marginal cost.
2. **Product market.** The model of supply and demand shows how consumer prices are determined. We look at the market equilibrium and explore the issue of market efficiency.
3. **Labor market.** The model of labor supply and demand shows how wages and employment levels are determined. We look at the market equilibrium and discuss efficiency issues.
4. **Consumer choice.** The consumer choice model shows how consumers maximize their utility when subject to constraints imposed by their income and consumer prices.
5. **Input choice.** The input choice model is the production analog of the consumer choice model. It shows how firms pick the cost-minimizing combination of production inputs.

1. THE MARGINAL PRINCIPLE

The marginal principle provides a simple decision-making rule that helps individuals and organizations make decisions. The marginal benefit of some activity is the extra benefit from a small increase in the activity; for example, the extra revenue from keeping a barbershop open for one more hour. The marginal cost is the additional cost from a small increase in the activity; for example, the additional expense incurred by keeping a barbershop open for one more hour. Therefore, the *marginal principle* can be defined as follows:

If the marginal benefit of an activity exceeds the marginal cost, do more of it. If possible, pick the level at which the marginal benefit equals the marginal cost.

Applying the marginal principle to the barber's problem, the barber should stay open for one more hour if the extra revenue from the additional hour is at least as large as the extra cost.

Thinking at the margin enables us to fine-tune our decisions. We can use the marginal principle to determine whether a one-unit increase in a particular variable would make us better off. Just as a barber could decide whether to keep the shop open for one more hour, you could decide whether to study one more hour for a psychology midterm, and a firm could decide whether to hire one more worker. When we reach the level where the marginal benefit equals the marginal cost, the fine-tuning is done.

1.1 Example: How Many Movie Sequels?

To illustrate the marginal principle, consider a movie producer who must decide how many sequels to produce. Suppose the original version of a movie is successful enough that we expect a sequel to be profitable too. If the sequel turns out to be profitable, the producer then has to decide whether to make a third movie, then a fourth, and so on. The producer could use the marginal principle to figure out when to stop, thus avoiding the banana problem: Beginning spellers know how to start spelling banana, but often don't know when to stop—ba-na-na-na-na-na . . . .

Figure A–1 has two curves, one showing the marginal benefit of movies in a series, and a second showing the marginal cost. Consider the benefit curve first. A general rule of thumb in the movie business is that a sequel generates about 30 percent less revenue than the original, and revenue continues to drop for additional movies. In Figure A–1, the marginal benefit is the revenue generated by each movie, which drops from $300 million for the first (original) movie (point b) to $210 million for the second movie (point a), to $125 million for the third movie (point y).

Consider next the cost curve in Figure A–1. The typical movie costs about $50 million to produce and $75 million to promote. At point c on the cost curve, the marginal cost of the first movie is $125 million. The marginal cost increases with the number of movies because film stars

FIGURE A–1 The Marginal Principle

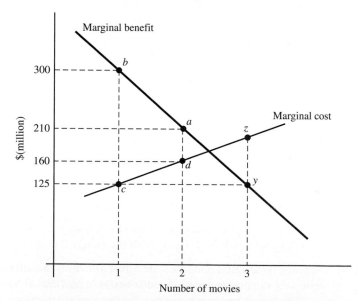

The marginal benefit of movies in a series decreases as revenue drops for each additional movie, while the marginal cost increases because actors demand higher salaries. The marginal benefit exceeds the marginal cost for the first two movies, so it is sensible to produce two, but not three movies.

typically demand higher salaries to appear in sequels. For example, Angelina Jolie was paid more for *Tomb Raider 2* than for *Tomb Raider,* and the actors in *Charlie's Angels 2, Legally Blond 2, and Bad Boys 2* received raises too. The marginal-cost curve is positively sloped, with a cost of $160 million for the second movie (point *d*) and an even higher cost for the third (point *z*), reflecting the rising cost of hiring movie stars for sequels.

In this example, the first two movies are profitable, but the third is not. For the first movie, the marginal benefit ($300 million) exceeds the marginal cost ($125 million), generating a profit of $175 million. Although the second movie has a smaller benefit and a bigger cost, it is profitable because the marginal benefit still exceeds the marginal cost by $50 million ($210 – $160). In contrast, the marginal cost of the third movie ($195 at point *z*)) exceeds the marginal benefit ($125 at point *y*), so the third movie is a losing proposition. In this example, the producer should stop after the second movie.

Although this example shows that only two movies in a series are profitable, other outcomes are possible. If the revenue from the third movie were higher or the cost were lower, the marginal benefit could exceed the marginal cost, and making a third movie would be profitable. Indeed, there are many examples of movies with multiple sequels and prequels, including *The Pink Panther, Star Wars,* and *Rocky.* Conversely, there are many examples of profitable movies that didn't generate any sequels. In these cases, the expected drop-off in revenues and run-up in costs were large enough to make a sequel unprofitable. In Figure A–1, if the marginal-benefit and marginal-cost curves were much steeper, the marginal benefit for the second movie would be less than the marginal cost, so a sequel would not be profitable.

1.2 Measuring the Surplus

The marginal approach allows us to compute the net benefit or surplus from a particular activity. In the movie example, the surplus is the sum of the profits from the two movies produced. The profit is shown by the gap between the marginal benefit and the marginal cost. The gap is $175 million for the first movie ($300 – $125) and $50 million for the second ($210 – $160), so the total surplus is $225 million. In general, to compute the surplus or net benefit, we add the gaps between the marginal-benefit and marginal-cost curves across the quantity produced.

Figure A–2 (page 370) shows how to compute the surplus when the quantity produced is larger. We can change our example to consider serial literature or comic books. In 1836 and 1837, Charles Dickens wrote monthly installments of *The Pickwick Papers,* and his decision each month was whether to write another installment. More recently, the producers of comic books decided each month whether to issue another installment of *Superman* or *Donald Duck.* In Figure A–2, as the number of issues increases, the marginal benefit decreases and the marginal cost increases. The marginal principle is satisfied at point *e*, with 100 issues.

The area between the marginal-benefit and marginal-cost curves provides a good approximation of the actual surplus from the serial. To compute the actual surplus, we would add the surpluses (the gaps between the marginal benefit and marginal cost) for the first issue, the second issue, and so on up to the 100th issue. The lightly shaded area (triangle *aeb*) is a good approximation because the number of issues is relatively large.

What happens if we go beyond the point that satisfies the marginal principle? For example, suppose the serial producer suffers from the banana problem (he doesn't know when to stop) and produces 140 issues. The loss associated with an excessive quantity is shown by the gap between

FIGURE A–2 Computing the Surplus

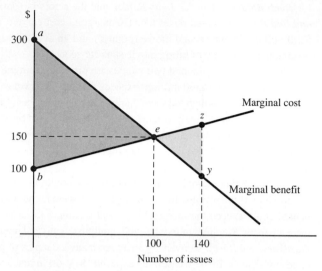

The net benefit or surplus from an activity is the area between the marginal-benefit and marginal-cost curves up to the quantity chosen. Triangle *aeb* is the surplus associated with satisfying the marginal principle at point *e*. Triangle *ezy* is the loss from going too far.

the marginal-cost and marginal-benefit curves beyond the point that satisfies the marginal principle. For example, for the 101st through the 140th issue this loss is shown by the lightly shaded area (triangle *ezy*). The net benefit or surplus from the entire serial is the area of triangle *aeb* (the surplus from producing the first 100 installments) minus the area of triangle *ezy* (the loss from going too far).

2. EQUILIBRIUM AND EFFICIENCY IN A PRODUCT MARKET

Economists use the model of supply and demand to determine equilibrium prices and quantities. In this book, we use the model in several chapters to explore the effects of public policies on product prices and quantities.

2.1 The Demand for a Product

Figure A–3 shows a market demand curve for seeing the circus. The demand curve is negatively sloped, indicating that an increase in the price decreases the quantity of people who see the circus. This occurs for two reasons:

- **Substitution effect.** An increase in the price of admission increases the cost of seeing a circus relative to the cost of other consumer goods. As a result, consumers will cut back on circus attendance in favor of seeing more movies, reading more books, or going to zoos or comedy clubs.

FIGURE A–3 Supply, Demand, and Equilibrium in the Circus Market

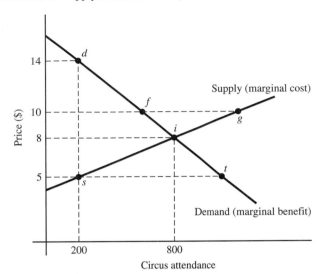

The demand curve is a marginal benefit curve, and the supply curve is a marginal cost curve. Equilibrium occurs at point *i*, where the quantity demanded equals the quantity supplied. The equilibrium price is $8. For a lower price (e.g., $5), there is excess demand, as shown by points *s* and *t*. For a higher price (e.g., $10), there is excess supply, as shown by points *f* and *g*.

- **Income effect.** An increase in price means that a consumer can no longer afford the original bundle of circuses and other goods (food, housing, entertainment). In other words, an increase in price decreases the consumer's real income. The consumer must cut back on something, and the circus is one candidate for cutting back. If circus attendance is a "normal" good, its consumption increases when real income increases and decreases when income drops.

The demand curve of a "normal" good is negatively sloped because the income effect reinforces the substitution effect. Both effects tend to reduce the quantity demanded when the price increases.

The demand curve shows the marginal benefit of consuming a good, so it is also a marginal-benefit curve. To see this, consider point *d*, which indicates that when the price is $14, a total of 200 people attend circuses. If the price were slightly higher (for example, $14.02), the 200th person won't go to the circus because the benefit is less than the $14.02 cost. But when the price drops to $14.00, this consumer goes to the circus because now the benefit exceeds the $14.00 cost. So in this case the marginal benefit of the circus for the 200th consumer must be $14.01, or as an approximation, $14. Similarly, the 800th person goes to the circus when the price drops to $8, so the marginal benefit for the 800th consumer is $8.

2.2 The Supply of a Product

Figure A–3 also shows the market supply curve for circus performances. The supply curve is positively sloped, indicating that an increase in price increases the number of people who can see the circus: Firms put on more shows and have them in larger venues, so more people can watch. The higher the price, the larger the quantity supplied.

The supply curve is also a marginal-cost curve, showing the marginal cost of entertaining people in circuses. To see this, consider point s, which tells us that when the price is $5, firms are willing to perform for a total of 200 people. If the price were slightly lower (for example, $4.98), no firm would serve the 200th person because the $4.98 price doesn't cover the firm's marginal cost. When the price rises to $5, a firm serves the 200th customer because the price is now high enough to just cover the cost. So in this case the firm's marginal cost must be $4.99, or as an approximation, $5. Similarly, a firm will serve the 800th consumer when the price reaches $8, so the marginal cost of serving the 800th consumer is about $8.

Why is the supply curve positively sloped? The supply curve is a marginal-cost curve, so it is positively sloped because of rising marginal cost. Consider the long-run, a period long enough that circus firms can change all their inputs, including labor and capital. The appeal of circus performers such as trapeze artists, elephants, and jugglers is their rarity. As the number of circus performances increases, circuses need more of these scarce inputs, and bidding among competing circuses pushes up the input prices. For example, the scarcity of bearded ladies means that as the circus industry expands, they earn higher wages.

The general idea is that a supply curve is positively sloped because as an industry expands, firms bid up the prices of scarce inputs. In the book, we discuss several markets subject to rising input prices, including housing and gasoline.

- **Housing and land prices.** The scarce input in the production of housing is land, and as the number of houses built increases, so does the price of land.
- **Gasoline and crude oil.** The scarce input in the production of gasoline is crude oil, the price of which rises with the total production of gasoline.

2.3 Equilibrium in the Product Market

As in other markets, equilibrium in the product market is shown by the intersection of the supply curve and the demand curve. In Figure A–3, this happens at point i, with a price of $8 and a quantity of 800 circus viewers. At any other price, the quantity demanded will differ from the quantity supplied, resulting in pressure to increase or decrease the price.

Consider first what happens when the price is below the equilibrium level. For example, at a price of $5, the quantity demanded (point t) exceeds the quantity supplied (point s), so there will be excess demand. Some consumers who want to see a circus at the relatively low price will be unable to do so. The long lines and disappointed consumers will produce pressure to increase the price. As the price increases, we move upward along the supply curve as firms stage more performances in bigger venues. At the same time, we move upward along the demand curve: Fewer consumers will want to see a circus at the higher price. The price will continue to rise until the excess demand is eliminated at point i.

Consider next what happens when the price is above the equilibrium level. For example, at a price of $10, there is excess supply, with the quantity supplied (point g) exceeding the quantity demanded (point f). In other words, there aren't enough consumers to fill the circus tents. Competition among firms will cause the price to drop. As the price decreases, we move downward along the demand curve because the lower price encourages more consumers to see the circus. At the same time, we move downward along the supply curve as circus firms reduce the number of performances, perform in smaller tents, or go out of business. The price will continue to drop until the excess supply is eliminated at point i.

2.4 Shifting the Curves

The demand curve shows the relationship between the price and the quantity of circus services demanded, *ceteris paribus* (all other things held fixed). What are the *cetera* (other things) that are *paria* (fixed in value) in drawing the curves? Once we've identified the other things, we have a list of other (nonprice) variables whose values determine the position of the curve. When the value of one of these other variables changes, the curve shifts to a new position.

On the demand side of the market, several variables are held fixed in drawing a particular demand curve. When the value of one of the variables changes, the curve shifts.

- **Consumer income.** An increase in income increases the demand for all "normal" goods, shifting the demand curve to the right.
- **Price of substitute products.** An increase in the price of a substitute good such as movies or books decreases the relative price of a circus and increases circus demand, shifting the demand curve to the right.
- **Price of complementary products.** An increase in the price of a complementary good such as peanuts or popcorn increases the total cost of an afternoon at the circus, decreasing the demand for circuses and shifting the demand curve to the left.
- **Preferences or tastes.** A change in preferences such as a greater desire to see jugglers and bearded ladies shifts the demand curve to the right.
- **Population.** If the market is defined geographically, an increase in the number of people shifts the demand curve to the right.

Panel A of Figure A–4 (page 374) shows the effects of an increase in demand. The demand curve shifts to the right, and at the original price of $8, there is excess demand: The quantity demanded (shown by point j) now exceeds the quantity supplied (point i). In the new equilibrium (shown by point k), the price is $9 and the quantity is 1,000.

On the supply side of the market, a number of variables are held fixed in drawing the supply curve:

- **Input prices.** Anything that increases the cost of producing a given quantity of output increases the marginal cost of production, shifting the supply curve upward. The sources of higher production costs include higher prices for raw materials (animal feed and fuel), higher capital costs (for tents and cages), and higher wages at each total output level. When production costs increase, firms are willing to supply less output at a given price, so the supply curve shifts to the left.
- **Labor productivity.** An increase in labor productivity means less labor time is required to produce each unit of output, so production costs drop, shifting the supply curve downward and to the right.
- **Technology.** Innovations that cut production costs shift the supply curve downward and to the right.

FIGURE A–4 Changes in Supply and Demand

A: Increase in demand increases the equilibrium price

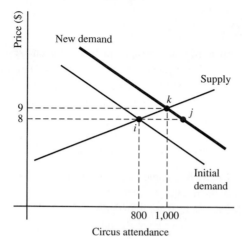

B: Increase in production cost decreases supply and increases the equilibrium price

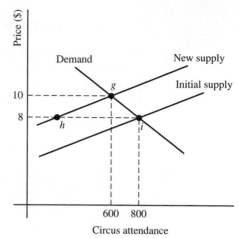

A: An increase in demand shifts the demand curve to the right, causing excess demand that increases the equilibrium price from $8 (point *i*) to $9 (point *k*).

B. An increase in production cost shifts the supply curve upward and to the left, causing excess demand that increases the equilibrium price from $8 (point *i*) to $10 (point *g*).

Panel B of Figure A–4 shows the effects of an increase in production cost. The supply curve shifts up and to the left, and at the original price of $8, there is excess demand: The quantity demanded (shown by point *i*) now exceeds the quantity supplied (point *h*). In the new equilibrium (shown by point *g*) the equilibrium price is $10 and the equilibrium quantity is 600.

2.5 Market Surplus

Earlier in the appendix, we used the marginal-benefit and marginal-cost curves to measure the surplus from an activity. We can use the supply and demand curves to measure the surplus or total value of the circus market. The demand curve shows the marginal benefit of the circus for the individual consumer. Assuming there are no external benefits from attending the circus, this is also the marginal social benefit of the circus. The supply curve shows the marginal cost of the circus, and assuming there are no external costs, it also shows the marginal social cost of the circus.

The market equilibrium shown in Figure A–5 maximizes the market surplus because it satisfies the marginal principle. At point *i*, the marginal-benefit curve (demand curve) intersects the marginal-cost curve (supply curve), and the market surplus is the shaded triangle *aib* between the demand curve and the supply curve. This is the best we can do. If we were to stop short of the equilibrium quantity, the marginal benefit of one more circus patron would exceed the marginal cost, so we could increase the surplus by moving toward the market equilibrium. If we were to go beyond the equilibrium quantity, the marginal cost would exceed the marginal benefit, so we could increase the surplus by moving back toward the market equilibrium.

FIGURE A–5 The Market Equilibrium Maximizes the Market Surplus

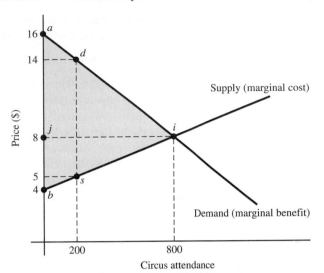

If there are no external costs or benefits, the market equilibrium satisfies the marginal principle, and the market equilibrium maximizes the market surplus, measured as the area between the demand (marginal benefit) and supply (marginal cost) curves. Consumer surplus is shown by triangle *aij* and producer surplus is shown by triangle *jib*.

2.6 Consumer Surplus and Producer Surplus

We can divide the market surplus into two surpluses, one gained by consumers and a second gained by producers. The surplus for an individual consumer equals the gap between the marginal benefit of consuming a product and the price paid for the product. The demand curve shows the marginal benefit to consumers. In Figure A–5, the 200th consumer has a marginal benefit of $14 (point *d*) and pays a price of $8, so that consumer's surplus is $6.

We can add the surpluses of individual consumers to get the market consumer surplus. In Figure A–5, the market consumer surplus is shown by the area between the demand (marginal benefit) curve and the dashed line at the equilibrium price of $8. In other words, the market consumer surplus equals the area of triangle *aij*. The area of this triangle is half its height times its base, or $3,200 = 0.50 · ($16 − $8) · 800.

The producer surplus is a measure of the net benefit of the market for producers. The producer surplus for an individual producer equals the price received for the product minus the marginal cost of producing it. The supply curve shows the marginal cost of producing the product. In Figure A–5, the firm that serves the 200th consumer has a marginal cost of $5 (point *s*) and gets a price of $8, so its producer surplus is $3. We can add the surpluses for different producers to get the market producer surplus. In Figure A–5, the market producer surplus is shown by the area between the supply (marginal cost) curve and the dashed line at the equilibrium price of $8. In other words, the market producer surplus is the area of triangle *jib*. The area of this triangle is half its height times its base, or $1,600 = 0.50 · ($8 − $4) · 800.

2.7 Inefficiency with Externalities

When the production of a product generates external costs, the market equilibrium does not maximize the market surplus. Recall the third axiom of urban economics:

Externalities cause inefficiency

As we saw in Figure A–5, in a market without externalities, the market equilibrium is efficient in the sense that it maximizes the total surplus of the market. Things are different when there are externalities.

Consider the market for gasoline. Using gasoline as a car fuel causes air pollution and generates greenhouse gases, so the marginal social cost of gasoline exceeds the marginal private cost of producing it. A gasoline producer pays its input suppliers, including workers and crude oil suppliers, and the supply curve (marginal-cost curve) includes these costs. The supply curve does not incorporate the cost of emissions, however, so the marginal social cost of gasoline consumption exceeds the marginal private cost. In Figure A–6, the marginal social cost curve lies above the supply curve, with a gap equal to the marginal external cost of pollution.

We can use Figure A–6 to show the socially efficient quantity of gasoline. To satisfy the marginal principle, we find the quantity at which the marginal benefit of gasoline (shown by the demand curve) equals the marginal social cost. This happens at point *e*, with 90 million gallons

FIGURE A–6 External Cost and Inefficiency

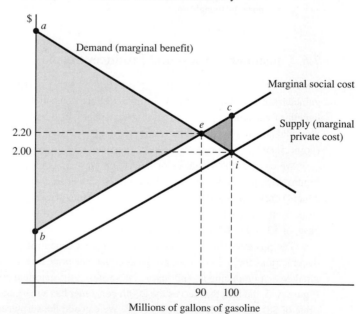

The marginal principle is satisfied at point *e*, so the total surplus of the market is shown by triangle *aeb*. The market equilibrium, shown by point *i*, generates an excessive quantity, with a loss from producing too much, shown by the triangle *eci*.

of gasoline. The total surplus of the market is the area between the demand curve and the marginal social cost curve, up to the socially efficient quantity. This is shown as the lightly shaded triangle *aeb*.

What happens if we go beyond point *e* and reach the market equilibrium at point *i*? For the last 10 million gallons, the marginal social cost exceeds the marginal benefit, so the surplus of the market decreases as the quantity increases. The loss associated with producing too much is shown by the darkly shaded triangle *eci*. This is the area between the marginal social cost curve and the demand curve, from the efficient quantity (90 million gallons) to the equilibrium quantity (100 million gallons). Point *i* violates the marginal principle, and triangle *eci* measures the social loss from going too far.

3. THE LABOR MARKET

Economists use the model of labor supply and demand to determine equilibrium wages and employment. In this book, we use the model in several chapters to explore various issues in the labor market.

3.1 The Demand for Labor

Figure A–7 shows a market demand curve for labor. The demand for labor comes from firms and other producers, and the demand for labor is derived from the demand for products. The labor

FIGURE A–7 Labor Market Equilibrium

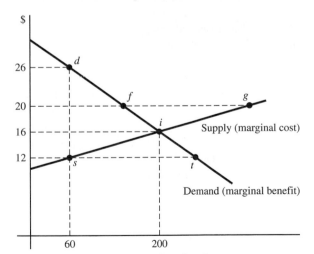

The demand curve is a marginal benefit curve, and the supply curve is a marginal cost curve. Equilibrium occurs at point *i*, where the quantity demanded equals the quantity supplied. The equilibrium wage is $16. For a lower wage (e.g., $12), there is excess demand, as shown by points *s* and *t*. For a higher wage (e.g., $20), there is excess supply, as shown by points *f* and *g*.

demand curve is negatively sloped, indicating that an increase in the wage decreases the quantity of labor demanded. This occurs for two reasons:

- **Substitution effect.** An increase in the wage causes firms to substitute other inputs (capital, land, materials) for the relatively expensive labor.
- **Output effect.** An increase in the wage increases production costs, increasing the prices of the products produced with labor. Consumers respond to higher prices by purchasing less output, so firms produce less and hire fewer workers.

The demand curve is negatively sloped because an increase in wages generates both a substitution effect and an output effect.

The demand curve is also a marginal-benefit curve. To see this, consider point d, which tells us that when the wage is $26, a total of 60 workers will be hired. If the wage were slightly higher (for example, $26.02), the firm would not hire the 60th worker because the wage exceeds the firm's benefit from the worker (the value of output produced). But when the wage drops to $26, the firm hires the worker because now the benefit is just above the wage. So in this case the marginal benefit of hiring the worker must be $26.01, or as an approximation, $26. Similarly, the firm hires the 200th worker when the wage drops to 16, so the marginal benefit of the 200th worker is $16.

3.2 The Supply of Labor

The supply of labor comes from workers who have the skills required for a particular job. In Figure A–7, the market supply curve is positively sloped, indicating that an increase in the wage increases the quantity of labor supplied. The supply curve shows the number of workers at different wages and implicitly assumes that each worker works the same number of hours, independent of the wage. This assumption simplifies matters because we don't have to keep track of hours worked by each worker, just the number of workers. The empirical evidence on labor supply suggests that an increase in the wage has a negligible effect on the aggregate hours worked: Some people work more and others work less, but on average, people work about the same number of hours.

Why is the labor supply curve positively sloped? If we ignore space and geography for the moment, the positive slope results from the fact that people have different opportunity costs of work time. At the low end of the supply curve, the 60th worker joins the labor market when the wage reaches $12, reflecting a relatively low opportunity cost of work time. Further up the supply curve at point i, the 200th worker joins when the wage reaches $16, reflecting a higher opportunity cost. In general, as the wage rises, the market attracts workers with progressively higher opportunity costs.

In an urban context, geography matters, and the supply curve reflects the migration of workers between cities. As one city's wage rises, the city becomes more attractive relative to other cities in the region. As a result, workers will migrate to the city, increasing the quantity of labor supply as the city moves upward along its labor supply curve. In this context, the positive slope indicates that a higher wage attracts more workers to a city.

The supply curve is also a marginal-cost curve for labor. To see this, consider point s, which tells us that when the wage is $12, a total of 60 workers are willing to work in the market. If the wage were slightly lower (for example, $11.98), the 60th person wouldn't work because the opportunity cost of working exceeds the wage. But when the wage rises to $12, the person joins the workforce because now the wage exceeds the opportunity cost. So in this case, the marginal cost of the 60th worker must be $11.99, or as an approximation, $12. Similarly, the 200th worker joins the market when the wage reaches $16, so the marginal cost is about $16.

3.3 Equilibrium in the Labor Market

As in other markets, equilibrium in the labor market is shown by the intersection of the supply curve and demand curve. In Figure A–7, this happens at point *i*, with a wage of $16 and 200 workers. At any other wage, the quantity demanded will differ from the quantity supplied, resulting in pressure to change the wage.

Consider first what happens when the wage is below the equilibrium level. For example, at a wage of $12, the quantity demanded (point *t*) exceeds the quantity supplied (point *s*), so there will be excess demand for labor. Some firms will be unable to hire as many workers as they want, and competition among firms for a relatively small number of workers will bid up the wage. As the wage increases, we move upward along the supply curve because more workers enter the market, attracted by the higher wage. At the same time, we move upward along the demand curve, because firms demand fewer workers at the higher wage. The wage continues to rise until the excess demand is eliminated at point *i*.

Consider next a wage above the equilibrium level. As shown by points *f* and *g*, the quantity of labor supplied exceeds the quantity demanded. There is excess supply of labor, so some people looking for jobs won't find any. Competition among workers for the relatively small number of jobs will bid down the wage. As the wage decreases, we move downward along the demand curve as firms hire more workers. At the same time, we move downward along the supply curve, with some workers dropping out of the market. The wage continues to drop until excess supply is eliminated at point *i*.

3.4 Shifting the Curves

The supply and demand curves in this case show the relationship between the wage and the quantity of labor supplied or demanded, *ceteris paribus* (all other things fixed). What are the *cetera* (other things) that are *paria* (fixed in value) in drawing the curves? Once we've identified the other things that are fixed, we have a list of other (nonwage) variables whose values determine the position of the curve. When the value of one of these other variables changes, the curve shifts to a new position.

Recall that the demand curve is a marginal-benefit curve, showing the benefit of hiring workers. The following changes will increase the marginal benefit of hiring workers, shifting the demand curve upward:

- **Price of output.** If the price of the product produced by workers increases, each worker will generate more revenue for the firm.
- **Productivity.** If output per worker increases, each worker will generate more revenue for the firm. The possible sources of productivity gains include an increase in labor skills or an increase in capital (machines and equipment) per worker.

These changes also shift the demand curve to the right: At a given wage, a firm will want to hire more workers.

FIGURE A–8 Changes in Labor Supply and Demand

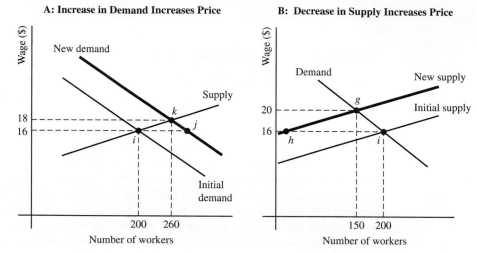

A: An increase in demand shifts the demand curve to the right, causing excess demand that increases the equilibrium wage from $16 (point *i*) to $18 (point *k*).

B. A decrease in supply shifts the curve to the left, increasing the equilibrium wage from $16 (point *i*) to $20 (point *g*).

Panel A of Figure A–8 shows the effects of an increase in demand. The demand curve shifts upward and to the right. At the original price of $16, there is excess demand: The quantity demanded (shown by point *j*) now exceeds the quantity supplied (point *i*). In the new equilibrium shown by point *k*, the price is $18 and the quantity is 260.

On the other side of the market, the labor supply curve shows how many workers participate in a labor market at each wage. In an urban context, anything that increases the relative attractiveness of a city (anything except the wage) will shift the entire curve to the right: More workers will be willing to work in the city. A city could become more attractive if it cuts pollution or improves public services. Conversely, anything that decreases the relative attractiveness of the city will shift the labor supply curve to the left.

In Panel B of Figure A–8, a decrease in labor supply shifts the supply curve up and to the left. At the original price of $16, there is excess demand: The quantity demanded (shown by point *i*) now exceeds the quantity supplied (point *h*). In the new equilibrium shown by point *g*, the price is $20 and the quantity is 150.

3.5 Market Surplus

We can use the supply and demand curves to measure the surplus or total value of the labor market. The demand curve shows the marginal benefit of labor for the firms that hire workers. Assuming there are no external benefits from labor, this is also the marginal social benefit of labor. The supply curve shows the marginal cost of labor to workers, and assuming there are no external costs, it also shows the marginal social cost of labor.

FIGURE A–9 The Labor Market Equilibrium Maximizes the Market Surplus

If there are no externalities, the market equilibrium satisfies the marginal principle, and the market equilibrium maximizes the market surplus, measured as the area between the demand (marginal benefit) curve and supply (marginal cost) curve.

The market equilibrium maximizes the surplus of the market because it satisfies the marginal principle. At point i in Figure A–9, the marginal-benefit curve (demand curve) intersects the marginal-cost curve (supply curve), and the market surplus is the shaded triangle between the demand curve and the supply curve. This is the best we can do. If we were to stop short of the equilibrium quantity, the marginal benefit of one more worker would exceed the marginal cost, so we could increase the surplus by moving toward the market equilibrium. If we were to go beyond the equilibrium quantity, the marginal cost would exceed the marginal benefit, so we could increase the surplus by moving back toward the market equilibrium.

4. THE CONSUMER CHOICE MODEL

The consumer choice model shows how consumers make decisions about how much of a product to buy. The idea is that a consumer maximizes his or her utility, subject to the constraints imposed by product prices and the consumer's income. To illustrate, consider the decisions of Maxine, a consumer who must decide how many movies and paperback books to buy each month. Maxine has a fixed income per month to spend on the two goods, so her options are limited by her budget. To decide how to spend her money, Maxine takes two steps:

1. She figures out her menu of options, the list of alternative combinations of books and movies her budget allows.
2. She picks the combination of books and movies that generates the highest level of satisfaction.

We'll start with a discussion of Maxine's budget options, and then discuss her preferences.

FIGURE A–10 Budget Set and Budget Line

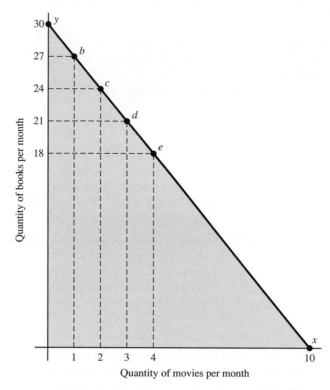

The budget set (shaded area) shows all the affordable combinations of books and movies, and the budget line (with endpoints x and y) shows the combinations that exhaust the budget.

4.1 Consumer Constraints: The Budget Line

Consider first the constraints faced by a consumer. Maxine's ability to purchase movies and other goods is limited by her income and the prices of movies and other products. Suppose Maxine has a fixed income of $30 per month, which she spends entirely on movies and used paperback books. The price of a movie is $3 and the price of a book is $1.

A budget line shows all the combinations of two goods that exhaust the consumer's budget. In Figure A–10, if Maxine spends her entire $30 budget on books, she gets 30 books and no movies (point y). At the other extreme, she can spend her entire budget on movies, getting 10 movies (point x). The points between these two extremes are possible too. For example, she could reach b (one movie and 27 books) by spending $3 on movies and $27 on books, or c (two movies and 24 books). A consumer's budget set is the set of all the affordable combinations of two goods. The budget set includes the budget line (combinations that exhaust the budget) as well as combinations that leave the consumer with extra money. In Figure A–10, Maxine's budget set is shown as a shaded triangle. She can afford any combination below the budget line but cannot afford combinations above it.

The budget line shows the market trade-off between books and movies. Starting from any point on the budget line, if Maxine buys one more movie, she diverts $3 from book purchases, reducing the number of $1 books she can purchase by three. The market trade-off equals the price ratio, the price of movies ($3) divided by the price of books ($1), or three books per movie. The market trade-off also equals the slope of the budget line, the "rise" (the change in books) divided by the "run" (the change in movies). If all consumers pay the same price for the two goods, they all have the same market trade-off of three books per movie.

4.2 Consumer Preferences: Indifference Curves

We've seen the consumer's budget set, which shows what the consumer can afford. The next step in our discussion of consumer choice is to look at what the consumer wants, what makes the consumer happy. Once we have a means of representing consumer preferences, we can show how a consumer makes her choice, picking the best of the combinations within the budget set.

We can represent the consumer's preferences with indifference curves. The idea behind an indifference curve is that there are different ways for a consumer to reach a particular level of satisfaction or utility. An indifference curve shows the different combinations of two goods that generate the same level of utility. In Figure A–11 (page 384), the indifference curve passing through points *b*, *z*, *m*, and *n* separates the combinations of books and movies into three groups:

- **Superior combinations.** All the combinations above the indifference curve generate higher utility than combinations on the curve. Maxine would prefer point *h* to point *z* because she gets more of both goods at point *h*.
- **Inferior combinations.** All the combinations below the indifference curve generate lower utility than combinations on the curve. Maxine would prefer point *m* to point *r* because she gets more of both goods at point *m*.
- **Equivalent combinations.** All combinations along the indifference curve generate the same utility. Maxine is therefore indifferent between combinations *b*, *z*, *m*, and *n*.

An indifference curve shows the preferences of an individual consumer, so indifference curves vary from one consumer to another. Nonetheless, the indifference curves of all consumers share two characteristics: They are negatively sloped, and they become flatter as we move downward along a particular indifference curve.

Why is the indifference curve negatively sloped? If we increased Maxine's movie consumption by one unit without changing her book consumption, her utility would increase. To restore the original utility level, we must take away some books, and that's what happens along an indifference curve. To keep utility constant, there is a negative relationship between books and movies, so the indifference curve is negatively sloped. The slope of an indifference curve is the marginal rate of substitution (MRS) between the two goods, the rate at which a consumer is willing to substitute one good for another. In Figure A–11, if Maxine starts at point *b* and we give her one more movie, we take away eight books to keep her on the same indifference curve. Therefore, starting from point *b*, her marginal rate of substitution is eight books per movie. When she starts with many books and only one movie, she is willing to trade a lot of books to get one more movie.

The indifference curve becomes flatter as we move downward along the curve. This reflects the assumption that consumers prefer balanced consumption to extremes. As we move down Maxine's indifference curve, movie consumption increases while book consumption decreases.

FIGURE A–11 Indifference Curve and the Marginal Rate
of Substitution

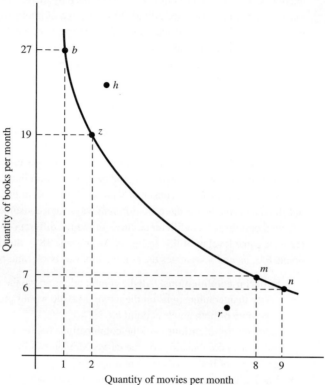

The indifference curve shows the different combinations of books and
movies that generate the same utility level. The slope is the marginal
rate of substitution (MRS) between the two products. The MRS is eight
books per movie between points b and z, but only one book per movie
between points m and n.

Starting from one extreme (few movies and many books), she is willing to sacrifice many books
to get another movie: The MRS is large and the indifference curve is steep. For example, starting
from point b, her MRS is eight books per movie. But as she gets more and more movies (and
fewer and fewer books), she isn't willing to sacrifice as many books to get more movies. As a result, her MRS decreases, and the indifference curve becomes flatter. For example, between points
m and n, the MRS is one book per movie.

An indifference map is a set of indifference curves, each with a different level of utility.
Figure A–12 shows three indifference curves: U_1, U_2, and U_3. As Maxine moves from a point on
indifference curve U_1 to any point on U_2, her utility increases. This is sensible because she can get
more of both goods on U_2, so she will be better off. In general, Maxine's utility increases as she
moves in the northeasterly direction to a higher indifference curve, from U_1 to U_2, and U_3, and
so on.

FIGURE A–12 Indifference Map

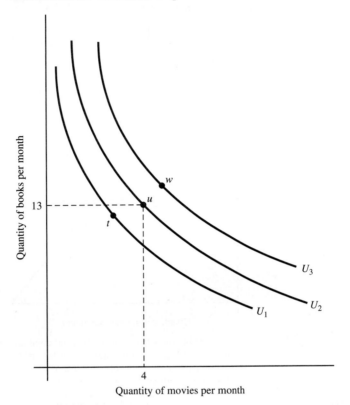

An indifference map shows a set of indifference curves, with utility increasing as we move northeasterly to higher indifference curves (U_1 to U_2 to U_3).

4.3 The Utility-Maximizing Rule

Maxine's objective is to maximize her utility, given her budget and the prices of movies and books. She can choose from many affordable combinations of books and movies, and she will pick the one that generates the highest level of utility. In graphical terms, Maxine will reach the highest indifference curve possible, given her budget set.

In Figure A–13 (page 386), Maxine maximizes her utility at point e, with four movies and 18 books. She achieves the utility level associated with indifference curve U_3. Why does she choose point e instead of other points such as z, b, or w?

- **Point z.** Maxine doesn't choose this point for two reasons. First, it is not on the budget line, so it does not exhaust her budget. Second, it is on a lower indifference curve than point e, so it generates less utility.
- **Point b.** Although point b exhausts Maxine's budget, it lies on a lower indifference curve than point e, so it generates less utility. Starting from point b, Maxine could reallocate her budget and buy more movies and fewer books. As she moves down her budget line, she

FIGURE A–13 Maximizing Utility: MRS = Price Ratio

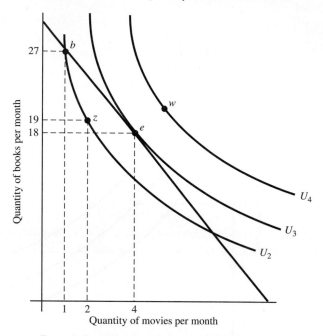

To maximize utility, the consumer finds the combination of books and movies where an indifference curve is tangent to the budget line. At the utility-maximizing combination (point *e*), the marginal rate of substitution (the consumer's own trade-off, shown by the slope of the indifference curve) equals the price ratio (the market trade-off, shown by the slope of the budget line).

moves to progressively higher indifference curves, ultimately reaching point *e* on indifference curve U_3.

- **Point *w*.** Although point *w* is on a higher indifference curve and thus would generate a higher utility level than point *e*, it lies outside Maxine's budget set, so she cannot afford it.

At point *e*, Maxine reaches the highest indifference curve possible, given her budget set. Notice that at point *e*, the indifference curve touches—but does not pass through—the budget line. In other words, the indifference curve is tangent to the budget line.

What is the economic interpretation of the tangency condition? At the point of tangency, the slope of the indifference curve equals the slope of the budget line. The slope of the budget line equals the opportunity cost of movies, computed as the movie price ($3) divided by the book price ($1), or three books per movie. The slope of the indifference curve is the marginal rate of substitution (MRS), so if the two curves are tangent at point *e*, the MRS is also three books per movie. In other words, the consumer's trade-off between the two goods (the MRS) equals the market trade-off (the price ratio) between the two goods:

$$MRS = \frac{\text{price of movie}}{\text{price of book}}$$

To show why the tangent point is best, suppose Maxine tentatively chooses a point where the MRS is not equal to the price ratio. For example, starting at point *b*, the indifference curve is relatively steep, and the MRS is eight books per movie: She is willing to give up eight books to get a single movie. But given market trade-off, she can actually get that movie by sacrificing only three books, so she will move down her budget line and consume more movies. The same argument applies to any combination for which the MRS (the consumer's own trade-off) is not equal to the price ratio (the market trade-off). Anytime Maxine is willing to trade at a rate that is different from market trade-off, it will be in her best interest to do so. The benefits of trading will be exhausted only when the MRS equals the price ratio. In Figure A–13, this happens at point *e*.

5. THE INPUT CHOICE MODEL

The input choice model shows how firms pick the best combination of inputs. There are many ways to produce a particular product, with different combinations of labor and capital (machines, buildings, and equipment). The idea behind the input choice model is that a firm will choose the input combination that minimizes the cost of producing a target quantity of output. To illustrate, Minnie produces catnip mice as cat toys, with a target production level of 100 toys per hour. She uses two inputs, capital and labor, and her objective is to minimize the cost of producing her target output level.

5.1 The Isoquant

An isoquant is the production analog of the consumer's indifference curve. It shows a set of production "recipes," different input mixtures that produce the same quantity of output (*iso* means equal in Greek). In Figure A–14 (page 388), the isoquant shows the different combinations of capital and labor that produce 100 toys. For example, Minnie can use 36 machines and two workers (point *b*) or 30 machines and three workers (point *z*). Further down the isoquant, points *e* and *w* show other input combinations that produce the target output.

The slope of the isoquant is the marginal rate of technical substitution (MRTS), the production analog of the marginal rate of substitution. The MRTS is the reduction in capital that offsets a one-unit increase in labor. For example, comparing point *b* to point *z*, if the firm adds one worker (going from two to three workers), it can reduce its capital by 6 units (from 36 to 30) and still produce the same quantity of output. As a firm adds more and more labor, the MRTS decreases. For example, the MRTS at point *e* is two units of capital per worker, and the MRTS at point *w* is less than one unit of capital per worker.

Why does the MRTS decrease as we move downward along the isoquant? A move down the isoquant increases the quantity of labor and decreases the quantity of capital. Starting from one extreme (many machines and few workers), adding a worker increases output by a large amount, so we can take away a large number of machines and produce just as much output: the MRTS is large and the isoquant is steep. For example, between points *b* and *z*, the MRTS is 6 machines per worker. But as we move downward along the isoquant to a point with more workers and fewer machines, there is less capital per worker, so adding another worker increases output by a smaller amount. Therefore, to keep output at the target level, we reduce capital by a smaller amount, for example 2 machines at point *e*.

FIGURE A–14 Minimizing Cost: MRTS = Input Price Ratio

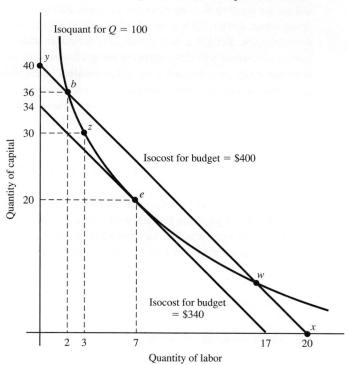

The isoquant shows the input combinations that produce the target output quantity ($Q = 100$). The isocost shows the input combinations that exhaust a given budget. The firm's objective is to reach the lowest feasible isocost, the one tangent to the isoquant. At point e, the cost of producing the target output level is minimized at $340, compared to a budget of $400 at point b or point w. The MRTS (the slope of the isoquant) equals the input price ratio (the slope of the isocost).

5.2 Isocost Lines

An isocost is the production analog of the consumer budget line. It shows the combinations of two inputs that exhaust a given budget. Suppose Minnie can rent machines for $10 per hour and pays her workers $20 per hour. In Figure A–14, the higher of the two isocost lines shows the affordable input combinations for a budget of $400. At one extreme, Minnie could spend the entire $400 by getting 40 machines (point y); at the other extreme, she could spend it all on labor and hire 20 workers (point x). At point b, she can spend $360 on machines ($10 · 36 machines) and $40 on labor ($20 · 2 workers).

5.3 Minimizing Cost: MRTS = Input Price Ratio

The firm's objective is to minimize the cost of meeting its production target. Minnie's target output is 100 toys, so she wants to get on the lowest isocost line that makes contact with the

$Q = 100$ isoquant. Suppose she starts at point b, with a budget of $400 spent on 36 machines and two workers. She could do better by moving from point b to point z. The MRTS between these two points is six machines per worker, so she can add one worker ($+$20$) and get rid of six machines ($-$60$), decreasing her total cost by $40. If she moves from point z to point e, she can cut her cost another $20, dropping it to $340. At point e, she has reached the lowest isocost that makes contact with the isoquant, so she cannot do any better. The isocost is tangent to the isoquant, so she is minimizing her cost.

What is the economic interpretation of the tangency condition? At the point of tangency, the slope of the isoquant equals the slope of the isocost. As in the case of the consumer budget line, the slope of the isocost equals the price ratio. The price of labor is twice the price of capital, so the slope of the isocost is two machines per worker. The slope of the isoquant is the marginal rate of technical substitution (MRTS), so if the two curves are tangent at point e, the MRTS is two units of capital per labor. In other words, the production trade-off between the two inputs (the MRTS) equals the market trade-off (the input price ratio) between the two inputs:

$$MRTS = \frac{\text{price of labor}}{\text{price of capital}}$$

To show why the tangent point is best, suppose Minnie tentatively chooses point b. At this point, the isoquant is steeper than the isocost line, with MRTS $=$ six machines per worker, compared to a market trade-off of two machines per worker. To keep output at the target level, she can eliminate six machines for each worker she hires (MRTS $=$ 6), and because workers are only twice as expensive (price ratio $=$ 2), substituting workers for machines cuts her cost. She will continue this input substitution until the production trade-off matches the budget trade-off of two machines per worker. This happens at point e, where the MRTS equals the input price ratio.

Index